# Understanding Medieval Primary Sources

Medieval society created many kinds of records and written material which differ considerably, giving us such sources as last wills, sermons, manorial accounts, or royal biographies. Primary sources are an exciting way for students to engage with the past and develop their own ideas about life in the medieval period.

*Understanding Medieval Primary Sources* is a collection of essays that will introduce students to the key primary sources that are essential to studying medieval Europe. The sources are divided into two categories: the first part treats some of the many generic sources that have been preserved, such as wills, letters, royal and secular narratives and sermons. Chapter by chapter each expert author illustrates how they can be used to reveal details about medieval history. The second part focuses on areas of historical research that can only be fully discovered by using a combination of primary sources, covering fields such as maritime history, urban history, women's history and medical history.

*Understanding Medieval Primary Sources* will be an invaluable resource for any student embarking on medieval historical research.

**Joel T. Rosenthal** is Distinguished Professor Emeritus, State University of New York at Stony Brook. He has published on the social history of late medieval England, looking into such topics as old age, families, popular religion, children and widows. He is the recent author of *Margaret Paston's Piety* (2010), and is the co-editor of *Medieval Prosopography*.

WITHDRAWN FROM THE LIBRARY
UNIVERSITY OF
WINCHESTER

KA 0350810 2

# Routledge guides to using historical sources

How does the historian approach primary sources? How do interpretations differ? How can such sources be used to write history?

The Routledge guides to using historical sources series introduces students to different sources and illustrates how historians use them. Titles in the series offer a broad spectrum of primary sources and, using specific examples, examine the historical context of these sources and the different approaches that can be used to interpret them.

**Reading Primary Sources**
*Miriam Dobson and Benjamin Ziemann*

**History Beyond the Text**
*Sarah Barber and Corinna Penniston-Bird*

**History and Material Culture**
*Karen Harvey*

# Understanding Medieval Primary Sources

## Using historical sources to discover medieval Europe

**Edited by**
**Joel T. Rosenthal**

Routledge
Taylor & Francis Group

LONDON AND NEW YORK

UNIVERSITY OF WINCHESTER
LIBRARY

First published 2012 by Routledge
2 Park Square, Milton Park, Abingdon, Oxon OX14 4RN

Simultaneously published in the USA and Canada
by Routledge
711 Third Avenue, New York, NY 10017

*Routledge is an imprint of the Taylor & Francis Group, an informa business*
© 2012 Joel T. Rosenthal

The right of Joel T. Rosenthal to be identified as author of this work
has been asserted by him in accordance with sections 77 and 78 of the
Copyright, Designs and Patents Act 1988.

All rights reserved. No part of this book may be reprinted or reproduced or
utilised in any form or by any electronic, mechanical, or other means, now
known or hereafter invented, including photocopying and recording, or in
any information storage or retrieval system, without permission in writing
from the publishers.

Trademark notice: Product or corporate names may be trademarks or
registered trademarks, and are used only for identification and explanation
without intent to infringe.

*British Library Cataloguing in Publication Data*
A catalogue record for this book is available from the British Library

*Library of Congress Cataloging in Publication Data*
A catalog record for this book has been requested

978-0-415-78073-5 (HB)
978-0-415-78074-2 (PB)

Typeset in Times New Roman
by Bookcraft Ltd, Stroud, Gloucestershire

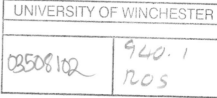

UNIVERSITY OF WINCHESTER

03508102      940. 1
              ROS

MIX
Paper from
responsible sources
FSC
www.fsc.org      FSC® C004839

Printed and bound in Great Britain by
CPI Antony Rowe, Chippenham, Wiltshire

# Contents

# Figures

# Contributors

The publications listed have been chosen to illustrate areas of interest; they are not a comprehensive guide.

**Bernard S. Bachrach** is Professor of History at the University of Minnesota. His publications include *Early Carolingian Warfare: Prelude to Empire* and a co-edited volume, *The Normans and their Adversaries at War*. He is a co-editor of *Medieval Prosopography* and founding editor of *Res Militaris*.

**Caroline M. Barron** is Professor Emerita, Royal Holloway University of London. She is the author of *London in the Later Middle Ages, 1200–1500* and co-editor of *Medieval London Widows, 1300–1500*.

**Roisin Cossar** is Associate Professor of History at the University of Manitoba. She is the author of *The Transformation of the Laity in Bergamo, 1265–c. 1400*.

**Katherine L. French** is J. Frederick Hoffman Professor of History at the University of Michigan. She is the author of *The People of the Parish: Community Life in a Late Medieval English Parish* and *The Good Women of the Parish: Gender and Religion after the Black Death*.

**Ralph A. Griffiths** is Professor Emeritus, University of Wales, Swansea. He is the author of *The Reign of King Henry VI: The Exercise of Royal Authority, 1422–1461*, co-author of *The Oxford Illustrated History of the British Monarchy*, co-editor of *Fifteenth-Century England, 1399–1509: Studies in Politics and Society*.

**David Hinton** is Professor of Archaeology at the University of Southampton. His publications include *Alfred's Kingdom: Wessex and the South, 800–1500*, *Medieval Jewellery from the Eleventh to the Fifteenth Century*, and *Twenty-five Years of Medieval Archaeology*.

**Hannes Kleineke** is Senior Research Fellow, History of Parliament, London, working on the fifteenth-century volumes of this project. He has recently published *Edward IV and Parliamentarians at Law*.

**Maryanne Kowaleski** is the Joseph FitzPatrick S.J. Distinguished Professor of History at Fordham University, director of Fordham's Medieval Studies programme, and (2012–13) President of the Medieval Academy of America. Her publications include *Markets and Regional Trade in Medieval Exeter*, co-editing *Medieval Domesticity: Home, Housing and Household in Medieval England*, and editing and compiling a volume of primary materials, *Medieval Towns: A Reader.*

**Sara Lipton** is Associate Professor of History, State University of New York at Stony Brook. Her *Images of Intolerance: The Representation of Jews and Judaism in the Bible* was awarded the John Nichols Brown Prize of the Medieval Academy of America.

**Lister M. Matheson** is Professor of English at Michigan State University. He has edited *Death and Dissent: Two Fifteenth-Century Chronicles* and he is the author of *The Prose Brut: The Development of a Middle English Chronicle.*

**Jinty Nelson** is Professor Emerita, King's College London. She is the author of *Charles the Bald* and *Rituals of Power in Early Medieval Europe*. She has edited and translated the *Annals of St Bertin*. She is a former president of the Royal Historical Society.

**Mark G. Pegg** is Professor of History at Washington University (in St Louis) and the author of *The Corruption of Angels: The Great Inquisition of 1245–1246* and *A Most Holy War: The Albigensian Crusade and the Battle for Christendom.*

**Carole Rawcliffe** is Professor of History at the University of East Anglia and author of *Leprosy in Medieval England* and *Medicine for the Soul: The Life, Death, and Resurrection of an English Medieval Hospital, St Giles's*. She is also co-editor of a two-volume history of Norwich.

**Joel T. Rosenthal** is Distinguished Professor Emeritus of History at the State University of New York at Stony Brook. He has published *Telling Tales: Sources and Narration in Late Medieval England* and *Margaret Paston's Piety*. He is also a co-editor of *Medieval Prosopography.*

**Philip Slavin** is a Mellon Fellow in the Department of Economics, McGill University. He has published on the environmental and economic history of late medieval Europe and has a forthcoming book on the provisioning of monastic communities in England.

**Anne T. Thayer** is the Diefenderfer Professor of Ecumenical Theology and Church History at Lancaster Theological Seminary. Her publications include *Penitence, Preaching and the Coming of the Reformation* and, as co-editor, *Penitence in the Age of Reformations.*

**Shona Kelly Wray** is Associate Professor of History, University of Missouri, Kansas City. She has co-edited *Across the Religious Divide: Women, Property, and Law in the Wider Mediterranean (ca. 1300–1800)* and is the author of *Communities and Crisis: Bologna during the Black Death.*

# Preface

Three sets of colleagues have helped to make this volume possible. The first group, of course, is those who have contributed the essays. Accepting the invitation to write turned out for almost all of us to be a more serious and difficult commitment in terms of time and energy than we had anticipated. Even historians who are immersed in using the primary sources of their field have to re-think their approach when they are asked to talk explicitly about those sources. The considerable variation in the way different essays deal with the assigned topic emphasizes the variety of the sources of medieval Europe, as well as the differences in how we use them. Letting each author do her or his 'own thing' seemed in keeping with the original mandate and the papers reflect this latitude.

The second group of people whom I wish to thank are the colleagues who, when asked if they would undertake to write an essay, declined to do so (for all sorts of reasons) but who were extremely helpful in steering me to others who could also do a good job, as they obviously have done. Since some of the essays and their authors lie well beyond any area of professional competence to which I have a personal claim, this advice about asking the right people has been essential in the compilation of this collection of papers.

The third group to thank are the members of the editorial staff at Routledge, Alison Yates, Eve Setch, and Laura Mothersole. In addition, thanks to a critical (crabby) anonymous reader of the proposal in an early stage; the need to answer some of the criticism gave the collection more focus than it otherwise might have had. Editorial encouragement has been particularly welcome because a collection of so many authors, working at different rates of progress and with different interpretations of their slice of the overall project, can be an awkward and slow-moving group to bring into the light of day.

# Introduction

*Joel T. Rosenthal*

The primary sources of medieval history discussed in this volume are presented as falling into several different groupings. In the first five chapters a few of the many categories of primary sources are explicitly treated – sources *qua* sources. Each essay deals with a particular genus (or a generic grouping) of primary source. In the second section, Chapters 6 to 14, some historical topics are dealt with to illustrate how historians use a mix of different sources to shed light on topics of interest. In this category the diversity of sources and the ways that historians use them are the major focus. And in the third section, Chapters 15 and 16, we step outside the historian's customary reliance on written sources and look, if but quickly, at what visual culture and archaeology add to the mix.

Primary sources are to the historian what molecules are to the chemist – the compounds from which larger constructions are assembled. While the chemist probes the nature of matter by combining molecules, the historian probes the past by a reading and analysis of the records left by the people, or at least by some of the people, of the period under discussion. Without such records the historian goes nowhere. These contemporary records are what we refer to as primary sources, that is, records from those who lived at the time under examination (while subsequent scholarly material is referred to as secondary sources). Primary sources are the foundation on which any examination of the past must rest – and where it must begin; even the first textbooks had to start there. And as scholarly and academic disciplines have developed and distinguished themselves from each other, it is the written records of that past that fall to the historian.

The records of medieval Europe, generated between the late Roman Empire in the fourth century and around 1500, and coming from a geographical span stretching from the eastern Mediterranean to Scandinavia, are voluminous. Though what has been preserved – what is extant – is obviously but a fraction of the writings and records of that medieval millennium, there are virtually mountains of sources of all sorts for us to study, many of them still unedited and unpublished. These sources can be divided, for our convenience, into a few major categories. One consists of narrative histories or chronicles – synthetic accounts that tell a tale in prose (in most cases). A second category consists of the records of government. This embraces an immense amount of material, emanating from the thrones, courts and chanceries of virtually every secular and ecclesiastical authority of medieval Europe. In their diversity and volume these records enable us to unravel the workings of the executive, administrative, legislative and policy-making aspects of public life and power. They take us up and down the socio-political ladder, from papal mandates to quarrels between peasants. A third major category is what we can lump together as private or personal records, with wills and family letters as good examples. Though other kinds of primary material could be added to the list, such as records of the early universities, these broad categories suffice for an introduction.

Were we to trace the history of modern scholarship regarding medieval Europe we would find that much of the work of the pioneers of the seventeenth and eight-eenth century was devoted to editing and publishing primary sources. This, they all agreed, was the way to begin a serious study of the Middle Ages. However, because much of this scholarship focused on political and diplomatic history it was the vast body of narrative chronicles and of government records that received most of the early attention. Our interest today has shifted and private or personal sources, along with familiar material now read for different purposes, stake a large claim. We look for windows into the worlds of women, family life, sex and sexuality, children, demography, health and other such areas. Anything and everything seems proper grist for the historian's mill, including the links between traditional written materials and visual sources (art history) and material remains (archaeology), as we shall see below.

\* \* \*

The purpose of this volume is to offer an introduction to some of the many kinds of primary materials that we use in our effort to understand the dynamics of medieval life. Though there are obviously more kinds of sources than any single volume can cover, and though we make no effort to give a reference book survey of extant materials, we try to give an idea of the complexity and variety of what has been preserved. The primary sources for medieval history vary widely, as does scholarly use of them. The essays in this volume are divided into three categories, a division emphasizing both the diversity of the material and the variations in how historians use them. We cover some traditional fields and sources that have been accepted as keys to medieval life; we also look at topics that would not have appeared had this volume been written a generation or two ago. Moreover, as well as a changing focus in the historians' agenda we have that steady outpouring of scholarly work: new editions of sources, new interpretive work based upon them. So we not only ask new and different ques-tions, along with the old ones, but we also have more resources at our disposal. Our view of medieval Europe continues to evolve in keeping with new scholar-ship and new scholars.

In the first group of essays we turn to some 'generic sources', as in a genus that contains a number of species. Wills or sermons or royal biographies or chroni-cles are the kinds of materials we have in mind. Though any category (or genus) of primary source admits of considerable variety within its boundaries, given the writings of ten centuries and of the many sub-cultures of Christendom, our premise is that there is sufficient similarity between material within a genre to allow for generalizations that cover the diverse examples. In a rough sense, a sermon is a sermon, whether it is a Latin sermon of a fourth-century Father of the church or a vernacular one from a parish priest of the fifteenth.

In the second group of essays we offer examples of how diverse kinds of sources are put together to talk to historical institutions or questions. We see how historians dip into a variety of sources and endeavour to synthesize them to illuminate a topic like manorial history or maritime activity or the role of women. The combination of sources drawn upon to study such topics gives them a sort of organic unity, though it is one imposed by the historian. A different combination of sources, or even a different reading of the same ones, might well result in a different picture with different conclusions. But it is the weaving of the different kinds of primary materials that gives us a nuanced picture of a complex topic like representative government or public health. And lastly, beyond the customary reliance on written sources, historians have long been encouraged to turn to related disciplines for a dialogue that crosses old boundaries. Since most of the people of medieval Europe would have been more immersed in the worlds of visual and material culture than in that of written materials, we conclude with two essays that explore the use of other kinds of primary materials, crossing the boundary lines of historical or disciplinary demarcation.

However, just because historians are at home with primary sources does not mean that essays devoted to their exposition have been an easy assignment. Each essay below is the result of its author's interpretation of the common task. Some authors have chosen to focus on what is in effect a detailed case study, as with military history, on the idea that a close analysis of a few sources opens up a method of inquiry that allows us to assess the mindset that created the sources under investigation. In other cases we have a broad survey of a given genre (as with royal biography), or perhaps a dip into many different kinds of sources that can be put together for a broad sweep (as with urban history).

Medieval England is much in evidence in many of the essays. England was a relatively well ordered country with a long practice of record preservation, and because of the accessibility of many of these sources a number of essays draw largely from English examples. But as those authors point out, comparable essays could be offered for many other states and cultures, including the Byzantine Empire (sadly omitted here) and even the world of Islam. No collection can cover all possible topics, just as no single essay can cover all the records that we still have.

\* \* \*

The introduction to a volume of essays offers some general reflections and gives an overview of what is to follow. It is fitting to begin with a discussion of some 'generic sources', as medieval thinkers worried about the very reality of categories. The classic statement (by Boethius) sums up the question: 'Now concerning genus and species, whether they have real existence or are merely and solely creations of the mind, and if they exist, whether they are material or immaterial, and whether they are separate from things we see or are contained within them – on all this I make no pronouncement.' We obviously do make a pronouncement, in favour of the reality of a genus: sermons, as we have said, or royal biographies, as real categories with a generic identity.

The first two essays look at familiar forms of primary sources – royal biographies, as Ralph Griffiths surveys the field, and narrative chronicles as the genre is presented by Lister Matheson. Kings set the tone for the medieval state and so their lives were seen as inviting ground for political as well as for personal or biographical treatment. Beginning with Einhard on Charlemagne in the ninth century we have biographical material on rulers across much of Europe: England, France, the Empire, Byzantium, and so forth. Whether it was a great king like Louis IX of France or lesser princes and middling-level nobles, many of them caught the biographer's attention. Contributions from Anglo-Saxon England, like Asser on Alfred, and from the Byzantine Empire, like Anna Comnena on her father the emperor Alexius, illustrate both the varieties of approach and the widespread appeal of such writing.

Matheson covers a broad canvas in a survey of (English) secular chronicles and historical narratives, explaining how much that we consider to be literature or romance had, for its intended audience, a serious historical component. Our line between 'history' and 'creative writing' was not a recognizable one in the Middle Ages. For those who read or heard the tales, Troy was as historical as William the Conqueror and the wide sweep of medieval ideas about a historical text serves notice that categories and genres are fluid matters, shaped by culture and interpretation. If the past is a different country, as we often say, to the medieval mind its narration had wider boundaries than our discipline-oriented view of such matters admits of.

But narrative sources are not our only carry-overs from the Middle Ages. Other types of primary materials are still with us and to a considerable extent in a recognizable form. While sermons rarely reach the level of popularity they once had as reading matter, they are still delivered as a matter of course in all manner of houses of worship, and a call from the pulpit can still be a powerful voice of conscience. Anne Thayer talks of the power and influence of the medieval sermon, their impact much enhanced in a world of limited literacy and with a great concern for orality (as well as for clerical authority). Everyone heard sermons; the learned also read them. For modern students medieval sermons are a window into how religious instruction on virtually every topic of spiritual and social concern was transmitted from the cleric to his flock. They were the bridge across which high theology was carried, very frequently in the vernacular, to the folk of medieval Christendom.

Other kinds of generic sources are also familiar to this day. Wills and letters are not all that different from their medieval form and use. A medieval will was designed to provide for the soul of the testator, to control the distribution of worldly assets and goods, and – for our eyes – to delineate a social network of family and friends and unnamed beneficiaries. As such, it is moulded and shaped by ecclesiastical injunctions, since testamentary matters fell largely within the Church's jurisdiction. It also reflects the conventions of secular society, standing at the intersection of social–spiritual norms and of individualized intention and volition. The two long examples with which Shona Kelly Wray and Roisin Cossar open their essay offer fuel for this analysis, though regional and cultural differences across Europe are highlighted by the distinctions between wills of the south and the north. The concept of posthumous social control – that of the dead over the living – is also a consideration when we think of the provisions of last wills and the many persons touched by their existence.

Letters, as the essay indicates, were for many centuries perhaps the basic form of communication between people at many levels of society and for no end of purposes. They were the instrument through which much of the business of rulers and states, both secular and ecclesiastical, was conducted. If the modern reliance on letters is narrower than the medieval usage and their literary pretensions no longer at a premium, their basic function as communication has endured, though admittedly with more alternatives today. Accordingly, both wills and letters, as generic sources, are familiar and still very much with us, whether on a regular basis, as with letter-writing, or as part of the closing chapter of the life-cycle.

*    *    *

When we turn to 'topical sources' we enter a different realm. Here we look, not at categories of sources but rather at areas of historical inquiry illuminated by an adroit combination of different kinds of sources. Here there is no single key to open the door. Rather – as with the chemist in our opening metaphor – the secret is in the combination. The choice of which sources to use, and in what mixture, is the challenge. Picking and choosing are skills the historian acquires through experience and in many cases through a good deal of trial and error.

The essays on topical questions illustrate some of the ways historians go about their business. Some are detailed case studies, with Bernard Bachrach's essay on military history as a prime example of this approach. An important narrative source, Dudo of St Quentin writing in early eleventh-century Normandy, recounted military operations of the tenth century but in terms of the institutions and conventions of his own day, a century after 'his' events had taken place. This anachronistic perspective, embedded in a vital primary source, was designed to please those for whom it was written. It has coloured our perception of what had really been the case with military operations of the early tenth century. The lesson is that we should use a source with attention to the circumstances surrounding its creation, a caveat of particular importance when the source is a narrative, since its literary form creates an air of credibility that we must learn to question.

It is a convention of historical writing that winners write history. Mark Pegg unpeels the layers of this onion in a discussion launched by a close analysis of the questions put to and the answers received from a young woman in an inquisitorial proceeding in mid-thirteenth-century France. Not only has the inquisition against 'heretics' been a field of modern contestations over the 'use' of history, with Catholic and Protestant interpretations at wide variance, but much of the agenda and the mindset of the inquisitors themselves reflects a 'reality' that they may well have constructed for their own purposes, one with little relationship to those being questioned regarding beliefs or practices. In reading these sources we must remember that their form and substance rest heavily on all sorts of preconceptions and the 'the objective fact of narrative habits' can – all too readily – make us inclined to take them at face value. This may have pleased the inquisitors but it is a dark window through which to see the complexity of the situation.

Though a king's main claim to his throne and all the privileges and powers that went with it usually rested on some sort of hereditary claim, a medieval monarch was a special person – anointed by the Church and having a role in a sacred and a political drama that ran both before and after his lifetime. Jinty Nelson explores the rituals and the liturgy devised by the Church and endorsed by the king himself that served to separate him from his subjects. At the same time, elements of a contractual theory of kingship can be found in the coronation oath, just as a popular element remains in the exaltation of the newly anointed and crowned ruler by the great figures of his realm. These rituals, across time and across much of Europe, are also a window on how one basic and virtually universal institution was shaped by differences in culture and well as in royal power and personality.

A wide sweep of the immense variety and volume of the sources that touch the gritty realities of rural life is offered by Philip Slavin, dealing with manorial and agricultural history. Though we talk about the problems posed by the loss of so many medieval sources, Slavin's coverage – touching both the quantity of extant material and its scope and level of detail – is a powerful reminder of how much we do have. The sheer volume of local case studies and statistical data on crops and crop yields, taxes, disputes between peasants and lords or other peasants, or touching inheritance and marriage patterns, along with moral injunctions about labour and its rewards, is overwhelming. The costs of labour and agricultural profits and surplus, for a pre-industrial world wherein some eighty per cent of the population lived on the land, are issues of great importance to both high and low. Most of what we know about these men and women of the countryside, given the sources, is top-down information: the lord's view of their economic potential, their tradition-bound social role, and of their efforts to assert an element of agency. The harsh reality is that most manorial records are about profit and loss, not about the people of the fields and villages.

Every textbook talks of the importance of maritime trade and seaborne commerce in medieval society. This major form of activity, involving international law, governmental policy, and a vast commitment of capital and human resources can only be adequately explored through the use of a variety of sources, as in Maryanne Kowaleski's wide ranging essay. She deals with legal and diplomatic conventions and regulations, fiscal accounts, and the records of notaries and merchants, among other sources. And beyond the records of costs and tonnage we have discursive sources: descriptions of voyages mixing sober travel lore with a perennial curiosity about the wonders of distant lands. We learn about and from shipwrecks and navigational charts, and for those unlucky mariners there are archaeological finds telling of lost ships and undelivered cargoes. A look at the environment and ecology of coastal towns and regions rounds out a complex story and emphasizes how many aspects of life were affected by the tale of the seas and those who ventured upon them.

The emergence and growth of towns (and cities) are among the most striking aspects of medieval life. Until the twelfth or thirteenth centuries most records of urban life are of a top-down sort, telling of the lords' willingness to exchange a degree of freedom and independence for monetary returns. Gradually, as life became more complex, competitive and profitable, the internal records of towns grew in variety, scope and sheer bulk; internal government, regulations covering crafts and guilds, rolls of citizens, urban customs and legal codes all took a place alongside those older royal, baronial or ecclesiastical charters that had granted a degree of autonomy. Caroline Barron also looks at how people came to take an interest in their own history, as they came to recognize their own importance and the value of recording privileges and customs for future use.

Sooner or later historians are apt to quote Thomas Hobbes to the effect that life is 'nasty, brutish, and short'. Against this grim view of society and nature Carole Rawcliffe shows that in medieval Europe both individuals and institutions were keenly aware of what we think of as public health and the general well-being of the population. In fact, they often moved to enact (and sometimes to enforce) measures for public welfare: the regulation of noisome crafts like butchering and tanning, and of urban waste as in provisions for privies, and in steps to reduce the threat of plague and disease with clean water and a quarantine of forty days. We find such regulations, especially in towns, and they concern kings and princes as well as urban councils and civic officials. Though all societies live with a gap between 'precept and practice', the variety of primary sources that highlight this salutary and easily-overlooked aspect of life show that public health was an issue of recognized importance. A royal decree or an ordinance of a municipal council about the quality of life, no less than the founding of a hospital to ameliorate the ravages of age and disease, tells us that Victorian generalizations about medieval life, like that comment of Hobbes, can be very wide of the mark.

No other aspect of medieval history has opened up or been 'discovered' to rival our current interest in women's history. Furthermore, what makes this vast area of historical writing so interesting is that virtually all the work of recent decades rests on primary sources long known and used by historians to delve into other questions about the past. But, as Katherine French points out, not only do women appear in significant numbers in so many of these sources, as in wills and grants of endowment, to give but two examples, but once we begin to look for and evaluate women's roles we encounter their presence and activity almost everywhere. They can be studied as agents in legal matters, in urban life and customs, in material about households, in peasant and manorial life, in studies of crime and violence, and – of course – in matters of sex and sexuality. Both what French categorizes as descriptive sources – telling us what people actually did – and prescriptive sources – focusing on what people are told they should do – open windows on aspects of life that affect both women and men. From queens and high-born matriarchs to those who only appear in the written record because, as part of the urban poor, they testified regarding the miracles of Louis IX of France, their voices are too many and too singular to be ignored. That historical research in earlier days was so focused on the male half of the population reminds that our own social and political agenda is not unrelated to our agenda as historians.

Historians are wont to say that the legacy of the Middle Ages is still with us in the guise of cathedrals, universities and parliaments. Parliaments, or representative government, have indeed come down to us by way of a zig-zag trail of trial and error as we trace today's institutions to their antecedents of the thirteenth and fourteenth centuries. Furthermore, though Hannes Kleineke concentrates on developments in England – given the great variety of English sources and the way they can be cross-referenced to fill in some of the gaps – a comparable tale could be told for much of medieval Europe. Kleineke illustrates how the interests of different parties and voices, and the sources that embody these different interests, can be woven into a tapestry that gives a fair glimpse of the larger tale, the development of representative institutions. The king, those of various ranks who were summoned to his great council (parliament), the towns that reimbursed those chosen to represent them, the chroniclers who wrote narrative histories, and even poets with an eye on the political scene, all did their share regarding the creation of sources, even if each party mostly cared about furthering his (or their) own interest.

\* \* \*

If the written primary source is the bread and butter of historical research, we should nevertheless remember that no society – let alone medieval society, with limited literacy and a difficult access to parchment and ink – is going to be fully explicated by such materials. The visual world and that of material objects, ranging from buttons and brooches to town walls and castles, were very much part of the experience of the people of our period. In keeping with this we conclude with two essays that look at different kinds of sources.

The riches of medieval imagery, at both the macro- and the micro-level, are obvious to anyone who has been to a museum, visited a medieval site, or even leafed through a good coffee-table book. But to see is not necessarily to understand, let alone to be able to set the object or image into the many contexts of interpretation that Sara Lipton offers. We may identify a visual depiction: St Roch with his bubo, Mary Magdelene of the long red hair, and so on. But many images and depictions are less clear-cut, as in Lipton's examples of royal sculptures or of probable Jews in manuscript margins. And beyond the question of identification we reach for deeper layers of analysis: what did the image mean to those who created it, who viewed it, who commented on it, and/or who commissioned and paid for it? These levels of interpretation are a challenge as we work to link visual culture to the written sources that cover the same world, the same culture. There are pitfalls and contradictions, but there are also opportunities to push ahead toward a more complex view of the society whence these images came.

Material culture is an academic way of talking about objects – things that have physical existence, and the study of such materials is the traditional realm of the archaeologist. But when the historical area being examined is one that is also richly embellished by written and visual survivals, then we look at how the archaeologist links that specialized form of research into those we are accustomed to unravel. David Hinton talks of material objects, from macro-structures like buildings and the outline of settlements, to micro-objects like buttons and animal bones. All of these physical remains, whether below the earth's surface or identifiable by way of aerial photography or field-walking, are keys to the past and invaluable supplements or complements to what we learn from our use of those more familiar written materials. We might think of the separate disciplines as being different paths leading, or so we hope, to an intersection of mutual enlightenment.

# 1   Royal and secular biography

*Ralph A. Griffiths*

Biography may not have been a term familiar before the seventeenth century, but fascination with the lives, deeds and histories of notable men and women – their *vitae*, *gestae* and *historiae* – was common in classical and medieval times. Plutarch, Suetonius, Tacitus and Cicero, and their lives of distinguished Greeks and Romans, were models for later ages, while the lives of saintly figures, both men and women, were at the heart of the Christian faith. Secular lives – especially of medieval emperors, kings and princes – were composed to impress and inspire, and were usually written within a generation or so of the subject's death. In those instances where authors were closely acquainted with their subjects or wrote with a hint of autobiography, their biographies seem especially vivid and to speak with greater conviction to modern historians. In Latin and Greek Europe, secular biographies became more common from the ninth century onwards. The difference between secular biography and the writing of history in the Middle Ages was inevitably blurred because most of these biographies were of notable rulers. The emergence of principalities and states, and the periodic resurgence of learning, encouraged the writing of collected histories of rulers' reigns (if not their lives). In the later Middle Ages, the renewed humanist emphasis on the individual who merited praise or whose example deserved to be emulated – or occasionally avoided – reasserted the importance of rhetorical writing and the use of Greek and Roman models.

Biographical writing varied greatly, depending on its purpose and the identity and motives of the writers: hagiography, commemoration and celebration, the writers' characters, knowledge and abilities, and the changing political and cultural circumstances in which they wrote, all are features that adjusted the nature of biographies from time to time. Some were blatant propaganda, while others were designed to entertain. In time, the writing of biography migrated from monasteries and churches to royal courts and scholars' studies, and vernacular languages were often favoured, while the context of individual combat and campaigning shifted towards political behaviour and more peaceful arts.

Many secular medieval biographies survive, and to judge by the manuscript copies in circulation they were popular reading and listening; others are known only indirectly or are fragmentary, while yet others may have been intended for a small courtly circle. Not all secular biographies that survive have been published in modern editions, still less in English translations, but their comparative study beckons.

Plutarch the Greek (*c.*AD 46–*c.*120), the most notable ancient biographer, composed a collection of short 'Parallel Lives of the Noble Grecians and Romans' whose characters and careers should inspire future generations; these lives certainly inspired later writers and continued to be a quarry for Shakespeare. The Roman Seutonius's 'Lives of the Caesars' (*c.*AD 120), though mainly descriptive and anecdotal, was even more influential on later writers, among them the Carolingian Einhard (*c.*770–840), through whom the rhetorical tradition passed into the medieval genre of royal biography.

Plutarch and Seutonius wrote what amounted to collected biographies of great men. In later centuries, authors also focused on notable kings and princes, and on Rome's successor kingdoms and principalities, while Christian hagiography concentrated on individual saints' lives. The revival of classical learning in the ninth century included the art of rhetoric and the writing of lives of secular rulers. The monk Einhard at the court of the Emperor Charlemagne is a beacon in the history of biography. His 'Life of Charlemagne' (*c.*830) took Suetonius as its model, rather than (but not in opposition to) the lives of Christian saints. No comparable life of a secular ruler which sought to convey an impression of its subject rather than a catalogue of his deeds had been written for centuries. For this reason it has been termed 'the greatest monument of secular biography of the Latin Middle Ages'. It proved to be of enduring popularity and today about eighty manuscripts of the life are known. As an author, Einhard set a pattern: an educated monk, poet and letter-writer who lived at Charlemagne's cultivated court and observed the emperor at close quarters: 'I was aware that no one could write about these things more truthfully than me, since I myself was present and personally witnessed them, as they say, with my own eyes'.[1]

Einhard vividly recalled Charlemagne's commanding presence and sought 'to speak of the character of his mind, his supreme steadfastness in good times and bad, and those things that belong to his spiritual and domestic life'.[2] Thus, he provided not only a portrait of Charlemagne – his early life and accession, his personal life, marriages and family, his visit to Rome and coronation there in AD 800, and his death, and last will and testament – but also judgements on his wars and relations with the North men and the Moors beyond his empire as well as the Saxons within: 'the king's greatness of spirit and steadfast determination – both in bad times and good – could not be conquered by [the Saxons'] fickleness or worn down by the task he had set himself'. In war the lessons for Charlemagne's successors were patent: 'Thus it was not his nature to give up in bad times or to be seduced by the false flattery of success in good times'.[3] Equal stress was laid on the emperor's determination to advance learning and the arts of peace: 'He avidly pursued the liberal arts and greatly honoured those teachers whom he deeply respected'. Yet Einhard was also aware of the personal limitations on Charlemagne in law-giving and encouraging learning: 'He also attempted to learn how to write and for this reason, used to place wax-tablets and notebooks under the pillows on his bed, so that, if he had any free time, he might accustom his hand to forming letters. But his effort came too late in life and achieved little success.'[4]

After Charlemagne's death, Einhard served his son and successor, Louis the Pious, for whom it is probable that the life was written, to celebrate the great emperor, legitimize Louis's rule of the Frankish empire, and to provide an exemplar of rulership. Its attractiveness lay in its brevity and 'powerful simplicity', its lightness of touch, and in the Ciceronian style which Einhard strove to emulate in order to praise a famous ruler, though inevitably it was selective in content and rarely criticized the emperor.

In the following two centuries, no secular person 'had a biographer who wrote of him in purely secular terms'. Those biographies that were written – of rulers in various parts of northern Europe, including Matilda, queen of Henry I of Germany, and Margaret, queen of Malcolm III of Scotland – generally saw their subjects in hagiographic terms and their political activities as of secondary importance. It is true that those who wrote lives of later Carolingian rulers sought to emulate Einhard, but they had few of his qualities and less of his range, and their biographies hardly breathed life into their subjects. Theganus (died *c*.848), a Frankish clerk of noble birth, composed a biography of Charlemagne's son, Louis the Pious; he used Einhard's biography as a model, but his work was more annalistic, and conventional in its description of Louis. Ermeldus Nigellus (died before 835), wrote a Latin historical poem 'In Honor of Louis, the Most Christian Caesar Augustus' to curry favour and he too used classical models for his individual portraits. Notker Balbus ('the Stammerer', *c*.840–912), a talented writer who was a monk at St Gall, wrote of Charlemagne's deeds; although he knew Einhard's work, he relied mainly on oral tradition and popular anecdotes in seeking to portray a wise and just emperor, an exemplar among rulers.

In Anglo-Saxon England, the writing of biography was a weaker tradition. Indeed, the three most noteworthy surviving biographies of kings – of Alfred, Cnut the Dane and Edward the Confessor – were probably written by, respectively, a Welshman and two Flemings. The first biography of an English monarch was Asser's life of Alfred. It certainly drew on the example of Einhard but was equally dependent on hagiographical tradition and Anglo-Saxon annals. As a result, it offers a more idealized, romanticized and stilted portrait than Einhard's. But at least Asser, a Welshman who was summoned to be bishop of Sherborne (Dorset), frequented Alfred's court, knew the king personally, and included some autobiographical details: 'At about this time I … was summoned by the king from the remote, westernmost parts of Wales … When I had been warmly welcomed by him, and we engaged in discussion, he asked me earnestly to commit myself to his service and to become a member of his household … '.[5]

Asser's life was written *c*.893 during Alfred's lifetime, and may have been composed at the king's request for the Welsh who had submitted to him; hence its extravagant dedication 'to my esteemed and most holy lord, Alfred ruler of all the Christians of the island of Britain, king of the Angles and Saxons'.[6] Its purpose was to celebrate the king's educational achievements, his just government and his military and naval campaigns against the Vikings. Scholarly arguments about its authenticity have been resolved decisively in its favour as a late ninth-century account, and its stories of Alfred's adversities seem authentic (though the tale of 'the cakes' is much later). Alfred emerges as a humane, Christian ruler, a lawgiver committed to advancing learning among his subjects:

[Alfred] used to affirm, with repeated complaints and sighing from the depths of his heart, that among all the difficulties and burdens of his present life this had become the greatest: namely, that at the time when he was of the right age and had the leisure and the capacity for learning, he did not have the teachers. For when he was older, and more incessantly preoccupied by day and night with – or rather harassed by – all kinds of illnesses unknown to the physicians of this island, as well as by the cares (both domestic and foreign) of the royal office, and also by the incursions of the Vikings by land and sea, he had the teachers and scribes to some small extent, but he was unable to study.[7]

Asser did not complete his biography and it never achieved the popularity of Einhard's life of Charlemagne. Its admiring assessment of Alfred is interestingly couched in a naval metaphor:

Yet once he had taken over the helm of his kingdom, he alone, sustained by divine assistance, struggled like an excellent pilot to guide his ship laden with much wealth to the desired and safe haven of his homeland, even though all his sailors were virtually exhausted; similarly, he did not allow it to waver or wander from course, even though the course lay through the many seething whirlpools of the present life. For by gently instructing, cajoling, urging, commanding, and (in the end, when his patience was exhausted) by sharply chastising those who were disobedient and by despising popular stupidity and stubbornness in every way, he carefully and cleverly exploited and converted his bishops and earldormen and nobles, and his thegns most dear to him, and reeves as well, … to his own will and to the general advantage of the whole realm.[8]

The lives of Cnut and the Confessor were written, unusually, in praise of their respective queens as well as for circulation at court. Each offered an idealized portrait that lauded the Christian hero-king as an example to others. In Richard Southern's view, these two authors 'most brilliantly imposed on recalcitrant material the dramatic unity and elevation of sentiment that the rhetorical ideal demanded. … They wrote as outsiders, and managed to express a mysterious depth of national feeling quite unlike anything we find elsewhere. They were serious artists and in their own way serious historians.'[9]

Queen Emma could hardly fail to be pleased by the account of the exploits and character of her husband, Cnut, and his Christian life, as described in the *Encomium Emmae*. Likewise, the *Vita Edwardi Confessoris* praised Queen Edith and her husband, and also her father Earl Godwin; their unity of endeavour benefited the kingdom while, instructively, their disunity all but destroyed it. Like Einhard and Alfred, these two biographers dwelt on the public and private lives of their subjects, with a nod towards the hagiographical and classical traditions, but in Edward's case the life also took the king to the threshold of sanctity by recording miracles.

The German empire and its rulers provided some of the best subjects for biography in the rhetorical tradition. Hrotsvitha von Gandersheim (*c.*935–*c.*1001/1003), an accomplished poetess, wrote her historical poem, *Gesta Ottonis*, *c.*968 at the request of Otto I's niece. As a history of Otto's reign, it showed knowledge of classical and religious literature and hagiography, without however being a comprehensive biography of the emperor. Liutprand of Cremona (*c.*920–72) moved to the Ottonian court and Otto I appointed him bishop of Cremona; his historiographical writings, including his deeds of 'the Great Emperor Otto', drifted at times into autobiography. Wipo's life of Conrad II, whose chaplain he was in the mid-eleventh century, did at least strive to paint a rounded picture of the emperor, though his intention was the spiritual instruction of his audience. The anonymous biography of the Emperor Henry IV, written *c.*1107, was squarely in the rhetorical tradition and spent more time on Henry's alleged holiness of character and good works than on his deeds as emperor.

At the other end of Europe, in the Byzantine Empire, the most extraordinary biography of the early Middle Ages was written by the daughter of the Emperor Alexius. Nothing in the Latin West could compare with it. Eulogies of Byzantine emperors had been written before – of Basil I (867–86), for example – and Michael Psellos (1018–*c.*1078), scholar, historian and statesman, produced a remarkable century-long history of the Byzantine imperial court, his *Chronographia*, with emperors at its heart, which drew on classical Greek models. More strictly biographical, however, was Anna Comnena's admiring epic of her father, the *Alexiad*, written soon after 1148 to record his deeds; it is well regarded by historians as a source for the emperor's reign and Byzantine relations in the Mediterranean and Near Eastern worlds in the age of the early crusades. A study of the empire constructed around the life of an individual, it is vivid and shrewd in its depictions of the imperial family and court, worldly and opinionated in its judgements of peoples and individuals, including Pope Gregory VII, the Latins of the West and Armenians. This is a human, rather than a spiritual, study of Alexius by a highly educated woman with unrivalled access to the court, and 'a masterpiece of Byzantine literature'. It records political struggles in Constantinople and the triumph of Byzantine arms against the Normans. If it omits much, digresses and lacks a firm chronology, it also has the virtues of immediacy and readability.[10]

Anna could rely on her own experiences and on the news and gossip of the court, and she injects herself into the narrative from time to time. Her sympathetic portrait of her father is luminous if biased:

> The physical appearance of the two rulers, Alexius and Irene [Anna's mother], was remarkable, indeed quite incomparable. A painter could never reproduce the beauty of such an archetype, nor a sculptor mould his lifeless stone into such harmony. … Alexius was not a very tall man, but broad-shouldered and yet well proportioned. When standing he did not seem particularly striking to onlookers, but when one saw the grim flash of his eyes as he sat on the imperial throne, he reminded one of a fiery whirlwind, so overwhelming was the radiance that emanated from his countenance and his whole presence. … The man's person indeed radiated beauty and grace and dignity and an unapproachable majesty. When he came into a gathering and began to speak, at once you were conscious of the fiery eloquence of his tongue, for a torrent of

argument won universal hearing and captivated every heart; tongue and hand alike were unsurpassed and invincible, the one in hurling the spear, the other in devising fresh enchantments.[11]

Her approach to writing the biography is mature: it shows an awareness of the dangers of eulogy, appreciates the value of history and its didactic quality, and seeks objectivity:

> In the course of this account, partly because of the nature of the history and partly because of the great importance of these events, I have forgotten that it is my father whose successes I am writing of. Often, in my desire not to incur suspicion, in the composition of my history I hurry over affairs that concern him, neither exaggerating nor adding my personal observations. I wish I were detached and free from this feeling for him, so that seizing on this vast material I might demonstrate how much my tongue, when released from all restraint, could delight in noble deeds. But the natural love I have for him overshadows my personal wishes; I would not like the public to imagine that I am inventing marvels in my eagerness to speak about my own family … I must avoid the subtleties of rhetoric, and like some unfeeling adamant or marble pass quickly over his misfortunes.

In describing her father's life, she gives assurance that 'The reader can rest assured that I would never betray the truth under the guise of history'.[12] Thus, Anna's portrait of Robert Guiscard, Alexius's Norman enemy, is not unflattering, rather portraying him as a worthy adversary of a great emperor: 'The truth is that Robert's manliness, his marvellous skill in war and his steadfast spirit are universally recognized. He was an adversary not readily vanquished, a very tough enemy who was more courageous than ever in the hour of defeat'.[13]

The portrait of Alexius is a secular one, using a maritime metaphor to assess his temporal achievements:

> … the emperor like a good helmsman guided his craft safely through the constant battering of the waves. Scarcely had he cleansed himself of the thick layers of brine (that is, set in good order the affairs of Church and State), when he was called upon to embark on fresh seas of tribulation. Indeed there was a never-ending succession of woes – an ocean of trouble, as it were – so that he was allowed no breathing-space, no chance whatever to rest.[14]

The intellectual revival of the twelfth century embraced secular biography as well as historical writing more broadly. Classical models were somewhat less influential than in the past though the interest in describing exemplary rulers in a Christian context was strong. King-centred history clarified the past and helped to ensure continuity of states' development. It was the court of Frederick I Barbarossa that inspired the most striking historical writing, including biography. Otto of Freising (*c.*1114–58), a Cistercian who became bishop of Freising, has been judged the greatest of German medieval historians. As a nephew of

Barbarossa, he was well placed to acquire information for his *Gesta Frederici*, whose deeds he was capable of placing in a historical context, both of the Hohenstaufen family and imperial rule. His picture of a strong, just ruler was in traditional mould, whereas his account of Frederick's establishment of peace in Germany and harmony between Church and state amounts to 'the most valuable surviving source for the early years of Barbarossa's reign'.[15]

In contemporary France, too, the writing of biography flourished vigorously from the late eleventh century onwards, reflecting the development of the French kingdom and the principalities associated with it. Classical, rhetorical and Christian influences were present, yet there was also a conscious striving after historical realism. William the bastard, duke of Normandy and king of England, was the subject of biographies by Norman clerks. William of Jumièges, a Benedictine monk, wrote his *Gesta Normannorum Ducum* in 1070–1 and originally dedicated it to William; centred on the dukes, it is a source for an entire century of Norman history. The *Gesta Guillelmi Ducis Normannorum et Regis Anglorum* of William of Poitiers (*c*.1020–*c*.1087/1100), is more tightly focused on William the Conqueror, but no contemporary copy of it now exists. Both clerks were well informed and well connected at William's court: their histories were pro-Norman and did not wholly abandon a panegyric style that portrayed William as a Christian prince.

The most notable English chronicles were in the form of collected studies of reigns rather than lives. The popular *Gesta regum Anglorum* of William of Malmesbury (*c*.1090–1143), a Benedictine monk of Norman and Saxon parentage, was written, with a supplement, *Historia Novella*, between 1118 and 1145, and amounted to a narrative of English history from the coming of the Anglo-Saxons. In writing of recent kings, especially William Rufus and his brother Henry I, hagiographic and classical influences as well as those of the Anglo-Saxon biographical tradition were apparent, and he was less interested in constructing a narrative than in describing personality and explaining motive. In this, he may be compared with Abbot Suger, his contemporary in Paris. William's aim was to record, educate and entertain without being unashamedly eulogistic. Though less successful or popular, the *gestae* of kings like Stephen and Henry II placed the lives of kings and their families at the heart of the events through which they lived.

Biographies continued to be written by clerks and royal chaplains, some associated with the lesser courts of, for example, counts of Anjou and counts of Hainault. Their predecessor seems to have been St Odo, abbot of Cluny, who *c*.925 wrote a life of the southern French noble, Count Gerald of Aurillac, which is regarded as the first, albeit hagiographic, biography of a medieval layman. Classical allusions were present in the life of Robert Guiscard, an epic poem on the early history of the Normans in southern Italy that was composed by William of Apulia (*c*.1100). William, a cleric, wrote at the request of Pope Urban II and dedicated his poem to Robert's son, Duke Roger of Apulia.

In Wales, where state formation was more hesitant, a posthumous Latin life of Gruffudd ap Cynan, king of Gwynedd, was composed *c*.1160 primarily to extol his prowess in winning his kingdom and in order to support the pretensions of

Gwynedd under his son Owain. Yet embedded in the flattery are realistic descriptions of Gruffudd the man:

> Contemporaries of Gruffudd reported that he was a man of moderate stature, with fair hair, a clever head, a round face, of good colour, eyes properly borne, fine eyebrows and a good beard, a round neck, fair skin, strong limbs, long fingers, straight legs, and comely feet; he was very polished in his education and outstanding at foreign languages; towards his soldiers he was kind and generous, towards his enemies spirited, and very brave in battle.

Even in commending his rule, there are elements that strike a realistic chord:

> After enduring such great labours, Gruffudd ruled for many years, affluent with wealth and rejoicing in a calm and unbroken peace, and was on the friendliest terms and greatest concord with neighbouring kings, namely Henry, king of England, Murchardh, king of Ireland, and the kings who ruled the islands of Denmark, and his name was famous not only in the adjacent kingdoms but even in the furthest lands … he governed his people with an iron rod but also encouraged peace and concord with kingdoms neighbouring him.[16]

Gruffudd is the only medieval Welsh king whose biography has survived; it has classical and biblical parallels, while underlining Gruffudd's Irish, Scandinavian and Norman connections as well as his Welsh heritage.

The monks of St Denis, near Paris, took the writing of royal biography a step further. They became official historians of the Capetian and Valois monarchs; the abbey's chronicle praised the French kings and was patronized by them. Thus, Abbot Suger, a confidant of Louis VI, wrote the king's biography, *Vita Ludovici grossi Regis*. Composed shortly after the king's death, Suger's aim was 'to celebrate the king and mourn his death' and to write 'of his devotion for the churches of God and his excellent government of the realm'. It was offered as advice to his young son Louis VII: to care for the Church and especially for St Denis, and then God would assist the new king in his enterprises as He had his father. Suger pointedly wrote that 'Louis, king of the French by the grace of God, could not put aside what he had grown accustomed to do in his youth, namely safeguarding the churches, protecting the poor and the needy, and working for the peace and defence of the kingdom'.[17] This suggests that the biography stands in the hagiographical Christian tradition of saints' lives, to whose ranks Suger prayed that Louis VI would be admitted; it was less influenced by the rhetorical tradition and classical writers like Suetonius, even by Einhard. Louis was presented in stylized colours as an exemplary Christian king, the protector of his people and Church and the dispenser of peace and justice. At the same time, Suger was an intelligent observer with inside knowledge, and he produced a vivid account of how the king set about exerting his authority in his royal domain and extending it over some of his greater vassals while keeping the English king and the German emperor at bay.

At the end of the twelfth century, St Denis was sponsoring what amounted to an official history of the French kings, *Historia regni Francorum*, a collection of royal biographies interwoven with the history of the kingdom. Its significance was confirmed by its transformation into the *Grandes Chroniques de France*, which was continued to the end of the Middle Ages. Rigord, monk of St Denis, and Guillaume le Breton, a royal chaplain, produced encomia of Philip Augustus in Latin verse; indeed it was Rigord, the court historiographer, who coined the term Augustus. Guillaume continued Rigord's *gesta* to celebrate Philip's victory over English and imperial armies at Bouvines in 1214. Though something of a panegyric, these were the first works of Capetian history produced at court in the interests of the French monarchy.

About 1250, a large compilation of Latin chronicles and *gestae* of French kings was made at St Denis. The abbey's official history was encouraged by Louis IX (canonized in 1298), and it was translated in 1274 into French for a courtly audience and presented to Philip III. Biographies of St Louis and later French kings were added to what became the *Grandes Chroniques*. This sequence of royal biographies, even including Einhard, provided a genealogical framework for the regal ideology and history of France: its purpose was didactic, revealing the intimate relationship between France and its kings.

Jean de Joinville's *Histoire de Saint Louis* is hard to classify: written in Old French (rather than Latin) by a minor nobleman, it is an account of Louis's crusading, a biography of the saintly king and, in part, an autobiographical memoir of Joinville who knew the king well and accompanied him on crusade in 1248–54. The personal reminiscences and anecdotes prevent it from being hagiography. Completed in 1309, long after Louis's death on crusade in 1270, it was commissioned by his widow (died 1295) and was initially addressed to his son and successor for his instruction. On one level it is a record of Louis's laudable reign and saintly life, yet the intimacy of a confidant, the conversational tone and Joinville's instincts as a historian give it great value as a historical source: 'I wish to make known to all that I myself actually saw and heard a great part of what I have told you here concerning the saintly king'. He notes that he had taken some material from a book written in French, very likely a chronicle: 'I am drawing attention to this so that those who hear this book read may have full confidence in the truth of what it says I saw and heard. As for the other things recorded here, I offer no guarantee of their truth, because I do not witness them myself.'[18] After a short account of Louis's early reign derived from another source, the personal observations are often vivid if prone to digression. The first part describes the king's piety and just government:

> I have sometimes seen him, in summer, go to administer justice to his people in the public gardens in Paris, dressed in a plain woollen tunic, a sleeveless surcoat of linsey-woolsey, and a black taffeta cape round his shoulders, with his hair neatly combed, but no cap to cover it, and only a hat of white peacock's feathers on his head. He would have a carpet laid down so that we might sit round him, while all those who had any case to bring before him stood about. Then he would pass judgement on each case, as I have told you he often used to do in the wood of Vincennes.[19]

Joinville emphasizes the king's wisdom, his concern to pacify the realm and his spiritual nature:

> After King Louis had returned to France from oversea he was very devout in his worship of our Saviour, and very just in his dealings with his subjects. That is why he made up his mind that it would be a very good and noble thing to undertake the reform of his kingdom of France. As a first step in this direction he drew up a general ordinance for all his subjects throughout the realm … [and Joinville then adds the long document].[20]

Louis's concern for the poor and his generosity towards the Church are stressed, and the biography ends with the process of canonization in 1298 which Joinville witnessed. But his admiration for the king was not uncritical – even to the extent (so he says) of contradicting the king to his face. Joinville's work is considered to be a monument of French prose and (in W.C. Jordan's view) 'the finest biography of the saint king'.

Secular biographies of other than kings and queens highlighted the chivalric and adventurous deeds of individual nobles. As early as *c.*1226, a verse history in French of William the Marshal, distinguished knight and statesman who ruled England during Henry III's minority, was written by a minstrel and commissioned by his son to commemorate William's life. It was the first in a series of biographies in romantic vein, designed to celebrate chivalric ideals, but at the same time tending to suppress unflattering details and thereby to distort historical reality. The History of William the Marshal portrayed a model of knightly virtue: its 19,000 lines focus on William's life as a perfect knight yet living in the real world of war-torn England, France and Ireland.

The Life of the Black Prince, a poem also in French by the herald of his retainer, Sir John Chandos, *c.*1385, was perhaps intended for recitation. It focuses especially on the prince's campaigns in Spain where Chandos served and the herald was an eyewitness; composed about ten years after the Black Prince's death in 1376, it was intended to commemorate the prince's accomplishments as a romantic hero. In similar vein was the biography of Bertrand du Guesclin, marshal of France, by Jean Cuvelier, written in 1385 soon after Bertrand's death; while a chivalric account of the deeds of Jean Boucicaut, knight errant, was written in 1409, during his own lifetime. These are far from the earlier works of Christian hagiography.

In the fourteenth century there was a revival of interest in classical antiquity, especially in Italy, and this included the lives of the ancients and later figures. Petrarch regarded Suetonius as the classic biographer, and Boccaccio wrote lives of illustrious men and women; Plutarch's 'Lives' was the prime model for biography by the mid-fifteenth century and was mined by Shakespeare in the sixteenth. The traditional arts of biography – even hagiography from the pens of clerical and secular writers – could be combined to recount the lives and deeds of distinguished men. In 1404, Christine de Pisan wrote an admiring biography of Charles V of France, *Le livre des faits et bonnes moeurs du roi Charles V le Sage*; thanks to him 'the English no longer dare to set foot in France'. There was no strong tradition of royal biography in England, though the reigns of kings provided a chronological structure for chronicles. The few biographies that were written – lives of Richard the Lionheart and Robert of Avebury's *Gesta* of Edward III – were eulogistic and intended to inspire.

To some degree, Henry V was treated similarly: though regarded as an exemplary chivalric hero in his lifetime, his biographers were also influenced by continental humanism. Henry could be viewed as a Christian, chivalric monarch and at the same time a great ruler. Thomas Elmham (1364–*c*.1427), scholar, historian and monk of St Augustine's, Canterbury, wrote a verse life of Henry in 1418, during the king's lifetime – in Latin in order to 'envelop [his work] in obscurity'. The *Gesta Henrici Quinti*, which, like Elmham, dealt with the first three years or so of Henry's reign, seems more overtly – even officially – propagandist yet well informed; the anonymous author was an Englishman in priestly orders and attached to the king's court. The purpose of this biography was to justify the king's deeds as those of a devout Christian prince whom God endorsed both at home and in the wars in France, especially in the victory at Agincourt.

> He applied his mind with all devotion to encompass what could promote the honour of God, the extension of the Church, the deliverance of his country, and the peace and tranquillity of kingdoms, and especially (because they were more closely connected and associated) the peace and tranquillity of the two kingdoms of England and France, which over a long and lamentable period of time have done injury to themselves by their internal conflicts, not without a great and grievous shedding of human blood.[21]

Like other *gestae*, it opens with the king's coronation (1413), not with his birth (1387). The writer's aim is to justify the king's policies and glorify his deeds. He repeatedly portrays the king seeking to enlist God's aid in his enterprises: at Harfleur, where the king's army landed in 1415, 'our king … called upon God as witness to his blameless quarrel'.[22] On the march towards Calais, 'our king – relying on divine grace and the justice of his cause, piously reflecting that victory consists not in a multitude but with Him for Whom it is not impossible to enclose the many in the hand of the few and Who bestows victory upon whom He wills, whether they be many or few – with God, as is believed, affording him His leadership, did nevertheless decide to make that march'.[23] And on the eve of Agincourt, he has Henry replying to a plea for more archers (with an echo perhaps in Shakespeare):

> 'That is a foolish way to talk … because, by the God in Heaven upon Whose grace I have relied and in Whom is my firm hope of victory, I would not, even if I could, have a single man more than I do. For these I have here with me are God's people, whom He deigns to let me have at this time. Do you not believe', he asked, 'that the Almighty, with these His humble few, is able to overcome the opposing arrogance of the French who boast of their great number and their own strength? as if to say, He can if He wishes. And, as I myself believe, it was not possible, because of the true righteousness of God,

for misfortune to befall a son of His with so sublime a faith, any more than it befell Judas Maccabeus until he lapsed into lack of faith and so, deservedly, met with disaster.'[24]

At the same time, there is no doubt that the author was an eyewitness for much of 1415–16, with access to public records, and so he provides one of the best accounts of these years, for all its providential and eulogistic air: 'I, who am now writing this and was then sitting on a horse among the baggage at the rear of the battle [of Agincourt]'.[25]

At the end of the fifteenth century, Philippe de Commynes's memoirs of King Louis XI of France is of a yet different order while incorporating features of earlier biographies: it is far from being an idealized life of the king or a glowing assessment of chivalric deeds. Rather does it offer a realistic analysis of the motives and self-interest of princes with virtues and flaws, from the perspective of a contemporary statesman, civil servant and chronicler; it is a personal account of the years 1464–98 showing a humanist's unvarnished appraisal of political behaviour. Commynes was a Burgundian noble who deserted the duke of Burgundy to enter Louis XI's service in 1472; he became close to the king but then fell from grace and was imprisoned during his son's reign and did not return to the court until 1490. He is scarcely an impartial witness and there is an embittered strain to his recollections. He dictated his memoirs in the 1490s and intended their moral and political observations to instruct and inform, somewhat in the tradition of 'mirrors for princes' to guide their behaviour but also, in Commynes's case, to justify his own career. He could both praise and criticize King Louis and Duke Charles the Rash of Burgundy; but his own motives mean that his memoirs fall short of complete reliability as a historical source. Commynes's prologue explains the circumstances of writing:

I can say nothing of [Louis's] youth except what I have heard from him; but from the time when I came into his service until the hour of his death, when I was present, I resided continually with him longer than anyone else, serving him at least in the capacity of a chamberlain and often being occupied in his most important business. In him, and in all other princes whom I have known or served, I have recognized good and evil for they are men just like ourselves and to God alone belongs perfection. But when a prince's virtues and laudable qualities exceed his vices, he deserves great praise, since princes are more inclined to act arbitrarily than other men. ...

As I do not wish to lie, it may happen that in certain parts of this account you may find things which are not at all to Louis's credit. But I hope that those who read of these matters will consider the circumstances I have mentioned already and, I dare to say, so much to his credit that in my opinion I have never known a prince in whose character there were, all things considered, so few faults.[26]

Commynes was less than frank when he noted that:

> Chroniclers usually write only praiseworthy things about those of whom they
> speak and they omit many things or are sometimes ignorant of the truth. I
> decided to speak about nothing that was untrue or which I had not seen or
> learned about from such important people that their words can be trusted,
> whether or not these things are praiseworthy.[27]

This did not prevent him from interpreting matters for his own purposes. He
was not blind to Louis's devious and manipulative qualities, albeit in his own and
France's interests:

> ... of all those whom I have ever known, the wisest in extricating himself
> from a tricky situation in an adverse time was our master, King Louis XI, and
> he was humblest in word and attire and one who ever worked to win over a
> man who could serve or do him harm. ... And these manners and qualities
> which he had, which I have just mentioned, saved his crown for him, seeing
> the enemies which he had acquired at his accession to the kingdom.[28]

In buying off the English king, Edward IV, who had invaded France in 1478,
Commynes reported that:

> The King [Louis] also had a good understanding of the king of England's
> character, that he liked his pleasures and comforts very much. From this
> it appeared that the King spoke more wisely than anyone else present and
> understood clearly the things he was talking about. ... Besides this the King
> said that there was nothing in the world he would not do to boot the English
> out of France, except that he would never consent to giving them any land.
> Before doing this he would rather hazard all.[29]

When Duke Charles of Burgundy died in 1477, Louis (according to Commynes)
strove to take full advantage of the situation, even reversing his policy and
spurning advice:

> He was pleased to tell me all about this because I had on previous occasions
> spoken to him and counselled him to adopt the other policy. ... He wanted
> me to understand his reasons for changing his mind and why this policy was
> more beneficial for his kingdom, which had suffered so much because of the
> greatness of the house of Burgundy. ...
>
> From a worldly point of view there was much substance in what the King was
> saying, but as a matter of conscience, I thought the opposite. Nevertheless
> the King's judgement was so much greater than mine or any others in his
> company that we could not comprehend his affairs as clearly as he could
> himself. For without doubt he was one of the cleverest and most subtle
> princes of his generation.[30]

Behind it all there lay a grudging admiration of the king:

> God had granted him one particular favour for he had endowed him with more sagacity, liberality and virtue in all matters than any other prince who ruled at the same time as he did, whether they were his enemies or neighbours, and as he surpassed them in all achievements so he exceeded them in length of life, although not by very much. ... In all of them there was good and bad, for they were all human. But without exaggeration it may be said he possessed more of the qualities needed by a king or a prince than any of the others. I have seen almost all of them and knew their abilities so I am not guessing.[31]

The lives of secular rulers, in all their variety, occupy but one niche in the systematic recording of historical events that is the medieval chronicle tradition which the next chapter exemplifies.

## Further reading

R.L. Benson (ed.), transl. T.E. Mommsen and K.F. Morrison, *Imperial Lives and Letters of the Eleventh Century* (New York: Columbia University Press, 2000).

E. Cochrane, *Historians and Historiography in the Italian Renaissance* (Chicago and London: University of Chicago Press, 1981).

R. Cusimano and J. Moorhead, transl. and introduction, *The Deeds of Louis the Fat* (Washington, DC: Catholic University of America Press, 1992).

D.S. Evans, *A Medieval Prince of Wales: The Life of Gruffudd ap Cynan* (Llanerch: Llanerch Enterprises, 1990).

C. Given-Wilson, *Chronicles: The Writing of History in Medieval England* (London: Hambledon and London Books, 2004).

A. Gransden, *Historical Writing in England, c.550–c.1307* (London: Routledge & Kegan Paul, 1974).

A. Gransden, *Historical Writing in England, II: c.1307 to the Early Sixteenth Century* (London: Routledge & Kegan Paul, 1982).

A. Gransden, 'Propaganda in English Medieval Historiography', *Journal of Medieval History*, 1 (1975), 363–81.

L. Grant, *Abbot Suger of St Denis* (London: Longman, 1998).

C.H. Haskins, *The Renaissance of the Twelfth Century* (Cambridge, MA: Harvard University Press, 1928), ch. VIII ('Historical writing').

D. Hay, *Annalists and Historians: Western Historiography from the VIIIth to the XVIIIth Century* (London: Methuen, 1977).

A.D. Hedeman, *The Royal Image: Illustrations of the Grandes Chroniques de France, 1274–1422* (Berkeley, Los Angeles and Oxford: University of California Press, 1991).

A.J. Holden (ed.), transl. S. Gregory, *History of William Marshall* (London: Anglo-Norman Text Society, 2002).

S. Kinser (ed.), transl. I. Caseaux, *The Memoirs of Philippe de Commynes*, 2 vols (Columbia, SC: University of South Carolina Press, 1969).

H.R. Loyn and J. Percival, *The Reign of Charlemagne* (London: Edward Arnold, 1975).

R. McKitterick, *Charlemagne: The Formation of a European Unity* (Cambridge: CUP, 2008).

C.C. Mierow and Richard Emery (transl.), *The Deeds of Frederick Barbarossa: Otto of Freising and his Continuator Rahewin* (Toronto: University of Toronto Press and Medieval Academy of America, 1994).

T. Reuter (ed.), *Alfred the Great: Papers from the Eleventh Centenary Conference* (Aldershot: Ashgate, 2003).

A.P. Smyth, *The Medieval Life of King Alfred the Great: A Translation and Commentary on the Text attributed to Asser* (New York: Palgrave, 2002).

L. Thorpe (ed.), *Einhard and Notker the Stammerer: Two Lives of Charlemagne* (Harmondsworth: Penguin, 1969).

## Notes

1  P. E. Dutton (ed. and transl.), *Charlemagne's Courtier: The Complete Einhard,* Readings in medieval civilizations and cultures 3 (Peterborough, Ontario: Broadview Press, 1998), p. 15.
2  Ibid., p. 27.
3  Ibid., pp. 20–1.
4  Ibid., p. 32.
5  S. Keynes and M. Lapidge (transl.), *Alfred the Great: Asser's Life of King Alfred and Other Contemporary Sources* (Harmondsworth: Penguin, 1983), p. 93.
6  Ibid., p. 67.
7  Ibid., pp. 75–6.
8  Ibid., pp. 101–2.
9  R.W. Southern, 'Aspects of the European Tradition of Historical Writing: 1. The Classical Tradition from Einhard to Geoffrey of Monmouth', *Transactions of the Royal Historical Society*, V series, 20 (1970), 186.
10  E.R.A. Sewter (transl.), *The Alexiad of Anna Comnena* (Harmondsworth: Penguin, 1969), p. 17.
11  Ibid., pp. 109–10.
12  Ibid., pp. 151–2, 478.
13  Ibid., pp. 195–6.
14  Ibid., p. 295.
15  J.R. Strayer (ed.), *Dictionary of the Middle Ages*, 13 vols (New York: Scribner, 1982–9), vol. 9, R.E. Lerner, p. 304.
16  P. Russell (ed.), *Vita Griffini filii Conani: The Medieval Latin Life of Gruffudd ap Cynan* (Cardiff: University of Wales Press, 2005), pp. 73, 87.
17  R. Cusimano and J. Moorhead (transl.), *Suger: The Deeds of Louis the Fat* (Washington DC: Catholic University of America Press, 1992), p. 64.
18  M.R.B. Shaw (transl. and introd.), *Chronicles of the Crusades: Jean de Joinville and Geoffroi de Villehardouin* (Harmondsworth: Penguin, 1963), pp. 352–3.
19  Ibid., p. 177.
20  Ibid., pp. 337–41.
21  F. Taylor and J.S. Roskell (transl.), *Gesta Henrici Quinti: The Deeds of Henry the Fifth* (Oxford: OUP, 1975), p. 3.
22  Ibid., p. 37.
23  Ibid., p. 61.
24  Ibid., p. 79.
25  Ibid., p. 85.
26  M. Jones (transl. and introd.), *Memoirs of Philippe de Commynes: the Reign of Louis XI, 1461–83* (Harmondsworth: Penguin, 1972), p. 57.
27  Ibid., p. 318.
28  Ibid., p. 98.
29  Ibid., p. 248.
30  Ibid., p. 317.
31  Ibid., p. 400.

# 2 Vernacular chronicles and narrative sources of history in medieval England

## Lister M. Matheson

The main objectives of this essay are twofold. First, I wish to consider briefly the term 'historical texts' from a primarily medieval point of view; second, I wish to offer a broad classification and survey of such texts within the cultural context of medieval England in relation to texts that are nowadays more commonly regarded as 'literary'. Similar studies could, of course, be made for every European country with a tradition of historical writing, but the present study concentrates on England writings in English for reasons of space and because of the richness of the relevant materials.

### The language background

Writers of all sorts and of whatever period are influenced by linguistic and socio-linguistic constraints in their choice of language in which to write, subject matter, literary form, and the appropriateness of literary form to subject matter. Historical writers are no exception, and the development of historical writings in medieval England parallels the fortunes of the English language and its social context. The linguistic period known as Middle English traditionally spans the years 1100 to 1500.[1] Historically, it is approximately bounded at its beginning by the Norman Conquest and the introduction of the feudal system and at its end by the advent of the English Renaissance and the rise of a mercantile economy, presaged by William Caxton's introduction around 1476 into England of that great instrument of cultural change, the printing press. Linguistically, the period sees a post-Conquest restriction in the use of written English in most areas in favour of Anglo-Norman and Latin, a restriction that prevailed for 250 years until, from around 1350 onwards, the English language began to reassert itself as the primary language for all kinds of writings.[2] Over this period of four centuries, English developed from an insular Germanic tongue into a cosmopolitan pot-pourri of native English, Scandinavian, Latin, French and Low German, with a dash of Cornish, Welsh, Irish and Scottish Gaelic, and even more exotic elements.[3]

### The problem with genres

The student of history might define 'historical texts' as 'those texts that are of value to the modern historian in establishing accurate historical facts'. But this is a modern, utilitarian viewpoint that disregards many of the texts – or even parts of texts – that medieval English men and women would have considered historical.

Part of the problem is the result of literary conditioning. Genre divisions dating back to the Renaissance formed the basis for a traditional hierarchy of fixed poetic 'kinds' until the end of the eighteenth century, from epic and tragedy at the top to short lyric, epigram and the like at the bottom. The development of new literary forms in the Romantic period drastically altered the conception and ranking of genres, and since then they have been thought of as convenient but rather arbitrary ways of classifying works of literature.[4] Criteria for the critical analysis and evaluation of literature have metamorphosed from rigid generic rules through 'sincerity, intensity, organic unity, etc.' to, from New Criticism on, the (supposed) non-evaluation on aesthetic grounds of texts of whatever type. Genre study may have become fluid or even been dismissed as irrelevant, but Middle English anthologies and literary histories have generally lagged behind the times in terms of what passes for cutting-edge literary criticism and theory. Editors often use genre as a convenient and pragmatic way of presenting their materials, but their terminology just as often betrays uneasiness with such divisions.[5]

The validity of applying Early Modern and later classifications to pre-Renaissance writings is doubtful. Renaissance literary criticism was based on the humanist rediscovery of the classics, including Greek theory. However, Aristotle's *Poetics* was not well known in the Middle Ages, and medieval literary theory, such as there is, was based on watered-down, sometimes misrepresented, classical theory. The primary concern was rhetoric, as exemplified by the *Speculum Doctrinale* of Vincent of Beauvais (1190–1264) and works by Radulfus de Longo Campo, Nicholas Trivet, John of Garland, and, put into practice, Geoffrey Chaucer.[6]

It is worth noting that the English word 'fiction' is first recorded as a descriptive division of literature only in 1599. In Middle English, the word meant 'artefact, something made or invented; lie, untruth'.[7] There was no single blanket term for 'literary fiction' in Middle English.

Medieval genre theory is vague and non-specific about individual works. However, in a series of important articles, Paul Strohm has shown, by close reference to what the writers themselves called their works, that medieval conceptions of different literary genres did not correspond to our modern terminology based on Renaissance critical theory.[8]

## An alternative textual classification

The following survey of 'historical texts' attempts to accommodate both the medieval Englishman's and the modern historian's interpretations of the historicity of texts, which frequently, though not always, reflect different perspectives on the meaning of history and different perceptions of historical truth.

Thus many narrative texts are included that are not traditionally regarded as primarily historical texts, and I have included poems with a historical or political content. Saints' lives and legends and biblical narratives have been included as texts which were historical from the medieval point of view. A major genre that is re-evaluated is the romance, which continues to be notoriously difficult to define; definitions have become increasingly wide and vague in order to accommodate the disparate nature of the works involved.[9] The main criteria for classification are subject matter and an estimate of authorial intent, the intended audience and the historical credence given to the works by their authors or readers.

Accordingly, texts that do not record historical narrative but which represent reactions to history or current events, such as a number of political poems, satires and elegies, have been excluded. In the widest interpretation, all Middle English texts can be considered as informational documents in one way or another. Thus Chaucer and William Langland are valuable witnesses in social history and are, indeed, first-rate social historians in their own right. Mystical, devotional and Wycliffite writings are important documents in ecclesiastical and spiritual history. Medical and scientific works are the factual evidence for the history of science. All are witnesses in intellectual history or the history of ideas; all texts, no matter what their subject matter or literary quality, and all texts, no matter how removed from the authorial original, are valuable for the history of the English language. However, many 'aesthetic' writers were also active historians by the standards of the time. Thus Chaucer is a historical writer from the medieval perspective in the Second Nun's Tale of St Cecilia, the miracle of the Prioress's Tale, and the moral stories of the Monk's Tale. John Gower and John Lydgate often narrate historical events, while Thomas Hoccleve is a frequent reporter of saints' lives.

Texts that are overtly and self-consciously fictional, such as Chaucer's tale of Sir Thopas, do not appear below, though their precise definition can be difficult.

Also excluded are official and public record texts and documents, such as wills, deeds, charters, indentures and account rolls; and official records, such as the Rolls of Parliament, the proceedings of the Privy Council, and Chancery and Exchequer records. Private and official letters also belong to this category. Such documents were not intended primarily as systematic records of history; they are, in general, non-narrative records of facts and transactions which by their nature have become primary historical sources of paramount importance to the modern historian.

## Medieval historical texts

In the present analysis, historical texts are defined as those texts whose primary authorial intent, as perceived by a medieval reader (or hearer), was to record the events of past or recent history. The subject matter is the political history of nations or of significant periods, the narration of important individual events in national or local history, ecclesiastical history, and the lives of historical or possibly historical persons. Taken together, these texts represent the sum of reliable history available to the medieval person in the vernacular, and thus help define the possible limits of his or her knowledge of history and the parameters of historical consciousness.

Chronicles and historical narratives are discussed first, followed by 'biographical' narratives, that is, texts focused on all or part of the life of an individual. Under 'Chronicles and historical narratives' I include verse and prose chronicles, various propagandist texts, and short historical poems and ballads. Under 'Biographical narratives' I include both religious texts (primarily saints' lives) and secular narratives of individuals, some of whom are now considered non-historical.

## Chronicles and historical narratives[10]

The most readily recognizable historical texts are the various secular chronicles of England. The audience for such works was originally upper-class or monastic, but widened in the fifteenth century to include members of the increasingly wealthy merchant class.

### Verse chronicles

The late eleventh- and twelfth-century prose continuations to the Peterborough copy of the *Anglo-Saxon Chronicle* represent the conclusion of the vigorous Old English tradition of chronicle-writing. A new tradition – in verse, however – of English chronicling arose in the thirteenth century, originally modelled on French verse chronicles such as those of Geffrei Gaimar and Wace, utilizing and expanding on the comprehensive history of Britain and England presented in Geoffrey of Monmouth's *Historia Regum Britanniae*. The result was, in approximate chronological order of composition, the comprehensive treatments of English history found in Laȝamon's *Brut* (early thirteenth century), the A and B versions of Robert of Gloucester's *Chronicle*, the *Anonymous Short English Metrical Chronicle*, Robert Mannyng of Brunne's *Chronicle* (all written during the early fourteenth century), Thomas Castleford's *Chronicle* (mid-fourteenth century), and the A and B versions of John Hardyng's *Chronicle* (mid-fifteenth century).[11]

Most verse chronicles of England begin with the founding of Britain by Brutus, either the son or the grandson of the Trojan hero Aeneas. This ultimate base for English history is paralleled in narratives of the Trojan War that are now often classified as 'romances' (see further below), such as the *Seege of Troye* (early fourteenth century), the *Gest Historiale of the Destruction of Troy* (late fourteenth century), the *Laud Troy Book* (*c.*1400), and Lydgate's *Troy Book* (commissioned as a historical work by the Prince of Wales, later King Henry V, and completed in 1420). All are based on what were for the medieval English reputable historical sources – Dares Phrygius's *De Excidio Trojae Historia*, Benoit de Sainte-Maure's *Roman de Troie*, and Guido delle Colonne's *Historia Destructionis Troiae* – and all are presented as serious historical narratives.

Lydgate's *Siege of Thebes*, which is found in association with the *Troy Book* in three manuscripts, was written as a supplement to Chaucer's *Canterbury Tales*. The historical account is overlaid with a good deal of topical political moralizing on war and peace.

The war waged by Titus and Vespasian against Jerusalem is recounted in two verse works. The alliterative *Siege of Jerusalem* interweaves Latin chronicles and legendaries, including among its sources Ranulph Higden's *Polychronicon* and the *Legenda Aurea*, while the couplet *Titus and Vespasian* utilizes the Gospels, the *Legenda Aurea*, the *Gospel of Nicodemus*, and the *History of Josephus*.

The *Sege of Melayne* lays claim to historical accuracy in several references to its source as 'the Cronekill,' and is partly intended as a glorification of the warlike Bishop Turpin, Roland's associate in the Charlemagne cycle.

*Prose chronicles*

The popularity of verse chronicles was small compared to that enjoyed by prose chronicles after their reintroduction in the late fourteenth century. As in the case of the verse chronicles, the earliest prose chronicles were originally translations, but as linguistic confidence and nationalist pride increased, they developed into independent English productions early in the fifteenth century.

The major published prose chronicles are John Trevisa's translation of Ranulph Higden's *Polychronicon* (and subsequent translations thereof), the various versions of the *Chronicles of London,* John Capgrave's *Abbreuiacion of Cronicles*, and the Prose *Brut*, the most popular and successful of all Middle English secular works. Major unpublished chronicles include translations of Geoffrey of Monmouth's *Historia Regum Britanniae* (a single manuscript) and Nicholas Trevet's *Cronicles* (a single manuscript), and prose paraphrases of Robert of Gloucester's *Chronicle* (two related manuscripts) and of Robert Mannyng of Brunne's *Chronicle*, Part 2 (a single manuscript).

William Caxton's *Recuyell of the Histories of Troy* (published 1473/74) is a prose counterpart to the verse narratives of Troy described above. Caxton's comments on his work make it clear that he regarded it as historical (with a topical moral), though he was aware of the variations to be found in different authors' accounts.

The Prose *Brut* became the first printed history of England when Caxton published it in 1480 (2nd ed. 1482) under the title *Chronicles of England*. The printer was probably the author of the final section in his edition, and he re-used this material in compiling a *Liber ultimus* for his edition (1482) of Trevisa's translation of the *Polychronicon*. Caxton makes a significant comment in the colophon to his continuation, that 'where as ther is fawte, J beseche them that shal rede it to correcte it. For yf J coude haue founden moo storyes, J wold haue sette in hit moo.'[12]

*Shorter prose chronicles*

Shorter prose chronicles focusing on specific events or periods include the *English Conquest of Ireland* (probably translated from a Latin chronicle ultimately based on the *Expugnatio Hibernica* of Giraldus Cambrensis), John Shirley's *Dethe of the Kynge of Scotis* (said to be translated from Latin), and the chronicle formerly attributed to John Warkworth, which is appended to two manuscripts of the Prose *Brut*.

Several shorter prose works cover the same subjects as the longer narratives described above. Two short narratives, occurring in the same manuscript and each abbreviated from the corresponding long poem by Lydgate, are the *Prose Siege of Troy* (with added details from Chaucer's *Troilus and Criseyde*) and the *Prose Siege of Thebes*. Three prose works deal with the siege of Jerusalem: the *Sege of Jerusaleme* in Aberystwyth, National Library of Wales, MS Porkington 10, abbreviated from the couplet *Titus and Vespasian*; a translation of Roger d'Argenteuil's *Bible en Francois* in Cleveland, Public Library, MS W q901.92-C468 (which also contains a Prose *Brut* text); and *The Dystruccyon of Iherusalem by Vaspazyan and Tytus*, printed by Wynkyn de Worde (1510?; 2nd ed. 1528) and by Richard Pynson (1513?).

Ecclesiastical history is represented by three dissimilar works. The *Book of the Foundation of St. Bartholomew's Church in London* piously relates the history of the church, with associated miracles. The *Chronicle of Popes and Emperors* (that is, of Rome) is a translation and abbreviation of Martinus Polonus's thirteenth-century *Chronicon Pontificum et Imperatorum*. A Lollard chronicle of the papacy presents a vitriolic account of the 'rablement of the popes' drawn from Higden's *Polychronicon*, supplemented by Martinus Polonus's chronicle. Clearly, the perceived historicity of the latter work would depend greatly on one's theological point of view.

## Political and propagandist newsletters and pamphlets

Unlike the ideal (at least) of modern historical writings, none of the above works is written from a totally detached viewpoint; the medieval chronicler does not hesitate to use history to state or draw his moral judgements or to show his political predilections. Even more consciously designed to influence are those short relations of recent or current events circulated as open newsletters or as propagandist pamphlets, particularly during the politically turbulent late fifteenth century. Official or semi-official accounts such as the *Chronicle of the Rebellion in Lincolnshire* (1470) and the short and long versions of the *Historie of the Arrivall of King Edward IV* (*c*.1471) use privileged inside information and official documents. The *Deposition of Richard II, Coumpleyntes ayens the Dewke of Suffolk*, and the *Claim of the Duke of York* (1460) are extracts or adaptations from the official records in the Rolls of Parliament that were circulated generally for partisan purposes, thus allowing their inclusion here as historical-informational rather than record texts (see below).

Genealogical chronicles of Edward IV, beginning with Adam, justified the legitimacy of the Yorkist claim to the throne. These are often quite elaborate, illustrated productions in roll format and may well have served as public manifestations of the political allegiance of the rich and powerful. Descriptive 'occasional' pieces are more neutral in motive, such as accounts of the death and funeral of Henry V or of the coronation of Elizabeth Woodville. Relatively few examples survive of this latter type of texts, which were nevertheless a major source of current information for the general populace; by nature ephemeral, no doubt many copies were passed from hand to hand and read to death.[13]

## Short poems and ballads

A number of relatively short poems qualify as historical-informational texts, paralleling in subject matter and intended audience the shorter prose texts described above. Although they are usually anthologized together under the rubrics 'historical' or 'political' poems, a distinction should be made between those poems that contain to some extent records of historical events – that is, true historical texts – and those that represent political or social interpretations or moral reactions triggered by historical events (see further above). Such historical poems are common from the beginning of the fourteenth century,[14] which was the heyday of the verse

UNIVERSITY OF WINCHESTER
LIBRARY

chronicle, until the end of the fifteenth century and beyond, and all are marked by some form of nationalist pride or partisanship.

Most similar in general outline to the prose chronicles, and quite possibly derived from a *Brut* chronicle, are Lydgate's highly popular verses on the *Kings of England*.[15] The *Battle of Halidon Hill* and John Page's eyewitness *Siege of Rouen* are verse narratives that are close in style to the prose chronicles in which they are frequently incorporated.[16] A poem in three parts describes the French campaign of Henry V, including the battle of Agincourt, and probably drew upon earlier ballads; in one manuscript (London, British Library, MS Harley 565) of the three surviving texts it is incorporated into a London chronicle. The war poems of Laurence Minot, written over a period of twenty years (*c.*1333–52), have been linked together in the surviving manuscript by short prose rubrics in the manner of the chapter-headings of a prose chronicle such as the *Brut*. The *Recovery of the Throne by Edward IV*, called 'the balet off the kynge' in the explicit, covers much the same ground as the short Yorkist prose *Historie of the Arrivall*.

Of varied historical value, both now and when originally written, and containing an uneven amount of historical detail, are short poems and ballads on the execution of Sir Simon Fraser, the siege of Calais, and the battles of Agincourt, Whitby, Northampton (cast in allegorical mould), Towton and Otterburn.[17] Although not all are contemporary with the events they describe, they were intended for popular consumption and their role probably approximated to that of the prose newsletters.

### Biographical narratives and related texts

Biography is a flexible medium for the conveyance of historical information, for it can be written at various levels to appeal to a variety of audiences.[18] In common with most other Middle English works, biographical narratives are a mixture of 'sentence and solas'. Many were intended for public reading aloud, and this fact, together with the literary forms employed, suggests that different categories of such works would reach a wide range of social classes, whose members – generally and individually – possessed differing degrees of sophistication in their perception of historicity. As a result, it is difficult, and in some cases impossible, to gauge precisely – or even guess – how much historical truth would or could have been accorded to certain works. I have, therefore, been tolerant in including such doubtful works in the following sections, on the principle that there are many people who will believe almost anything, especially if it is written down and bases its claims to truth on ancient authority.

Almost all the narrative works classed here as biographical narratives are saints' lives (or 'legends' as many were called) or romances and, as Strohm has demonstrated, such works were considered historically true in the Middle Ages.[19]

### Religious texts: saints' lives

The lives of saints and of Christ and the Virgin, accounts of miracles, narrative works based on biblical or apocryphal sources, and even the Bible itself can be considered as historical texts, although, as in other medieval historical works, there are other motives and purposes involved as well.[20] Their claim to historicity was inherent and self-evident, and the overwhelming majority of readers or hearers of such works would have accepted their historical truth without question. Saints' lives constitute the vast majority of such texts, and it is on them that I concentrate here.

In the preface to his *Lives of Saints*, the Anglo-Saxon abbot and scholar Aelfric asserts the historicity of his hagiographical narratives (quoted here in modern translation):

> We say nothing new in this book, because it has stood written down long since in Latin books, though lay-men knew it not. Neither will we feign such things by means of falsehoods, because devout fathers and holy doctors wrote it in the Latin tongue, for a lasting memorial, and to confirm the faith of future generations. ... We shall describe many wonders in this book, because God is wonderful in His Saints, as we said before, and the miracles of His Saints glorify Him, because He wrought hem by their means.[21]

There is no reason to doubt that Aelfric's convictions were shared without question by the great majority of English men and women throughout the medieval period.[22] For many persons, both lay and religious, hagiographical narratives were one of their two main sources of historical information (the other being the popular romances).

## Saints' lives in verse

Beyond a few early works in prose, legacies from the Anglo-Saxon period, the majority of saints' lives were written in verse until the fifteenth century. Several large collections and many individual lives have survived, testifying to their saturating influence on medieval intellectual life.

The various versions of the massive *South English Legendary*, whose over fifty extant manuscripts span the late thirteenth to the mid-fifteenth centuries, were intended for the oral instruction of an unsophisticated, largely illiterate audience.

The sources of the material in the versions of the Legendary are diverse, and the progressive accretion of *sanctorale* and *temporale*[23] narratives in some texts suggests the same principle is at work as in Caxton's chronicle continuation to the *Polychronicon* – if more stories can be found, then they should be included. In addition to the recognized, though fluid, types of saints' lives such as *vita*, *vita et passio*, and *passio*, there are exotic romance-like narratives such as those of St Thomas of India, St Katherine of Alexandria, or the tales of St Thomas Becket's parents. There are stories common to the Legendary and to the full-scale chronicles; thus the story of St Brandan is paralleled in Robert of Gloucester's *Chronicle*, while the story of the martyred St Ursula and the Eleven Thousand Virgins and miracles associated with Thomas Becket and Duke Thomas of Lancaster are factually recorded in the later chronicles such as the *Brut*.

The intention of popular oral instruction is continued in the fourteenth century in another large compilation of *sanctorale* and *temporale* material, combined with verse sermons and moral tales, in the different versions of the *Northern Homily Cycle*. One of the manuscripts containing this work is the Vernon Manuscript (Oxford, Bodleian Library, MS Eng. poet. a.1), which also contains a verse translation of selected items from the *Legenda Aurea* of Jacobus de Voragine. Direct address in the Vernon *Golden Legend* shows that it was intended originally for oral presentation to a mixed lay audience, though the manuscript in which the text is preserved was probably intended for private reading.

At the same time, there survive many verse lives (for example, those of Sts Katherine, Gregory, Alexis and Mary Magdalene) designed primarily for entertainment – and presumably for pecuniary profit – written in the minstrel tradition. The life of St Marina in London, BL, MS Harley 2253 has a typical beginning:

> Herk[n]eþ hideward & beoþ stille,
> y preie ou, ȝef hit be or wille,
> & ȝȝe shule here of one virgine.

One of the minstrel copies of *St. Gregory* concludes with a true professional's claim:

> Alle þat herden þis storie rede
> Wiþ herte and deuocioun ...
> Þe pope haþ graunted hem to mede
> And hundred dawes to pardoun.

In saints' lives composed in the late fourteenth and fifteenth centuries by experienced authors such as Chaucer, Lydgate, Osbern Bokenham and Capgrave, a shift to a more educated audience of a higher class can be observed, although texts of the *South English Legendary* continued to be copied and were thus still available for public instruction. Popular verse lives designed for public performance also continued to be written or reworked (for example, lives of Sts Margaret, Katherine, Erasmus and Alexis, who remained a perennial favourite) in the fifteenth century. Again, several were clearly for minstrel recitation, and use direct exhortations similar to those found in fourteenth-century lives and in minstrel romances to attract and keep a restless, peripatetic crowd.

The diversity of audience is illustrated by three lives of St Anne designed for public reading aloud. The stanzaic version in Minneapolis-St Paul, University of Minnesota, MS Z.822.N.81 is an addition to a *Northern Homily Cycle* collection, designed to be read in church, and begins: 'Herkens now to me. / A lytill tretice ȝe sall her.' The version in rhyme royal in Cambridge, Trinity College, MS 601 is a paraphrase of *lectiones* for St Anne's day in the Sarum Breviary and is addressed to an audience of male religious, the author's 'most dere brethern'. A third version in Oxford, Bodleian Library, MS Tanner 407 (based on the *Legenda Aurea*) is written in quatrains for a guild celebration, possibly for the St Anne's Guild in the parish of St Peter at the Skinmarket in Lincoln.

Fifteenth-century lives of English saints with local connections were written primarily for special-interest audiences. The lives of St Etheldreda and St Editha were written by a resident of Wilton Abbey and are remarkable for their conscious-ness of historical context and attention to the claims of historicity. Thus the life of St Etheldreda begins with a long introduction setting the story in the historical context of the seven Anglo-Saxon kingdoms and gives marginal references to Bede as an authority. A similar introduction and references are also found in the life of St Editha, which also appends a list of historical reference works, or *auctoritates*, including 'Legenda s[an]c[t]e Edithe virginis' among chronicle sources.[24]

The *Legend of St. Wolfade and Ruffyn*, written at the monastery of Stone in Staffordshire, recounts the lives of Wulfhad and his brother Ruffin and the foun-dation of the monastery; as sources are cited 'the cronakle' and a tablet that hangs in the church.

The *Life of St. Cuthbert* was intended for a gentle audience, and the author care-fully identifies his sources, including Bede's *Vita Sancti Cuthberti* and *Historia Ecclesiastica*, which he combines to form 'a collection of previously existing lives, thrown into English verse'.[25] The writer describes his method of compila-tion and acceptance of hearsay evidence thus:

> ... diuers othir cronykill
> Of cuthbert and his, tell I will,
> Þe whilk writen I haue sene,
> And herde tell of whare I haue bene.

The *Metrical Life of St. Robert of Knaresborough* was probably written by a brother of the Trinitarian Order at its house at Walknoll, Newcastle, and the authen-ticity of the source – 'a boke / That was sentt me by a frere / Fray ['from'] Sayntt Robertys to me her' – is referred to throughout the work. The poem associates itself with the minstrel romances 'Of Arthure, Ector, and Achilles' by attacking their seriousness, not their historicity, relative to the present subject matter.

## Saints' lives in prose

Saints' lives in English prose do not begin to be written until the early fifteenth century. They fall into two groups according to whether they are connected with the *Legenda Aurea* or whether they are independent of that immensely popular collection.

More than 700 pan-European manuscripts survive of Jacobus de Voragine's Latin *Legenda Aurea*, which was probably completed by 1267. Its huge influence in England extended from the late thirteenth century to the Reformation.[26]

Prose lives of two individual saints are based, directly or indirectly, on the Latin *Legenda Aurea*: St Dorothea (in possibly three separate versions) and the first chapter of a life of St Jerome in a work commissioned by Margaret, Duchess of Clarence.[27]

In 1438, the *Legende Doree* of Jehan de Vignay, a close translation into French of the *Legenda Aurea*, was translated into English as the *Gilte Legende*, possibly by a monk of St Albans. The full *Gilte Legende* consists of 178 items (in 179 chapters, since Cecilia is duplicated). Three of the eleven surviving manuscripts contain a set of additional lives, mostly of English saints, that are with one exception prose redactions from the *South English Legendary*. The constant interweaving of religious and secular history is illustrated in the chapter heading that begins 'the life of S. Pelagien, with Geestis of Lumbardie'.

Caxton published his version of these works in 1483 (2nd ed. 1487) under the title the *Golden Legend*. He combined a Latin *Legenda Aurea*, a French *Legende Doree*, and an expanded English *Gilte Legende* and added a set of lives of Old Testament figures, possibly taken from an unidentified English *Temporale*, and, when that text ended, he translated items from the Vulgate Bible.[28] The underlying principle is again, as in his *Polychronicon* continuation, one of all-inclusiveness. The implicit historicity of the narratives and lives is reinforced by Caxton's frequent omission of sceptical comments found in Jacobus de Voragine and generally retained by Jean de Vignay.[29]

Saints' lives independent of the *Legenda Aurea* are few. A life of St Anthony in London, BL, MS Royal 17.C.xvii was intended for oral presentation either to the congregation of a church dedicated to the saint or a monastic community. The lives of Sts Elizabeth of Spalbeck, Christina Mirabilis of St Trudons, Mary of Oignies and Katherine of Siena were translated from Latin by a monk, possibly at the Carthusian monastery of Beauvall in Nottinghamshire, who stresses the authenticity of his sources.[30]

Capgrave's *St. Augustine* was written for an unnamed gentlewoman, presumably for private reading; his *St. Gilbert* was made at the indirect request of Abbot Nicholas Reysby of Sempringham for the use of his nuns, 'whech vnneth can vndyrstande Latyn, þat þei may at vacaunt tymes red in þis book þe grete vertues of her maystyr.'

A prose life of the popular saint and king, Edward the Confessor, fills all fifty-two leaves of Oxford, Trinity College, MS 11. That the work constitutes a complete manuscript by itself suggests that its interest was less religious than purely biographical; the miracles associated with Edward are simply accepted as facts in his life.

Two translations by Caxton belong here.[31] His account of 'the decollacion, the lyf after, and the translacion of Saynte Wenefrede' was translated *c.*1485, probably from a Latin life of St Winifred by Prior Robert of Shrewsbury (*c.*1140), to which an account of the saint's translation was added.[32]

According to Wynkyn de Worde, who printed the work in 1495, Caxton finished his translation of the *Vitas Patrum* on his death-day in 1491. It is a sprawling, ill-organized work, as is its French source, *La Vie des Pères*, published in 1486/7, whose purpose was the spiritual amendment of its readers.[33] The lives of a number of desert Fathers are supplemented by the lives of other early saints and of the twelfth-century French Saint Christian of Maine, together with much anecdotal and admonitory material.

### Secular texts

Romances were extremely popular with all levels of society in medieval England and were written in various styles to cater for different audiences and modes of delivery (oral or read).

The close relationship between chronicle and romance can be observed best in the interweaving and borrowing of material and the association of texts in manuscripts.[34] Thus some romances, such as *Havelok*, were incorporated wholesale into chronicles and the English verse romance *Arthur* is interpolated in a Latin chronicle on the kings of England in a Longleat House manuscript. Even the romance hero Sir Bevis of Hampton turns up as the name of an Arthurian knight in Robert Mannyng's *Chronicle*.

The association of texts in manuscripts is often telling. The verse romance *The Siege of Troy* immediately precedes the unedited translation of Geoffrey of Monmouth's *Historia Regum Britanniae* in London, College of Arms, MS Arundel 22, and presumably serves as a kind of amplified introduction to the latter work. London, Lambeth Palace, MS 491 contains a Prose *Brut* text, *The Siege of Jerusalem*, the prose *Three Kings of Cologne*, and the *Awntyrs of Arthur*, while Oxford, Bodleian Library, MS Digby 185 has another copy of the *Brut*, together with the prose romance *Ponthus* and Hoccleve's stories of the emperor Gerelaus and of Jonathas.

The reverse case is where a romance is set within its own framework of history, as in the introductory synopsis of the Trojan ancestry of Britain and the concluding references to Troy in *Sir Gawain and the Green Knight*. The poem 'zooms in' to focus sharply on a specific story (and it is interesting to note that the year taken by Gawain's adventure corresponds to the primary unit of historical time for medieval man) before 'zooming out' again at the end, thus situating the narrative in a larger world/British/Arthurian historical context. Taking these points with the setting of the story in a real and concretely described locale, I would suggest that a veneer of possible historicity is being established.

### Verse secular lives

We may consider here the great majority of Middle English romances, which were written solely in verse until the fifteenth century, when their counterparts in English prose first began to be produced (see below).[35]

Many of these biographical romances are set in Arthurian times and should be read in the context of the chronicle accounts of King Arthur, especially of the twelve-year period of peace in England that the chronicles skip over.[36] Several are closely associated with chronicles, such as the short *Arthur* interpolated in a Latin prose chronicle in a Longleat manuscript and the alliterative *Morte Arthure*, which was partly based on chronicle sources. Others, such as *Arthur and Merlin* and Henry Lovelich's *Merlin*, cover segments of their protagonists' careers, while yet others feature exploits of individual knights such as Gawain, Ywain, Lancelot, Perceval and Tristram.

Minor groups of romances that act as historical biographies include those associated with characters like Firumbras, Roland and Otuel from the Charlemagne cycle, usually derived from French *chansons de geste*, and Alexander the Great. A few romances feature English heroes such as Horn, Havelok (also found in chronicles), Bevis of Hampton, Guy of Warwick (in several versions), and Richard Coer de Lyon (in several related versions, some of which emphasize the supernatural and one of which is embedded in a prose chronicle). The Robin Hood narratives are similarly associated with historical figures and events.

We might also consider here works like Chaucer's *Legends of Good Women* and the series of short 'biographies' that constitute the Monk's Tale, as well as Lydgate's *Fall of Princes*. In Scotland, John Barbour's *Bruce* and 'Blind' Harry's *Wallace* function as panegyric historical narratives.

## Prose secular lives

The first examples of prose lives of secular historical figures written in Middle English appear in the early fifteenth century with works such as John Rous's Warwick Roll and the *Pageant of the Birth, Life, and Death of Richard Beauchamp, Earl of Warwick, K.G., 1389–1439.*[37] Only tantalizing traces remain of English lives of Henry V and Edward IV. Lydgate's *Serpent of Division*, composed in 1422, is essentially a biographical narrative (entitled in the colophon of one text 'the cronycule of Julius Caesar') but, like other historical texts, it also presents a strong political moral.

Prose romances began to appear around the middle of the fifteenth century but remained few in number before 1500. The major works of this sort are *King Ponthus*, a version of the Horn tale; the *Prose Merlin*; and Thomas Malory's *Morte Darthur* (finished before 1470). This last work was printed by Caxton in 1485 and it is significant that the printer rewrote Malory's account of Arthur's war against the Romans to accord with that found in his editions of the *Chronicles of England* (1480; 1482).

## A case in point: texts printed by William Caxton

Examples of most of the types of texts already mentioned were published in the late fifteenth century by William Caxton, and Caxton's comments in his prologues can be taken as representative of what a fairly well-educated Englishman considered to be the range of acceptable historical texts.[38] Less educated people – the majority of the population – had, presumably, commensurately wider limits of belief. Caxton's view on the usefulness of history, given in the prologue to the *Polychronicon* (1482), is that history acts as a moral spur and an admonition to men of all ages and stations by presenting the lives and actions of individuals. The *Golden Legend* and the *Polychronicon* are equally described as 'historye', containing within them 'many noble historyes' and 'many wonderful historyees' respectively. The history of Jerusalem and the life of Godefroy de Bologne in *The Siege of Jerusalem* (1481), the life of Charlemagne in *Charles the Grete* (1485), and 'the cronycle & hystory' of *The Four Sonnes of Aymon* (1489?) are presented as authentic historical works. Even the romance of *Blanchardyn and Eglantine* (1489?) is represented as true (and morally proper); its emphasis on the steadfastness of love relative to deeds of derring-do is due to the youth of its projected gentle readership. Scepticism concerning the authenticity of King Arthur is discussed and rejected in the printer's prologue to his edition of Malory, though the reader is allowed to form his own opinion, however misguided, of the veracity of the book – 'for to gyue fayth and beleue that al is trewe that is conteyned herin, ye be at your liberte.' Caxton's comments here on the number of vernacular and foreign accounts of Arthur and his knights and in the prologue to *The Siege of Jerusalem* – 'O blessyd Lord, whan I remembre the grete and many volumes of Seynt Graal, Ghalehot, and Launcelotte de Lake, Gawayn, Perceval, Lyonel, and Tristram, and many other of whom were overlonge to reherce and also to me unknowen' – suggest a predisposition to consider as true almost anything found in written form. When two sources disagree in *The Historie of Jason* (1476/77) as to a proper name, Caxton simply records the fact of the disagreement. Hearsay evidence makes Caxton question in *The Mirrour of the World* (1481) the visions supposed to be experienced at St Patrick's Purgatory, but he tempers this scepticism by the observation that 'hit may wel be that of auncyent tyme it hath ben thus as a fore is wreton, as the storye of Tundale & other witnesse.'

## Conclusion

The foregoing survey attempts to define the historical consciousness of medieval England and suggests that a large segment of medieval writings functioned as vehicles for the transmission of historical information, overlaid with the proper moral interpretation. Even those romances whose possible historicity might have seemed incredible to medieval audiences were usually cast in a historical mould. In the same way that a romance could set itself in a framework of history, so a saint's life could be established within a larger historical context. It is easy to understand why medieval audiences might lack a touchstone for critical historical judgement. They might hear the true life of a saint, replete with miracles, read out and expounded in church on a feast day, then hear the life of the same saint, with essentially similar details, recited two days later in popular tail-rhyme form at the fair, immediately followed by a romance of a chivalric hero in the same tail-rhyme form and with similar claims to authenticity. As for marvels, in a circumscribed local world who knows what wonders might have occurred far away or long ago? *Mandeville's Travels* and the encyclopedia of Bartholomaeus Anglicus are full of them.

The sixteenth century was a watershed: the Reformation put paid to saints' lives (and altered irrevocably the sense of 'legend'), changing literary tastes doomed the romance, and more 'sophisticated' approaches to historiography condemned the earlier sections of many chronicles as fanciful legends. Until then, however, chronicles established the framework of history. Historical narratives, romances, saints' lives, and other works formed an interlocking nexus of texts that fleshed out the details of history. History was very much a succession of individual lives. Even the chronicles of England are a series of royal lives, where the major formal unit is an individual reign. The well-being of the nation depended upon the character of the ruler; wider trends and abstract forces in the movement of history were simply not recognized. History was personal, filled with good stories and moral exempla; it was not restricted to what a seventeenth-century playwright dismissively termed the 'leaues of a worme eaten Chronicle.'[39]

# Further reading

## *General*

The Medieval Chronicle Society website, http://medievalchronicle.org/

## *Bibliographical reference works*

D'Evelyn, Charlotte and Frances A. Foster, 'Saints' Legends' in *A Manual of the Writings in Middle English 1050–1500*, J. Burke Severs (ed.), Vol. 2 (Hamden, CT: Archon Books, 1970).
Donovan, Mortimer J. *et al.*, 'Romances' in *A Manual of the Writings in Middle English 1050–1500*, ed. J. Burke Severs (ed.), Vol. 1 (New Haven: Connecticut Academy of Arts and Sciences, 1967).
Embree, Dan and Holly Johnson, *Repertorium Chronicarum. A Bibliography of the Manuscripts of Medieval Latin Chronicles*. http://nt.library.msstate.edu/chronica/
Graves, Edgar B. (ed.), *A Bibliography of English History to 1485*. (Oxford: OUP, 1975).
Kennedy, Edward Donald, 'Chronicles and Other Historical Writing' in *A Manual of the Writings in Middle English 1050–1500*, Albert E. Hartung (ed.), Vol. 8 (Hamden, CT: Archon Books, 1989).

## *Discussions of chronicles and related narratives and topics*

Brandt, William J., *The Shape of Medieval History: Studies in Modes of Perception* (New Haven: Yale U.P., 1966).
Given-Wilson, Chris, *Chronicles: The Writing of History in Medieval England* (London: Hambledon Continuum, 2004).
Goldstein, R. James, *The Matter of Scotland: Historical Narrative in Medieval Scotland* (Lincoln, NB: University of Nebraska Press, 1993).
Gransden, Antonia, *Historical Writing in England c.550–c.1307* (Ithaca, NY: Cornell University Press, 1974).
Gransden, Antonia, *Historical Writing in England. II. c.1307 to the Early Sixteenth Century* (Ithaca, NY: Cornell University Press, 1982).
Heffernan, Thomas J., *Sacred Biography: Saints and Their Biographers in the Middle Ages*. (New York: OUP, 1988).
Keeler, Laura, *Geoffrey of Monmouth and the Late Latin Chroniclers, 1300–1500* University of California Publications in English 17.1 (Berkeley: University of California Press, 1946).
Kingsford, C.L., *English Historical Literature in the Fifteenth Century* (Oxford, 1913; repr. New York: Franklin, 1972).
Le Goff, Jacques, *The Medieval Imagination*. Trans. Arthur Goldhammer (Chicago: University of Chicago Press, 1988).
Matheson, Lister M., 'Historical Prose' in *Middle English Prose: A Critical Guide to Major Authors and Genres*, ed. A.S.G. Edwards. (New Brunswick: Rutgers U.P., 1984).
Matheson, Lister M., 'The Arthurian Stories of Lambeth Palace Library MS 84' in *Arthurian Literature* V, ed. Richard Barber. (Cambridge: Brewer, 1985), pp. 70-91.
Matheson, Lister M., 'Printer and Scribe: Caxton, the Polychronicon, and the Brut', *Speculum* 60 (1985), 593–614.
Matheson, Lister M., 'King Arthur and the Medieval English Chronicles' in *King Arthur through the Ages*, ed. Valerie M. Lagorio and Mildred Leake Day. 2 vols (New York: Garland, 1990).

Matheson, Lister M., *The Prose Brut: The Development of a Middle English Chronicle* (Tempe, AZ: Medieval & Renaissance Texts & Studies, 1998).

Matheson, Lister M., 'The Chronicle Tradition' in *A Companion to Arthurian Literature.* ed. Helen Fulton (Chichester: Wiley-Blackwell, 2009).

McLaren, Mary-Rose, *The London Chronicles of the Fifteenth Century: A Revolution in English Writing* (Woodbridge: Brewer, 2002).

Moll, Richard J., *Before Malory: Reading Arthur in Later Medieval England* (Toronto: University of Toronto Press, 2003).

Summerfield, Thea, *The Matter of Kings' Lives: The Design of Past and Present in the early fourteenth-century chronicles by Pierre de Langtoft and Robert Mannyng.* Costerus New Series 113 (Amsterdam: Rodopi, 1998).

Taylor, John, *English Historical Literature in the Fourteenth Century.* (Oxford: OUP, 1987).

Turville-Petre, Thorlac. *England the Nation: Language, Literature, and National Identity, 1290–1340.* (Oxford: OUP, 1996).

# Notes

1   See Kemp Malone, 'When did Middle English begin?,' *Curme Volume of Linguistic Studies*, James T. Hatfield *et al.* (ed.), Language Monographs 7 (Baltimore: Johns Hopkins U.P., 1930), pp. 110–17; Richard Jordan, *Handbook of Middle English Grammar: Phonology* Eugene J. Crook (transl. and rev.), (The Hague: Mouton, 1974), pp. 1–2; for the fifteenth century, see J. H. Fisher, 'Chancery and the Emergence of Standard Written English in the Fifteenth Century,' *Speculum* 52 (1977), 870–99; M. L. Samuels, 'Spelling and Dialect in the Late and Post-Middle English Periods,' in *So Meny People Longages and Tonges: Philological Essays in Scots and Mediaeval English Presented to Angus McIntosh*, Michael Benskin and M. L. Samuels (eds), (Edinburgh: Edinburgh U.P., 1981), pp. 43–54 (repr. in *The English of Chaucer and His Contemporaries: Essays by M. L. Samuels and J. J. Smith*, J. J. Smith (ed.), (Aberdeen: Aberdeen U.P., 1988), pp. 86–95; E. J. Dobson, 'Early Modern Standard English,' *Neuphilologische Mitteilungen* 67 (1966), 122–32.

2   See Albert C. Baugh and Thomas Cable, *A History of the English Language*, 5th edn. (Upper Saddle River, NJ: Prentice Hall, 2001), pp. 108–57; Basil Cottle, *The Triumph of English 1350–1400* (New York: Barnes and Noble, 1969).

3   See Mary S. Serjeantson, *A History of Foreign Words in English* (London: Kegan Paul, 1935); Erik Björkman, *Scandinavian Loan-Words in Middle English* (Halle a. S.: Niemeyer, 1900, 1902).

4   See Brian Joseph Duffy, *The English Language and English Literary Genres in Transition, 1475–1600* (New York: Garland, 1987). A traditional but still useful survey of genres appears in Marlies K. Danziger and W. Stacy Johnson, *An Introduction to Literary Criticism* (Boston: D. C. Heath & Co., 1961), pp. 66–90; see also René Wellek and Austin Warren, *Theory of Literature*, 3rd edn. (Harmondsworth: Penguin, 1966), chapters 5 and 17. Northrop Frye proposed a new mode of generic theory, in which four major genres – comedy, romance, tragedy, and satire – reflected the archetypal myths correlated with the four seasons (*The Anatomy of Criticism*, Princeton: Princeton U.P., 1957, pp. 158–239).

5   Compare Polonius's trenchant survey of the theatre: 'tragedy, comedy, history, pastoral, pastorical-comical, historical-pastoral, tragical-historical, tragical-comical-historical-pastoral, scene indivisible or poem unlimited' (*Hamlet*, Act 2, Scene 2, lines 398–401). For the problems of anthologists, see Thomas J. Garbáty's divisions and his introductory remarks in *Medieval English Literature* (Lexington: D. C. Heath & Co., 1984), pp. 6, 8, 12, 14, 27–28, 29, 30 note, and the combinations of terms on pp. 53, 92, etc.

6   See A.J. Minnis, A. Brian Scott, and David Wallace, *Medieval Literary Theory and Criticism, c.1100–c.1375: The Commentary-Tradition* (Oxford: Clarendon, 1988); Alex Preminger, O.B. Hardison, and Kevin Kerrane, *Classical and Medieval Literary Criticism: Translations and Interpretations* (New York: Frederick Ungar, 1974); Joseph M. Miller, Michael H. Prosser, and Thomas W. Benson, *Readings in Medieval Rhetoric* (Bloomington: Indiana U.P., 1973); and, *in toto* and on the specified pages for the individual rhetoricians mentioned here, James J. Murphy, *Rhetoric in the Middle Ages: A History of Rhetorical Theory from Saint Augustine to the Renaissance* (Berkeley: University of California Press, 1974), p. 179; Charles Sears Baldwin, *Medieval Rhetoric and Poetic (to 1400) Interpreted from Representative Works* (New York: Macmillan, 1928), pp. 175–76; Clifford Leech, *Tragedy* (London: Methuen, 1969), pp. 2, 4.

7   See OED, *s.v.* fiction, where the earliest quotation is 1599 Richard Linche, *The fountaine of ancient fiction*, trans. 1780 [1781 in Bib.] James Harris, *Philological inquiries* (publ. in Works [1841]): 'Dramatic fiction copies real life.' For the medieval senses, see MED, s.v. ficcioun.

8   See Paul Strohm, 'Storie, Spelle, Geste, Romaunce, Tragedie: Generic Distinctions in the Middle English Troy Narratives,' *Speculum* 46 (1971), 348–59; 'Some Generic Distinctions in the Canterbury Tales,' *Modern Philology* 68 (1971), 321–28; 'Passioun, Lyf, Miracle, Legende: Some Generic Terms in Middle English Hagiographical Narrative,' *Chaucer Review* 10 (1977), 62–75, 154–71; 'The Origin and Meaning of Middle English Romaunce,' *Genre* 10 (1977), 1–28; 'Middle English Narrative Genres,' *Genre* 13 (1980), 379–88.

9   For example, 'a story of adventure – fictitious and frequently marvelous or supernatural – in verse or prose' (A. C. Baugh); 'a narrative about knightly prowess and adventure, in verse or in prose, intended primarily for the entertainment of a listening audience' (Elaine Newstead); 'secular narratives, with a hero, designed for entertainment' (Derek Pearsall). Formal classifications are attempted in Dieter Mehl, *The Middle English Romances of the Thirteenth and Fourteenth Centuries* (London: Routledge & Kegan Paul, 1968 [i.e., 1969]) and Derek Pearsall, 'The Development of Middle English Romance,' *Medieval Studies* 27 (1965), 91–116. Pearsall splits off 'historical epics' from 'romances'.

10  The spelling of titles of medieval works in the rest of this essay follows that of their standard modern editions, as listed in the bibliographical reference works in the Further reading section.

11  Many of these works survive in manuscripts of later date than the presumed composition date, thus showing their continuing popularity.

12  Quoted from Lister M. Matheson, 'Printer and Scribe: Caxton, the *Polychronicon*, and the *Brut*,' *Speculum* 60 (1985), p. 614.

13  Official proclamations and public declarations would also have played a similar role when facts or situations were described.

14  See Rossell Hope Robbins (ed.), *Historical Poems of the XIVth and XVth Centuries* (New York: Columbia U.P., 1959), p. vii.

15  Lydgate makes frequent appeals to historical authority, such as 'thus saith the Cronicler' and the like. In some copies made after Lydgate's death in 1449 the material is extended up to the present king; sometimes the poem is incorporated into a chronicle or is found in the same manuscript as a chronicle.

16  Halidon Hill is only found in the second translation of the Prose *Brut*. Most Siege of Rouen texts form part of a continuation to the first translation of the *Brut*, in which tradition the poem was subsequently paraphrased in prose. Indeed, the scribe of London, BL, MS Harley 753 copied out the poem as prose. There are occasional traces of ballad originals underlying sections of the *Brut*, such as the description of the battle of Agincourt; this is an interesting example of attitudes to such texts as valid historical sources.

17  A second poem on the siege of Calais occurs in a version of the *Brut*.

18 The English word 'biography' is a modern invention, first recorded in 1683 in Dryden, but narratives of the lives of eminent persons have an ancient pedigree. For England, see Donald A. Stauffer, *English Biography before 1700* (Cambridge, MA: Harvard U.P., 1930).

19 See the articles cited in note 8 above.

20 We could also consider a number of other works in verse and/or prose, such as lives of biblical persons other than saints and the Holy Family; histories of sacred objects, places, etc.; miracles and visions; moral tales, collections thereof, and religious works using these; and even the Corpus Christi cycle plays, which can be seen as dramatized histories of God's plan for mankind. For reasons of space these are not considered here; their general development, however, parallels that of the saints' lives.

21 *Aelfric's Lives of Saints, Being a Set of Sermons on Saints' Days Formerly Observed by the English Church*, Walter W. Skeat (ed.), Part 1, EETS o.s. 76, with facing-page translation by Misses Gunning and Wilkinson (London, 1881), pp. 5, 7.

22 See Thomas J. Heffernan, *Sacred Biography: Saints and Their Biographers in the Middle Ages* (New York: OUP, 1988) and Charles W. Jones, *Saints' Lives and Chronicles in Early England* (Ithaca, NY: Cornell U.P., 1947). Sceptical comments occasionally appear, as, for example, in the *South English Legendary* and the *Legenda Aurea* about the devil swallowing St Margaret (noted in D'Evelyn and Foster [see Further reading], p. 418).

23 *sanctorale*: 'That part of the breviary and missal which contains the offices proper for saints' days' (OED); *temporale*: 'That part of the breviary and missal which contains the daily offices in the order of the ecclesiastical year, as distinct from those proper for Saints' days' (OED).

24 There is also a series of learned notes in Latin on the history of Wilton Abbey.

25 J.T. Fowler (ed.), *The Life of St. Cuthbert in English Verse, C. AD1450*, Surtees Society, vol. 87 (Durham, 1891), p. vi.

26 Among the verse texts, the *Legenda Aurea* was used as a source in the early development of the South English Legendary and by Bokenham. Chaucer's Second Nun's Tale of St Cecilia is also based in large part on 'Frater Jacobus Januensis in Legenda'.

27 Wife of Thomas of Lancaster (1388?–1421), the second son of Henry IV by Mary de Bohun, created Duke of Clarence in 1412.

28 See N.F. Blake, 'The Biblical Additions in Caxton's Golden Legend,' *Traditio* 25 (1969), 231–47 (repr. in N.F. Blake, *William Caxton and English Literary Culture* (London: Hambledon Press, 1991), pp. 213–29).

29 See N.F. Blake, *Caxton and His World* (Elmsford: London House and Maxwell, 1969), pp. 119–20. Caxton's generic terms for the varied types of narrative in the *Legenda Aurea* is 'hystoryes,' though he also speaks in the prologue of 'eche hystorye, lyf, and passyon' and characterizes the book in the epilogue as containing 'alle the hygh … hystoryes and actes'.

30 Her life was also printed from a mid-fifteenth-century translation by Wynkyn de Worde.

31 The lives of St Katherine and St Elizabeth, printed by Wynkyn de Worde in 1493, may have been Caxton's translations.

32 Include this work as a saint's life rather than a miracle narrative since the 'virgyn and martir' survives for fifteen years as a nun after St Beunow has restored her to life after her beheading, which begins the narrative.

33 The French text is a translation of the *Vitas Patrum*, printed in 1478 at Nuremberg, which is in turn a combination of the *Vitas Patrum* attributed to St Jerome and the *Historia Monachorum* of Rufinus of Acquileia. The three texts, Latin, French and English, represent up-to-the-minute European hagiography of the late fifteenth century.

34 For further discussion, see Lister M. Matheson, 'King Arthur and the Medieval English Chronicles,' in *King Arthur Through the Ages*, Valerie M. Lagorio and Mildred Leake Day (eds), 2 vols. (New York: Garland, 1990), 1, pp. 259–63.

35  Works that deal generally with the sieges of Troy, Thebes, Jerusalem and Milan are noted above in relation to verse and prose chronicles; none of these narrates the deeds of one central character throughout.

36  See Richard J. Moll, *Before Malory: Reading Arthur in Later Medieval England* (Toronto: University of Toronto Press, 2003) for a full discussion of the complex relationships between chronicles and romances.

37  Some earlier Latin lives survive, such as Eadmer's twelfth-century life of Anselm (more hagiography than secular biography, however); Robert of Avesbury's mid-fourteenth-century *Chronicle*, entitled *De gestis mirabilibus Regis Edwardi Tertii*; the *Historia vitæ et regni Ricardi II. Angliæ regis*; and several Latin lives of Henry V.

38  We can also compare the work of the compiler of the greatly amplified *Brut* text in London, Lambeth Palace, MS 84 and his work in his two other known manuscripts.

39  *Everie Woman in her Humor* (1609), in *A Collection of Old English Plays*, ed. Arthur H. Bullen, IV (1885), C 4 b.

# 3 The medieval sermon: text, performance and insight

*Anne T. Thayer*

'The sermon represented the central literary genre in the lives of European Christians and Jews during the Middle Ages.'[1] So begins Beverly Mayne Kienzle's Introduction to the key reference work in the field of medieval sermon studies, *The Sermon*. Many scholars describe medieval preaching as the 'mass media' of the day since it was foundational to the broad dissemination of ideas for centuries. While huge quantities of preaching materials must be assumed to be lost, there are still thousands of sermons extant in manuscripts and early printed books, most of which remain unedited. It is hard to imagine an aspect of medieval history that is not in some way illuminated by sermons, yet sermons bear most direct witness to the religious culture of the Middle Ages.[2] Along with providing important historical insights, sermons offer a distinctive challenge as sources for, as Kienzle continues, 'Modern scholars face the dilemma of analyzing the written vestiges of an essentially oral and highly performative genre.'[3]

What is a sermon? This is not an easy question to answer because the genre is fluid and overlaps with many others, such as biblical commentary, religious treatises, letters, hagiography, synodal speeches, and so on. Kienzle defines the sermon thus:

> 1) The sermon is essentially an oral discourse, spoken in the voice of a preacher who addresses an audience, 2) to instruct and exhort them, 3) on a topic concerned with faith and morals and based on a sacred text.[4]

Medieval sermons as they come down to us are the written form of such a discourse. Over the course of the Middle Ages, more and more preaching took place and more and more sermon texts have survived. The turn of the thirteenth century is a watershed in the history of preaching and sermon production. Prior to that, most of the extant sermons come from monastic contexts, although we do know that there was popular preaching being done by the secular clergy as well. Once the Franciscans and Dominicans come on the scene in the early 1200s, communities, especially cities, 'discovered the importance and almost the intoxicating quality, as it were, of public discourse.'[5] There was a veritable boom in preaching and the production of aids for preachers. While mendicants worked across Europe, their largest numbers were found in France and Italy; consequently more sermons survive from these areas than others. Ironically, none of the sermons of Francis or Dominic have survived, although there are descriptions of their preaching in other sources, such as the *Little Flowers of St. Francis* and the *Libellus* of Jordan of Saxony.

Sermons were woven into the fabric of medieval culture and thus their study is inherently interdisciplinary. While sermons have been traditionally mined for the history of theology, the study of rhetoric, and glimpses into historical life, more recent scholarship has expanded into studies of performance, art, audience, women, devotional practice, spirituality and other topics. Many key works in the field are collaborative efforts. For example, *Speculum Sermonis* has as its goal 'to illustrate how different disciplines study medieval sermons and reciprocally, how the sermon informs the discipline's conclusions about the Middle Ages.'[6] The authors of the essays in the volume come from the fields of social history, archaeology, liturgical studies, history of theatre, linguistics, literature, manuscript studies, music, patristics, political science and art history. A survey of articles from the last decade of the journal *Medieval Sermon Studies* shows scholars discussing the content of medieval sermons to illuminate theological, pastoral and social issues. There is significant interest in stylistic considerations and the use of resources in the composition of sermons, suggesting an ongoing interest in the training and formation of preachers. Sermons are also used to gain access to the concerns, interests and religious formation of particular audiences such as urban and rural laity, nuns and women. While close and careful reading of the text is essential, it is nearly always the case that the significance of a given sermon and important factors pertaining to its interpretation are more fully illuminated through the use of additional sources.

## Textual issues

The two most commonly used labels for texts recording preaching are 'sermon' (*sermo*) and 'homily' (*homilia*). These terms were often used interchangeably throughout much of the medieval period, but historians have tended to use them more specifically to designate styles of discourse. A homily is structured by the biblical text on which it is based. The preacher takes the passage or pericope (a designated scriptural passage, usually from the gospels or epistles), reads a word, phrase or sentence at a time and offers commentary as he goes along. He need not stay close to the text (homilies are replete with what may seem to be tangents or digressions), but the framework of the discourse is provided by the text. This style of preaching was the norm in the early centuries of Christianity and continued through the early Middle Ages in both monastic and parochial settings. Homilies continued to be foundational to preaching in subsequent centuries, and saw a resurgence at the end of the Middle Ages.

By the late twelfth century, sacred oral discourses were becoming more complex in structure. Soon after 1200, they settled into a stylized form, designated the 'sermon'. Scholarly literature often provides such additional descriptors as thematic (based on a theme), modern (self-consciously departing from the old homily style), scholastic (sharing a passion for organized knowledge with scholastic theology), university (often disseminated from university centres), or mendicant (the major users of this form). The structure of such discourse was vital to its aesthetic and pedagogical intentions. At the heart of this style of preaching was the theme (a biblical or liturgical verse) and its division, the points to be made from or concerning it. For example, a sermon of the Franciscan John of Werden for the Sunday after Christmas has Luke 2:47 as its theme: 'They marvelled at his teaching and his answers.' The division of the text announces that there are four things which are to be marvelled at by the whole world: 'the incarnation of Christ (*Christi incarnatio*), the contrition of sinners (*peccatorum contritio*), the change of the world (*mundi mutatio*), and the glorification of the elect (*electorum glorificatio*).'[7] Note the rhyming of the divisions; this was a common technique to aid both preacher and hearer to remember the sermon. The bulk of the sermon then consists of the confirmation, elaboration and driving home of these points. Sometimes the body of a sermon is preceded by an introductory section, the protheme. Frequently a sermon ends with an exemplum or narrative tale. A contemporary genre of works known as the *artes praedicandi* (art of preaching) gave explicit instructions on how to construct such a sermon.[8] While the *artes* describe multiple modes of 'dialating' or 'expanding' the divided theme, the fundamental methods were by providing authorities, scriptural and patristic citations which confirm the points; proofs of reason for the points; and exempla to underline the moral message. The thematic sermon provided the main form of sermonic expression for 300 years, 1200–1500, and was used for preaching to all audiences.

There are basic facts about a sermon which one would like to know (although this is often not possible), such as author, date, location within the liturgical year, venue and audience. Many sermon texts have informative rubrics. For instance, a sermon contained in a manuscript in the *Biblioteca Palatina* in Parma is announced as, 'Preached by Brother Giordano, in 1303, on the 5th day of August, the feast day of St. Dominic, in Santa Maria Novella after nine.'[9] Scholars know a good deal about Giordano of Pisa and his preaching schedule; we also have a number of other sermons by him for stylistic comparisons. But, as with other medieval primary sources, such attributions should always be tested against other sources when possible.

Many rubrics are far less illuminating. For Latin sermons of the high and late Middle Ages, the *Repertorium der lateinischen Sermones des Mittelalters* of J.B. Schneyer is essential.[10] Schneyer identified over 100,000 individual copies of sermons copied between 1150 and 1350. For each he gives the manuscript and its location, early printed edition (if available), place within the liturgical calendar, biblical theme (if relevant), and the opening and closing words. It is possible to search the *Repertorium* by author, religious order (for anonymous sermons), theme, or name of sermon collection, enabling one to see where a particular sermon fits in an author's body of sermons, to read other medieval sermons on the same topic, to make a first stab at discovering whether a particular text has a known author, and so on. This masterful work has been extended with sermons to 1500 by L. Hödl and W. Knoch.[11] For all of their massive size and erudition, these works are not complete or fully reliable; other confirmations need to be sought.[12]

Sermons were written down in a variety of formats. One cannot simply assume that the text at hand corresponds to what was preached, or indeed that it was preached at all, although one might demonstrate that a sermon was not preached in the form in which it was recorded from internal evidence (too short, too long, in a different language). A sermon transmitted as a complete or full text may have been written out prior to delivery, or later on from memory or in consultation with notes made by the preacher or a listener. It may have received careful editing and/or elaboration, departing significantly from its oral form. Even when the extant text of a sermon is an autograph (a manuscript written by the author), it may depart from the sermon as actually preached. For instance, in an autograph sermon by Matthew of Aquasparta, there is a simple notation to 'tell the story of the boy from Modena'. Thanks to a listener's notes, we know that when Matthew preached, he told his own tale about an encounter between a wary provincial and a zealous candidate for the Franciscan order.[13] Some complete sermons may never have been delivered, but were composed for devotional reading, even though they adopt many of the features of oral delivery that characterize a live sermon, such as direct address, contemporary allusions, and comments on the community or audience.

A second format for sermon transmission includes summary reports, outlines and *sententiae*. The texts here are shorter than those in the previous category, often giving just the main structure of the sermon and the biblical and patristic authorities used to support its points. This format is very common, suggesting that these elements were considered to be the critical features of a sermon. Again, summaries might be prepared before or after preaching; a full text sermon might be abridged in this form.

A third format is the live report known as a *reportatio*. The survival of the notes taken by a listener during the delivery of a sermon is extremely rare; cleaned up copies of the notes are somewhat more frequent. Varying with the interests and skill of the reporter, these may include the preacher's gestures and the response of the crowd, along with the outline, authorities and tales told in the sermon. *Reportationes* began to appear in the thirteenth century. Occasionally, more than one reporter took notes on the same sermon, making possible a more complete picture of the preaching event. Such is the case for sermons preached in 1425 in Siena by the famous Franciscan, Bernardino of Siena. An anonymous reporter took notes in Italian; a civil servant named Iacopo di Nanni di Iacopo di messer Griffolo took notes in Latin. Iacopo concentrated on doctrine and scriptural citations, while noting what happened in the pulpit and piazza. The anonymous notetaker summarized Bernardino's scriptural citations, took interest in his narrative digressions, and commented on gesture and mimicry in the sermon.[14]

The fourth major format is the model sermon. Model sermons are the works of seasoned preachers designed to help others with the basics of the task. In the early medieval period, patristic homilies were often gathered into collections to exemplify good preaching and to be read aloud in parish and monastic settings. The most prominent of these was the collection of Paul the Deacon, an eighth-century Carolingian reformer. It includes sermons by Ambrose, Augustine, Bede, Gregory, Leo and Maximus of Turin. With the advent of the Friars in the early thirteenth century, huge numbers of model sermons were produced and circulated in collections: *de tempore* (for the Sundays and major festivals of the liturgical year), *de sanctis* (for the feast days of the saints) and *quadragesimales* (for Lent). A preacher could use these sermons whole, or mine them for outlines, authorities or stories. Model sermons were effectively published by multiple copying schemes and, once printing was invented, they were bestsellers well into the seventeenth century. These are often considered the 'typical' medieval sermons, for although model sermons do not tell us what was preached by any particular preacher in any particular place at any particular time, because of their widespread and routine use, they reveal what many European parishioners heard from the pulpit in both style and content.

A given set of sermons might pass through or be found in several of these formats. For example, St Bonaventure preached live in various places, including Paris. During his sermons, notes were taken by Marco da Montefeltro and others. While the original *reportationes* are no longer extant, abbreviated forms of the sermons copied from them survive. Bonaventure then chose 'a sermon for each Sunday from the *reportationes* and reworked them, drawing on his exegetical and theological works, to form a collection designed to help preachers.' He may have undertaken this work himself or he may have asked Marco to do it. The result was his collection, the *Sermones dominicales*.[15] Once in circulation, the whole collection could be copied; a few sermons might be copied along with those of other authors; they might be changed or abridged when copied, and so on.

Such variety raises the question of the reliability of a given sermon text. For coming as close as possible to the text the author actually wrote or first authorized, the path of manuscript transmission is traditionally determined by the stemmatic method. This creates a genealogical chart showing which manuscripts were copied from which earlier ones by tracking the transmission of scribal errors.[16] However, the earliest form of a text may not be the one which was most widely disseminated and thus had the most influence. During the thirteenth century, the *pecia* system for copying manuscripts was developed and used to great advantage in such university and preaching centres as Paris. A student or preacher interested in owning a manuscript could rent a piece of it (*pecia*) from a stationer, copy and return it. Since any given manuscript could be in the process of being copied by a large number of persons at one time, it facilitated the production of numerous copies of a single exemplar. Indeed it was the *pecia* system which enabled sermon texts to function as contemporary mass media.[17] From his experience with *pecia* and other manuscripts, David d'Avray has proposed an alternative method, which others are now using, for arriving at a reliable text using selected portions of a widely disseminated exemplar in conjunction with manuscripts from different textual families.[18] The goal of such editing protocols is ultimately to make more medieval sermons available for study.

The vast majority of medieval sermons have been preserved in Latin. Early on Latin was the vernacular, as reflected in the sermons of Caesarius of Arles (d. 542). After Latin and the vernacular diverged, Latin continued to be the language of delivery in several venues. In many male monastic settings, sermons were read and delivered in Latin, except on major liturgical festivals when lay brothers joined the congregation. Similarly, in university settings Latin was likely to be used, except on those occasions when the local populace was in attendance. Near the end of the Middle Ages, the revival of classical rhetoric prompted the delivery of new Latin sermons, especially at the papal court.[19]

The vernacular should be assumed to be the language of delivery for sermons to the laity (*ad populum*) in keeping with the mandates of church councils from Carolingian times onward. Such sermons, however, were often recorded in Latin. Latin shaped the mindset of medieval religious culture. It was the language of the Bible, the church Fathers and theological education; the liturgy of the mass and many key prayers were in Latin. The Latin scribal tradition had standard-ized a number of abbreviations to speed up the job of manuscript copying. Many preachers and reporters used these even when preparing or recording vernacular sermons. Latin also served as the international language among the mendicants, who could thus share preaching materials for use in a variety of vernaculars. The interplay between international Latin and various vernaculars is confirmed by the use of translators on occasions when the language of the preacher's sermon did not match that of the audience, as when Pedro, bishop of Lisbon preached in Latin to Crusaders from England, Germany and elsewhere.[20] Despite the preponder-ance of Latin, there are sermons preserved in the vernacular. In general, the later Middle Ages have more of these than the early centuries; once sermons begin to be printed, this trend accelerates.[21]

## Interpretive issues

A vital feature of the sermon as a primary source for medieval studies is its reli-giously committed and persuasive, at times even polemical, nature. Sermons do not constitute 'objective' historical records. Preachers sought to convey a reli-gious message to their audiences effectively. Sermons need to be read closely and interpreted as 'engaged literature',[22] as enactments of Christian faith and practice. They thus can reveal the beliefs, commitments, ideals and values of their various communities. The more one can learn about medieval culture in general and reli-gious culture in particular, the better one will be able to interpret a given sermon or sermon collection.

In order for a sermon to be effective in conveying its religious message, it needed to come from an authorized source. Contemporary theologies of preaching stressed that the preacher needed both the personal authority of a godly life and the institutional authority that came with ordination and licensing.[23] Outside monasteries, according to canon law, the responsibility for preaching belonged fundamentally to bishops, who in turn were expected to delegate this to others in order to make preaching widely available. Within a monastery, the abbot (and sometimes the abbess) was the key preacher. However, with the rise of apostolic life movements in the twelfth and thirteenth centuries, growing numbers believed that a call to preach was inherent in the call to Christian discipleship. Groups such as the Waldensians and Cathars came into conflict with Roman Catholic officials by claiming the priority of personal authority. The Friars adopted the ideal of apostolic holiness and were granted special authorization to preach, sometimes in direct competition with the secular clergy. Women also engaged in activities that would have been labelled preaching if done by men, but were labelled 'prophecy', 'teaching', 'exhortation' and so on when valued by their hearers and 'wanton behaviour', 'heresy' etc. when not.[24]

Sermon texts themselves offer clues to how a preacher understood his or her authorization; often these can be more fully appreciated by the coordinate use of other sources. Catherine Mooney's study of Humility of Faenza (d. 1310) offers a good example. She was a Vallombrosan nun for whom 180 pages of sermons were recorded by one or more nuns in her convent during her lifetime. By carefully studying the sermons along with *vitae* (hagiographic biographical texts) prepared for her canonization, Mooney finds that Humility was quite a forceful personality. Although Humility offered some of the typical disclaimers about being unworthy to speak, she seems to have been less troubled by her call to preach than other women such as Catherine of Siena or Birgitta of Sweden. Those who wrote about her life did not accentuate traditional female virtues, but stressed 'her strength, willfulness, independence, and creative gifts' and 'her power and leadership'. Humility was not mandated to write her words by a male confessor, nor did such an authorizing male take them down. She attributes her words to the three persons of the Trinity as well as to the Virgin Mary and John the Evangelist. Such a range of heavenly sources is unusual among both men and women. Humility spoke boldly to both nuns and monks, conveying the confidence gained from her self-understanding as a divinely empowered preacher.[25]

Essential to the sermon's nature as engaged literature, and closely tied to the authority of the preacher, is the frequent citation of authorities from the Christian tradition. Uniqueness or innovation was not valued by the authors, compilers or transmitters of medieval sermons, but continuity of message, going all the way back to Christ, was. The centrality of authorities to medieval sermons is evidenced, as noted above, by the fact that when sermons were condensed for transmission, the authorities cited continued to be recorded. The writers of medieval sermons were passionate about the word of God. This was true in the early Middle Ages when homilies followed their pericopes, and with the mendicants a 'passion ... for incessantly quoting the Bible' blossomed.[26] In addition to the Bible, earlier Christian writers were frequently cited to confirm the division of the theme of the sermon and provide the latticework of the sermon's basic structure. For example, John Herolt, a fifteenth-century Dominican, cites the following authorities to answer the question, 'What is contrition?' in a sermon for the fourth Sunday of Lent: Thomas Aquinas, Romans 8, Bernard of Clairvaux, Augustine, Psalm 127, and Peter of Tarentaise.[27] Many preachers drew their quotations from works such as Gratian's Decretals, Lombard's Sentences, and the various *florilegia* (collections of useful materials for preachers) produced after 1200.

Were the sermons of authorized preachers with authoritative messages effective? From a sermon text itself, it is very difficult to assess whether or not the sermon achieved its aim. One cannot simply assume that all hearers adopted the preached theology as their own, abandoned the sins decried by the preacher, or became devout recipients of the sacraments. Sometimes a reporter included comments about audience reaction (positive or negative) that ended up in the transmission of the sermon. Some of the *exempla* recounted testify to a preacher's own experience and indicate audience responses to sermons. Further information of this type can be gleaned from other sources such as chronicles, hagiography or local legislation. Repentance, individual and corporate, was perhaps the quintessential desired outcome of medieval sermons. Individuals might be moved to tears on the spot, converted from heresy, make a devout confession, go on crusade or join a religious order. On a corporate level, a community might be moved to destroy a site associated with superstitious practices, burn 'vanities' such as fancy dress clothes or playing cards, or even take a vow of peace to end factional violence. Occasionally we hear of miraculous endorsements of a preacher's message, but sometimes he was heckled and driven out of town.[28]

As a way to gain greater access to the oral nature of the preaching recorded in a sermon, scholars are increasingly turning to performance theory. Beverly Kienzle has gathered the insights of several theorists whose work is being appropriated by sermonists. J.L. Austin's categorization of types of utterances draws attention to the high incidence of 'illocutionary' verbs in sermons, that is, speech that seeks to have an effect and generate a response. The concept of framing, articulated by Gregory Bateson, points to the importance of 'the conceptual framework that the mind uses to interpret actions or messages', drawing attention to issues of authorization, expected language, and so on. Medieval preaching had much in common with ritual and, judging by complaints about certain preachers, also with theatre. Thus Richard Schechner's distinction between ritual, which aims at effectiveness, such as the moral or spiritual transformation of the hearers, and theatre, which aims to entertain, is useful. Similarly, because live sermons employed gesture, vocal modulation and occasional visual effects, and called for a corporate response, Manfred Pfister's understanding of the 'multimediality' of dramatic texts contributes to the goal of moving from a written text to appreciation of live preaching. Maurice Bloch's work on the 'relationship of performance and authority' underscores the importance of preaching's conformity to established patterns of formalized speech. For both preacher and audience, sermons played a role in shaping individual and communal identity, and so performance theory makes use of various postmodern theories of social construction. To all of these tools, Kienzle argues that the scholar must add the performance expectations of medieval preachers themselves. These are often articulated in the *artes praedicandi*, a critical element of which she calls 'moral performance'. Attention to gaining the goodwill of the audience, moderation in gesture, well-told narratives, etc. were highly valued.[29] Mary Swan summarizes, 'Interpreting them as performative texts makes the committed nature of homilies the point of our analysis … and encourages us to deal in a scholarly way with the question of belief.'[30]

Thus, carefully used, performance theory can be quite illuminating, even for sermons designed for reading where the 'performance' takes place within the mind of the reader. Yet there is a potential pitfall. This approach may be most easy to use on material that is atypical, where the flamboyance of the preacher is a known factor. But many sermons as we have them, especially those that served as models, are predictable, even boring. They tend toward the abstract, formulaic and general. Yet this is a significant part of their value. D'Avray suggests that 'it was precisely the detachment of the content from any immediate social context that enabled them to 'travel'.[31] They reveal what was standard, what was likely to become assumed knowledge or common sense through being preached year in and year out. Routine preaching provides the background against which eloquence or charisma like that of Bernard or Bernardino stands out. D'Avray writes of an anonymous thirteenth-century collection of Franciscan sermons:

> There is not much colour in the Legifer collection, but it is a particularly good representative of some forms of thought characteristic of thirteenth-century preaching. It helps save one from the process of natural selection by which historians are attracted away from the more essential parts of a sermon by the patches which are entertaining or which tell him about social habits and customs.[32]

Recognizing these forms of thought is an essential part of the interpretation of a medieval sermon. D'Avray's works have been seminal in this area. While a thematic sermon begins with a single text, it then 'fanned out' from there, with the theme providing a 'matrix of ideas'.[33] These ideas were then combined freely and developed in aesthetic ways that valued symmetry, parallelism and ordered combinations, much like the structure of a cathedral or the patterns in a kaleidoscope. Although the rules for combining ideas were often unconscious, the results were often familiar to sermon audiences. The parallel between microcosm and macrocosm was a favourite, as was interpretation according to the multiple senses of scripture. Customary triads of understanding include *intellectus, affectus, effectus* (understanding, affect, effect) and *corde, ore, opera* (in thought, word, deed).[34] Because of such analytical conventions and the repeated use of traditional authorities, sermons are fruitful ground for the study of the use *topoi*. One needs a sense of the doctrinal continuities passed on in sermons in order to recognize individual aspects of creativity or new combinations of old *topoi*. D'Avray avers, 'Only comparisons can bring out the difference between short-term trends and the *longue durée* of Western preaching; the similarities and the differences are equally interesting.'[35]

Such comparisons may be pursued in diverse ways. The growing availability of electronically searchable texts offers new opportunities to find and count certain types of repetitions and stylistic conventions. While this will never substitute for the careful reading of texts, Martine De Reu asserts:

> It is a complementary way to look at texts. 'Counting' offers a more objective basis to 'intuitive' feelings occurring while reading texts. In those cases where statistical methods yield unexpected results, they exhort us to return to the texts and start reading them over again from a new point of view.[36]

De Reu demonstrates the fruitfulness of this method by analyzing occurrences of virtues and vices in sermons of the early Middle Ages. She finds that in comparison with the Merovingian period and the tenth and eleventh centuries, the intervening Carolingian period showed an emphasis on the virtue of faith 'achieved at the expense of all the other vices and virtues'.[37] Among the vices, Carolingians gave most attention to anger, while the centuries on either side of this period lifted up pride as the key vice. The distinctive emphases of the Carolingian period are confirmed by comparing the frequency of these words in sermons with that in other contemporary sources such as biblical commentaries, treatises, scientific works, letters and historical writings. Thus Carolingian preachers gave their sermon collections a contemporary and characteristic identity, even while borrowing heavily from their predecessors. What prompted this? De Reu highlights the influence of Charlemagne's legislation mandating the preaching of the Christian faith and the threat that anger posed to the imperial desire for order and justice.[38]

The practice of dating medieval documents via the liturgical calendar is well known; sermons provide powerful evidence for a corresponding calendar of ideas, regularly disseminated on a set of customary topics. Although there were variations in lectionaries, the time-honoured pairing of particular texts with particular days and particular preaching themes yielded a common set of expectations and a familiar body of knowledge. For instance, the story of Jesus turning water into wine at the wedding in Cana (John 2:1–11) was read on the second Sunday after Epiphany, and this became a traditional time to preach on marriage. This pairing was in place by the thirteenth century and continued into the seventeenth. Such continuity enables one studying ideas of marriage in the Middle Ages to track what was preached over time, to compare one preacher to another, and to assess 'typical' teaching on marriage. Other Sunday themes are similarly predictable. The first Sunday after the octave of Easter with its pericope of the Good Shepherd often brought preaching on what makes a good cleric or church leader.[39] Sermons for the dedication of a church regularly discuss how to worship properly.[40] The endurance of the lectionary texts and associated themes continued for Catholics and Lutherans through the sixteenth century, thus ensuring that model sermons remained key vehicles for the shaping of religious discourse in that contested age.[41]

A study of the differences among model sermon collections on a given theme can highlight the historical ramifications of such varied inculcation. Following Lateran IV's call for annual confession for all Christians, the standard features of the penitential process were preached all across Europe. All were expected to undergo careful self-examination, cultivate sorrow for their sins and confess them to their parish priest who would pronounce absolution and assign works of satisfaction. By examining geographically diverse popular model sermon collections, Anne Thayer has shown that the relative balance struck by preachers between the penitent's responsibility for successful forgiveness of sins and the grace offered in the sacrament of penance differed significantly in different regions of Europe in the decades prior to the Reformation. This in turn correlated with varied lay receptivity to new theologies of forgiveness in the sixteenth century. Thayer concludes:

> Based on pervasive and influential sources, this study provides insight into the religious mindsets created in various regions of Europe by the preaching of mendicants and parish clergy. ... Preaching was a powerful shaper of late medieval religious culture, contributing to its varied vulnerabilities and strengths.[42]

The more one knows about the sermon itself, the author, and the religious culture in which the sermon was produced, the richer and more insightful one's interpretation can be. No single text or approach can exhaust a sermon or sermon collection. A recent example of a study that brings together a wealth of learning to a series of sermons is Beverly Kienzle's study of the gospel homilies of Hildegard of Bingen. Hildegard was a twelfth-century Benedictine abbess from whose hand, along with a number of other works in various genres, we have fifty-eight extant homilies on twenty-seven gospel pericopes. These are for Sundays and feast days and were delivered to the nuns of her community, probably in the chapter house, in the 1160s and 1170s.[43] Kienzle explores Hildegard's visionary authorization for her exegetical work in a religious culture that did not authorize women to preach. She then illuminates Hildegard's homiletic pedagogy and interpretation of scripture through careful presentation of her cultural milieu, the sources available for her use, and the ways she dramatized the voices of biblical characters and glossed the text to create a continuous narrative. Hildegard's theological understanding of the history of salvation pervaded her homilies and undergirded her denunciation of contemporary Cathar heretics. Kienzle examines the relationship of the gospel homilies to Hildegard's other works, and is able to highlight the distinctive features of Hildegard's exegesis, compare her with contemporary preachers such as Bernard of Clairvaux, and discuss the homilies beside other works written by medieval women for female audiences.[44]

## Contemporary interests

The study of sermons is often guided by developments in the broader world of medieval scholarship. Contemporary interests include women, heretical groups, 'popular' religion, spirituality and images. Augmenting those already given, a few more examples suggest the fruitfulness of sermons as primary sources for such topics.

Sermons were vital to the cultivation, diffusion and social significance of popular religious devotions. Katherine Jansen's study of devotion to Mary Magdalen relies heavily on mendicant sermons. A careful reading of the sermons themselves, augmented by the use of other forms of evidence available for the later Middle Ages, such as letters, hagiography, testamentary bequests and artistic commissions, shows how the saint's persona was presented, her cult was shaped, and laypersons responded to the preachers' message. In the newfound zeal for preaching of the thirteenth century, sermons present Mary Magdalen as symbolic of the 'apostolic life', as well as a contemplative mystic. '[T]hrough the process of symbolic gender reversal the mendicants identified themselves with the faithful and humble Magdalen in opposition to the institutional church, as symbolized by Peter, prince of the apostles, who faithlessly had denied Christ.'[45] But the message of the Magdalen continued to evolve so that she became emblematic of the sin of lust. Jansen argues that 'preachers and moralists of the later Middle Ages invented a Magdalen to address philosophical and social exigencies: the nature of Woman, the care and custody of women, and the ever-increasing problem of prostitution.' Concurrently Mary also became the ideal penitent, and thus a powerful symbol of hope, adding to her appeal.[46] Overall, this careful longitudinal study

shows why Mary Magdalen (after the Virgin Mary) was the most important female saint of the period and how her cult exemplified, reflected, and
refracted some of the most important social issues, theological questions, and
pressing politics of the later Middle Ages.[47]

The relationship between sermons and economic issues is a complex one. The
thirteenth and early fourteenth centuries saw a changing economic pattern in
Europe, with the growth of a moneyed economy, the development of banking, and
the growth of cities where the very wealthy lived side by side with the very poor.
It was suggested some years ago that urban money-making shaped the mentality
of mendicant preaching.[48] There are indeed numerous examples of marketplace
imagery and discussions of merchants and business in thirteenth-century mendicant sermons, often casting Christ as a good merchant and the Devil as an evil
one.[49] However, d'Avray warns against assuming that this arose directly from
the preachers' urban context, since such images may also be found in sermons
originating outside urban areas and could be readily drawn from concordances
of biblical imagery. Additionally, mendicant sermons also use political and royal
images, reflecting the political pressures on medieval people. He writes:

> The image of Christ as the good merchant was obviously evocative, but there
> is no reason to be surprised to meet him in the guise of the innocent and just
> son of a good prince, who lets him be a hostage in order to redeem a captured
> and imprisoned army.[50]

D'Avray concludes that commercial imagery was simply a subset of social
imagery which was a subset of preachers' overarching tendency to use images.
Even so, mendicants preached directly to both rich and poor about their status
in life. Jussi Hanska's study of sermons on the story of Lazarus and Dives (Luke
16:19–31, assigned for the first Sunday after Trinity), shows that in keeping
with prior Christian tradition, the poor were assumed to be more likely to be
good Christians than the rich, 'yet the sermons and other writings of mendicant
brothers arguably present this ethos more frequently, intensively and concretely
than Christian writers of any century before or after that time.'[51] The preachers
kept the salvation of their audiences in the forefront of their efforts. Thus they
consoled the poor with hopes of better things to come and urged them to be patient
and persevere, in effect turning their suffering into the voluntary poverty that the
mendicants valued so highly. The rich were blamed for the oppression of the poor
and warned by being told of the torments of hell; if they did not repent in generosity and care, the tables would be turned on them in the next life. Such preaching
did not do much to disrupt the emerging status quo, but it did convey the spiritual
value of life in this world.[52]
Medieval artwork bore witness to preaching, and sermons themselves drew on
visual images. A regular visual tool of the preacher and an integral part of live
preaching events was the pulpit. While there was great variety in the styles and
placement of pulpits throughout the Middle Ages, Nirit Debby has shown that the
iconography of pulpits in Renaissance Italy was quite closely correlated to the

content of the sermons preached in them. Many featured images of saints; some commented on social issues such as clashes with Muslims or local relationships with neighbouring states.[53] Lina Bolzoni has studied the way visual imagery was a part of a cluster of rhetorical, logical and mental tools used to facilitate the recall of sermons both by preacher and hearer.[54] While model sermon collections do not often refer to images other than the crucifix, which could reliably be found in any church, *reportationes* reveal that some preachers explicitly discussed the visual imagery found nearby in their sermons. Bernardino of Siena, for instance, preaching in Siena on 15 September 1427, the Feast of the Annunciation, said that on account of Mary's modesty, she was hesitant when the angel appeared to her. He asked his hearers,

> Have you ever seen the Annunciation in the Duomo above the altar of Saint Sano, next to the sacristy? That certainly seems to me to show the most beautiful attitude, the most reverent, and the most shy that I have ever observed in an Annunciation. You see how she dares not look straight at the Angel; how she shrinks away in an attitude almost of fear? … Draw a lesson from this, girls, regarding what you should do yourselves. Never speak to a man if your father or your mother is not present.[55]

Such details illuminate how the preacher helped his hearers visualize the biblical story while at the same time giving them an interpretation of a readily accessible picture to help them remember his message. Such cross-referencing underscores the embeddedness of the medieval sermon and its audience in mental and visual religious environments.

Sermons are very rich sources for the study of many aspects of medieval religious culture. The most critical approach to a sermon is also the most obvious – read the text very carefully, recognizing it as a persuasive expression of faith. Any interpretation must be built on the sermon's content as understood in context through various textual, linguistic and performative considerations. The context is as broad as the Middle Ages, for everything from theology to politics bears on the sermon; no sermon was created without precedent, and no extant sermon was without some kind of transmission and influence. Hence, the field of sermon studies is inherently multidisciplinary and interdisciplinary. Happily, it is also characterized by a great deal of collegiality and international cooperation, making possible projects that go far beyond any individual's contribution. Read, learn, interpret, consult, re-read, revise and enjoy!

## Further reading

Andersson, Roger, *Constructing the Medieval Sermon* (Turnhout: Brepols, 2007).

Bataillon, Louis Jacques, 'Approaches to the Study of Medieval Sermons', *Leeds Studies in English*, 11 (1980): 19–35.

Bériou, Nicole and David L. d'Avray (eds), *Modern Questions about Medieval Sermons: Essays on Marriage, Death, History and Sanctity* (Spoleto: Centro italiano di studi sull'Alto medioevo, 1994).

Berkey, Jonathan Porter, *Popular Preaching and Religious Authority in the Medieval Islamic Near East* (Seattle: University of Washington Press, 2001).

Cunningham, Mary B. and Pauline Allen, *Preacher and Audience: Studies in Early Christian and Byzantine Homiletics* (Leiden: Brill, 1998).

Donavin, Georgiana, Cary J. Nederman, and Richard Utz (eds), *Speculum Sermonis: Interdisciplinary Reflections on the Medieval Sermon* (Turnhout: Brepols, 2004).

d'Avray, D. L. *The Preaching of the Friars: Sermons Diffused from Paris before 1300* (Oxford: Clarendon, 1985).

Kienzle, Beverly Mayne (ed.), *The Sermon. Typologie des Sources du Moyen Age Occidental*, fasc. 81–3 (Turnhout, Belgium: Brepols, 2000).

Kienzle, Beverly Mayne, and Barbara Walker (eds.), *Women Preachers and Prophets Through Two Millennia of Christianity* (Berkeley: University of California Press, 1998).

Medieval Sermon Studies. Leeds, 1991+

Muessig, Carolyn (ed.), *Medieval Monastic Preaching* (Leiden: Brill, 1998).

Muessig, Carolyn (ed.), *Preacher, Sermon and Audience in the Middle Ages* (Leiden: Brill, 2002).

Roberts, Phyllis 'Sermon Studies Scholarship: The Last Thirty-five Years', *Medieval Sermon Studies* 43 (1999), 9–18.

Saperstein, Marc, *Jewish Preaching 1200–1800: An Anthology* (New Haven: Yale University Press, 1989).

Saperstein, Marc, *Your Voice Like a Ram's Horn: Themes and Texts in Traditional Jewish Preaching* (Cincinnati: Hebrew Union College Press, 1996).

## Notes

1  Beverly Mayne Kienzle (ed.), *The Sermon*, Typologie des Sources du Moyen Age Occidental, fasc. 81–83 (Turnhout, Belgium: Brepols, 2000), p. 143.

2  Due to the vast quantity of extant material, this essay will limit its discussion to Christian preaching in the West, although the suggestions for further reading contain recommendations for Byzantine, Jewish and Muslim preaching.

3  Kienzle, *The Sermon*, p. 143.

4  Kienzle, *The Sermon*, p. 151.

5  Carlo Delcorno, 'Medieval Preaching in Italy (1200–1500)', in Kienzle, *The Sermon*, p. 450.

6  Georgiana Donavin, 'Introduction', in *Speculum Sermonis: Interdisciplinary Reflections on the Medieval Sermon*, Georgiana Donavin, *et al.* (eds.), (Turnhout: Brepols, 2004), p. xiii.

7  John of Werden, Sermon 6, *Sermones dormi secure de tempore* (Nurnberg: Anton Koberger, 1498).

8  See Marianne G. Briscoe, *Artes Praedicandi. Typologie des sources du Moyen Age occidental*, fasc. 61 (Turnhout, Belgium: Brepols, 1992).

9  Predicò frate Giordano M.CCC.IIJ. di. V. d'agosto *il dì di sancto Domenico in Sancta Maria Novella dopo nona*. Palatino 23, 68vb–71va. For the full text of this sermon see Delcorno, 'Preaching in Italy', pp. 543–59.

10  Johannes Baptist Schneyer, *Repertorium der lateinischen Sermones des Mittelalters für die Zeit von 1150 bis 1350*, 11 vols. (Münster: Aschendorff, 1969–90).

11  Ludwig Hödl and Wendelin Knoch, *Repertorium der lateinischen Sermones des Mittelalters für die Zeit von 1350 bis 1500*, CD-ROM (Münster: Aschendorff, 2001).

12  For publication information on widely disseminated printed sermon collections in the decades prior to the Reformation, see Anne T. Thayer, *Penitence, Preaching and the Coming of the Reformation* (Aldershot: Ashgate, 2002), chapter 2.

13  Louis-Jacques Bataillon, OP, 'Approaches to the Study of Medieval Sermons', in *Leeds Studies in English*, 11 (1980), 22.

14  Delcorno, 'Preaching in Italy', pp. 498–9.

15  Summarized in D. L. d'Avray, *The Preaching of the Friars: Sermons Diffused from Paris before 1300* (Oxford: Clarendon, 1985), p. 97.

16  See Paul Mass, *Textual Criticism*, transl. Barbara Flower (Oxford: Clarendon, 1958).

17  See d'Avray, *Friars*, 3, pp. 160–62, 273–81.

18  D.L. d'Avray. *Medieval Marriage Sermons: Mass Communication in a Culture without Print* (Oxford: Oxford University Press, 2001), 38–47.

19  John W. O'Malley, *Praise and Blame in Renaissance Rome: Rhetoric, Doctrine and Reform in the Sacred Orators of the Papal Court, c. 1450–1521* (Durham: Duke University Press, 1979).

20  Beverly Mayne Kienzle, 'Medieval Sermons and their Performance', in *Preacher, Sermon and Audience in the Middle Ages*, Carolyn Muessig (ed.) (Leiden: Brill, 2002), p. 110.

21  For further information on vernacular preaching and sermon texts, see the essays in Kienzle, *The Sermon*, on Italian, Old English, Middle English, Old Norse-Icelandic, French, Spanish, Portuguese, Catalan and German sermons. The ever-growing SERMO project aims to provide a thorough record of extant vernacular sermons. *A Repertorium of Middle English Prose Sermons* has been published (Turnhout: Brepols, 2007), which gives sermon contents, patterns of transmission, exempla, biblical and patristic citations, as well as bibliographical references. Similar works for other vernaculars are in process.

22  I take this phrase from Mary Swan, 'Men ða leofestan: Genre, the Canon, and the Old English Homiletic Tradition', in *The Christian Tradition in Anglo-Saxon England: Approaches to Current Scholarship and Teaching*, Paul Cavill (ed.), (Woodbridge: D.S. Brewer, 2004), pp. 185–92.

23  Claire Waters, *Angels and Earthly Creatures: Preaching, Performance, and Gender in the Later Middle Ages* (Philadelphia: University of Pennsylvania Press, 2004), p. 15.

24  See Beverly Mayne Kienzle and Barbara Walker (eds.), *Women Preachers and Prophets Through Two Millennia of Christianity* (Berkeley: University of California Press, 1998).

25  Catherine M. Mooney, 'Authority and Inspiration in the *Vitae* and Sermons of Humility of Faenza', in *Medieval Monastic Preaching*, Carolyn Muessig (ed.), (Leiden: Brill, 1998), pp. 123–43.

26  d'Avray, *Friars*, pp. 236–7.

27  John Herolt, Sermon 43, *Sermones discipuli de tempore* (Strasbourg: [Martin Flach], 1492).

28  Kienzle, 'Sermons and their Performance', pp. 118–19.

29  Kienzle, 'Sermons and their Performance, pp. 90–103.

30  Swan, 'Men ða leofestan', p. 191.

31  d'Avray, *Friars*, p. 158.

32  d'Avray, *Friars*, p. 277.

33  d'Avray, *Friars*, p. 246.

34  d'Avray, *Friars*, pp. 246–8.

35  d'Avray, *Friars*, p. 255.

36  Martine De Reu, 'A Statistical Treatment of Sin and Holiness in Sermons from the Early Middle Ages (500–1100), in Donavin, *Speculum Sermonis*, p. 340. This essay includes helpful bibliographical references on using computers in the study of medieval texts.

37  De Reu, 'Statistical Treatment', p. 350.

38  De Reu, 'Statistical Treatment', pp. 356–7.

39  Jussi Hanska, 'Reconstructing the Mental Calendar of Medieval Preaching: A Method and Its Limits – An Analysis of Sunday Sermons', in Muessig, *Preacher, Sermon and Audience*, pp. 293–311.

40   Anne T. Thayer, 'Learning to Worship in the Later Middle Ages: Enacting Symbolism, Fighting the Devil and Receiving Grace', *Archive for Reformation History* 99 (2008): 36–65.
41   See John M. Frymire, *The Primacy of the Postils: Catholics, Protestants, and the Dissemination of Ideas in Early Modern Germany* (Leiden: Brill, 2010).
42   Thayer, *Penitence*, pp. 194–5.
43   Beverly Mayne Kienzle, *Hildegard of Bingen and Her Gospel Homilies: Speaking New Mysteries* (Turnhout: Brepols, 2009), pp. 2–3.
44   Kienzle, *Hildegard*, pp. 19–21.
45   Katherine Ludwig Jansen, *The Making of the Magdalen: Preaching and Popular Devotion in the Later Middle Ages* (Princeton: Princeton University Press, 2000), p. 15.
46   Jansen, *Magdalen*, p. 15.
47   Jansen, *Magdalen*, p. 17.
48   Barbara H. Rosenwein and Lester K. Little, 'Social Meaning in Monastic and Mendicant Spiritualities', *Past and Present* 63 (1974): 4–32.
49   d'Avray, *Friars*, pp. 208–12.
50   d'Avray, *Friars*, pp. 217–25, quote on p. 225.
51   Jussi Hanska, *'And the Rich Man also died; and He was buried in Hell': The Social Ethos in Mendicant Sermons* (Helsinki: Suomen Historiallinen Seura, 1997), p. 168.
52   Hanska, *Social Ethos*, pp. 168–74.
53   Nirit Ben-Aryeh Debby, *The Renaissance Pulpit: Art and Preaching in Tuscany, 1400–1550* (Leiden: Brepols, 2007), pp. 177–9.
54   Lina Bolzoni, *The Web of Images: Vernacular Preaching from its Origins to St. Bernardino da Siena* (Aldershot: Ashgate, 2004), pp. 2–9.
55   Quoted in Bolzoni, *Web of Images*, p. 138.

# 4    Wills as primary sources

*Shona Kelly Wray and Roisin Cossar*

**Example I**

Testatrix: Anastassu, widow of Nicolaus Caravello
Place: Venetian-governed Crete
Date: 30 July 1328.

In the name of eternal God, amen … in Candia, on the island of Crete. Since the time of the end of life is known to no one, and there is nothing more certain to us than the fact that we know we cannot avoid death, it is necessary for all of us to dispose of our earthly goods carefully. And so, I, Anastassu, widow of Nicolaus Caravello, an inhabitant of Candia, healthy in mind and body, fearing lest I die intestate, desiring to leave my estate well-ordered, called to me Andrea de Bellamore, a notary, so that he could write my testament. I named as my executors Iohannes Secreto, son of Lorenzo Secreto and Rosa Secreto, my beloved nephew, and Aniza Fontanela, my beloved niece, both inhabitants of Candia, that they might carry out my wishes after my death. First, I leave for my soul, 50 *iperpera* to be given to those who have been imprisoned for debt, giving 5 or 6 *iperpera* to each prisoner. Then, I leave ten *iperpera* to the monastery of Sinaita in Candia for my soul. Then, I leave ten *iperpera* to the lepers of S. Lazzaro for clothing to cover them. Then I leave 6 *iperpera* to the congregation of S. Tito in Candia for my soul. Then, I leave one of my bed-covers, some sheets (to be selected by my executors) and three *iperpera* each to the sick in the hospital of S. Maria Maiore in Candia. And I desire that the slave that I have kept be freed on my death. And if she wants to return to her own region, she should be given enough for the journey from my belongings. I ask that 20 iperpera be spent on my burial, so that I may be buried honorably and well. I leave Agnetus de Bellamore ten *iperpera*. I leave Sophie, the daughter of Simenachus, whom I baptized, 15 *iperpera* so that she may marry. I leave the priest Emmanuelus Saclichus two *iperpera* so that for one year from the day of my death he may celebrate one mass each Saturday for my soul. I leave the priest Simenachus the same amount for the same reason. I leave the priest Constantino de Chera Pissiotissa the same amount for the same reason. [These bequests to individual priests continue; there are 13 in all]. Then, I leave five *iperpera* to the nuns of the church of S Caterina for [pious] works. I leave Calus, the illegitimate ['natural'] son of Michale Mazamurdi, my late brother, five *iperpera*. Then, I leave 100 *iperpera* to

Iohannes de Rizo, my nephew, to be given to him when he receives his father's goods. And if he dies before this happens, I wish that my bequest devolve to Nicolotas Rizo, his sister, if she is alive. Otherwise the money goes to Iohannes Secreto. Then I leave to Aniza, my niece and executor, 25 *iperpera*. Then I leave to Andrea de Bellamore, the notary, 10 *iperpera* for writing this will. I ask and order that all of the abovementioned legacies be distributed within 9 days after my death. I also ask that all of my *massaria* (household goods), namely sheets, linens, cauldrons, and all other things in my house except those made of gold or silver, or any money, be divided equally between my nephews Iohannes Secreto and Marcus Secreto. ... [she then gives her executors the power to act on her behalf after her death, and she establishes that the will is to be her last will].

... I, Nicolaus de Alexandrio, witness, signed this [with a cross].

... I, Iohannes Alexandro, witness, signed this [also with a cross].

[Notarial sign] I, Andreas de Bellamore notary, completed and validated [the act].

**Example II**

Testatrix: Christina Rous, widow
Place: York, England
Date: 17 March, 1342

In the name of God, Amen. On Saturday after the Feast of Saint Gregory Pope [March 12], 1342. I, Christina Rous, widow of John Rous of York, make my testament in this manner. I commend my soul to God, Holy Mary and all of the saints and I leave my body to the cemetery of the church of Saint Peter at York, for burial next to my late husband John. And I leave my best dress for mortuary fee. Item I leave four pounds of wax for candles around my body. I leave 12 pennies for poor clerics and widows. Item I leave 12 pennies for my parish chaplain. Item I leave 6 pennies for my parish clerk (*clerico*) and 3 to the under-clerk (*subclerico*). Item I leave 12 shillings to the four mendicant orders of York to be divided equally. Item I leave to Mariota of Quelpdale a big leaden vessel. Item I leave to my sister Annicia a feather bed with a coverlet. Item I leave her two sheets and two coverlets. Item I leave to Mariota Urry a feather bed with a sheet and a carpet. Item I leave to Robert of Newenham a cloth of 4 lengths and a towel of three lengths in measure. Item I leave to William of Apperby, clerk, a good quality coverlet. Item I leave to Cecilia of Roucliff a new carpet. Item I leave to Isabelle Balle a coverlet. [Five other bequests of sheets or coverlets to individuals follow.] Item I leave to Peter the Potter a checkered cloak. Item I leave to John of Berwys a white cloak. Item I leave to Thomas son of Peter Denenys a coverlet with a sheet. Item I leave to Robert Coltebay a coverlet with a sheet. And all the rest I leave to Amicia my sister so that she may discharge all my legacies and debts equally. I name as my executors, my sister Amicia and Peter the Potter, with the counsel and aid of William of Appelby, so that they may carry out all. Enacted at York.

## The will as a document shaped by different legal traditions

Will-making was common across Europe in the Middle Ages. From the thirteenth century on, canonists and other authorities agreed that individuals who were legally independent and possessed of reason could make wills, and the practice became increasingly popular among laypeople, both men and women, in the fourteenth and fifteenth centuries. Archives across western Europe thus contain large numbers of wills similar to the examples we have cited above, and the records have become increasingly popular as a primary source for both historians and literary scholars of the Middle Ages. It is tempting to see these wills as expressions of the inner desires of individual testators, and a number of historians have taken this perspective in their work with wills. We see this view as too simplistic, however, and in this essay we will examine both the formation and the content of the will in order to demonstrate how wills were shaped by the confluence of a testator's wishes, the desires of family and friends, and established legal and pious conventions. Furthermore, while wills are a valuable source for medieval scholars, we argue that they must be read in tandem with other material from the period in order to understand their significance.

The format, purpose and contents of wills were largely influenced by legal traditions that varied across Europe. These traditions comprised a complex matrix bounded not only by the broad distinctions of Roman, canon and common law but also by local and regional custom and norms. Broadly speaking, Roman law governed wills in southern Europe and the Mediterranean littoral and island regions, as in the example of Crete above, while central-northern European wills were influenced by customary law (*coutume de pays*). English wills, such as the one in our example, fell under the restrictions of common law and the supervision of ecclesiastical courts working with canon law.

Perhaps the single largest legal difference apparent in wills across Europe is that testators in England and northern Europe, bound by common law or customary law on inheritance, did not use a will to devolve patrimonial property (i.e. inherited property). Instead, wills in that part of Europe contained bequests of chattels or 'movables' such as clothing, furniture, tools, jewellery and books. Indeed, after the thirteenth century in England, there developed the practice of making two documents: a 'testament' for the disposal of chattels and a 'last will' for tenements or other property. Example II, above, is a testament, since it deals solely with movables. In contrast to northern Europe, in the south inheritance was not governed by customary law, and thus was supposed to be the principal concern of testators; the fundamental purpose of the Roman *testamentum* was to name a universal heir or heirs. That means that wills in the south could (and do) contain long lists of 'immovable' property, including houses and land, as well as bequests of movables, such as items used in the household or for work. Example I above mentions only movables, not because of the nature of the document, but because the testatrix probably had no immovable property to leave to her heirs.

The contrast between the legal restrictions on the will in northern and southern Europe is not as clear-cut as we have just suggested, however. Local law and custom in all parts of Europe could allow exceptions for testators wishing more

UNIVERSITY OF WINCHESTER LIBRARY

freedom to dispose of their property. Thus, some English boroughs upheld deviations from the common law principles of property devolution, and testators in these jurisdictions could more freely distribute land by wills. Similarly, testators themselves found ways to get around the restrictions of common law by employing devices such as the concept of 'use' that enabled them to distribute property to heirs of their choosing as 'enfeofees' or trustees who had to follow instructions concerning use and distribution of property outlined by the testator in the will. Similarly, testators in the Low Countries and areas of northern France found their desires to transfer property freely by a will hampered by the *coutume de pays*, but they too worked out solutions to free up devolution. Here, the generous customary arrangements for wives that resulted from the community of goods regime governing marital property could be altered by husbands through marriage contracts that dictated property arrangements. It is thus important to keep this interplay between legal forms and local realities in mind when first approaching wills as sources.

## Testators, witnesses, and notaries

Law influenced not only the purpose of the will and the type of property, but also who could be a testator. The influential Italian notarial textbooks, following Roman law, decreed that testators must be in their rational minds, not be under the legal control of anyone else, and be able to express themselves clearly. These restrictions kept from testating groups ranging from children, slaves and criminals to the deaf and mute, the insane and those who had taken religious vows. Married women were allowed to make wills under Roman law, and many did so. But except for Venice, where scholars have found married women making wills with each pregnancy, wives did not make wills ('testate') as frequently as their husbands. Where rates of testation by gender are available, it appears that usually about 60 per cent of wills were by men. In late medieval Venice, however, the ratio is reversed. While Roman law permitted married women to testate, they were not allowed to do so in England where common law regarded a wife's property as belonging to her husband. Only widows were allowed to make wills, as in our example. Likewise, peasants were viewed as technically unable to hold property in England and thus were legally barred from making wills.

But as we noted above, legal norms were not the only factor shaping the creation of the will, nor, in this case, the identity of the testator. Local custom often played a significant role in determining who could make a will. For example, although Italian wives living under Lombard law needed the permission of their husband or a guardian to make a will, scholars see this restriction largely as *pro forma*; it did little to keep women from making wills. And across Europe, including England, many peasants also made wills, which were accepted or at least recognized by the courts. In particular, by the fifteenth century more people of lower social status could be found making wills in both northern and southern Europe, sometimes to leave property to a hospital or other institution which had housed them (and might have required them to make a will as they neared death) or because they belonged to a religious guild or confraternity which similarly encouraged its members, of whatever social rank, to make a will in order to leave it a bequest. One legal restriction appears to have been followed everywhere in Europe; nowhere could children make wills without the permission of their parents, and children's wills are almost never found in the archives.

Another restriction that was usually followed concerned the religious, those who had taken vows of personal poverty when they entered a monastery. Gratian had pronounced on the question of the 'testamentary freedom' (*ius testandi*) of the religious in his twelfth-century compilation of canon law texts, the *Decretum*. Anyone who had entered a monastery had given up this freedom, since his personal possessions had become the property of the religious institution. On the other hand, religious living outside monasteries, such as anchorites or hermits, might have property of their own and thus were able to make wills. By contrast with the restrictions on monks, priests and other 'secular' clerics could make wills bestowing their patrimonial property (that is, not property that had come to them through their benefice) on their chosen heirs. Officials at church councils from the early Middle Ages discussed what constituted the property of clerics. By the twelfth century, it was generally agreed that any extra income from a cleric's benefice should be returned to the church itself. But some believed that clerics had the right to direct some of the income from their benefices to charitable institutions or their servants. In the early Middle Ages, clerics had been instructed not to name anyone outside the church as a recipient of a legacy, while by the twelfth century it was acceptable for clerics to name both relatives and the church itself as heirs. The *Liber Extra*, the thirteenth-century collection of papal decretals, noted that clerical testators could not bequeath the goods of the church to others but they were permitted to bequeath movables from their patrimonial property to family members and others in their wills. In some places, such as the northern Italian city of Treviso, fourteenth-century bishops tried to restrict the clerical *ius testandi* by requiring any cleric who wished to make a will to obtain a letter of permission from the bishop. Only if this permission was obtained would the will be accepted as authentic; lack of such permission could be asserted as the reason to contest a cleric's will.

Where and in what state was the testator when he or she finally came to make the will? Rolandino Passaggeri, the writer of a famous textbook on notarial law in medieval Bologna, assumes that the testator was ill, identifying him as *aegrum*, or an invalid, and most testators followed this model, dictating their last wills on their sick- or deathbed. But testators might also be healthy, as in our first example above. Sometimes they were embarking on risky endeavours such as pilgrimage, commercial voyage or military campaign. During the recurrent plague outbreaks following the Black Death, more individuals seem to have prepared wills in advance of the onset of illness, as well. Childbirth was another risky venture, and women sometimes dictated their wills before going into labour (scholars of Venice have found this to be the case), and the modern tendency to make one's will long in advance of illness or death was not a common medieval practice.

While the testator was usually ill and confined to a sickroom, when the time came to make the will both legal scholars and local custom agreed that he would not make it alone. Witnesses were crucial figures in this event, and their number, capacity and gender were restricted by law. Here, too, important regional differences played a role in determining the number and identity of witnesses. The Roman testament required witnesses who were legally capable males (that is, not subject to the testator's authority), and established their number as seven in towns and five in the countryside. The influential medieval notarial formularies of Bologna followed these requirements exactly. Canon law also included statements about witnesses, easing the requirements for wills containing pious donations. The *Liber Extra* stated that a legal will could be drawn up by a parish priest and two or three witnesses, and in Perugia some fourteenth-century testaments included only two witnesses. In late medieval Hungary, where canon law governed wills, the three witnesses were carefully selected by the testator and considered significant. There, witnesses were of higher social status than the testator. Leading officials might ask the mayor and judges, while most citizens asked members of the town councils. Less well-off inhabitants living in the suburbs made do with their neighbours and acquaintances. Elsewhere in European cities, witnesses could be one's neighbours, one's compatriots (in Italian towns, such as Bologna, immigrants from towns outside the city often came to the bedsides of their compatriots), or business associates. Almost everywhere witnesses were to be male. In fact, the Italian notarial formularies prohibited women (as well as hermaphrodites with ambiguous gender identity) from acting as witnesses. Medieval Hungary, however, did allow some, but not all, witnesses of a will to be female, and in a few instances in Italy the presence of women at the dictating of a will might be noted by the scribe or notary.

Also present at the testator's bedside was usually (though not necessarily) a priest, who often was the testator's confessor; the notary, or, outside of southern Europe, a scribe; and family members, who could not be witnesses, but whose presence is sometimes noted in the will. While many wills report the minimum number of witnesses present, many lists of witnesses included a dozen or more people. A testator, then, was surrounded by people as he made his will, and it is likely that they could influence the choices listed in the document. For the most part, readers of wills cannot know the influence of witnesses on a testator, but some wills from late medieval Hungary took the form of word-for-word report of the dictation and included prompts from witnesses. In those wills in which witnesses' urgings were recorded, the record reveals the testator defiant in his or her resolve not to follow their suggestions (for example, to disinherit a child or disregard traditional charitable donations), so it appears that this information was noted down by the scribe in case the will was later contested.

While witnesses were important presences in the moment of the creation of the will, in most parts of southern Europe only their names, and not their signatures, were required, since its authenticity was guaranteed by the notary who prepared it. The notary was a potentially powerful influence on the content of testament and choice of bequests in the will. The preambles, or introductory religious statements found in many wills, may often have been the product of notaries, rather than testators. Likewise, the modern reader would be justly suspicious of eloquent pious flourishes included as the words of dying testators. These were also likely the product of the notary, who would offer – at a price – his learned abilities to embellish and solemnize the written document. It is important, however, not to overemphasize the assumed role of notaries in determining the content of testators' last wishes. The notary was charged by law – as notarial manuals strongly emphasize – to ensure that the testators' wishes were authentically and accurately reproduced in the document. Rolandino Passaggeri stressed that the testator should not be coerced by the witnesses, and that any instructions, particularly those pertaining to the widow or the children, be carefully recorded and that the notary make absolutely certain the testator was mentally fit enough to make a will (again, so that the testator be able to state his or her own wishes and not those of others). Robert Brentano (1990), contemplating the question of the notary's influence over the testator, also noted that even if notaries did shape the testator's bequests in some ways, these 'currents of conventional piety caught in a notary's cartulary are, very much, things historians want to know'. While they were prohibited from shaping the actual content of a testator's bequests, notaries were responsible for creating the will in its final written form, and after it was redacted they could also be charged with the responsibility of making civic or ecclesiastical authorities aware of its content. At the 1331 Council of Benevento, for instance, it was agreed that notaries or scribes and priests would bring the names of heirs to the attention of their local bishop within one month of a testator's death.

Scholars working in the south of Europe, in particular Italy and southern (but not northern) France and Spain, thus need to keep notaries in mind as they consider how the will was created. In England and the rest of northern Europe, on the other hand, a scribe, often a priest or other cleric, was normally responsible for preparing the written record. One of the major results of this distinction is related to the preservation of documents. Notaries were responsible for maintaining their records, and thus often (although see below for some important caveats) substantial numbers of notarial registers, containing many wills, have survived. Scribes were not responsible for storing or housing their own records, and thus their documentation may not survive to the same degree. In addition, scribes in northern Europe could prepare a will as a 'chirograph', meaning that several copies of a will (usually two or three) would be copied onto the same piece of parchment, which would then have the term *chirographum* written in large letters across its reverse side. The parchment would be cut and then the pieces could be put back together to prove their authenticity at a later date. In comparison to the wills dictated to scribes or notaries just before death, chirograph wills were normally made by relatively wealthy people long before their deaths, perhaps because such arrangements took time to make and the will itself cost more to create.

At times, wills appear to be composed by the testator, in that they are recorded in the first person (as are both of our examples), but in most parts of Europe wills were almost never physically set down by the testator or testatrix themselves. Instead they were dictated orally and thus are known as 'nuncupative'. Testator-written or 'holographic' wills were forbidden in Roman law and did not begin to appear until the sixteenth century, and then only sporadically. The issue in law was the difficulty of determining whether the will was genuine or a forgery. The script of wills written by a known scribe or notary could be checked against other similar documents. In addition, the scribe or notary would be held up to

professional standards which forbade him to forge documents, and the consequences of enacting such forgeries could be severe. One variation on the dictation of the will was found in Venice and its subject territories. Venetian testators
sometimes wrote down their wishes and then give these to a notary to recopy with
the addition of correct legal formulas. In the spring of 1348, for instance, Marinus
Quirino, a Venetian living in Crete who lay dying (possibly of plague), called the
notary Angelo Bonconotolo to him and presented him with a text which Marinus
himself had written in a small register (*cedula*) written in his own hand (*scripta
manu mea propria*). The notary then rewrote the will for the testator, retaining the
first-person form and the vernacular form of the bequests themselves and adding
Latin formulas to the beginning and end of the will.

## The nature of testamentary bequests and devolution of property

In southern Europe, as we have already established, wills followed Roman law,
which stated that the fundamental purpose of the *testamentum* was to nominate
an heir to succeed 'universally', that is, in assets and liabilities, to the testator.
The primary heir was *sui heres*, that is, the child or children of a parent, for the
patrimony of a father passed to his child as if to himself. The laws of the emperor
Justinian stated that children succeeded their parents equally, whether they be
male or female. If there were no children, intestacy law then assigned property
by relations of degree to the testator, to siblings and their children (as in our first
example), then cousins and aunts or uncles and their children, and on to collat-
erals. Jurists and lawmakers of southern Europe in the thirteenth century and after
followed Roman testamentary norms, except for the Justianian equality of heirs
– daughters no longer succeeded as sons. This legal development went hand in
hand with the revival of the Roman dowry and the rise of commercial life in
towns in Italy and southern France and Spain, as Diane Owen Hughes (1978) has
shown. As the medieval communes of central and northern Italy made statutes
governing urban life, they stipulated that patrimony must be passed patrilineally,
and daughters who had received their dowries from their fathers (*filiae dotate*)
were excluded from the patrimony, that is, that they must be *contentas* with their
dowries alone. This principle of *exclusio propter dotem* functioned in much of
Italy and, contrary to the earlier Justinian principle of equality, served to disinherit
daughters. Of northern Italy, Venice alone maintained the Justinian principle in
paternal inheritance. The result was that in Venice, mothers provided the funds
for their daughters' dowries, as Chabot and Bellavitis (2005) argue, in order to
protect the bulk of the paternal inheritance for sons. Thus, at least according to the
law, testators in southern Europe used the testament principally to name an heir.

Naturally, testators had several other concerns that were also included in
their testaments. Many testators from all over Europe left instructions in their
testaments, as do both of our examples, regarding their burial. In fact, both
civil jurists and canonists, such as Gratian, saw this as a principal purpose of
the testament. Testators often made donations to the church where they would
be buried; according to Michael Sheehan (1963), this was a type of alms called

*sawolsceatt*, and was required by law in Anglo-Saxon England. Wills of the élite could contain elaborate descriptions of funerals and tomb construction. The privileged and powerful left payment for tombs, either new constructions or ancestral ones. Scholars such as Jacques Chiffoleau (1980), who has worked on wills from the French region of Comitat, and Samuel K. Cohn (1992) working on Tuscan wills, have examined the elaborate instructions for burials and tombs in wills, interpreting them as a late medieval concern for earthly memorialization. Many testators also left property to cover the cost of food to be distributed and prayers and masses to be said at the annual anniversaries of their deaths (such as in our first example). Others might set aside sums for large numbers of poor to attend their funerals, and fourteenth- and fifteenth-century sumptuary laws attempted to restrict the number of mourners at funerals, as well as their dress and behaviour.

Testators with minor children often named a guardian (*tutor*, *tutrix*) for those children in their testaments. Thus, wills served as powerful tools to ensure the continuity of the testator's desires for their family and even for the memory of themselves after they had passed away. In this regard, perhaps the most important decision was the naming of the testator's executor who was to supervise the distribution of bequests, make arrangements for the burial, and generally act on behalf of the testator after his or her death. Testators often relied on their male and female relatives, whether by blood or marriage, to assist them after death (as our examples do), but many also nominated a cleric, notary or business associate. In Italian wills, testators usually named more than one executor. Wives often were assisted by clerics or other male family members when they were appointed as executors. Tutors always were named executor, sometimes also with the help of additional executors.

The salvation of one's soul was especially on the mind of many late medieval testators. After either the standard clause 'sick in body but healthy in mind' or a more elaborate preamble noting the inevitability of death and such, testators often commended their soul to God and the saints and left a payment for tithes. Some also added a donation made 'for ill-begotten gain' (*male ablata*). Generally this was a token amount, but testators worried for the future of their soul and mindful of possible usury could leave more substantial sums in order to pay back interest on usurious loans. Bequests 'for the soul' were also an important component of many wills. Some scholars have seen the will as primarily an articulation of the needs of a testator's soul, but it would be over-generalizing to make this statement for the whole of Europe. Nevertheless, many testators and testatrices did consider the needs of their souls as they dictated their wills, and bequests intended to benefit their souls and those of their close family members were very common. Such *pro anima* bequests were often, but not always, directed to religious individuals or institutions. Common recipients of these bequests included members of the mendicant orders, local hospitals and other charitable associations (confraternities or religious guilds) and paupers. Parish churches and parish clergy were also important recipients of bequests. Some testators named all of the hospitals, confraternities or guilds in their communities and left a similar amount of cash or something else (often grain or wine) to each, while others were more discriminating, and might even direct bequests to very specific works within a church, such as a painting or fresco. But a *pro anima* bequest did not have to be directed to a religious institution: a bequest to any individual which was designated as 'charitable' could also benefit the testator's soul. Many testators identified individuals in their wills as recipients of such bequests; these were sometimes poor inhabitants of a local community, or relatives of the testator, and in slave-holding regions such as Crete, the manumission of one's slave was a religious act, as seen in our first example.

## Where to find wills, their preservation and dissemination

Finding wills in the archives requires a lot of time and some imagination. It is useful to begin by consulting the finding aids or indices prepared by archivists. These are sometimes only available in paper copies on site. But increasingly such indices or even databases containing references to individual wills are available online, and searches of archival websites can yield some useful data even before a research trip begins. Wills are available in manuscript form in the archives of both ecclesiastical and secular institutions across Europe. In the south (that is, southern France, Spain, Italy, Dalmatia/Croatia and some eastern Mediterranean sites) wills are found most often in the protocols, or bound registers, of notaries whose job, as we have seen, was to record the testator's final wishes for the distribution of his/her estate. Notarial registers include a wide variety of 'documents of practice' and are not generally indexed. Researchers seeking wills in these volumes must resign themselves to turning a great many pages during the initial phase of research. Wills containing bequests directed to pious and religious institutions were also preserved in their final parchment form by those institutions. In some cases selections of these parchments have been edited and published, although they are seldom translated into modern languages. In some cities, wills were registered with local authorities and can be found in the public records of those communities. For instance, the city registers of thirteenth- and fourteenth-century Bologna, known as the *Libri Memoriali* and contained in the State Archive (*Archivio di Stato*) of Bologna today, contain copies of thousands of wills and notarial contracts made by notaries working for the city's bureaucracy, while the original protocols of the local notaries are much more sparse. Similarly, in fourteenth-century Venice, notaries deposited testaments in the office known as the *Cancelleria Inferiore* at the request of the Venetian government, and these documents are now located in the section known as *Cancelleria Inferiore: Notai* in the Venetian Archivio di Stato.

In medieval England, wills were subject to 'probate', meaning that either an ecclesiastical court or a manor court had to first grant an executor the power to make the disbursements named in the will. Thus, copies of wills are found in the records of these 'probate' courts. (The church in England took more control over wills and the question of succession and/or inheritance in the twelfth and thirteenth centuries than did the church on the continent, although the English church courts dealt exclusively with questions of the inheritance of land, not moveable property or chattels.)

While archives in continental Europe have generally not made wills available online, in recent years, some English wills have been made available in digital form. Readers without paleographic skills should be aware that such deposits are simply images of the original records. A few collections of wills have also been edited and published by scholars wishing to make this valuable source more accessible. Again, English wills seem more available than those from the continent, with sites such as www.british-history.ac.uk/ providing access to wills from the thirteenth century and after.

## Historians' approaches to wills

Because medieval wills, especially from the later Middle Ages, survive in very large numbers, some historians have found them suitable for quantitative analysis. The work of Samuel K. Cohn (1992) stands out in this camp, for he has gathered information from thousands of late medieval wills and subjected them to regression analysis and statistical processing to reach conclusions in several of his studies. Cohn is interested in religious mentalities and compares bequests and burial choices in wills from Tuscany with other Italian and northern European cities. This statistical methodology does have its critics, such as Martin Bertram (1995), Antonio Rigon (1985) and Agostino Paravicini Bagliani (1980), who charge that the will does not have the rigorously standard form that modern computer statistical software demands. Rigon cites the potential 'homogenization' of data as another of the risks of quantitative analysis. He, along with other readers of wills such as Robert Brentano (1990), eschews graphs and data sets to read the declarations of testators as evidence of (to quote Brentano) 'the color of men's souls'.

Wills have been used by many historians of women to uncover aspects of the lived experience of ordinary women in the medieval past. Our two examples contain myriad details about the household organization and property of women in two regions of Europe. In particular, studies examining how female testators (testatrices) deployed bequests of their movable property (such as clothing, jewels and household goods) have raised the issue of women's agency within the patriarchal societies of medieval Europe. Women who left tablecloths and other household items to adorn the statues and altars of their parish churches, argues Katherine French, were making important statements about their place in the devotional and liturgical life of the church. In France and Italy, too, women left clothing and household textiles to churches to be used as altar cloths. Joelle Rollo-Koster (2010) provides an example of a wealthy French widow of Avignon who left several of her clothes to various altars: 'The clothes she wore would be placed on an altar, thus linking her presence to the holy sacrament.'

Wills, with their quasi-narrative qualities, could be used as a source by those writing chronicles and histories in the later Middle Ages. Antonio Rigon (1985) notes that in Italy the same men who worked as notaries writing testaments for their co-citizens were also the men who wrote the chronicles and histories of their communities. He has identified examples of chroniclers from the city of Padua who used testaments as sources for their other writings. Guglielmo Cortusi, who chronicled events in Padua and Lombardy in the thirteenth and fourteenth centuries, includes a long passage about the death of Marsilio da Carrara which reads, almost verbatim, as a copy of Marsilio's will. Wills were thus known to and used by writers of the Middle Ages as they composed accounts of the political and social events of their communities.

## The problem of the will as document

As we have seen, wills are an attractive primary source for scholars working on medieval and early modern history across western Europe and beyond. Nevertheless, as Clive Burgess (1990) has warned, these documents can be very misleading about testators' piety. Since wills come at the end of life and mark one moment of giving in a testator's life, they do not record any *pre obit* charity and may omit plans for large donations, such as the foundations of hospitals, that testators would have arranged elsewhere. Indeed, Burgess claims 'wills are perniciously deficient as indicators of the longer-term services that the wealthy commissioned' (1990, pp. 14–33). Working in the legal climate of southern Europe, Thomas Kuehn (2008) has also questioned the utility of wills for historical analysis, because wills could be contested in court. Kuehn argues that wills are only one part of a legal process and that they could always be repudiated by the heirs. Still other scholars emphasize the need to read the bequests contained in a will in the context of the entire document. Attilio Bartoli Langeli (2006), for instance, argues that careful comparison of all aspects of a will can reveal the relationship between its character as a legal document and other purposes, such as pious goals, which the testator may have had in mind. Finally, although we have large numbers of wills available in archives across Europe, scholars should keep in mind that what remains is only a small percentage of the original documentary record. Andreas Meyer has pointed out that the surviving records represent only a small portion of the original documentation because notarial archives were often kept in the hands of individual households, and the damage to a storage room or neglect by an owner often resulted in catastrophic losses of historical material. Finally, Martha Howell (1996) has identified wills as 'rhetorically complicated compositions', and she argues that they were only one player in a 'meta-drama' of the management of property, protection of social status, and control of women in the medieval Low Countries. These careful assessments underscore the need to see medieval wills in conversation with other records to create a fuller picture of piety, social ties, inheritance strategies, and indeed of the historical record itself.

## References

Bagliani, Agostino Paravicini (1980) *I testamenti dei cardinali del Duecento*. Rome, Presso la Società.
Bertram, Martin A (1995) '"Renaissance Mentality" in Italian Testaments?' *Journal of Modern History* 67 (June): 358–69.
Brentano, Robert (1990) *Rome Before Avignon: A Social History of Thirteenth-Century Rome*. Berkeley: University of California Press.
Burgess, Clive (1990) 'Late Medieval Wills and Pious Convention: Testamentary Evidence Reconsidered,' in *Profit, Piety and the Profession in Later Medieval England*, Michael Hicks (ed.), Gloucester: Sutton 1990.

Chabot, Isabelle and Bellavitis, Anna 'A proposito di 'Men and Women in Renaissance Venice' di Stanley Chojnacki,' *Quaderni Storici* 118 (2005): 203–38.

Chiffoleau,Jacques (1980) *La comptabilité de l'au-delà: les hommes, la mort, et la religion dans la région d'Avignon à la fin du moyen âge (vers 1320–vers 1480),* Rome: École Française de Rome.

Cohn, Samuel Kline (1992) *The Cult of Remembrance and the Black Death: Six Renaissance Cities in Central Italy*, Baltimore, Johns Hopkins U.P..

Howell, Martha C. (1996) 'Fixing Movables: Gifts by Testament in Late Medieval Douai', *Past and Present* 150: 3–45.

Hughes, Diane Owen (1978) 'From Brideprice to Dowry in Mediterranean Europe,' *Journal of Family History* 3: 262–95.

Kuehn, Thomas (2008) *Heirs, Kin and Creditors in Renaissance Florence,* Cambridge: CUP.

Langeli, Attilio Bartoli (2006) *Notai: Scrivere documenti nell'Italia medievale* (I Libri di Viella, 56.), Rome: Viella.

Rigon, Antonio (1985) 'Orientamenti religiosi e pratica testamentaria a Padova nei secoli XII–XIV (prime ricerche),' in A. Bartoli Langeli, *Nolens Intestatus Decedere: Il testamento come fonte della storia religiosa e sociale,* Perugia: Archivi dell'Umbria: pp. 41–63.

Rollo-Koster, Joelle (2010) 'The Boundaries of Affection: Women and Property in Late Medieval Avignon' in Jutta Sperling and Shona Kelly Wray (eds.), *Across the Religious Divide: Women, Property and the Law in the Wider Mediterranean (ca. 1300–1800)* New York: Routledge.

Sheehan, Michael (1963) *The Will in Medieval England: From the Conversion of the Anglo-Saxons to the End of the Thirteenth Century*. Toronto: University of Toronto Press.

# 5    Letters and letter collections

*Joel T. Rosenthal*

Until the electronic revolution of recent decades reduced the importance of letter writing in hard copy, letters were a main form of communication in literate societies around the world.[1] This had been the case for hundreds, if not for thousands of years, even as we perhaps near the end of a longstanding reliance upon this artefact of discourse, one devised and used to over-leap the distance separating writer and recipient. Letters have long been recognized as a fall-back alternative to speaking face to face – a 'substitute for conversation' – and personal letters written over the centuries indicate this in mode of address and content. If one could neither see nor hear the one with whom one had business or personal dealings one could write a letter; many did, and with considerable frequency, and to many categories of recipient.

We think of modern letters and letter-writing practices as falling into two distinct categories (with room for overlap and exceptions): business letters and personal letters. Business letters can carry welcome news – admission to college or an income tax refund, or less cheerful information – rejection of that college application or a notice of unpaid taxes. Many business letters are matter-of-fact, formulaic and impersonal, sent simultaneously to many recipients and of the 'summoned to jury duty' sort. In the realm of personal letters, love letters come to mind, though probably most personal letters covered social and family news and exchanged platonic greetings rather than commitments of the heart. If medieval love letters are not found in large numbers, and they hardly represent a significant proportion of what has been preserved, we do encounter them. When family letter collections begin to appear in the fifteenth century we have real touches of intimacy, even though almost all medieval letters were dictated to a scribe. During the course of her first pregnancy a young wife wrote to her absent husband: 'I am discovered of all men that see me. … Ye have left me such a remembrance that maketh me to think upon you both day and night when I would sleep.'[2]

But if the overwhelming bulk of medieval letters seem dry – and most are official documents of government – there are not only interesting exceptions but also many variations in expression and in the conventions regarding the articulation of friendship. Furthermore, even official (or business) letters conveying peremptory orders might be wrapped in an outerwear of courtesy at odds with their substance, whereas dry and hectoring phrases from an ecclesiastical prince might cover the writer's passion about the subject matter and regard for the recipient. The

recipient of a letter from St Bernard had to be moved by its personalized salutation, though he was only known through intermediaries: 'To Thomas ... a youth
of great promise, that he may learn by the example of his namesake, the apostle
[Thomas], from Bernard, the servant of the Poor of Christ at Clairvaux'.

Neither personal nor business letter-writing, let alone that which we think of
as official letter-writing, originated in medieval Europe. But as a convenient form
of élite and official communication – across distance, thanks to literacy (and the
common use of Latin) – letters played a major role in how men, women and
governments communicated across the face of the medieval and Mediterranean
world. We can divide medieval letters into three basic categories. The first is those
letters of eminent men and women, written as literary, pedagogical and spiritual
documents, composed with great care and subsequently preserved and collected.
As such these usually conformed to formal rules of rhetoric and were meant to
display the writer's erudition and piety, as part of or in addition to what we read
as their message. Letters of this sort are found in the 'collected letters' we associate with famous spiritual and intellectual figures: the collected letters of John of
Salisbury (d. 1180) or of Arnulf of Lisieux (d. 1182), to name but two of many.
In their collected form they reveal the author's views as expressed (and as they
evolved) over years of letter-writing, touching any number of events or topics.
These collections have been preserved because either their authors or devoted
followers made a copy when the letter was written or, at some later date, they were
moved to gather and reassemble them for an edition that might circulate in dozens
or scores of manuscripts.

The second major category of letters is that of the countless letters by means
of which the business and the wishes of rulers and the actions of government
were conveyed – those official letters that emanated from every seat of authority,
secular or ecclesiastical, for centuries. Such 'letters', like the thousands of close
or patent letters of the English chancery, or as copied in vast numbers into the
papal registers, are basic records showing us how rulers conducted their affairs.
Through the various kinds of letters orders were given, privileges granted or
confirmed, petitions approved or denied, policies enunciated, ideas circulated (or
denounced). They might be directed to an individual recipient or they might be
the medieval version of an open letter, a public proclamation. They have been
preserved because they were enrolled or copied as the normal procedure of a
chancery, the secretarial office of secular and ecclesiastical authorities. As Lister
Matheson says in this volume (Chapter 2), such letters can be thought of as 'non-
narrative records of facts and transactions which by their nature have become
primary historical sources of paramount importance to the modern historian.'

The third category consists of the miscellaneous collections of personal and
family letters. Though they might aspire to a serious level of literary polish and
learning, they were mostly written for in-house consumption, intended for the
recipient or perhaps to a known circle of relatives and friends (and often to be
read aloud). They cover all manner of subjects: personal, domestic, commercial,
family gossip, and so forth. Their numbers increased exponentially in the later
Middle Ages, testifying to the growth of lay literacy and to the need, for personal
and commercial reasons, to keep in touch. We have them in the vernacular and,

increasingly, from women as well as men when we reach the fourteenth and fifteenth centuries. Many letters of this private or family-letters category have been preserved in what we can think of as a family archive rather than in a self-conscious formal collection. We have letters of this more personal sort from princes and queens along with those of merchants and gentry families, all opening windows on private thoughts and private lives.[3]

This categorization gives us convenient bins for sorting the thousands of medieval letters that have been preserved. However, there is an element of arbitrariness here and it is not certain that medieval letter-writers would have understood or agreed with our distinctions. Furthermore, many if not most of those official letters that we have in such abundance are far from our idea of a letter, often being an announcement or a public decree. But they were missives written and sent, either on an individualized or on some wider basis, considered at the time, and referred to by all parties, as letters. The collected letters of men and women of exalted stature and position perhaps occupy some sort of middle ground, claiming the territory of a business letter or even an official letter and yet with touches of personal letter as well. They were written to instruct the recipient (and others to whom it would be transmitted) on any and all matters on which the esteemed writer chose to comment. Daily problems and ephemeral issues, along with views about faith and doctrine or ecclesiastical personnel or human frailty were all likely to be found in these self-conscious productions of what are quasi-public documents. Many purposes could be served by a single letter, widely circulated and straddling that line between the private and the official. A famous letter, like that of Charlemagne to Abbot Baugulf on educational reform, has variously been interpreted as a letter to an individual, as a form letter intended for many recipients besides Baugulf, or as a court circular proclaiming royal policy throughout the realm. Papal letters to 'all people of the Province of the Old Saxons' or a papal call for a crusade sent to 'all the faithful in Flanders' can be thought of as medieval versions of a website posting or an encyclical from the Vatican.

Medieval letter-writers recognized their literary debt to their predecessors. This debt, touching the proper form and style, was traced back to Cicero (d. 43 BC), the epitome of pagan learning and eloquence (the *magister eloquentiae*). Thence came a chain of epistolary tradition built on by such towering figures as St Augustine (d. 430) and St Jerome (d. 420), with supporting roles for St Ambrose of Milan (d. 397), Pope Gregory I (d. 604), and Cassiodorus (d. 540s) among others. It is ironic that the twenty-two books of the New Testament in the form of epistles were not widely cited in the extensive literature on the 'how to' of letter-writing. Presumably the epistles attributed to Paul, James, Peter, John and Jude were held to be beyond the realms of emulation or analysis, standing unto themselves and not on the table in a discussion of literary forms and models.

One aspect of a personal letter we tend to assume is that the parties in the exchange know each other, or at least know of each other, whereas the medieval convention was that many such letters were really in the nature of 'open letters' from lord to subject or from subordinate to would-be pupil. The intimate letter quoted above was from Paston husband to Paston wife in fifteenth-century England. But we also see a comparable element of intimacy in the twelfth-century letters of Abelard and Heloise – former lovers now torn asunder by his castration and their separate enclosure within monastic walls. Abelard to Heloise, 'To his dearly beloved sister in Christ, from Abelard her brother in Him'; Heloise to Abelard, 'To her lord, or rather father; to her husband, or rather brother; from his handmaid, or rather daughter; from his wife, or rather sister'. Mixed identities, no doubt, but using a language of deep affection in their search for a new life course.[4] And in many instances the language of strong affection was wholly spiritual, bridging distance and gender. When Boniface in the eighth century advised an abbess about her proposed pilgrimage to Rome, he opened with a greeting of some warmth: 'To the beloved lady, Abbess Bugga, sister and dearest of all women in Christ, Boniface, a humble and unworthy bishop wishes eternal salvation in Christ', and he continued in this fashion.

It is when we turn to the vast range of official or impersonal letters, those used by people in positions of authority to disseminate policy or to issue an order (like a summons to parliament) that we come to the realm of public information and government business, being conveyed in some version of letter form. The English chancery had ten different kinds of letters for the king's affairs, each with its level of formality and the seal used for authentication.[5] A typical patent letter (an open-faced parchment sheet) of November, 1325, indicated royal favour and privilege: 'exemption for life of Robert de Malo Lacu from being put upon assizes, juries … or from appointment as sheriff, coroner, or other minister against his will'.[6] For an imperial letter that was in reality a summons, we have Emperor Henry IV to the bishop of Verdun in 1084 and couching his orders in terms of amity and fellowship:

> If you do not find it burdensome to do what we wish, we ask you to come to us at Augsburg after the feast of the apostles Peter and Paul. … Make an effort, therefore, to come to us, as you can gladden us by your coming.

In truth, to decline this request was to declare against the Emperor in a time of civil war.

Fortunately for the historian, both chanceries and countless individuals chose to keep their letters. Though recipients saved letters for a variety of reasons – depending on the nature of the correspondence, the author, and their own predilection for hanging on to old paper (though usually it was parchment until the fourteenth or fifteenth century) – the happy result is that so many letters of all sorts have been preserved (with many as yet unedited and unpublished). Of course, we can never determine what proportion of a given individual's output, or even that of a papal or imperial chancery, has been preserved. However, various factors work in our favour and we think we probably have about half of the output of St Bernard or Alcuin of York (against the ill fortune of having no letters at all from Ailred of Rievaulx, a major spiritual figure of twelfth century England).[7] Though we rarely have the original of a medieval letter – the actual parchment as written and sent – for official letters we have copies (or abbreviated versions) enrolled in the records; for those of individuals we have those collected letter enterprises (and family archives) that stand us in such good stead.

The 'collected letters' bracket covers the letters of women and men of prominence, usually public intellectuals and/or powerful voices in ecclesiastical and scholarly circles. Since virtually all letters were dictated, we may have a copy made by the scribe. Such a letter might also have been saved by the recipient, given the celebrity of its author, and it might have been reunited with its fellows for the collection. A letter from archbishop Lanfranc of Canterbury (d. 1089) or from John of Salisbury would have trophy value, apart from its substance; this militated in favour of preservation. To a considerable extent it is his collected letters that make a bishop like Herbert Losinga of Norwich (1090–1119) a figure to reckon with for the Anglo-Norman Church, though he lamented that he had not kept copies of letters to friends. And it is through the preservation of his letters that a fifteenth-century mayor of Exeter, one John Shillingford, has any celebrity status at all.

The collected letters of the great letter-writers are a window into their world-view as it unfolded and developed over time: the wisdom and opinions of three or four decades. Some letter-writers were personally concerned to collect and edit their letters; others just knew it was being done on their behalf. Alternatively, the collecting might be a posthumous tribute, though Peter of Blois (d. 1203) assiduously collected his own letters to edit and 'publish' them in a series of revised editions. These new editions kept his name in lights, and for each new edition he eliminated old letters and added new ones. None of his other writings ever neared the popularity of his collected letters and the many manuscripts still extant attest to his bestseller status long after his death.[8]

When we talk about the written sources of medieval society we must also acknowledge our good fortune. While the major letter collections were the fruit of deliberate efforts to gather and publish them (and 'publish' means putting manuscripts into circulation), and while official letters had a practical and a legal value that argued for retention, the miscellaneous letters of individuals or families just happened to be preserved. The rich family collections from fifteenth-century England bear this out. The Plumptons' letters have been preserved because they were held by the court during a disputed inheritance; those of the Stonors because of a sentence of attainder. The richest of all, the Paston letters, were assembled in a haphazard fashion because family affairs necessitated keeping track of each other through letters. These collections are closer to family archives than to literary collections; they illuminate family affairs rather than transmit pearls of wisdom. And for perhaps the best example of good luck, the world of Mediterranean trade is revealed in innumerable ways thanks to the preservation of a treasure trove of letters to and from the Jewish merchant community of Cairo.[9]

Though letters were written throughout the Middle Ages, there are several major periods of epistolary activity in terms of both quantity and quality. This is a sweeping generalization; many letters and letter collections have been preserved from drier periods, whereas official registers – once they became a regular part of bureaucratic and secretarial practice in the twelfth or thirteenth century – took little account of changing literary fashions. Early medieval letter-writing picked up on the heels of Roman literary practice, and though the Church worried about pagan culture, both classical and Christian letter-writing flourished between the fourth and sixth centuries; scores of writers have been identified, hundreds of letters from all sorts of individuals have been published. A second great age of letter-writing came with the Carolingian renaissance of the eighth and ninth centuries, a time of relative internal peace, of educational reform, and of a need for communication across Charlemagne's vast dominions.

However, it is when we come to the renaissance of the twelfth century and the origin of the universities that letters really come into their own, both as a major form of literary expression and as a basic instrument of government. R.W. Southern described the letter collections of the twelfth century as having a special place in the history of medieval correspondence, 'distinguished by their learning and their vivacity'. From this golden age of epistolary creation at least a few letters have survived from almost every literary figure of note, and from many, as Giles Constable described them, of no note at all (though there is poor Ailred of Rievaulx). We have those letters and letter collections of distinguished figures and the roughly simultaneous development of letter-writing as a formal part of higher education and vocational training. This formalization was spelled out in scores of 'how to' manuals, the *ars dictaminis*. They elaborated rules for a proper letter, and, as teaching guides, they usually included model or form letters for all sorts of circumstances (as we shall see below).

By the later Middle Ages the grip of academic formalism was loosening. When we come to the fourteenth and fifteenth centuries we find letters being written (or dictated) by a wide range of individuals up and down the social pyramid: male and female and from both northern and southern Europe. As literacy spread and crossed social and gender barriers, women alongside their brothers and husbands turned to this form of communication (or discourse). Whether we look at figures of the Italian Renaissance or of northern humanism or of those secular English families, letter-writing for business, for private exchange, and as an in-group or family newsletter now claimed space on the literary stage. Letters in the vernacular were becoming common, whether in Tuscan Italian (as for Catherine of Siena), or London English, or Parisian French. Even the manuals used at late medieval Oxford included a 'how to' for business letters – a far cry from the rhetorically determined boundaries and rhyming lines of earlier models.[10]

The letter-writing of the early Middle Ages differed from that of pagan or classical antiquity more by the introduction of a Christian agenda than by any great change in form. As the role models for subsequent letter-writing, it is interesting to learn that Sts Augustine and Jerome, the two great church Fathers, corresponded but never met face to face as they sought to build *amicitia* (friendship) through their correspondence. We must remember that letter-writing was a serious enterprise, claiming both time and energy. Alcuin of York, a central figure in Charlemagne's world, wrote hundreds of letters on virtually every aspect of public and private policy. To manage this he acknowledged that he often copied his own words, thereby also revealing that he (or his secretaries) kept copies as he went along. As tireless a writer as Bernard of Clairvaux said 'let our wits have a rest from dictating, our lips from talking, our fingers from writing' (indicating that he might have written some himself). On the other hand, comments about being pressed for time and having to cut off short were but a common convention, as likely to be found in letters of a hundred lines as in a short note. A statement like '(only) a few words because there was not enough time for more' (from Adam Marsh) was mere boilerplate, as was Agnes Paston's 'Wrettyn in haste at Norwich the Thorsdaie aftir Candelmasse Daie'.

The twelfth century stands as the high water mark of medieval letter-writing, as we have said, and it can be dealt with in terms of those two kinds of letters, the literary letters of the great and famous and those of academic training. The training of men who would serve the ever-growing secretarial needs of secular and ecclesiastical government was now a matter of considerable importance. It became an integral part of the humanistic curriculum, as the 'how to do it' approach to letter-writing assumed the role of an art form. The rules regarding a proper letter had been spelled out by Alberic of Monte Cassino in the 1070s (perhaps following Pope Sylvester II, d. 1003) and these formalities were further codified by the grammar masters of the University of Bologna in the twelfth century. Men like Buoncompagno wrote manuals on written eloquence, with their five parts of a formal letter becoming the model to be followed for centuries – a sort of party line on rhetoric and epistolography.

A formal letter was to consist of five parts. According to the 'Anonymous of Bologna' (c. 1135) it was to open with a salutation or greeting (*salutatio*), leading in turn to a longer formal greeting (*capitatio benevolentia*), which in turn led to an explanation of the background or specific reason for the letter (*narratio*). This finally opened the way for the request – what it really was about, the petition (*petitio*) – followed by some sort of conclusion (*conclusio*). These rules would raise letter-writing to a full-fledged liberal art; the *ars dictaminis* (the art of letter-writing), alongside the *ars praedicandi* (art of preaching), and the *ars poetriae* (the rhetoric of verse writing). Two further precepts, not in the rules and probably more honoured in the breach, were that the letter was to be kept short, and to be focused on a single subject. The letter in which Walter Daniel excused his temerity for writing a biography of Ailred of Rievaulx runs to sixteen pages in a modern edition; so much for brevity. The other point is one of omission; there is nothing in the rules about dating. Indeed, most private and personal letters were undated, bedevilling modern editors if not medieval recipients.[11]

The how-to-do-it manuals were wont to carry a selection of sample letters. They make amusing reading as aids in the quick training of those going on to clerical careers. And as student manuals, many of the form letters talk of student problems – young men away from home, balancing academic demands against expensive temptations. A letter could cover a request for money, perhaps triggering parental exasperation: 'a student's first song is a demand for money ... there will never be a letter which doesn't ask for cash', as one parent supposedly said. Variations covered requests for money for bedding, for unexpected travel expenses (after he had been robbed or swindled along the way), or for a ham or a pair of hose. More money might mean more years of study, more time 'in the camp of Pallas' as one letter put it, or the reminder, 'science once lost can never be recovered'. When a father proved hard-hearted, the supplicant might turn to others in the family or even to ecclesiastical intercessors, though this must have been a last resort. The manuals talked to issues of decorum, with the status of writer and of recipient encoded in the salutation and mode of address. There was the proper greeting for pope to emperor, emperor to pope, priests to a bishop, bishop to bishop, and so forth. A letter to one of higher rank was to devote considerable space to the niceties before getting down to the business; one going down the scale could talk with greater directness.[12]

Though the manuals were serious and with a practical purpose, they also have an element of make-believe in their textbook regulations. When we contrast form letters with the powerful and influential letters of the great and famous of the day the prescriptions seem stilted, schoolroom exercises. For letters that offer a sustained barrage – virtually an on-going campaign of advice and wisdom – we can turn to those of a figure like St Bernard, one of the great voices of the twelfth century. Among his many roles, he was a letter-writing industry. His secretary Geoffrey began collecting the letters even before Bernard's death, with something like 200–300 letters in the first edition of what quickly proved to be a very popular text, and this number has been roughly doubled by subsequent scholarship. One editor points out that:

> almost anyone in difficulties seemed to think that he could appeal to the abbot of Clairvaux. Sandwiched between letters to popes and kings one finds letters to poor and insignificant people … [Bernard] himself tells us that he made a point of answering every letter.[13]

The index to a collection of the letters lists scores of recipients: five popes, the patriarch of Jerusalem, Peter the Venerable of Cluny; and down the celebrity scale to 'a monk Drogo', 'a lady of rank', and finally, 'someone who broke his word'. The sweep of these letters reveals Bernard's attacks on heresy, the Cistercian–Cluniac rivalry, proselytizing for a crusade, his mystical exaltation of the Virgin, and much more. A full agenda, evolving and changing over the years in some respects, fixed and unyielding in others.

\* \* \*

No primary source is perfect, in the sense that it tells us all we wish to know, and medieval sources are usually more problematic than modern ones.[14] One obvious problem with letters is their uneven and partial preservation. There is no major writer, no significant collection (not even papal or royal chanceries) for which we can be confident that we have everything. Sometimes the lost letters might not change our view of their world, though they would tell more. Anselm, archbishop of Canterbury, was a major player in church–state relations. Since we have the bulk of his theological work it seems unlikely that his lost letters would tell us much more about his intellectual and spiritual role. They might, however, shed light on his difficult relations with his kings over ecclesiastical independence and reform. John of Salisbury was a major letter-writer and close to Thomas Becket, with a good account of Becket's last days and death. But whereas others cover much the same ground on Becket, John's letters are our only sources for some of Henry II's negotiations with Frederick Barbarossa. However, we can rarely pinpoint the gaps like this precisely. For a more prosaic example regarding lost letters, we can turn to Margaret Paston. There is nothing in her hundred letters from just before or after her husband's unexpected death in 1466. When we might hope for some glimpse into how a widow had to cope with orphaned children and unfinished projects, we have a complete blank for some months.

Another problem with letters, particularly acute with those letter collections, is the editorial hand of whoever assembled them, letter-writer or follower thereof. Since virtually every collection is the result of such assembling, we have both the missing letter dilemma and that of editorial choice regarding inclusion (and exclusion). The collecting does testify to the serious efforts made to run down the letters, and it reminds us – as some writers were known to point out – that the collection would be shaped to show the writer in the best possible light. Authors and/or their disciples were free to omit letters and to tinker with the text. St Catherine of Siena, a powerful fourteenth-century voice for ecclesiastical reform, wrote – without benefit of official position – to a great many recipients (as we shall see below), and often with extreme candour. When it came time to promote her canonization her followers toned down some of her language and omitted some of her more abrasive letters. Our interest in having access to as many letters as possible, warts and all, clearly differs from the interests of those who collected them, much though we stand in their debt. In keeping with R.W. Southern's reflection that 'a collection of letters was essentially a memorial to the learning of a single man', we just have to accept the hard fact of different motives and different interests.

Forgery is another problem, though this applies more to charters and deeds than to letters. To whose profit was it to forge a letter, we ask, and the answer is that when letters granted privileges and conferred esteem, altering or even manufacturing them could be of considerable advantage. The literate world of the Middle Ages was one of forgery, and an early invention like the Donation of Constantine had a serious role in shaping the ground of high politics. When the monks of Christ Church Canterbury sought to assert their primacy over the nearby monastery of St Augustine, what better than a forged letter from an early pope in support of their claim? And if this ruse gave them a leg up against a rival monastery, why not a letter asserting the primacy of Canterbury over York?[15] Such forgeries were manufactured for a specific purpose, in contrast to 'The Letter from Heaven', purportedly written by God himself and brought to earth in the sixth century by the archangel Michael.[16] Versions of this droll fabrication were produced from time to time over the centuries, usually to enjoin sabbatarian observance or a crusade or plain old moral regeneration, with threats of dire punishment for those who ignored its warnings, as most clearly did. Though denounced by ecclesiastical authorities as a fraud from the start, it had a long life, with variations in Latin, Greek, Norse, Anglo-Saxon, French, Spanish, German and Slavic languages into the fourteenth century.

Letters intrigue us because people write letters to express themselves: to indicate beliefs and feelings, to enlighten or instruct or scold, to show off literary skills. An editor of Jan Hus' fifteenth-century letters says they were 'written spontaneously to personal friends and not intended for publication, revealing the writer's intimate feelings and personal characteristics not to be found in his formal writings', and this holds true in almost every case. Letters became more personal as well as more mundane in the later Middle Ages, and these later ones often reveal an interior world that the lofty correspondence of the great writers of an earlier day never did. To illustrate the distinction between public and private letters we can contrast the letter-writing circle of Catherine of Siena with that of Margaret Paston. Catherine's letters went to many recipients as her powerful voice rang out on many issues: mystical piety, returning the papacy to Rome, rebukes to princes who ignored her advice, and more along these lines. In letters of a twelve-month period (1374–75), all dictated in Italian, we see her range of recipients. At the top we have queen mother Elizabeth of Hungary, urging her support for a crusade; Barnabo Visconte, ruler of Milan, with separate letters to his wife; the bishop of Florence; Sir John Hawkwood, a famous mercenary soldier; and the lord of Sanseverino, also advocating a crusade. Spiritual recipients included the abbess of Santa Maria in Siena; the prior of the Oliventan house in Florence; numerous priests and friars; a hermit of Lecceto; and Catherine's first confessor, Tammaso della Fonte of Siena. This list can be extended: letters to men considering monastic vows (one of whom ignored her and chose marriage); to a senator in Siena; to young women about to enter religious life; and to still others, male and female, some in the Church and some in the world. Moreover, 1374–75 was a typical year as Catherine's letter-writing seemed to go.

By way of comparison with this pattern we have the private or family letter, as in the tight circle of the Pastons. The three most prolific Pastons are Margaret (c. 1420–1484), her eldest son John II (1442–1479), and her second son, John III (1444–1504+). Their letters were not about the woes of Europe but about family business: of Margaret's 101 letters, sixty-nine were to her husband John I (d. 1466), nineteen to John II, ten to John III, and but three to non-family members. Nor did her sons – men of the world and out and about on many projects – cast an appreciably wider net. John II wrote six letters to his father, thirty-eight to John III with whom he was very close, thirty-one to his mother, two to other family members, and but five to outsiders. John III followed this pattern: five to their father, thirty-six to John II, eighteen to his mother, two others to family members, seven to non-family. The difference between letters as a voice of conscience to the powers of Europe and letters as family newsletters could hardly be more striking, taking us from the papal court to Norfolk manor houses.

The number of current scholarly projects devoted to editing, translating and explicating medieval letters indicates their continuing fascination. Those who use the letters often extol their special status, the insights they alone provide. A scholar like Charles Langlois said almost a century ago that public and private letters together give us one of our most valuable sources for the study of medieval society. They have so many points of interest, even when they seem remote and convoluted by our standards. Modes of speech that seem stilted and artificial survive to give us the author's voice. In the pious rhetoric of the day Cuthbert, archbishop of Canterbury, reported the death of St Boniface in 754:

> although this bitter sorrow tortures our heart, nevertheless a certain triumphant, exulting joy softens and quiets our grief as we … render thanks that the English

people were found worthy ... to send out this gifted student of heavenly learning ... for the salvation of many souls through the grace of almighty God. [17]

In stark contrast to this ornate speech stands a laconic passage in a Paston letter of the plague year, 1479. The family was hit by many deaths:

Sore tidings are come to Norwich that my grandmother is deceased, whom God assoil ... [a messenger came] at such time as we were at mass for my brother Walter, on whom God assoil ... My sister is delivered, and the child passed to God, who send us his grace.

A lot of grim news for one letter, and not much concern here for its five proper parts.[18]

Given that even a long letter is likely to be brief compared to a full-fledged treatise, it is in letters that we often find one-liners that sum up larger issues. A letter 'brings it home', and a few lines here can give a pithy summation of a large issue. Sidonius, in 474, tells of waiting for the other shoe to drop – that of Germanic invasion: 'Rumor has it that the Goths have occupied Roman soil ... their menacing power has long pressed us hard ... we of Clermont know that all these ills befell your people of Vienne.' It is a commonplace that St Jerome had a morbid fear of sex and sexuality, and a one-liner in a letter sums up his hundreds of pages on this: 'I praise marriage, I praise conjugality, but because for me they produce virgins.' These are but random examples; many more could be offered from the letters of the great, as in a letter to Edward II of England from his sister, requesting his intercession in the choice of a prioress for her nunnery.

\* \* \*

In conclusion, we can turn to an aspect of the study of medieval letters that puts them in line with some current scholarly interests. This has to do with women as letter-writers, as we now recognize the extent to which letters were a medium that so many women, in different stations of life, used to express themselves. Perhaps because they did not have to come into public space to do so, their epistolary voice seems to have been accepted. From empresses and queens to religious mystics and Italian matriarchs to women of the English gentry, women wrote letters. We noted the wide sweep of Catherine of Siena, and centuries before we have Hildegard of Bingen (d. 1179), a prolific correspondent in a world where a woman's voice could sometimes make itself heard, and with her own high-flying list of recipients: Bernard of Clairvaux, Pope Anastasius IV, the bishops of Bamberg and of Salzburg, the archbishop of Mainz, emperors Conrad III and Frederick Barbarossa, Henry II of England, among others, and including another famous mystic, Elisabeth of Schöngau.

But Hildegard and Catherine were women who, somehow, fought their way to the top of the world of (female) piety; theirs were public and outspoken voices on matters of wide concern. In some ways it is the letter-writing of so many women of lesser status that is striking, as they took to this form of self-expression whether for personal, business, intellectual, religious or family reasons. We have seen some of the personal touches that the Paston women put into their letters, letters vital for the coordination of family business. We can turn to the letters of many other women of varying status: nuns at a twelfth-century German convent, women of high-ranking Italian families, English women combining news and family concerns with personal feelings.[19] If letter-writing provided an opportunity for so many forms and styles of self-expression, for so many personalized comments (like Alessandra Strozzi's 'I like the deVerna match, but from what I've heard she is clumsy and looks like a peasant'), for a glimpse at women playing many roles with dignity and success, we can understand why they sought to master the medium and to take advantage of the opportunities it offered. The sheer number of women who were letter-writers, considering their diversity of erudition, ease of expression, and level of informed observation, gives us confidence about placing them within that expanding world of literacy that came to view epistolary communication as an effective way to reach across space – that long-established alternative to face-to-face speech with which we began.

## Further reading

The basic introduction to medieval letters is Giles Constable, *Letters and Letter Collections,* published as Fascicle 17 in the *Typologie des Sources du Moyen Âge Occidental* (Turnhout: Brepols, 1976), with another good introduction, Alain Boureau, 'The Letter-Writing Norm, a Mediaeval Invention', in Roger Chartier *et al.* (eds), *Correspondence: Models of Letter Writing from the Middle Ages to the Nineteenth Century* (transl. Chrisopher Woodall), (Princeton: Princeton University Press, 1997), pp. 24–58. Because the study of letters and letter-writing is tied to studies of literacy, Michael Clanchy, *From Memory to Written Record,* 2nd edn, (New York: Blackwell, 1993), and Rosamund McKitrick (ed.), *The Uses of Literacy in Early Mediaeval Europe* (Cambridge: CUP, 1990) are basic. For the *ars dictaminis:* E.J. Polack, 'Dictamen', in *Dictionary of the Middle Ages,* J.R. Strayer (ed.), (New York: Scribner, 1982–89), iv, pp. 173–77: James J. Murphy, *Rhetoric in the Middle Ages: A History of Rhetorical Theory from St Augustine to the Renaissance* (Berkeley: University of California Press, 1974), especially pp. 194–268; Carol Poster and Linda E. Mitchell (eds), *Letter Writing Manuals and Instructions from Antiquity to the Present* (Columbia, SC: University of South Carolina Press, 2007); the essays of Malcolm Richards, Martin Camargo and Gideon Burton for medieval epistolography. Old but not superseded: Charles Homer Haskins, *Studies in Mediaeval Culture* (New York: F. Ungar, 1958). Two important aspects of letters and letter-writing largely omitted here for reasons of space are seals (sigillography) and forgery. For seals, a recent survey is offered by Elizabeth A. New, *Seals and Sealing Practices,* Archives and the User, No. 11 (London: British Records Association, 2010); for a broader discussion, Brigitte Bedos-Rezak, 'Medieval Identity: A Sign and a Concept', *American Historical Review* 105 (2000), 1480–533. On forgery, A. Hiatt, *The Making of Medieval Forgeries: False Documents in Fifteenth-Century England* (British Library:

London and Toronto, 2004). For English exempla, Martha Carlin and David Crouch (eds and transl.), *English Society, 1200–1250: Lost Letters of Everyday Life* (Philadelphia: University of Pennsylvania Press, forthcoming). To go a bit farther afield, Adrian Gully, *The Cult of Letter-Writing in Pre-Modern Islamic Society* (Edinburgh: Edinburgh University Press, 2008), and for a recent collection on a theme, Malcolm Barber and Keith Bale (transl.), *Letters from the East: Crusaders, Pilgrims, and Settlers in the 12th and 13th Centuries* (Aldershot: Ashgate, 2010).

## Notes

1  Thanks to Sara Lipton for helpful criticism and advice on this essay.
2  In the seventeenth century love letters were such an accepted vehicle of communication that they became a fixture in Dutch painting; Peter C. Sutton *et al.*, *Love Letters: Dutch Genre Paintings in the Age of Vermeer,* The Bruce Museum of Arts (London and Greenwich, CT: Francis Lincoln, 2004).
3  For the unofficial letters of a public figure, J.H. Hamilton, 'The Character of Edward II: The Letters of Edward of Caernarfon Reconsidered', in *The Reign of Edward II: New Perspectives,* eds Gwilym Dodd and Anthony Musson (Woodbridge: Boydell & Brewer, with Centre for Medieval Studies, University of York, 2006), pp. 6–21.
4  On the authenticity of the Abelard–Heloise correspondence, the current consensus is in their favour: Michael Clanchy, *Abelard: A Medieval Life,* 2nd edn (Oxford: Blackwell, 1997), pp. 50–6. These famous letters continue to draw attention: Constance J. Mews, *The Lost Love Letters of Heloise and Abelard: Perceptions of Dialogue in Twelfth-Century France* (New York: St Martin's Press, 1999), and Bonnie Wheeler (ed.), *Listening to Heloise: The Voice of a Twelfth Century Woman* (New York: St Martin's Press, 2000).
5  On the various categories of chancery letters, A.L. Brown, *The Governance of Late Medieval England, 1272–1461* (Stanford, CA: Stanford University Press, 1989), pp. 42–52.
6  Close letter – sealed as a closed sheet of parchment – might deal with business not meant for the public eye, as in a letter of 4 July, 1361: 'To the sheriff of Norfolk. Order to cause a coroner for that county to be elected in place of Walter Broun, incapacitated by age and infirmity.'
7  In an unusual turn-around, for Adam Marsh, an important thirteenth-century English Franciscan, we only have his letters: C.H. Lawrence (ed. and transl.), *The Letters of Adam Marsh* (Oxford: Clarendon, 2006).
8  John D. Cotts, *The Clerical Dilemma: Peter of Blois and Literate Culture in the Twelfth-Century* (Washington, DC: Catholic University of America Press, 2009). About 250 manuscripts of Peter's letters floated around medieval Europe. He was instrumental in introducing the *ars dictaminis* into the English curriculum; R.W. Southern, 'Peter of Blois: A Twelfth Century Humanist' in his *Medieval Humanism and Other Studies* (Oxford: Blackwell, 1970).
9  S.D. Goitein (ed. and transl.), *Letters of Medieval Jewish Traders* (Princeton: Princeton University Press 1973), is the easiest introduction to a world that Goitein explicated in a number of studies. There is a reference to the Datini letters in Chapter 10, below, by Maryanne Kowaleski. For an English version of merchants' letters, Alison Hanham (ed.), *The Cely Letters, 1472–1488* vol. 273 (London: OUP, 1975).
10  H.G. Richardson, 'Business Training in Medieval Oxford', *American Historical Review,* 46 (1941), 259–80.
11  Dating is a peculiar problem. Most personal letters were undated with no indication that this was worrisome. Official letters, perforce, had to be dated: 'Given at Brieux the Sunday before the feast of Saints James and Christopher in the year of Our Lord 1250',

as the archbishop of Rouen concluded a missive. Many Paston letters are undated, bedevilling their editors, though Margaret Paston did date almost all her 100 letters, usually by a saint's day: 'Wretyn at Norwhick yn the Tuesday next be-fore Mydlent Sonday', or 'Wretyn in hast on the Monday next aftyr Seyn Andrewj'. The year often has to be filled in by context and external references.

12  Protocol questions had a long life: Giora Sternberg, 'Epistolary Ceremonials: Corresponding Status at the Time of Louis XIV', *Past and Present,* 204 (2009), 33–88.
13  Bruno Scott James, transl., *The Letters of St Bernard of Clairvaux* (Chicago: Henry Regnery, 1953), p. xi.
14  As well as editions of letters there is scholarship looking at letters as the key to a career or as a study of language: Anne Duggan, *Thomas Becket: A Textual History of His Letters* (Oxford: Clarendon, 1980); Dom Adrian Morley and C.N.L. Brooke, *Gilbert Foliot and His Letters* (Cambridge: CUP, 1965); Christof Rolker, *Canon Law and the Letters of Ivo of Chartres* (Cambridge: CUP, 2010); Lena Wahlgren, *The Letters of Peter of Blois: Studies in the Manuscript Tradition* (Gothenburg: Acta Universitatis Gothoburgensis, 1993).
15  Diplomacy by way of letters was especially sensitive regarding authenticity and the trustworthiness of the messenger's oral delivery: Michael Jucker, 'Trust and Mistrust in Letters: Late Medieval Diplomacy and its Communication and Practice', in *Strategies of Writing: Studies in Text and Trust in the Middle Ages,* Petra Schulte *et al.* (eds), (Turnhout: Brepols, 2008), pp. 213–36.
16  Robert Priebsch, *Letter from Heaven on the Observance of the Lord's Day* (Oxford: Blackwell, 1936); W.R. Jones, 'The Heavenly Letter in Medieval England, *Medievalia et Humanistica,* n.s. 6 (1975), 163–78; Dorothy Haines (ed. and transl.), *Sunday Observance and the Sunday Letter in Anglo Saxon England* (Woodbridge: Boydell & Brewer, 2010).
17  *The Letters of St Boniface*, Ephraim Emerton (ed. and transl.), New York: Norton, 1976 (reprinted from Columbia University Press, NY, 1940).
18  One aspect of letters not dealt with is delivery: the messengers who carried them and who often supplemented the written word with an oral message that might be the real substance of the matter, the written missive perhaps just vouching for his (or her) *bone fide* status. Giles Constable talks of the use of messengers: see Further reading; Mary C. Hill, *The King's Messengers, 1199–1377: A Contribution to the History of the Royal Household* (London: Edward Arnold, 1961); C.A.J. Armstrong, 'Some Examples of the Distribution and Spread of News at the Time of the Wars of the Roses', in *Studies in Medieval History presented to F.M. Powicke,* R.W. Hunt *et al.* (eds), (Oxford: Clarendon, 1948), pp. 429–54.
19  Among others, James Daybell (ed.), *Early Modern Women's Letter Writing, 1450–1700* (New York: Palgrave, 2000); Karen Cherewatuk and Ulrike Wiethaus (eds), *Dear Sister: Medieval Women and the Epistolary Genre* (Philadelphia: University of Pennsylvania Press, 1993); Jane Couchman and Ann Crabb (eds), *Women's Letters across Europe, 1400–1700: Form and Persuasion* (Aldershot: Ashgate, 2005); Heather Gregory (ed.), *Selected Letters of Alessandra Strozzi* (Berkeley: University of California Press, 1997); Alison Beach, 'Voices from a Distant Land: Fragments of a Twelfth Century Nuns' Letter Collection', *Speculum* 77 (2002), 34–54; Joseph I. Baird and Radd K. Ehrman, *The Letters of Hildegard of Bingen* (New York: OUP, 1994), for a translation of material edited in 1991 in the *Corpus Christianorum* series; Anne L. Clark (ed.), *Elisabeth of Schönau: The Complete Works* (New York: Paulist Press, 2000), pp. 235–54 for the letters; Margaret King and Albert Rabil, Jr. (eds), *Her Immaculate Hand: Selected Works by and about the Women Humanists of Quattrocento Italy* (Binghamton, NY: Center for Medieval and Early Renaissance Studies, State University of New York at Binghamton, 1983).

# 6 Writing military history from narrative sources

## Norman battlefield tactics, *c.* 1000

*Bernard S. Bachrach*

Relatively few of the large number of administrative documents produced by governments concerning military matters have survived from pre-Crusade Europe. This is the case largely because various *acta* issued for particular campaigns like those issued for other administrative tasks generally were time conditioned. As a consequence, their usefulness ended when military operations drew to a close or shortly thereafter, and relevant documents of this type were destroyed, usually by scraping the highly valuable parchment for subsequent use.[1] As a result of this immense lacuna in the evidentiary record, scholarly study of military history in the pre-Crusade era depends, in large part, on information provided by various types of narrative sources, such as histories, chronicles and annals, which were written by contemporaries and near contemporaries.[2] The authors, for the most part male, generally were clerics with a strong aversion to warfare and mixed feelings if not outright hostility in regard to those who lived the violent life of a professional soldier, i.e. a *miles*.[3]

The biases inherent in medieval narrative accounts, however, do not *prima facie* cripple modern scholarly efforts to use these texts in order to write the military history of the pre-Crusade era.[4] As will be seen below, these narratives must be dealt with cautiously and their *parti pris* must be examined in specific detail. Clerical bias, for example, often is identifiable in regard to the supposedly large number of innocent people, especially monks, nuns, and priests, killed by 'bad' people. In this context, God often is depicted as punishing such bad people with defeat, disease, and death. Another theme that often is exaggerated by clerics focuses on the destruction of churches and monasteries, as well as upon the devastation of estates belonging to the clergy.[5] Finally, some clerics, concerned with preparing their readers for the Apocalypse, which they believed to have been imminent, greatly exaggerated the impact on life and property of all kinds of disasters, and especially those resulting from war.[6]

The problems caused by particular biases in regard to exaggeration often can be controlled, at least in part, by the use of *Sachkritik*. This method, developed largely by the German military historian Hans Delbrück during the later nineteenth century, introduces the element of 'brute fact' to help us control the information provided by the sources.[7] For example, a soldier, in order to maintain himself in combat-ready condition, requires on average approximately 3,000 calories per day. This nutrition can be provided most efficiently by a daily ration of a kilogram of milled wheat.[8] An army of 10,000 men required 10,000 kilograms of milled wheat per day, which under best-case land transport conditions in pre-Crusade Europe required twenty carts each drawn by two oxen.[9]

This type of 'brute fact', e.g. nutrition minima and maximum hauling capacity for a cart, can be used effectively to control claims regarding the size of armies and the duration of campaigns. For example, it was asserted in the mid-sixth century that in AD 451, Attila the Hun invaded Gaul with 700,000 men, and from other evidence it is clear that he campaigned there for about a month. An army of this order of magnitude would have required, during the period that the Huns and their allies operated west of the Rhine, approximately 21,000 metric tons of milled wheat. In turn, this volume of grain would have required the use of some 42,000 carts each drawn by two oxen. As Delbrück showed, however, the operation of such a large number of men in Gaul during the stipulated period of time was not possible in an objective sense in light of the speed of troop movement and the technology available to provide them with supplies.[10]

The use of *Sachkritik*, when augmented by the deployment of material evidence that has been identified by archaeologists, can be effective in establishing the accuracy, or more often than not the inaccuracy, of clerical reportage concerning destruction and devastation that is to be found in the narrative sources. For example, claims by a clerical author that a particular late Roman fortress city, such as Metz, was destroyed by barbarians and turned into a 'ghost town' can be undermined by providing a balanced treatment of the archaeological evidence. In such a context, it is necessary to examine the material evidence independently of the claims found in the narrative sources. In addition, it is crucial to discuss all of the archaeological finds, not merely a selection intended to validate an account found in the written sources.[11] The question as to why a particular author, contrary to the widely accepted teachings of Isidore of Seville, provided inaccurate information, either in general, or in a particular case, is another very important matter, and runs the gamut from religious prejudice to political bias and most everything in between.[12]

## Dudo of St Quentin

The work of Dudo, a monk of St Quentin, is particularly challenging in regard to the problems inherent in using narrative sources to write military history. First, it must be noted that the impetus behind Dudo's work was a commission by the Norman ruler Richard I (d. 996) to write a history of his Norse forebears who had settled in the region that came to be known as Normandy.[13] It is obvious that Dudo's patron and members of the ducal entourage had to be pleased sufficiently by the work in order to see it published, that is, to make it public. The result was *De Moribus et Actis primorum Normanniae ducum* (sometimes referred to by scholars as *Gesta Normannorum*), which, in fact, was completed and published early in the eleventh century, during the reign of Richard I's son and successor Richard II (d. 1026).[14]

Although Dudo's patrons commissioned him to write a history in praise of their ancestors, everyone was aware that these people were Vikings who were known far and wide for their destructive violence, and who, in addition, were widely condemned by the clerical authors who wrote about them.[15] The published version of *De Moribus*, nevertheless, was found to be convincing by the ruling family and the Norman court over which they presided.[16] In this context, Duke Richard II not only saw *De Moribus* published, but rewarded its author handsomely, and likely played a role with other members of the ducal family in encouraging copies of the text to be made.[17] In addition, Dudo's posterity among the writers of history in Normandy and England during the Middle Ages, such as William of Jumièges, Robert of Torigny, Wace and Benoît of St Maure, also found the text convincing and either copied large parts of it into their own works or deployed extensive paraphrases.[18] Modern scholars, by contrast, have shown that *De Moribus* is filled with inaccuracies, especially in regard to the kind of factual detail that Clio's contemporary practitioners find to be so valuable for reconstruction of the past.[19]

These errors, it appears, were generated, in part, by Dudo's ignorance of events that occurred in the more distant past, that is, beyond the direct and perhaps indirect memory of those at the Norman court who provided him with at least some of the information that found its way into *De Moribus*. It seems, as well, that the hostile bias toward the Vikings of many of the written sources available to Dudo impinged upon the accuracy of *De Moribus* as he found it necessary either to ignore or manipulate these sources so as not to displease those who commissioned his work.[20] In short, Dudo's reliability in regard to telling the truth, recording what happened, as this imperative has been understood from the time of Isidore of Seville (d. 636), is often suspect.[21] As a result, serious challenges are faced by modern scholars, who would seek to use Dudo's narrative in order to write about the military history of those Norsemen, who settled in the *Francia Occidentalis*, the French kingdom, in 910.

In considering *De Moribus* for the purpose of treating Norman military history, it is of signal importance that Dudo was writing within a tradition of rhetorical plausibility that had been revived in the cathedral schools in the northern parts of the French kingdom during the second half of the tenth century.[22] Dudo was taught, following arguments that Cicero had championed a thousand years earlier, an imperative to provide accurate information when possible, but when this was not possible to provide information that, at the least, would likely be regarded as plausible by his audience.[23] In discussing matters concerning which he knew his audience at the Norman court to be well informed, such as contemporary buildings which they saw regularly and documents which they used frequently, Dudo worked diligently to provide accurate information.[24] This tactic was intended to gain the confidence of his audience which would then be more likely to accept as true such information about which they were uninformed but which was consistent with what they already believed to be true.

*De Moribus* was patronized by the Norman rulers and was intended initially for oral presentation at their court in Rouen.[25] As a result, it is not surprising that the discussion of military matters dominated Dudo's account. Both Richard I and Richard II, it should be emphasized from the outset, were primarily military leaders, *duces* in a traditional sense, as well as the rulers of a significant polity within the French kingdom.[26] They were exceptionally interested in having a history written that depicted the glory won by the martial exploits of their fore-bears. This was accomplished by Dudo in sufficiently simple Latin so that the prose portions, which were historical in nature, of *De Moribus* could be read aloud for the edification and entertainment of the duke's courtiers and foreign visitors.[27]

In addition to numerous clerical functionaries and ecclesiastical dignitaries who frequented the ducal court, it is important, in the present context, that the Norman duke was surrounded, in large part, by military officers and various members of the ducal military household. These men served as a standing army and represented the core of the professional armed forces of Normandy.[28] Among these men, who served under the command of the dukes, it has been shown that a great many were likely to understand Latin when read out to them with a familiar 'romance' accent.[29] Because these men were part of the court, Dudo had to be exceptionally careful in providing information regarding military matters that, if not historically true, that is, actually happened, were at least plausible to those who were well versed in the realities of war.[30]

In contrast to Dudo, the authors of the various histories, chronicles and annals of the previous century, written in various parts of the French kingdom, not only often suffered from the types of religious bias discussed above, but, in general, were implacably hostile to the pagan Norsemen and their Norman posterity. These Christian writers provided information concerning the Norsemen as 'the other', an enemy force like a violent storm or other natural catastrophe. They did not provide details that were either reliable or plausible regarding the 'inside' of Norse history, for example how Rollo, Richard I's grandfather, and his followers organized their military forces, planned their strategy, or executed their tactics.[31]

Dudo needed to provide a view of the Norse and their Norman descendants from the inside, and to do so from a positive perspective. Of course, over the past century or more prior to Dudo's arrival at the ducal court, the Normans had transmitted orally stories about their past. Dudo used aspects of some of these, but for the most part they added an epic flavour indicative of oral tradition and did not provide the kind of information that was needed for the writing of a 'proper' history of a people and a ruling family.[32] In addition, these stories did not provide the kind of detail that was needed to present a structured view of military matters, such as military organization, strategy, and tactics as these were understood at the Norman court *c.* 1000.

As has been shown in several cases, Dudo responded to the difficulties he faced, both informational *lacunae* and the imperative to maintain rhetorical plausibility, by immersing himself in an understanding of contemporary Norman military insti-tutions. These were the well-known structures concerning which his audience was best informed, and about which Dudo was able to acquire accurate and detailed information. He then projected what he knew about commonly known present practice backward into the previous century and earlier.[33] As a result, what we see of military matters from Dudo's *De Moribus*, by and large, concerns Norman warfare as practised in the two or so decades surrounding the millennium, that is, within the living memory of his informants at the Norman court. In general, there is rather little accurate information pertaining to two centuries earlier when the Norse began their attacks on the mainland and initiated a process that over time ultimately would result in them being able to secure a place to settle in the French kingdom.

## The Norman military

During the century between the Norman settlement in *Francia occidentalis* led by Rollo in 910 and the reign of Duke Richard I, who recruited Dudo to write *De Moribus*, the Normans adopted and maintained Carolingian military institutions, which had been well established throughout the Frankish kingdom for centuries.[34] At the most fundamental level, all able-bodied men, whether free or unfree, were required to participate in the local defence. In addition, those able-bodied men, whose real or movable wealth reached a legally stipulated minimum, were required, when called upon by the government, to serve as members of an expeditionary levy, or to find substitutes, for military operations beyond the locality in which they resided. All those who possessed multiples of the minimum wealth requirement were obliged, when called upon, to provide numbers of troops consistent with the value of their holdings. Finally, the king, or in the case of Normandy the duke, and his magnates, both lay and ecclesiastical, maintained military households composed of professional soldiers. These forces were an important element in the contingents which the great landholders were required to mobilize at ducal command for military action of an expeditionary nature in consonance with their great wealth.[35]

These institutions had been conditioned for the long term by the massive fortification throughout Gaul during the later third and fourth centuries of more than one hundred *urbes*.[36] These great fortress cities, by and large, were maintained in defensible condition throughout the Middle Ages.[37] In addition, numerous lesser strongholds, e.g. *castra* and *castella*, were also built by the Romans, and many of these endured well into the medieval era.[38] Other strongholds were constructed in later years. In the aggregate all these fortifications combined with the elaborate Roman road system, which, in general, was kept in repair, dominated the military topography of what would become the French kingdom.[39] As a result of the imperial heritage, long-term military strategy in the Norman duchy, as throughout the rest of the erstwhile Carolingian empire, was dominated by the defence of fortifications and offensively by mobilizing the large expeditionary forces that were required to besiege or storm enemy fortress cities and lesser strongholds.[40]

Because military strategy during the tenth and early eleventh centuries was focused on the defence and capture of fortifications, which were fundamental to the control of territory, battles in the field, as commonly understood, were few and far between.[41] Indeed, even those comparatively few battles in the field that did take place, generally were fought in the context of a siege. The most common occurrence of this type was a battle between a besieging force and a relief column that was trying to raise the siege by forcing the enemy to retreat or defeating it in the field. In order to maintain the investment of a stronghold, it was necessary for the besieging force to meet the relief force in the field or give up the siege. Other instances occurred when an army on the defence tried to block a force that was marching toward a particular fortification with the aim of establishing a siege.

Finally, in some cases the defenders of a besieged fortification would sally out of their stronghold to attack the besieging force.[42]

The domination of warfare by sieges meant that fighting men were deployed overwhelmingly on foot. Obviously, this was the case when the attacking forces were assigned to shoot arrows or bolts from bows or crossbows, respectively, and to launch stones or spears from various types of catapult. Defenders operated in much the same manner against the besieging army. When an effort was made to storm an enemy stronghold, the attacking forces advanced on foot across a so-called 'killing field' with ladders and siege towers in order to over-top the walls. They also deployed battering rams to smash the gates, and sappers to undermine the walls. In general, the defenders had little or no opportunity to use mounted troops, with the possible exception of a sortie against a poorly defended siege position or against parties of ladder-carriers who were advancing against the walls. For the besieging forces, mounted troops were used largely for intelligence purposes. They were deployed to identify places where forage might be obtained and to ascertain if there were a relief force on the march to raise the siege.[43]

## Dudo and Norman battlefield tactics

Although Dudo recognized that contemporary warfare was dominated by sieges, he does provide examples of situations during which a siege evolved into a battle. In one noteworthy case, Dudo tells a story about the Norse leader Rollo, who, in command of a very large army (*magnus exercitus*), composed of both mounted and foot soldiers (*equites* and *pedites*), decided to lay siege to the old Roman fortress city of Chartres.[44] Rollo began by deploying the bulk of his army composed of foot soldiers around the city and followed this up by having many if not most of his mounted troops dismount and join his foot soldiers. Further efforts were undertaken with the preparation of fences (*saepes*) and walls (*parietes*) to protect his forces from a sortie launched from the besieged garrison or a relief force.[45]

While the greater part of his army was being deployed at Chartres, Rollo dispatched some mounted elements of his force to forage throughout the Chartrain and the nearby region of the Châteaudunois in order to gather foodstuffs to sustain the siege.[46] Among the quantity of booty collected by this force were numerous animals – cattle, asses, goats and sheep – that were to be used to sustain the besieging army. In addition, the foragers also seem to have acquired horses, which likely were not to be used for food unless absolutely necessary as they were valuable for transport purposes. The livestock were kept at Lèver, the site of an abandoned monastery about three kilometres north of Chartres.[47]

While Rollo began to deploy his forces to besiege Chartres, Walter, the count-bishop of the city, whom Dudo characterizes as 'a very religious man', sent messengers to seek aid from Richard, the duke of the Burgundians, to Ebalus, the count of the Poitou, and to the Franks.[48] As the siege progressed and the forces at Chartres maintained their positions within the fortress city, a relief force was on the march. When Rollo learned that this relief force, composed of Burgundians and Franks, was drawing close to Chartres, he recalled his troops, who were harassing the men defending the walls of the city, and deployed them into a deep infantry formation to undertake a battle in the field. As Duke Richard's forces came into sight, Rollo took the offensive and advanced on the enemy column pushing it back, if not, in fact, breaking into its marching column before the men could redeploy into a battle line.[49]

After this initial clash, which Dudo claims Rollo was winning, the relief force began to reform and to hold its own against the Norse. As these two groups of tightly packed men fighting on foot pounded against each other in the open field, Walter, the count-bishop of Chartres, sortied from the city to attack the Norse from the rear. Walter's force was composed of two units, *cives*, from the local levies, who fought on foot like most militia troops, and heavily armed professional soldiers (*ferrates*) from the garrison. These men also advanced into the fray on foot in a closely packed formation ('aciebus constiaptus'). When Rollo realized that his forces had been caught in a pincer, he ordered his men to withdraw from the field by fighting their way out through the lines of the Burgundians and their Frankish allies. This was accomplished, and interestingly, there is no mention of a pursuit of the retreating Norse. This permits the inference that the latter retired in good order.[50]

This siege and the battle between the Norse and the relief force are treated by Dudo in a timeframe as having taken place about a century prior to the writing of *De Moribus*, that is, during the career of Rollo. However, it is problematic whether these events occurred, much less the details of deployment.[51] What is important here is that Dudo is telling a story that was plausible to his audience at the Norman court in regard to the details of military operations. Dudo easily maintained plausibility concerning the siege of Chartres and the engagement between Rollo's men and the relief force because the Normans of his day, like all other military forces in the erstwhile Carolingian empire, as noted above, frequently engaged in sieges and sometimes battles in the field that resulted during such operations.

The details regarding how the Normans and their adversaries at Chartres fought in the field *c*. 1000, that is, with phalanxes of men fighting on foot, is corroborated by many other examples in *De Moribus*. For example, in another engagement, Dudo indicates that when any force approached in its battle line, 'Rollo and those who were with him knelt down ... and waited to begin the combat protected by a wall of shields and packed together in close formation'[52] In yet another case, Dudo notes that 'The Norse gathered themselves in a close formation and crouched' awaiting the enemy attack. Thus, the Franks dismounted and prepared their 'battle line' to attack on foot, knowing that a mounted assault on a phalanx was little likely to succeed.[53]

Although set-piece battles in the field unconnected to sieges were very rare, actions of a less structured nature did take place. For example, after completing a campaign of ravaging the area of the upper Loire river valley, Rollo set out for Paris. However, local levies from the recently devastated region, *rustici*, abandoned their traditional role of remaining at home as a purely defensive force and joined together into a very large army with expeditionary levies (*pedites*) and professional mounted troops (*equites*) in order to pursue the Norse. Rollo, whose own column of foot (*pedites*) and horse (*equites*) likely were moving slowing because of the booty that they had collected during the above-mentioned raid, caught sight of the pursuing forces, which the Norse commander judged to be very large because of the immense dust cloud that was raised by their marching column.[54]

With this intelligence in hand, Rollo, as Dudo explains the situation, devised a plan, an ambush of sorts, that was intended to discourage the pursuing force. Rollo initiated his plan by ordering his units of foot soldiers (*pedites*) to press forward on the march so as to increase the distance between them and the pursuing force should the latter manage to continue its march. Rollo himself retained command of his mounted troops (*equites*) and deployed them so that when the enemy column, unaware of the Norse presence and unprepared for battle (marching in column rather than deployed as a battle line as a phalanx), came into view, he would charge and scatter them. In carrying out this plan, Rollo ordered his mounted troops to charge, with special attention to the *villani* (a subgroup of the *rustici*), who were the least well trained among the enemy and were the most likely to break and run. As a result of this surprise attack, the entire enemy column was thrown into confusion and, according to Dudo, Rollo's troops inflicted massive casualties and ended the enemy pursuit.[55]

## Conclusions

When Dudo was able to unearth sound information regarding the Norse past of his Norman patrons and their entourage, or plausible information which they provided to him, he worked diligently throughout the prose sections of *De Moribus* to provide accurate detail or at least detail that he believed to be accurate. However, as modern scholars have made clear, much of the detail that he obtained in this way often was not accurate. It is evident, however, that when Dudo knew that he lacked reliable information, and this was the case especially concerning the early military history of the Norse, he described matters such as tactics and strategy, such as those undertaken by Rollo, in contemporary terms. In this context, Duke Richard II and the members of his military household were no better informed than Dudo regarding Norse tactics and strategy in the distant past. As a result, Dudo was able to maintain rhetorical plausibility by describing past practice, such as tactics, in the way in which they were undertaken in the present. This made possible Duke Richard II's embrace of *De Moribus* as a true history, the publication of the text, and its widespread acceptance by later medieval writers.

Dudo's technique of assuring rhetorical plausibility and, thus, the acceptance his information regarding military matters as truthful by the audience for *De Moribus*, undoubtedly has undermined the value of this text for modern scholars in their efforts to illuminate early Norse history. Paradoxically, because Dudo found it necessary to describe military matters of the past as these were understood by the audience in his present, *De Moribus* can be relied upon as providing an accurate presentation of Norman military institutions, strategic thinking and battlefield tactics as these existed *c.* 1000. In addition, because the duke and his military household also were well aware of the military institutions, strategy and battlefield tactics of their adversaries, we also can rely upon Dudo to have presented these in an accurate manner.

UNIVERSITY OF WINCHESTER
LIBRARY

## Notes

1 See, for example, the discussion by Bernard S. Bachrach, 'Are They Not Like Us? Charlemagne's Fisc in Military Perspective', in *Paradigms and Methods in Early Medieval Studies* (The New Middle Ages), Celia Chazelle and Felice Lifshitz (eds), (New York: Palgrave Macmillan 2007, pp. 319–43, with the extensive scholarly literature cited there.

2 Note the discussion by Bernard S. Bachrach, '"Verbruggen's Cavalry" and the Lyon-Thesis', *Journal of Medieval Military History*, 4 (2006), 137–63.

3 The path-breaking work of Walter Goffart, *The Narrators of Barbarian History (550–800). Jordanes, Gregory of Tours, Bede, and Paul the Deacon*, (Princeton: Princeton University Press, 1988), remains basic. For a broad survey of the writers of history during the tenth and eleventh centuries, see Robert-Henri Bautier, 'L'Historiographie en France au Xe et XIe siècles', *Settimane di Studio del Centro Italiano di Studi sull'alto Medieovo*, 2 vols (1970), 1, 793–850. With regard to *milites* as professional soldiers during the period under discussion here, see David S. Bachrach, 'Memory, Epistemology, and the Writing of Early Medieval Military History: The Example of Bishop Thietmar of Merseburg (1009–1018)', *Viator*, 38 (2007), 63–90.

4 See the discussion by Bernard S. Bachrach, '"A Lying legacy" Revisited: The Abels-Morillo Defense of Discontinuity', *The Journal of Medieval Military History*, 5 (2007), 154–93.

5 See Bernard S. Bachrach, 'Early Medieval Military Demography: Some Observations on the Methods of Hans Delbrück', *The Circle of War*, Donald Kagay and L.J. Andrew Villalon (eds), (Woodbridge: Boydell, 1999), pp. 3–20.

6 See, for example, Richard Landes, *Relics, Apocalypse, and the Deceits of History: Ademar of Chabannes, 989–1034* (Cambridge, MA: Harvard U.P., 1995), who discusses in detail Ademar's obsession with the end of days.

7 An excellent discussion of *Sachkritik* is provided by Gordon Craig, 'Delbrück:The Military Historian', in *Makers of Modern Strategy: From Machiavelli to the Nuclear Age*, Peter Paret *et al.* (eds), (Princeton: University of Princeton Press, 1986), pp. 326–53, esp. pp. 332–6. See also Bachrach, 'Early Medieval Military Demography', pp. 3–20.

8 See, for example, Bernard S. Bachrach, 'Crusader Logistics; from victory at Nicaea to resupply at Dorylaion', in *Logistics of Warfare in the Age of the Crusades*, John H. Pryor (ed.), (Aldershot, UK: Ashgate, 2006), pp. 43–62, with the extensive literature cited there regarding the feeding of the troops.

9 See the discussion by Bernard S. Bachrach, 'Carolingian Military Operations: An Introduction to Technological Perspectives', in *The Art, Science, and Technology of Medieval Travel*, eds Robert Bork and Andrea Kann (Aldershot, UK: Ashgate, 2008), pp. 17–29.

10 Craig, 'Delbrück', p. 334, discusses Delbrück's arguments in this situation. For several more examples discussed in detail, see Bachrach, 'Early Medieval Military Demography', pp. 3–20.

11 A useful example of the misuse of archaeological evidence in order to support biased narrative sources is provided by Guy Halsall, *Settlement and Social Organization: The Merovingian Region in Metz* (Cambridge: CUP, 1995). For an exposé of Halsall's methods, see Bernard S. Bachrach, 'Fifth Century Metz: Later Roman Christian *Urbs* or Ghost Town?', *Antiquité Tardive* 10 (2002), 363–81.

12 See, for example, Goffart, *The Narrators of Barbarian History*; and Bachrach, '"A Lying legacy" Revisited', pp. 154–93.

13 Concerning the recruitment of Dudo, see Eric Christiansen, *Dudo of St. Quentin, History of the Normans* (Woodbridge: Boydell, 1998), pp. ix–xiii.

14 The basic edition remains *Dudo: De Moribus et Actis primorum Normaniae ducum* (Caen: F. Le Blan-Hardel, 1865–1872). Gerda C. Huisman, 'Notes on the Manuscript Tradition of Dudo of St. Quentin's *Gesta Normanorum*', *Anglo-Norman Studies*, 6 (1984), 122–35, has promised a new edition. In addition, Christiansen, *Dudo of St.*

*Quentin* has provided a complete and, in general, highly satisfactory translation with a useful introduction and helpful notes. Unfortunately, in dealing with technical military matters the translation is sometimes misleading and occasionally wrong. This is especially the case, for example, with regard to the term *miles* which he does not seem to recognize as a problem (p. xxxvi). See on this topic Bernard S. Bachrach, 'The *Milites* and the Millennium', *The Haskins Society Journal*, 6 (1994), 85–95; and for the continued problematic use of *miles* to mean 'knight' into the Anglo-Norman period and beyond see William Delehanty, '*Milites* in the Narrative Sources of England, 1135–1154', (unpublished diss. Minneapolis, MN: 1975).

15 Horst Zettel, *Das Bild der Normannern und der Normanneneinfälle im westfränkischen, ostfränkischen und angelsächsischen Quellen des 8. bis II. Jahrhunderts* (Munich: Wilhelm Fink, 1977), provides a very useful treatment of these matters.

16 There is a wide range of views regarding how Dudo accomplished his task of pleasing the Norman ruling family. See, for example, Henri Prentout, *Étude critique sur Dudon de S. Quentin et son Histoire* (Paris, 1916); Eleanor Searle, 'Fact and Pattern in Heroic History: Dudo of St. Quentin', *Viator*, 15 (1984) 75–85; Felice Lifshitz, 'Dudo's Historical Narrative and the Norman Succession of 996', *Journal of Medieval History*, 20 (1994), 101–20; and Leah Shopkow, 'The Carolingian World of Dudo of St. Quentin', *Journal of Medieval History*, 15 (1989), 19–37.

17 Huisman, 'Notes on the Manuscript Tradition', p. 124, lists the rather large number of manuscripts, but does not search out *fragmenta* that would indicate that perhaps other now lost *mss.* copies had been made. An excellent example of a work that was found unacceptable by the patron, the *auctor* going unrecognized and the project damned to obscurity, is the Bayeux Tapestry. On this, see Bernard S. Bachrach, 'Some Observations on the Bayeux Tapestry', *Cithara*, 27 (1987), 5–28.

18 Albu [Hanawalt], 'Dudo of Saint-Quentin', p. 112, notes that Dudo 'was so convincing that virtually everyone believed him for over 800 years'. These matters are discussed in detail by Bernard S. Bachrach, 'Dudo of Saint Quentin as a Military Historian', *The Haskins Society Journal: Studies in Medieval History*, 12 (2002), 155–85.

19 For easy access to the lengthy modern tradition of finding fault with Dudo's works, see David C. Douglas, 'Rollo of Normandy', *The English Historical Review*, 57 (1942), 417–36 and reprinted in David C. Douglas, *Time and the Hour* (London: Methuen, 1977), pp. 121–40. Christensen, *Dudo*, pp. xxiii–xxvii, also summarizes much of this scholarship.

20 See Christensen, *Dudo*, pp. xxiii–xxvii, where much previous scholarship is effectively summarized.

21 Regarding Isidore's highly influential dictum, see *Etymologiae* W.M. Lindsay (ed.), (Oxford: OUP, 1911), I, 44.5.

22 Of great importance in this context is Justin C. Lake, 'Truth, plausibility, and the virtues of narrative at the millennium', *Journal of Medieval History*, 35 (2009), 221–38, which deals with Dudo among others. See, for background, Richard W. Southern, 'Aspects of the European Tradition of Historical Writing: 1, The Classical Tradition from Einhard to Geoffrey of Monmouth', *Transactions of the Royal Historical Society*, 5th series 20 (1970), 173–96. See also Geoffrey Koziol, *Begging Pardon and Favor: Ritual and Political Order in Early Medieval France* (Ithaca, NY: Cornell U.P., 1992), pp. 139–55, who groups Dudo with the other rhetorical historians of the later tenth and early eleventh centuries; Leah Shopkow, *History and Community: Norman Historical Writing in the Eleventh and Twelfth Centuries* (Washington DC: Catholic University of America Press, 1997), p. 130; and Christiansen, *Dudo*, pp. xxi–xxiii.

23 Lake, 'Truth, plausibility, and the virtues of narrative at the millennium', pp. 221–38.

24 See the scholarly works cited by Bernard S. Bachrach, 'Dudo of Saint Quentin and Norman Military Strategy', in *Anglo-Norman Studies*, 26 (2004), 21–36.

25 Bernard S. Bachrach, 'Writing Latin History for a Lay Audience *c.* 1000: Dudo of Saint Quentin at the Norman Court', *The Haskins Society Journal*, 20 (2008), 58–77, with the literature cited there.

26 David Bates, *Normandy Before 1066* (London: Longman, 1982).
27 Bachrach, 'Writing Latin History for a Lay Audience', pp. 58–77.
28 Bernard S. Bachrach, 'Dudo of Saint Quentin as a Military Historian', *The Haskins Society Journal: Studies in Medieval History*, 12 (2002), 155–85, with regard to Norman military organization, which will be discussed in more detail below.
29 Bachrach, 'Writing Latin History for a Lay Audience', pp. 58–77.
30 Regarding Dudo's care in these matters, see two studies by Bernard S. Bachrach, 'Dudo of Saint Quentin's Views on Religion and Warfare, ca. 1000. A *mise au point*', in *Foi chrétienne et églises dans la société de l'Occident du Haut Moyen Âge (IVe–XIIe siècle)*, Jacqueline Hoareau-Dodinau and Pascal Texier (eds), (Limoges: Pulim, 2004), 241–52; and 'Dudo of Saint Quentin and Norman Military Strategy', in *Anglo-Norman Studies*, 26 (2004), 21–36.
31 For a useful survey of the writing of history by Dudo's contemporaries, see Bautier, 'L'Historiographie en France au Xe et XIe siècles', pp. 793–850; and with specific attention to treatment of the Vikings, see Zettel, *Das Bild der Normannern und der Normanneneinfälle*.
32 A substantial literature has developed regarding the supposed oral traditions available to Dudo and especially those that putatively had a Norse saga background. See the useful discussion by Christiansen, *Dudo*, pp. xvi–xvii.
33 See, for example, Bernard S. Bachrach, 'Dudo of Saint Quentin's Views on Religion and Warfare, ca. 1000. A *mise au point*', in *Foi chrétienne et églises dans la société de l'Occident du Haut Moyen Âge (IVe–XIIe siècle)*, Jacqueline Hoareau-Dodinau and Pascal Texier (eds), (Limoges: Pulim, 2004), pp. 241–52; and *idem.*, 'Dudo of Saint Quentin as a Military Historian', pp. 155–85.
34 Bernard S. Bachrach and Charles R. Bowlus, 'Heerwesen', in *Reallexikon der Germanischen Altertumskunde*, Heinrich Beck *et al.* (ed.), (Berlin and New York: De Gruyter, 2000), 14, cols. 122–36.
35 See, for example, Bachrach, 'Dudo of Saint Quentin as a Military Historian', pp. 155–85; J. Yver, 'Les premières institutions du duché de Normandie', *Settimane di Studio del Centro Italiano di Studi sull'alto Medieovo*, 16 (1969), 299–366; and Bates, *Normandy Before 1066*.
36 Bernard S. Bachrach, 'The Fortification of Gaul and the Economy of the Third and Fourth Centuries', *Journal of Late Antiquity* 3.1 (2010), 38–64, with the extensive literature cited there.
37 Stephen Johnson, *Late Roman Fortifications* (Totowa, NJ: Barnes & Noble, 1983); and Bernard S. Bachrach, 'Imperial walled cities in the West: an examination of their early medieval *Nachleben*', in *City Walls: The Urban Enceinte in Global Perspective*, James T. Tracy (ed.), (Cambridge: CUP, 2000), pp. 192–218.
38 In general, see *L'Architecture de la Gaule romaine. Les fortifications militaires*, Documents d'Archéologie Française 100, directed by Michel Reddé with the aid of Raymond Brulet, Rudolf Fellmann, Jan-Kees Haalebos and Siegmar von Schnurbein (Paris-Bordeaux: MSH/Ausonius, 2006), *passim*.
39 *L'Architecture de la Gaule romaine*, eds Michel Reddé, *et al.*, *passim*, and for background regarding Normandy, see the invaluable work of Jean Yver, 'Les châteaux forts en Normandie jusqu'au milieu du XIIe siècle. Contribution à l'étude du pouvoir ducal', *Bulletin de la Société des Antiquaires de Normandie*, 12 (1957 for 1955–1956), 28–115, 604–9.
40 Bachrach, 'Dudo of Saint Quentin and Norman Military Strategy', pp. 21–36.
41 With regard to the German kingdom, see Bernard S. Bachrach and David S. Bachrach, 'Saxon Military Revolution, 912–973: Myth and Reality', *Early Medieval Europe*, 15 (2007), 186–222; concerning Anjou, see Bernard S. Bachrach, 'L'art de la guerre angevin', in *Plantagenêts et Capétiens: confrontations et héritages* Martin Aurell and Noël-Yves Tonnerre (eds), (Turnhout, Belgium: Brepols, 2006), pp. 267–84; concerning the Norman duchy, see Bachrach, 'Dudo of Saint Quentin and Norman Military Strategy', pp. 21–36; and with regard to the frontier of the German kingdom,

see David S. Bachrach and Bernard S. Bachrach, 'Early Saxon Frontier Warfare: Henry I, Otto I, and Carolingian Military Institutions', *Journal of Medieval Military History*, 9 (2011), forthcoming.

42 Jim Bradbury, *The Medieval Siege* (Woodbridge, UK: Boydell, 1992), whose study remains the state of the question; and Bernard S. Bachrach, 'Medieval Siege Warfare: A Reconnaissance, *Journal of Military History*, 58 (1994), 119–33; reprinted in Bernard S. Bachrach, *Warfare and Military Organization in Pre-Crusade Europe* (London: Brill, 2002), with the same pagination, where the earlier literature is surveyed.

43 See, for example, several studies by Bernard S. Bachrach, 'On Roman Ramparts, 300–1300, in *The Cambridge Illustrated History of Warfare: The Triumph of the West* Geoffrey Parker (ed.), (Cambridge: CUP, 1995), pp. 64–91; 'Early Medieval Europe', in *War and Society in the Ancient and Medieval Worlds: Asia, The Mediterranean, Europe, and Mesoamerica*, Kurt Raaflaub and Nathan Rosenstein (eds), (Cambridge, MA: Harvard U.P., 1999), pp. 271–307; and 'The Culture of Combat in the Middle Ages', *Cithara*, 47 (2007), 3–24.

44 *De Moribus*, bk II, chs. 22–23 (p. 162). Regarding the history of the fortifications at Chartres, see Johnson, *Late Roman Fortifications*, pp. 99–101.

45 *De Moribus*, bk II, ch. 24 (p. 164).

46 *De Moribus*, bk II, ch. 22 (p.162).

47 *De Moribus*, bk II, ch. 24 (p. 165).

48 *De Moribus*, bk II, ch. 23 (p. 162).

49 *De Moribus*, bk II, ch. 23 (p. 162).

50 *De Moribus*, bk II, ch. 23 (p. 162).

51 Cf. Jules Lair, *Le siège de Chartres par les Normands* (Caen: H. Delesques, 1902).

52 *De Moribus*, bk II, ch. 9 (p. 150).

53 *De Moribus*, bk II, ch. 15 (p. 156).

54 *De Moribus*, bk II, ch. 22 (p. 156).

55 *De Moribus*, bk II, ch. 22 (p. 156).

# 7  Historians and inquisitors

## Testimonies from the early inquisitions into heretical depravity

*Mark G. Pegg*

I

In the year as given above [1245], on [Friday] 22 December, Aimerzens, wife of Guilhem Viguier of Cambiac, sworn as a witness, said that it was a good twenty-three years ago that her aunt, Geralda de Cabuer, led her to Auriac to the house of na [from *domna*, lady] Esquiva Aldric, wife of the knight Guilhem Aldric. And she saw two female heretics in the house. And then everyone in the house, Geralda, Esquiva and Guilhem Aldric, and their son Guilhem, adored the female heretics in the same way (with the witness instructed by Esquiva), genuflecting thrice, saying, 'Bless us, good women, pray God for these sinners.' She also said that later the same day, R[aimon] de Auriac and others visited the female heretics in the house. All of them and the witness listened for a long time to the preaching of the female heretics, and then everyone adored them, just as previously stated. And the female heretics said to the witness, in front of everyone, that because she was a pregnant adolescent she was carrying a demon in her belly. And then everyone was seized with laughter.

Likewise, she said that many times she saw heretics enter the house of Raimon Vassar by night. And when she saw the heretics enter the house, there were there [waiting for them] Bernart Doat, Arnaut de Chaubles, Arnaut Sabatier, Peire Arnaut, Helias Gausbert, Esteve Auger and his wife Bernarta, Valentia, wife of P[eire] Valentia, Peire Viguier, Guilhem Viguier, husband of the witness, Guilhem Girbert and his sister Aicelina, Guilhem Sais, brother of Jordas Sais, Pons Aimers de Francavila, son-in-law of Jordas Sais, and Jordas himself. All the aforesaid she saw enter the said house many times when the heretics were there around two years ago. And the witness herself saw all of them adoring the said heretics and listening to their preaching. And for a week the witness closely watched all this inside the said house as the house is next to the house of the witness. Nevertheless, she said that the said Pons Aimers she only saw with the heretics twice, whereas all the others she saw many times just as she said. She also said that Guilhem Viguier, her husband, warned her that she had to love the heretics, just as he and everyone else in the village did, but she did not wish to love the heretics after they told her that she was pregnant with a demon. And for that reason her husband thrashed her many times, yelling many insults, because she would not love the heretics.[1]

So begins na Aimerzens Viguier's testimony in the surviving record of the great inquisition undertaken by the Dominicans Bernart de Caux and Joan de Sant-Peire between May 1245 and August 1246. She was among almost six thousand men and women questioned about heretics (living or dead) in the Romanesque cloister of the abbey-church of Saint-Sernin in Toulouse. She confessed much more than her youthful humiliation by the 'good women' or what she recently saw going on next door – indeed, she testified three times that Friday – and yet what is so marvellous and problematic about studying inquisition records is already exemplified by her opening statements. Is it a glimpse into the expired reality of a woman who if it were not for the inquisition would have left no evidence of her existence? Or is it a story so compromised by the circumstances that elicited it, so shaped by the questions and assumptions of the inquisitors that, for all intents and purposes, na Aimerzens Viguier might as well be a fictional character, no more 'real' than Elizabeth Bennet or Emma Bovary? Is there a compromise between these two positions? What methods, skills, or even ethics, are necessary when using inquisition records? Is there a particular way of viewing historical writing when using this kind of evidence? Does the historiography of medieval heresy, especially the enduring falsehood of 'Catharism', overly determine what historians read in (and into) such testimonies? In the end, though, do inquisition records expand our vision of the medieval world or fracture it with too much specificity, too many marginal perspectives, too many stories about demons in bellies?

## II

Less than sixty years ago no historian studied inquisition records for insight into a woman like na Aimerzens Viguier. Of course, such documents were known, and even edited, but mostly they were examined for what they revealed about the evolution of western law, the 'Inquisition' as an institution, and the governing structures of the medieval Church. What was actually in testimonies was less important than that such testimonies existed. The records of medieval inquisitors were to be analysed in so far as they revealed evidence about a momentous shift in western legal and religious institutions after 1250. From the late nineteenth century such analyses were frequently defined by confessional allegiances between Roman Catholic and Protestant scholars. Generally speaking, and never forgetting that many of these scholars were learned and subtle thinkers, the former justified the inquisitors as responding to a genuine threat to the Church from organized and militant heretics, whereas the latter censured them as zealots hunting down spiritual individualists and religious dissenters who were clearly the forebears of the Reformation. In both cases it was taken for granted that descriptions of heretics in more erudite sources (polemics, treatises, law codes, histories, chronicles, papal letters) were accurate and that, for the most part, it was unnecessary to read inquisition records for information about heresy. Sometimes a testimony was quoted or edited by a scholar (especially the more thoughtful and paleographically gifted) but never as the starting point from which to understand the heresy of the testifying individual, merely as the confirmation of what other sources argued a heretic must believe. Surprisingly, some of these attitudes remain to this day.

In the 1960s and 1970s with the emergence of social history, especially among historians in Great Britain and the United States, inquisition records were read in conjunction with other archival sources (land contracts, wills, cartularies, petitions, gifts to religious houses, *dotal* agreements, judicial records, *enquêtes*) for evidence of familial relationships within communities and for prosopographical details of town and village notables. Testimonies provided evidence of local political and institutional formation, particularly within the towns of northern Italy and southern France. They were studied with little or no interest in religion or heresy. What other scholars had been saying about heretics since the nineteenth century was accepted as not so much conclusive as mostly irrelevant in writing political and social history. Despite such a limited perspective on what was worth studying, historians found the vivid anecdotal evidence within inquisition testimonies hard to ignore, even if they were not quite sure what to do with stories of village courtliness, sexual innuendo, magical charms and heretical holy men. Slowly but steadily, the sense of revelation of what lay within inquisition records, especially for the history of ordinary people, inspired some historians to approach the testimonies with methods derived from anthropology.

These anthropological methods were mixed, and varied from the neo-Durkheimian functionalism of Mary Douglas to the hot-house structuralism of Claude Levi-Strauss to the interpretative 'thick description' of Clifford Geertz. Underlying these different ethnographic approaches is an assumption that very large conclusions can be drawn from small seemingly irrelevant facts. In a wink is a world. Historians must be prepared to be 'heroically consequential', swiftly seeing connections between the seemingly unconnected, effortlessly leaping over the dualism of text and context.[2] Only through emphasizing the particular (however pedestrian, however peculiar) could anything general (however global, however grandiose) be said. Evidence that had once been dismissed as too fragmentary, too obscure, or too full of mundane people chattering about mundane things, now seemed to offer dazzling insight into the past. (Despite the importance of anthropology for historians in the 1960s and 1970s, it should not be forgotten that Marc Bloch, for instance, was writing anthropologically-inclined medieval history more than four decades earlier.) As anthropologists wrote about the pangolin cult of the Lele, or Amazonian mythologies, or cockfighting in Bali, so historians wrote about the cult of the saints in sixth-century Tours, the magical killing of cows in fifteenth-century Kent, or the rites of violence in sixteenth-century Lyon. These histories, especially when they used inquisition testimonies, came to be known as 'microhistories'.

These microhistories typified the promise and peril of 'postmodernism' for many historians in the United States forty years ago.[3] Two books in particular were celebrated and attacked: Emmanuel Le Roy Ladurie's *Montaillou, village occitan de 1294 à 1324* (1975; English translation 1978) and Carlo Ginzburg's *Il formaggio e i vermi: il cosmo di un mugnaio del '500* (1976; English translation 1980).[4] Pathbreaking studies using the inquisition testimonies of a fourteenth-century village in the Pyrénées and a sixteenth-century miller in the Friuli. Of course, Le Roy Ladurie and Ginzburg never assumed they were engaging in postmodernism as understood by scholars self-consciously doing it at the time (or since) and which, give or take a philosophical addendum here and there, is the idea that language is not a crystalline reflection of the world as it is (or was), rather it is only through language that the world exists as it is (or was). Why they exemplify postmodernism for some historians, and what links them with a philosopher like Michel Foucault (especially his earlier studies on the 'archaeology' of the human sciences), is the apparent emphasis on the marginal, the obscure, the deviant, the sick, and the persecuted as the subject of history. Microhistories were unfairly accused (and almost always by intellectual historians) of accentuating what was seen at the time (and still is by some scholars) as the shift away from the grand synthetic historical vision to the myopically small, petty and inarticulate.

## III

In 1233 Pope Gregory IX sent two letters (Wednesday, 20 April, and Friday, 22 April) to the Dominicans in France and Provincia (the papal name for the vast region between the Garonne and Rhône rivers in what is now southern France) instructing them to eradicate heresy through *inquisitiones heretice pravitatis*.[5] Although it was only four years since the Albigensian Crusade (a savage twenty-year holy war against the count of Toulouse and the heretics supposedly infesting his lands) ended in triumph for the Church and the kingdom of France, the pope feared the 'serpent' of heresy was rising again. These 'inquisitions into heretical depravity' were *ad hoc* investigations rather than the tribunals of an autonomous institution. They are not to be confused with the Inquisitions (especially the Roman and the Spanish) of the fifteenth and sixteenth centuries. They are definitely not to be confused with the dark fantasy of the Inquisition in Enlightenment polemics and Gothic novels. Of course, the procedures, punishments and documentary practices of later Inquisitions, whether in Europe or the Americas, were derived and developed from these earlier inquisitions. This is why the inquisition of Bernart de Caux and Joan de Sant-Peire is so important. Many of the forensic techniques that were eventually formalized in the following centuries were being tried and tested. Most of what it meant to confess about oneself and about others was still new and unusual for a woman like na Aimerzens Viguier. More to the point, what it meant to testify and to see your testimony recorded, well aware that it would be read now and in the future, was an innovation with lasting consequences for the western world.

The original parchment inquisition registers of Bernart de Caux and Joan de Sant-Peire are lost. Fortunately, two other Dominican inquisitors, Guilhem Bernart de Dax and Renaud de Chartres, had the testimonies copied onto paper some time after October 1258, although no later than August 1263. This copy has been in the Bibliothèque municipale of Toulouse since 1790. It is currently catalogued as manuscript 609. Yet even this massive manuscript (260 folios, 291 millimètres high, 236 millimètres wide, and roughly thirty-nine lines of cursive minuscule recto and verso) consists of only two books, five and four, arranged in that order, out of an estimated ten. The other eight have disappeared, like so many documents of the early inquisition. Apart from some parchment fragments, usually no more than a folio or two, the only remaining inquisition testimonies from these years are those transcribed in the late seventeenth century from medieval manuscripts that no longer exist. These transcriptions (250 volumes in large, elegant, flourishing cursive with the Latin respelled *style classique*) are catalogued as the Doat Collection in the Bibliothèque nationale of France.

Whether an inquisition testimony is read in a manuscript or in a modern edition, how it has survived to the present, as parchment original or paper copy (medieval or early modern), must always be kept in mind. Although na Aimerzens Viguier's testimony is one of nearly six thousand, so many more are missing, and while this should neither constrain nor hinder any arguments about her or anyone else questioned by the inquisitors, whatever a scholar wishes to argue, he or she must implicitly take into account the possibility of being challenged, confounded, or even disproved by one of those missing testimonies.

## IV

All testimonies at Saint-Sernin began with a person first abjuring heresy and then taking an oath that he or she would 'tell the full and exact truth about oneself and about others, living and dead, in the matter of the fact or crime of heresy or Waldensianism'. Sometimes this formula was recorded in a confession (Aimerzens' did not). After being sworn as a witness, an individual was asked a standard series of questions. Occasionally a testimony reported these questions (Aimerzens did not). Extrapolating from these transcribed questions, and from the *formula interrogatorii* that Bernart de Caux and Joan de Sant-Peire recommended in a small pamphlet on inquisitorial methods written two years after their inquiries at Saint-Sernin,[6] a procedural template can be outlined, a script to be followed by inquisitors and their assistants during interrogations.

'Did you see a heretic or a Waldensian?' 'If so, then where and when, how often and with whom, and who were the others present?' 'Did you listen to the preaching or exhortation of heretics?' 'Did you give heretics lodging or arrange shelter for them?' 'Did you lead heretics from place to place or otherwise consort with them or arrange for them to be guided or escorted?' 'Did you eat or drink with the heretics or eat bread blessed by them?' 'Did you give or send anything to the heretics?' 'Did you act as the representative, messenger, or assistant of the heretics?' 'Did you hold any funds or anything for a heretic?' 'Did you receive the peace from a heretic's book, mouth, shoulder, or elbow?' 'Did you adore a heretic or bow your head or genuflect and say "bless us" before the heretics?' 'Did you participate, or were you present at their *consolamen* and *aparelhamen* [*consolamentum* or *apparellamentum* in Latin]?' 'Did you ever confess to another inquisitor?' 'Did you believe the heretics to be good men and women, to have a good faith, to be truthful, to be the friends of God?' 'Did you hear, or do you know, the errors of the heretics?' 'Did you hear them say that God had not made all visible things, that there was no salvation in baptism, that marriage was worthless, that the Host was not the body of Christ, and that the flesh would never be resurrected?' 'If you did believe these errors, and also believed the heretics to be good, then how long have you persisted in these beliefs?' 'And when did you first begin to believe in the heretics and their errors?' 'Did you leave the sect of the heretics?' 'How long ago did you leave and did you ever see the heretics after this time?' 'Did you ever agree to keep silent about all these things?' 'Did you ever hide the truth?'

These questions focused more on behaviour than ideas. In stressing what men, women, and children did rather than what they thought, these questions articulated a 'social theory' of heresy. This was a vision of heresy not only permeating but being propagated through the ordinary habits and the inescapable structures of society. Or rather what the inquisitors decided were ordinary habits and inescapable structures. Inquisition records are unparalleled in allowing historians to reconstruct the intricacies and complexities of everyday existence in medieval society, yet discovering such intricate and complex social patterns requires disentangling them from the overbearing social theory of the inquisitors. Of course, sometimes the inquisitorial social model perceptively reflected the social order it was investigating and classifying. More often it did not. Almost always, though, the inquisitors attempted to remake individuals and communities according to their notion of a Christian society.

This emphasis on behaviour by Bernart de Caux and Joan de Sant-Peire was not from a lack of interest in heretical ideas. Rather the inquisitors seemed to have taken it for granted that to be guilty of heresy through habit indicated that an individual was guilty of heresy in thought. Moreover, the inquisitors knew precisely what these heretical doctrines were even if most of the individuals they questioned either did not coherently understand what they were accused of believing or never considered statements like 'the Devil made visible things' or 'marriage is worthless' as dogmatic principles within an overarching dualist theology. At least since the end of the twelfth century what the heretics in the lands of the count of Toulouse supposedly believed was outlined in polemics, histories and sermons by Latin Christian intellectuals. Importantly, what these heretics were accused of believing was what all heretics were accused of believing no matter where they lived in Latin Christendom. Even if the social details of heresy may have varied somewhat from the Po to the Rhine to the Garonne rivers, the doctrines did not. (Although some Churchmen readily argued that all heretics, no matter where and even when they lived, followed the same familial, sexual, or ritual patterns.) The inquisitors were less concerned with ideas because they already knew what they would find. What really interested them was the social geometry in which these essential heretical beliefs existed.

This stress upon behaviour by the early inquisitions, while never disappearing from investigations into heresy, diminished as the primary forensic focus after 1250. By the turn of the fourteenth century what an accused heretic believed or what he or she knew others believed was what mattered most to an inquisitor. It was not so much that inquisitors were now unsure of what heretics were thinking, although this was sometimes the case, rather that heretical doctrines and the men and women who thought them were no longer exclusively understood within a framework connecting all heretics back to ancient dualists like Manichaeans and Arians. The intellectual conviction that heretics all thought the same way, carried over from late twelfth-century schoolrooms into early thirteenth-century inquisitions, slowly dissipated into a pedantic scholastic awareness of the heterogeneous potential of heterodoxy. Inquisition testimonies gradually became more and more detailed about the beliefs and ideas of a testifying individual. This doctrinal precision, at once genuine punctiliousness by individuals consciously

knowing they were thinking (or had heard) heretical thoughts and the sharp prod-
ding by inquisitors for confessions to be more notionally exact, also means that
by the end of the thirteenth century a significant number of testimonies from
southern France actually do outline seemingly coherent dualist philosophies.
However, for the inquisitors such doctrines were now just one set of heretical
beliefs amongst others. This interrogatory shift was allied with an inquisitorial
policy of questioning fewer individuals over longer periods of time. Le Roy
Ladurie's *Montaillou*, for example, is based on fourteen testimonies from the
inquisition of Jacques Fournier, Cistercian bishop of Pamiers, into sixty-six men
and forty-eight women between 1318 and 1325. It is only through recognizing
these changing assumptions about heretical ideas on the part of inquisitors and
those they questioned that the historian can even begin to extrapolate from a
confession what a man or woman truly believed.

Questions are culturally specific predictions about knowledge and inductive
habits, exemplifying routine notions of truth, predictable rules of inference, and
habitual methods of deduction. Answers justify questions by completing their
sense and purpose. Questions and answers, like inductive habits derived from
precise evidence and deductive techniques framed by general assumptions, get
confirmed, and acquire validity, from being brought into agreement with each
other. Questions get amended, discarded, or reworded, if they yield answers that
individuals and communities are reluctant to understand or unwilling to accept.
The process of justifying particular questions, which the inquisitors not only had
to do for themselves but also for those they interrogated, was a careful exercise
in making mutual adjustments between what was asked and what was inferred.
Selecting the right questions was as much a moral and intellectual test of an
inquisitor searching for truth about heresy as giving the right answers was a moral
and intellectual test of a woman confessing or concealing this truth during a trial.
Every confession was judged and largely shaped by the analytic formula implicit
in the questions asked by the inquisitors. The questions asked of na Aimerzens
Viguier justified the deductive methods and the principles of analysis by which
her interrogators delineated not just the past, present and the future of heresy but
also who they thought she was as an individual (and as a woman) before, during
and after her interrogation.

Some historians view the question-and-answer format underlying all inquisition records as being analogous to the field-notes of an anthropologist. Le Roy
Ladurie and Ginzburg, for instance, both argued for such a likeness.[7] Although an
interesting analogy, it is ultimately misleading. The radical asymmetry and moral
tension of the relationship between anthropologists and their subjects is present in
inquisition texts; nevertheless, testimonies were not elicited as the opening methodological gambit in an enterprise of trying to see the world through 'native' eyes.
The inquisitors and those they questioned took it for granted that they were part
of the same world, even if neither of them saw or felt about that world in the same
way. Inquisitors confidently possessed *a priori* assumptions about the men and
women they questioned (and although the same can easily be said about anthropologists, part of their way of doing things is to try and overcome such presup-
positions). An interrogation was not really a dialogue, except in the most limited

sense. An inquisitor said nothing about himself, ending testimonies where and when he thought necessary. The men and women he questioned talked as much or as little as they were allowed, or could get away with. A few tried manipulating the 'conversation' with lies, digressions, gossip and second-guesses about what they thought an inquisitor expected to hear. Either way, inquisition records are not field-notes or dialogues in the strict sense of the term.

## V

Na Aimerzens Viguier was questioned in Occitan (or Old Provençal as it is also known), that is to say, she was interrogated in the vernacular. She answered in the first-person vernacular. A scribe or notary simultaneously translated what she said into third-person Latin. He did not scribble a literal word-for-word translation of what she said, rather he used a form of Latin tachygraphy, a style of rapid writing where he abridged and abbreviated what he heard. This translation and transcription of testimonies into Latin by the inquisition was, despite the obvious moral and coercive implications, immensely practical. It was the only language with a fully developed method of reporting speech, the only language with simplified versions of itself, so that the spoken word, even if not in Latin, was easily and quickly represented. Many testimonies were often just abbreviations or formulaic phrases – 'Aforesaid year and day, Joan Fabre said that he never saw heretics unless captured, nor believed them, nor adored them, nor gave them anything, nor sent them anything' – a scribe swiftly getting through the business at hand. At the end of Aimerzens' interrogation her testimony was read back to her, with the scribe translating his Latin transcription back into the vernacular, so that she could confirm the veracity of what was recorded of what was testified. Such confirmation allowed a testimony to become a notarized document, witnessed by the scribe and at least one other person. (Aimerzens' witnesses were the Dominicans Guilhem Pelhisson, Peire Rasoiret, Esteve Rechaut and Bernart de Caux.) Inquisitorial records were similar to other notarized documents. Lawful authenticity, whether an interrogation for heresy or a transaction for a vineyard, was signified in the procedures of the notariate.

No one questioned by Bernart de Caux or Joan de Sant-Peire would have thought a Latin transcription resembling a vernacular confession was beyond their experience. Latin was a language listened to, looked at and translated for most of these men and women on a regular basis. Charters, wills, oaths, bequests, deeds, debts, accounts, contracts, letters, all acts of existence that needed notarized authentication were, more often than not, written in Latin, even if an individual was unable to read the language. Latin was a vigorously living language, in that so much depended on its ability to faithfully record the wishes of a dying man, the size of a house being sold, the length of a field, or the freedom of a manumitted woman. Most people knew a modicum of Latin, recognizing a few words here and there, and they certainly knew the look and feel of a Latin parchment document. The inquisition enhanced every assumption about the relationship of Latin and the vernacular. Latin was not just a language giving legal verisimilitude to existence, it was now a threatening arrangement of words, abbreviations, and quill-strokes, with the potential to persecute and punish.

(All this scribal translation of the first-person into the third in a recorded and notarized testimony means the historian can occasionally choose what is the most appropriate pronoun in the translation of a text. If the purpose of a translated extract from a confession is to suggest the individual actually testifying before an inquisitor, then it is entirely proper for a translation to be in the first person. Otherwise, a straightforward translation in the third person is the rule.)

## VI

There is nothing natural about narrative. Humans are not inherently storytellers. There is no innate reason why na Aimerzens Viguier talked about herself in the way that she did. The twenty-first canon of the Fourth Lateran Council in 1215 may have mandated that all Christians must confess to a priest once a year, but it took more than two centuries for most medieval men and women to even begin accepting that talking about oneself was a routine part of being Christian. Yet many historians presume that narrative is natural and this presumption of the naturalness of narrative (underlying much of the so-called 'linguistic turn' and the postmodern challenge to history in the 1980s) is pervasive amongst studies using inquisition testimonies. This view of narrative justifies a critical and ethical stance which assumes reality (past and present) is a text, or an ensemble of texts, to be read. This narrative innateness supposedly gives the historian an impermeable analytic position outside the vagaries of historical contingency. What was once thought to be the objective fact of social habits (politics, religion, serfdom and the subjugation of women) is really no more than the objective fact of narrative habits (the discursive strategies framing politics, religion, serfdom and the subjugation of women). Accordingly, there is only fiction in the archives, only the stories that long-dead people once told about themselves and about others – and, ultimately, only the stories of historians telling these stories. These ideas are misguided. Any reflection upon the past beginning with the supposition that some things are universal in humans or in human societies is more than just a retreat from seriously explaining the rhythms of existence in previous centuries, it is the very antithesis of what it is to be an historian.

The way that na Aimerzens Viguier talked about herself was as much (if not more so) the result of the framework imposed upon her testimony by the questions she was asked as by her own assumptions about what it meant to talk about (and so imagine) herself as a person. Nevertheless, why she supposedly digressed or went off on tangents in her testimony, why she apparently said things that inquisitorial questions did not require her to say, should not be seen as narrative 'excess' or 'surplus' as some historians have argued.[8] Deciding what is excessive or superfluous in a testimony because such anecdotes or statements do not conform to a historical model of what it means to tell a now-this-now-that story is to impose a normative narrative ideal on both the inquisitors and those they questioned. Aimerzens talking about her pregnancy, the mockery of the good women, or being beaten by her husband, while not obviously required by the interrogatory formula of the inquisitors, were not exercises in excess or surplus, they were quite deliberate narrative manoeuvers at once deriving from (and so only understood by the historical evocation of) the world in which she lived and as a canny response to existential assumptions of the inquisitors.

Existence was resiliently linear to the inquisitors. No relationship, action, or thought, was contingent, random or accidental. There was no separation of cause and effect in the confession of an individual life. A meeting with two heretics in 1223, even if it had never happened before or would never happen again, was still the effect of something in the past and could still be the cause of something yet to occur. Everything was potentially implicated in everything else for inquisition. By contrast, existence for Aimerzens was a constantly shifting and changing labyrinth and not a straight line. The adolescent girl was not accountable to the mature woman in this nonlinear universe. An individual life was made from innumerable transient and mutable episodes that, while meaningful and intense at specific times and places, did not necessarily proceed, sequentially, one into the other. This was a notion of the self as sung by the troubadours and as enacted in *cortezia*. Individual identity was closer to a vernacular lyric than the Latin prose of an inquisitor. Nevertheless, the way in which the inquisitors viewed the world, apart from eventually winning out over the decades, was at least partially understood by Aimerzens (and by many others) and clearly manipulated for confessional advantage. The challenge when reading any inquisition testimony is always trying to discern the 'reality' imposed upon a witness during an interrogation (and in the text recording the testimony) and in the 'reality' of the individual as she or he understood it outside the courtroom.

## VII

Who were the 'good women' who mocked na Aimerzens Viguier? Over a century of scholarship has mistakenly identified such women as the female religious leaders of the sect of Catharism. This is more than a case of mistaken identity, it is a fundamental misunderstanding of these women and of the holiness they thought they personified and of the heresy the inquisitors thought they revealed. The thoroughly modern story of Catharism usually begins with Bogomil missionaries travelling from the Byzantine Empire and covertly spreading a doctrine of dualism in northern Italy and southern France in the eleventh century and then, somehow or other, by the beginning of the thirteenth a 'Cathar Church' exists with an elaborate episcopate from the Mediterranean to the North Sea. The inquisitions into heretical depravity were, according to this scenario, set up to eliminate the 'Cathars' and their followers in the aftermath of the Albigensian Crusade. Unfortunately, if this through-the-looking-glass story is accepted, it is almost impossible to read an early inquisition testimony as saying anything other than what this scholarly narrative says it must be saying. Ironically, even though the historiography of Catharism was set in place in the late nineteenth century with very little reference to the records of the inquisition, a great deal of the scholarship on medieval heresy over the last forty years has valiantly struggled to make these records fit this storyline. Indeed, even the simple fact that the word 'Cathar' was never uttered by anyone questioned by the inquisition is often passed over in silence.[9] Many histories of heretics and inquisitors are little more than exegeses on this fanciful plot. The modern fabrication of Catharism has come to constitute 'what really happened' for many historians – and yet this is to confuse the realism of good fiction for the reality of good history.

The present-day narrative of Catharism in seemingly saying everything that need be said about heresy (certainly before 1300) has had the effect of diminishing the historical necessity of trying to grasp why certain ideas had meaning for particular societies at specific times and places. In a number of recent studies using inquisition testimonies there is insufficient effort put into working out the relationship between what men and women habitually did and what they habitually thought. Of course, something like society exists for these historians, although it largely functions as a one-dimensional backdrop to the in-the-round vividness of ideas and discourses. More than that, these historians take it for granted that heresies and religions are defined by scriptural consistency and theological cogency, rather than the poorly articulated thoughts and anomalous opinions frequently to be found in the records of the inquisition. They are always searching for the unchanging pure doctrines of Catharism. Weightless and above the demands of historical contingency, a doctrine like dualism was simply 'in the air'.[10] Any (equally weightless) history can be strung together if you assume ideas float about like clouds or specks of pollen. This intellectualist bias was the explicit approach in studying heresy and religion a century ago and, despite the social historical emphasis of the 1960s and the postmodern turnings of the 1980s, remains the implicit method to this day.

Paradoxically, Le Roy Ladurie's *Montaillou* reinforces (as only a famous book can) the enduring bias that heresy and religion have nothing to do with society by barely mentioning the former (five paragraphs about Albigensians and Cathars in the Avant-propos) and treating the latter as relatively unimportant. This was the approach of the Annales school of historians in the 1960s (and only slightly altered a decade later with a dash of structuralist anthropology) where, after dismissing traditional historical narrative as *l'histoire événementielle*, systematic historical truth was to be found in the hierarchical layering of, first and foremost, economic, geographic and demographic data, followed by social structures, with ideas, politics, culture, and religion (and so heresy) drifting on top as windswept flotsam. It is easily forgotten that *Montaillou* is not really interested in individuals, despite all the wonderful testimonial extracts, it is about excavating the immutable structures of rural existence. There is an underlying assumption that if the material world is unchanging, as physical existence in the medieval countryside is frequently thought to be, then the beliefs concerned with that world are assumed to be unchanging as well. Rural communities, tied to the soil, trapped in the cyclical movement of the seasons, forever dwelling in an eternal present and so denied the virtues of linear time, never change the way they do things, never change the way they think things. These premises are as unsound in the treatment of inquisition testimonies as is the bias towards ideas.

A dichotomy between ideas and society, matter and metaphor, what was done and what was thought, has always existed within the discipline of history. It has always needed to be overcome. Anthropology seemed to offer some promise in this direction in the 1960s and 1970s, if for no other reason than that it suggested this chasm not only should be bridged but also could actually be traversed without any loss of disciplinary identity for the historian. This promise is still unfulfilled. As far as the records of the inquisition are concerned, not only did methodological innovation stall in the early 1980s but, in an odd turn of events, these sources were studied less than they had been a decade earlier. This was reversed in the late 1990s with a renewal of interest in heretics and inquisitors. Much of this newer scholarship is superb, and not at all lacking in sophistication, yet what seemed so promising about anthropological methods almost half a century ago is still missing. (Although some historians have adopted the relentless authorial self-reflexiveness from recent anthropology and literary theory, along with the morally and intellectually dubious arguments for using the relentless 'I'.) This is not nostalgia for a historiography that might have been, or even regret for the idealist paths many scholars followed in the 1980s. Rather, this false dichotomy between ideas and society must be actively overcome, or at the very least acknowledged as an enduring problem, if anything new and worthwhile is to be said by the historian.

Past worlds can only be understood if evoked as fully as possible. No bias towards ideas. No dismissal of what is not the stuff of thoughts. A world exists from one day to the next, from one decade to another, because of an interweaving of thoughts and actions so individually intimate, so communally strengthening, that the relations a person (or thing) maintains in the material realm entrenches the relations he or she (or it) maintains in the metaphoric, and vice versa. In other words, how men and women owned property, dressed themselves, lay in bed, or greeted each other, were inescapably tied to what they knew about heresy, holiness, the question of evil, or the sufferings of Christ. Moreover, this histor-ical evocation of a world adds up to nothing unless it coalesces into an aesthetic whole. History is more art than science, striving for the precision of the imagi-nation. Only through imaginative rigour does imaginative sympathy occur. In training the imagination at overcoming the sheer incomprehensibility of the past by an effort at once intellectual and aesthetic, the historian moves closer to a more exacting and truthful vision of an expired reality. Historians should always aspire to the truth, even if they know they will never achieve it, even if they know that it is (as it must be) forever out of reach.

## VIII

What does na Aimerzens Viguier's testimony reveal about her and her world, the inquisitors and heretics? The good women, for a start, cannot be understood without first understanding the 'good men'. A good man (*bon ome* in Occitan, *bonus homo* in Latin) was a 'heretic' for the inquisitors by the middle of the thir-teenth century. A good man knew and accepted this about himself by 1250, as did any person who welcomed or sheltered him. A hundred years earlier this was not the case. Apart from 'good man' being a courteous epithet for any man in the lands of the count of Toulouse, in every village there were one or two very special good men who were the embodiments of courtliness, honour and holiness. These holy good men did not think they were heretics, and even after 1170 when travelling Cistercian preachers accused them of heresy, they and most villagers dismissed the accusation. These good men lived and preached openly. In all the confessions to Bernart de Caux and Joan de Sant-Peire by any man or woman over forty, every person remembered being courteous to the holy good men, recalled genuflecting thrice and saying: 'Bless us, good men, pray God for us.' The holy *cortezia* given to the good men was the idealized version of the daily cycles of *cortezia* shaping the lives of every man, woman, and child. The vernacular term for courtesy given to the good men was *melhoramen* – transcribed by inquisitorial scribes as *melioramen* or *melioramentum* – and it meant, at one and the same time, improvement, betterment, perfection, moderation, accumulation of honour, the accrual of wisdom, and the reciprocal process of giving and receiving holiness. The inquisitors classified the *cortezia* given to the good men as 'adoration' – recalling the worship and liturgies of ancient heretics – obscuring the meaning, complexity and sheer ubiquity of courtliness.

Unlike the good men, the good women before the thirteenth century were all noble matrons and prepubescent girls. Thousands of noble little girls were made into good women for as little as a few weeks or for as long as three or four years. All these holy children, after their months or years of being good women, married upon reaching their majorities at twelve. No woman was a good woman during her years of fertility, the years of her youth, the years when she married, had children, and was a wife. Marriage was an episode in the lives of all women, a fecund season to be survived. The older noble matrons were women beyond the years of fertility, no longer able or willing to marry, sometimes widows, sometimes separated from elderly husbands, living together in twos or threes in tiny houses, nursing and teaching little girl good women. These older good women rarely left their houses, never preached, and were given few if any courteous greetings. Even the name 'good woman' was a very faint echo of the social and moral complexities resounding within 'good man'. The good women, infants or adults, never thought that they were heretics.

Little girls were no longer becoming good women when na Aimerzens Viguier was led by her aunt to the village of Auriac in 1223. The two good women she met were vagrant fugitives, who understood that they were now heretics. What is so fascinating was that these good women preached and received the *melhoramen*, both of which would have been almost unthinkable only two decades earlier. Equally inconceivable was that an adolescent like Aimerzens needed instruction in holy decorum towards the good women. The fact that *cortezia*, holy or otherwise, was losing some of its meaning and power was vividly illustrated in the humiliation of Aimerzens by the good women. This is why it was not the thought of a demon growing inside her that so upset Aimerzens, such a metaphor of capricious growth and reproduction was the very definition of a fertile adolescent, rather it was the disgrace of being mocked over such an unavoidable fact of feminine existence, that severed all love and loyalty the girl had for the holy good women. Even if the good women themselves thought their little joke was also making fun of what Catholic intellectuals accused them of believing – as in the Devil made the world and there was no virtue in marriage – they still knew as noble women themselves that they were rude and disrespectful to a noble girl in a room full of nobles. Aimerzens may not have known how to be courteous in the right way to the holy good women herself, but she certainly knew they were meant to be the epitomes of *cortezia*, however faded this ideal was by 1223.

All good men and good women were fugitives by the time na Aimerzens Viguier met the good women in the village of Auriac. They were furtive figures, wandering throughout the countryside, mostly at night, from one hiding place to another. The communal structures of honour and courtesy that once needed (and made) them were largely broken by more than a decade of holy war. They now personified social and sacred nostalgia. This hearth and holy sentimentality applied to the men and women who consciously became 'believers of heretics'. Some good men were called 'deacons' around 1210 (although possibly this title was used here and there a few years earlier); more remarkably, a handful even anointed themselves 'bishops' by 1220. The adoption of such titles were attempts at holding onto deteriorating honour and at reshaping their identities amidst the communal and holy chaos around them. The good men and good women, formerly at the very centre of the moral and civic rhythms of their communities, were now marginal individuals; in short, they were now heretics not only to their accusers but to themselves. It is a cruel irony that the heresy investigated by Bernart de Caux and Joan de Sant-Peire was no more than atrophied nostalgia for the complex and distinctive world of the good men and good women before the Albigensian Crusade. The early inquisitions into heretical depravity persecuted a heresy of fatalistic sentimentality no more than two decades old.

All this (and much more) is not just the context in which na Aimerzens Viguier's testimony needs to be read, it is also where her testimony leads the thoughtful reader. Her confession makes clear the shift in the meaning and behaviour of the good men and good women before, during and after the Albigensian Crusade. It captures the atmosphere in villages and towns with the arrival of the inquisitors. Men, women and children closely watched their neighbours, counting the comings and goings in houses, remembering what they overheard through walls. Everyone was alert to doing nothing that might arouse the suspicion of heresy. Aimerzens addressed this worrisome issue at the very beginning of her testimony. The story she told of meeting the good women, with its emphasis on her need to be instructed in politeness towards them and their lack of courtesy towards her, established the narrative arc of her confession. She was not a 'believer' in the heretics and never had been, despite the abuse and beatings of her husband. Her overall testimonial narrative was not being rigidly linear, jumping back and forth through the decades. Yet she deliberately framed her memories within a plot line that simultaneously stressed her past innocence as an adolescent girl and her present reliability as a mature woman giving witness about the heretics and their believers. (Although the inquisitorial scribe perhaps imposed his narrative structure upon Aimerzens' testimony, she nevertheless approved the structure when he read it back to her.) Aimerzens willingly (and intelligently) shaped her personal history within the interrogatory template of the inquisitors, knowing that it was only through the artfulness of her confession that the truthfulness of what she said and did might be believed.

## IX

Inquisition records are demanding documents to read and use, but difficulty is not the same as impenetrability. More than any other primary sources from the Middle Ages, they are exceptional in allowing historians to evoke former ways-of-being-in-the-world as fully as possible, particularly amongst ordinary men, women and children. This is what makes them such wonderful and profound documents; this is why, far from limiting our vision of the past, they open it up in unexpected and exciting ways.

### Further reading

Christine Caldwell Ames, *Righteous Persecution: Inquisition, Dominicans, and Christianity in the Middle Ages* (Philadelphia: University of Pennsylvania Press, 2008).

Peter Biller, 'Christians and Heretics', in *Christianity in Western Europe, c. 1100–c. 1500* Miri Rubin (ed.), (Cambridge: Cambridge University Press, 2009), pp. 170–86.

Leonard E. Boyle, 'Montaillou Revisited: Mentalité and Methodology', in *Pathways to Medieval Peasants*, J.A. Raftis (ed.), Papers in Medieval Studies (Toronto: Pontifical Institute of Medieval Studies, 1981), 2, pp. 119–40.

James B. Given, *Inquisition and Medieval Society: Power, Discipline, and Resistance in Languedoc* (Ithaca and London: Cornell University Press, 1997).

Richard Kieckhefer, 'The Office of Inquisition and Medieval Heresy: The Transition from Personal to Institutional Jurisdiction', *Journal of Ecclesiastical History*, 46 (1995): 36–61.

Robert I. Moore, *The Formation of a Persecuting Society: Authority and Deviance in Western Europe, 950–1250*, 2nd edn. (Oxford: Blackwell, 2007).

Mark Gregory Pegg, *The Corruption of Angels: The Great Inquisition of 1245–1246* (Princeton: Princeton University Press, 2001).

Mark Gregory Pegg, *A Most Holy War: The Albigensian Crusade and the Battle for Christendom* (New York: Oxford University Press, 2007).

Edward Peters, *Inquisition* (New York and London: The Free Press, 1988).

### Notes

1  Toulouse, Bibliothèque municipale, MS 609, fol. 239v.
2  Peter Brown, '*SO* Debate: *The World of Late Antiquity* Revisted', *Symbolae Osloenses* 72 (1997): 21–2, aptly summarizing what the anthropology of Mary Douglas (and anthropology more generally) demands of the historian. Despite the thrill of Douglas' demand for 'utter consequentiality', Brown never totally succumbed. 'It always seemed to me that something was lost in the lightning speed with which she would make connections between ritual, social structure and possible varieties of religious experience in the charmed bell-jar of her rigorously neo-Durkheimian vision of society.'
3  Anthony Grafton, 'History's Postmodern Fates', *Daedalus* 135 (2006): 54–69.
4  Emmanuel Le Roy Ladurie, *Montaillou: The Promised Land of Error*, transl. Barbara Bray (New York: George Braziller, 2008); and Carlo Ginzburg, *The Cheese and the Worms: The Cosmos of a Sixteenth-Century Miller*, transl. John and Anne Tedeschi (Baltimore: The Johns Hopkins Press, 1995).
5  Yves Dossat, *Les crises de l'Inquisition Toulousaine au XIII$^e$ siècle (1233–1273)* (Bordeaux: Imprimerie Bière, 1959), pp. 118–21, 325–9.
6  Ad. Tardif, 'Document pour l'histoire du *processus per inquisitionem* et de l'*inquisitio heretice pravitatis*', *Nouvelle revue historique du droit français et étranger* 7 (1883):

669–78, and translated by Walter Wakefield in his *Heresy, Crusade and Inquisition in Southern France* (London: George Allen & Unwin, 1974), pp. 250–8.

7   Carlo Ginzburg, 'The Inquisitor as Anthropologist' in his *Clues, Myths, and the Historical Method*, transl. John and Anne C. Tedeschi (Baltimore: The Johns Hopkins University Press, 1989), pp. 156–64. Cf. Renato Rosaldo, 'From the Door of His Tent: The Fieldworker and the Inquisitor', in *Writing Culture. The Poetics and Politics of Ethnography* James Clifford and George E. Marcus (eds), (Berkeley, Los Angeles and London: University of California Press, 1986), pp. 77–97.

8   John H. Arnold, *Inquisition and Power: Catharism and the Confessing Subject in Medieval Languedoc*, The Middle Ages Series (Philadelphia: University of Pennsylvania Press, 2001), esp. pp. 11–15 on 'excess'; and Caterina Bruschi, *The Wandering Heretics of Languedoc*, Cambridge Studies in Medieval Life and Thought, 4th series (Cambridge: Cambridge University Press, 2009), esp. pp. 21, 29–44 on 'surplus'.

9   Carol Lansing, 'Popular Belief and Heresy', in *A Companion to the Medieval World*, Carol Lansing and Edward D. English (eds), (Oxford: Wiley-Blackwell, 2009), p. 287, although acknowledging that 'Cathar' was rarely used in the twelfth and thirteenth centuries, confusingly argues that this inappropriate term should still be used as it is 'less value-laden' than historically specific terminology and so less disconcerting to unwary (and incurious) scholars.

10  Peter Biller, 'Cathars and the Material World', in *God's Bounty? The Churches and the Natural World*, Peter Clarke and Tony Claydon (eds), (Woodbridge: Ecclesiastical History Society/Boydell, 2010), p. 106.

# 8  Coronation rituals and related materials

*Jinty Nelson*

Coronations have become rare, but as objects of study and interest, they have never lost their charm.[1] In the European Middle Ages, as in the ancient world, ritual practices surrounding kings and emperors attracted writers and their audiences. Again, from the sixteenth to the eighteenth centuries, as Europeans looked more critically on their own world, past and present, and compared oriental Old Worlds and the New World too, they noted rulers' inauguration rituals that seemed familiar, others that were alarmingly strange. In London, over the dinner table, probably some time in the 1640s – that is, in the midst of the English Civil War – an English lawyer reputed 'most learned' in his day, John Selden (d. 1654), had this to say about church rituals, or liturgies, in his own time and in other times: 'To know what was generally believed in all Ages, the way is to consult the liturgies, not any man's private writings.'[2] This thought-provoking claim is still worth thinking about by those of ordinary apprehension interested in medieval Europe, and not least in regard to coronations.

From the early Middle Ages onwards, the scripts for such rituals were written down in books, especially those used by bishops for the most important church services – books known as pontificals (from pontiff, meaning bishop). The surviving manuscripts are often large and beautifully written, as befitted the wealth and power of bishops and the most solemn rites of the Church. Each type of service that only a bishop could perform, which ranged from confirmation (a regular fairly frequent occurrence since every Christian baptised by a priest had also to be confirmed by a bishop), to king-making (which was much less frequent and normally required at least one archbishop plus a number of bishops), would be written out as a series of performance instructions often in red ink, known for that reason as rubrics. For instance:

> Two bishops lead [the king] by the hand from the assembly of the senior men into the church. And the clergy, with the two bishops going ahead and singing, sing the antiphon …

or:

> Then the highest of the bishops taking the ring and putting it on her [the queen's] finger must say [this].

These rubrics about ritual actions were interspersed with the texts of ritual words, that is, prayers, written in black ink, for instance:

> Holy Lord, omnipotent Father, eternal God, who consecrated your servant
> Aaron as a priest through anointing of oil, and thereafter in pouring of this
> anointment made priests, kings and prophets for the ruling of the people
> of Israel, and predicted through the prophetic voice of your servant David
> that the face of the Church would be made joyful with oil, so we ask that
> through this oil-anointing you come down to sanctify by your blessing this
> your servant [here the text often has 'N.', to signify: 'insert the appropriate
> name'] ... and cause him to secure the height of the kingdom in the counsels
> of knowledge and the judgement of fairness, so that through the anointing of
> oil and your blessing, you make him have, with your help, a face of joyful-
> ness prepared for the whole people.

These examples illustrate how the bishop's book gave instructions for big and complicated rituals, and so helped make good performance possible.[3] They also suggest how a cluster of rituals might interconnect, and belong in a broader context of belief and practice.[4] Books were important in preserving and stabilizing ritual forms, even if practice was never wholly standardized. But medieval written culture existed within an oral culture, or, as it has been called in a recent study of ritual, a 'presence culture': a term emphasizing the fundamental importance of face-to-face interaction.[5]

Can these rituals be read as expressions of 'what was generally believed'? In post-Reformation London in the 1640s, the liturgies with which Selden was familiar were in English. I translated the words quoted above from Latin. In the lands of the Catholic Church of Rome (and this remained true until 1965), all rituals were spoken in Latin. This fact must affect a historian's judgement as to how far laypeople attending the performance understood what was going on, and how far they felt themselves to be participating in, or 'believed' in, what was going on. Many medieval historians have become curious about these questions. Yet coronation rituals have featured in a curiously on-off way in modern historiog-raphy, bursts of interest and active research being followed by phases of neglect, and scepticism as to how far rituals reflect reality. The existence of rule-books is no proof that the rules were actually followed in practice. And even if they were, were they actually more 'private' than 'general' writings, to be understood only by clergy, or even in some cases, just one particular clerical group? What can histo-rians do with coronation rituals? In this chapter I want to revisit Selden's claim, and pursue the implications for our understanding of medieval mentalities. In the main section, I shall examine four case-studies from the earlier Middle Ages, and consider different ways in which modern historians have approached them.

But to start with, the special characteristics of coronation-rituals are worth comparing with those of other types of evidence for the medieval world. Laws, for instance, are prescriptive; that is, they set out what ought to be the case, rather than descriptive, recording what authors observe, or claim, is the case. They certainly have much to say about norms and values and about ideas of social power, but legal practice has to be looked for in actual cases. Ritual texts are in some ways prescriptive, as it were instructions for use: if you want to make a king, here's what to do. The assumption here, we note, is that a king has to be made. To use the language of more modern times, a king's son may have been heir-presumptive for years, or a king's rival may have been nursing a claim for years, but the old king's death is not followed immediately, or automatically, by a simple announcement of a new king's take-over. Cries of 'The king is dead: long live the king!' did resound at the funerals of kings in late medieval France, but they meant, not that succession was automatic, but that the kingship, unlike the individual king, never died.[6] There was often a gap of many months, or even longer, between one king's death and the inauguration of the next. Meanwhile royal documents were dated from the old king's death, and no break, or interregnum, was legally acknowledged. Modern historians have sometimes tied themselves in knots over which acts were constitutive, that is, made a king, and which were simply affirmative, declaring what had already happened. The distinction is legalistic. Medieval people, before and after the advent of a legal profession from the twelfth century on, seem to have thought in terms of a process including several stages, all of which mattered somehow or other, rather than assigning exclusive or overriding importance to just one. Churchmen have often been credited by historians with clear ideas quite distinct from the fuzzy ideas of laymen, and with the clear aim of asserting their own authority over laymen. Yet especially for the earlier Middle Ages, this approach seems unhelpful. From the ninth century, archbishops of Rheims claimed, with near-consistent success, the privilege of performing royal consecrations in France. But as will become clear, they never claimed a monopoly of king-making. Consecration-anointing, like other forms of liturgical anointing, according to church law could only be performed by bishops. It was important in making kings legitimate in the eyes of laypeople. Also important, though, were the legitimating acts of laypeople, sometimes in large numbers and in some cases including women, within coronation rituals, as will become clear below, and outside them – in watching kings as they rode round their kingdoms after their accessions, for example, or in processions welcoming kings into towns, in collective oath-swearings, in the offering of gifts, or, for a few, shouting their consent to the king's coronation before it could happen.

By the fifteenth century, there is more evidence for views other than those of clerical élites or legal experts. How did Joan of Arc, the seventeen-year-old daughter of a peasant couple in Lorraine, know that the king of France must be consecrated at Rheims?[7] The likely answer is that she was born and brought up in the village of Domrémy, whose church was dedicated to St Remy, alias Remigius, bishop of Rheims, who was believed to have received oil brought by a dove from heaven to consecrate Clovis (or Louis), the first Christian king of the Franks. In 1429, supporters of the English king's claims to rule France had the upper hand. Yet Joan arrived at the court of the French claimant Charles (VII) already with a passionate conviction, which she shared with her elders and social superiors, that only consecration by the archbishop of Rheims using that oil brought from heaven could transform Charles into the legitimate heir (his own mother was among many who doubted his paternity) and lawful king. Wartime conditions made the correct regalia unavailable; a substitute crown had to be found. No such problem arose in the case of the oil. Contemporary chroniclers record in detail the fetching of the holy oil 'according to custom' from the monastery of St-Rémy where it had always been kept safe, and the abbot's carrying of it from there up the road into the cathedral. Great crowds filled the city and its environs. It is a striking fact that though Rheims and its region were not within Charles' political control, no one attempted to stop the consecration, nor the visit to St-Marcoul near Rheims where French kings 'touched' scrofula sufferers with healing power thought to be received through the oil from heaven.[8] By the fifteenth century, a cluster of beliefs had solidified around the French ritual of royal anointing, generalized through a range of written texts and practices associated with the cult of Rémy and Rheims, with dynastic legitimacy that had been contested and had to be defended, and with an idea that the French as a nation were special.[9]

Used for the whole ritual process of king-making, 'coronation' is an anachronism, though I have used it in my title and shall continue to use it in what follows because it is well understood. It is true that crowning and crown-wearing were such visible acts, and crowning was so closely linked metaphorically with anointing, that in pontificals from the tenth century on, though the term *consecratio* remained more usual, the term *coronatio* did sometimes appear as the heading for the whole service, and in non-liturgical texts it increasingly often stood for the whole king-making process.[10] Nevertheless, in the Church's view, the anointing made the crowning possible. What Joan cared about above all was *le sacre du roi*, the king's consecration, that is, the anointing that infused the king with God's special grace. The ninth-century prayer text quoted near the beginning of this chapter makes very clear the biblical roots of anointing, and its exemplars, Aaron the priest and David, the king and prophet. Despite the prevalence of 'coronation' in modern English, the anointing, wherever and whenever practised (and this varied in Latin Europe) was, and has always remained at the very heart of the religious meaning of royal inauguration: as the Bible said of Saul newly-anointed by Samuel (I Sam 10: 9–10), 'God gave him another heart', and 'the spirit of God came upon him'. This meant that king-makings were rites of passage, or status-changing rites, later defined by church lawyers as sacraments, like baptism, or confirmation (associated with coming of age in many societies), or marriage, or the ordination of priests and bishops. All these rituals, in spiritual terms, made the recipient new, thanks to divine grace that was summoned and transmitted by clergy. Christians, as it were, bought a whole package, and the meanings of all these items were interconnected symbolically.[11]

*   *   *

The first early medieval case-study comes from the ninth century, and, as it happens, includes the first appearance of the story of Rheims' holy oil in a coronation ritual. This was the consecration of the Carolingian king Charles the Bald of West Francia (France) as king of Lotharingia (Lorraine), the 'middle' kingdom created by earlier family divisions of the Frankish empire.[12] The death of Charles' nephew Lothar in 869 without a legitimate male heir, and the presence of supporters of Charles among Lotharingia's lay and clerical élite, triggered a long-wanted opportunity of expansion and Charles grabbed it. He marched quickly on the Lotharingian centre, Metz, and his chief counsellor and ecclesiastical fixer Archbishop Hincmar of Rheims was ready with an appropriate ritual. Hincmar had already written consecration-rites for Charles' daughter as queen of Wessex on her marriage to the West Saxon king, and for Charles' wife Ermentrude, who having seen four of her six sons die (a fifth had been tonsured as a cleric), sought a special queenly consecration in 866.[13]

For Charles himself, Hincmar wrote a composite script:[14]

> Charles entered Lothar's kingdom and received the bishops at Verdun, then Metz. They came to the church of St Stephen[15] on 9th September.
>
> Before Mass, the bishop of Metz announced the following capitula.
>
> The bishop stated the Lotharingians' wish to have a king who could rule them well and lead them to salvation.
>
> The bishop stated their willingness to have Charles as king.
>
> The bishop asked Charles to spell out with his own words what his faithful people wanted to hear from him.
>
> Charles responded with the following announcement.
>
> He undertook to keep for all of them, clerical and lay, 'their law and rights, according to their due laws', asking for their continued help in return.
>
> After this Hincmar announced the following capitula.
>
> Hincmar justified his own presence at Metz.
>
> Hincmar gave further justifications.
>
> Hincmar added another justification.
>
> Hincmar declared Charles' qualifications to rule and asserted that the Lotharingians had commended themselves to him of their own free will just as all living creatures had assembled themselves into Noah's ark, signifying the church, without anyone compelling them to do so. He said that Charles' father the emperor Louis (Hludowicus) had been 'descended from Clovis (Hludowicus) the famous king of the Franks who had been converted along with his whole people, 3,000 Franks, not counting women and children, through the catholic preaching of Remigius the apostle of the Franks, and baptised on the vigil of Easter in the metropolis of Rheims, and then anointed and consecrated king with oil brought down from heaven, of which we still have some'.

Hincmar asked the assembled laity if it pleased them that the bishops should now crown Charles and consecrate him with a holy anointing. 'If you agree, please shout.' And when they all shouted together, Bishop [Adventius] said: 'Let us all give thanks to God with one accord, singing: Te Deum laudamus (We praise thee O God ...).'

Blessings: Bishop Adventius and five other episcopal colleagues each briefly invoked God's blessing on Charles

Hincmar uttered four slightly longer blessing-prayers.

At these words, 'May the Lord crown you', Archbishop Hincmar anointed him with chrism (consecrated oil mixed with sweet-smelling balsam) on the head, at his right ear and across his brow and down to his left ear.

'May the Lord crown you in his loving-kindness and his mercies, and may he anoint you with the oil of the grace of his holy spirit...'; and three further substantial blessings.

At these words 'May the Lord crown you', the bishops placed the crown upon his head.

'May the Lord crown you with glory and justice ... ' At these words, 'May the Lord grant that you will ... ', they gave him the palm and the sceptre.

'May the Lord grant that you may want and be able to do what he commands'. [The prayer-texts of the Mass follow.]

This has recently been called 'a very peculiar ceremony'.[16] It could equally well be said that, for a particular critical juncture, Hincmar produced a hybrid masterpiece of ritual composition and management. He brought together in 869 elements he himself distinguished as legal: teacherly episcopal expositions and overtly political exchanges involving king and lay élite set out with numbered headings (*capitula*) – and quasi-liturgical: blessings, consecration and investiture with regalia, but with the stage directions in the past rather than the present tense, hence giving an air of reportage rather than prescription. Hincmar combined stylized negotiation, as practised by successive Carolingian rulers, none more successfully than Charles the Bald, and a full-blown ecclesiastical coronation ritual, as choreographed by Hincmar. The resultant performance was opportunistically angled to the political needs of the moment, but also perfectly tailored to the 'presence culture'. There was a dimension beyond this: Hincmar set the whole thing into the annals in which, more or less contemporaneously year by year, he wrote up Charles' reign.[17] His presentation of the events at Metz was transmitted in several more manuscripts than the three that have survived. This helped ensure not just the diffusion of the story of the heaven-sent oil and its preservation at Rheims (not to mention the myth that the Carolingians were descended from the preceding Merovingian dynasty), but some very long-lasting effects on subsequent French coronations.

At this point I want to pause and reflect on what is problematic about 869. I am not referring to the fact that the apparent public relations success of Charles, and Hincmar, was short-lived. In 870 Charles had to settle for a partitioning of Lotharingia with his brother; and within a few decades, the West Frankish king lost the remaining part of the middle kingdom as well. I am concerned, rather, with a methodological question. Hincmar in 861 had taken over the writing of what he called 'the deeds of our kings', a continuation of the annals that recounted the history of the Frankish kingdom from 714 (when the Carolingian dynasty definitively emerged). These annals branched into different versions after 830, and the branch continued by Hincmar was the West Frankish one (the so-called *Annals of St-Bertin*).[18] He produced a year-by-year record, written up more or less contemporaneously, king-focused, and with audiences in view that included his own entourage, but also, very probably, the royal court, and great churches that were court-connected. Hincmar was sometimes economical with the truth, often highly tendentious, self-justifying on a heroic scale, as in 869, and capable of forging texts to score legal points in his frequent disputes over his church's privileges. The fact that Hincmar put the Metz coronation into these annals, far from establishing the truth of his 869 story, arguably puts a large question-mark against it. Historians in recent years have stressed – belatedly, perhaps – that medieval annalists were not like themselves, aiming at objective analysis, but wordsmiths, with literary and rhetorical agendas, writing to persuade. Annalists were not analysts. When they wrote about rituals, whose meanings were symbolic, slippery and contestable, they were particularly liable to twist, over-interpret, and occasionally invent. Because Hincmar's report on 869 is just one such authorial construct, obeying no professional rules of scientific method, it can be neither verified nor falsified. An episode in Hincmar's annal for 864 is in fact the star construct deconstructed in a recent book by the French-American scholar Philippe Buc. Another contemporary annal-writer, Buc notes, in a different account of the same episode, gave it a different meaning. How to know 'what, if anything, had really happened'? Buc's answer is: 'One should give up the attempt to reconstruct the events ... and rather concentrate on the meanings different authors wanted to convey in recounting them.'[19]

I favour doing both, and more. That meanings are disputed presupposes a context of shared expectations and understandings. Plural accounts can also cross-validate each other. The ritual at Metz was mentioned by two other annalists, one contemporary (the East Frankish *Annals of Fulda*), another writing a generation later (Regino of Prüm).[20] Both offered much shorter accounts of the ritual, and what they chose to say differed; but they converged on the point that Charles was consecrated at Metz, and that his objective was to acquire Lotharingia. Charters, formal legal documents usually giving things or judgements, form another type of evidence, equally subject to deconstruction, but with internal rules that make historicity testable. Charles issued a charter 'on 9 September 869, in the first year of our succession to Lothar's kingdom' – the original still survives in the archive of the Metz area – granting lands to the church of St-Arnulf at Metz, the burial-place of Charles's father Louis. The beneficiary was the abbot of St-Arnulf, Charles's son Carloman to whom he had just granted the abbacy. A few weeks later, Charles acted as ruler in the middle kingdom: he notified the archbishop of Vienne that he had granted the bishopric of Grenoble to a former palace cleric of Lothar's, and shortly afterwards, in another charter dated in the first year of his Lotharingian succession, he settled the affairs of the church of St-Evre at Toul, so that they returned to their happy state in the reign of Louis, Charles's father.[21] In these documents, meanings converge. Hincmar the annalist says Charles then went to the palace at Aachen. Regino the chronicler says the same, adding, 'because Aachen was seen as the seat of the empire, and many more people flooded to him there'.[22]

Case-study two is an event long regarded by German historians as foundational: the coronation in 936 of Otto I, which 'the [East] Franks and the Saxons had determined was to be held at the palace at Aachen, the place of universal election'. The information comes from the monk and historian Widukind of Corvey in Saxony.[23] Given that the tenth century was a period generally poor in sources by comparison with the ninth, German historians have mostly welcomed Widukind's detailed two-part near-contemporary account, because it seems more precisely datable and locatable, and exudes a stronger sense of actuality, than any coronation-*ordo*:

> The dukes, the leading men among the counts and a crowd of the more important warriors assembled in the yard of Charlemagne's church, placed the new ruler on the throne which had been constructed there, gave him their hands and offered their fidelity, and promising help against all his enemies, they made him king according to their custom. Meanwhile Archbishop Hildebert of Mainz, the clergy and the laypeople waited inside the church. ... When the new king had processed in, the archbishop advanced to meet him, touched the king's right hand with his left, then led the king into the middle of the church and turned to the people standing about them: 'Look, I bring before you Lord Otto, elected by God, already designated by [his father] Henry, now made king by all the leading men. If this election pleases you, signify by raising your right hand to heaven'. At this, all the people raised their right hands to heaven, and with a loud shout called down prosperous things on the new leader. The king, dressed in a close-fitting tunic according to the custom of the Franks, was led behind the altar on which lay the royal insignia: sword with swordbelt, cloak and armills [arm-rings], sceptre and staff, and diadem.

After emphasizing Hildebert's eminent qualifications for his role ('he was a Frank, a man of wondrous sanctity and superior understanding'), Widukind gave the texts of the prayers uttered by the archbishop as he invested the new king with the various insignia. Only after these came quite brief statements about Otto's anointing and coronation, and enthronement. After mass, the king walked to the palace, and

> ... sat down with the bishops and all the people while the dukes waited on them: Duke Gislebert of Lotharingia was chamberlain, Duke Eberhard of Franconia steward Duke Herman of Swabia cupbearer, and Duke Arnulf of

Bavaria, marshal; Count Siegfried, highest of the Saxons and brother-in-law of Henry [therefore Otto's uncle] was governing Saxony [and therefore not at Aachen] at this point, against enemy attacks, and he was minding the young Henry [Otto's younger brother]. Then, the king, after honouring each of the great lords with an appropriate gift according to royal munificence, dismissed the multitude with great good cheer.

As in 869, a striking element in the ritual process was a kind of election. In 936, this was done in separate parts: outside the church, the acceptance of the new king by the dukes, counts and warriors and their offering of fidelity, 'according to their custom', and inside the church, the question-and-answer between arch- bishop and people, reminiscent of 869, at the beginning of proceedings. Though Widukind expresses no special interest in consecration, he does say that an anointing occurred, having earlier in his work said that Otto's father had refused anointing. This contrast implies that Otto was more keen than his father to play up continuity with Frankish precedent, a theme that runs through this whole set- piece narrative. There is some liturgical evidence, in the form of an early tenth- century coronation-*ordo*, known to historians as 'the Early German *ordo*', to set alongside Widukind's account.[24] Both *ordo* and historical narrative convey the idea that Otto and his people considered election and anointing complementary rather than somehow opposed. The author of the *ordo*, like Widukind, repeatedly uses the phrase *clerus et populus*, a stock phrase in liturgy and law which had special salience for these writers; the *ordo*, like Widukind, stresses the position of a *designatus princeps*, or king-designate, has stage directions for an elective question-and-answer procedure, and uses the term 'king' only after the anointing. The insignia in this *ordo*, as in Widukind's account, have a military aspect: in both texts, the armills and the military cloak appear as a pair of items; in both, there is a giving of a sword, which, though the *ordo* provides no prayer at this point, could hardly be other than a warrior's symbol. The first part of the sword-prayer as given by Widukind borrows directly from the Second Book of Maccabees 15: 16, in the Vulgate Bible: 'Receive this holy sword, a gift from God, with which you may drive out all the enemies of my people Israel' – Widukind substitutes for that last phrase, 'the enemies of Christ, barbarians and bad Christians', adding 'by the divine power given to you and by the power of the whole empire of the Franks'. Finally, the coronation-feast picks up once again on elective themes. Bishops and laymen sat at the king's coronation feast, no doubt in a hierarchical order and just possibly in ethnic sections, but at the same table. The late Tim Reuter wryly pointed out that the way Widukind depicted the dukes as representing their own peoples as well as serving them 'probably did their own … position within their duchies little harm'.[25] These features taken together suggest some consensus on 'what was generally believed' about the point of Otto's coronation. In the nineteenth and earlier twentieth centuries, there was a comfortable historians' consensus too: as evidence for 936, liturgy did not lie, and neither did Widukind.

In recent years the deconstructive turn of historical criticism has left consensus quite severely mauled. It is not hard to spot discrepancies between the *ordo*'s account and that of Widukind, who mentions the anointing only briefly and places it *after* the handing-over of the insignia.[26] To suppose the pursed-lipped author at work with the *ordo* on his desk, changing or omitting parts of it to suit an ideological agenda, rests on an unprovable assumption. A learned monk could have invented prayer-texts. His historical accuracy or otherwise cannot be measured by checking him against an *ordo* he may not have known, nor against any other more nearly-contemporary accounts of 936. Yet one strictly contemporary year-by-year annalist, Flodoard of Rheims, did have something to say about the circumstances:

> because Henry I [Otto's father] had died [2 July 936], there arose a conflict over the kingdom among his sons, as a result of which the highest position fell to his son who was better by birth.[27]

This is just what Widukind implies by commenting on the absence from the coronation, and specifically from the feast, of Count Siegfried of the Saxons, who was 'minding' Otto's younger brother Henry. Widukind's account of the feast, therefore, not only takes up the theme of the opening section, the general agreement to Otto's elevation as king, but also adds the specific suggestion that the leaders of the duchies and their men assented to an *undivided* succession. This gives a much more plausible reading of Widukind's precisely calibrated emphases than modern suggestions that he wanted to downgrade the anointing's 'constitutive' significance and 'reduce' the bishops' role because of his own 'secular' outlook. *Saxon Deeds* of more kinds than one were indeed the theme of his *Three Books*.

Case-study three shifts the scene to England and the coronation of Edgar in 973 at Bath, an unprecedented location for such an event. Edgar's and Otto's coronations can be compared as regards the nature of the two major types of evidence historians have to go on, a narrative author and an *ordo*; but in the Anglo-Saxon case, so it has recently been alleged, the use of an *ordo* by the narrator, Byrhtferth, was so obviously extensive that the 'credibility' of the narrative, the Life of St Oswald, simply cannot be checked against it. This need not mean, though, that the *ordo* should be left out of consideration as evidence for 973, that the question of what did happen in 973 should be abandoned as unanswerable, and that a wise historian should retreat to analysis of the author's narrative and intent. The coronation ritual used for Edgar in 973 has been fairly convincingly identified as a particular version, B, of what is known as the Second English *Ordo*. By 973, that *ordo*'s basic form seems to have been in use for West Saxon, or English, coronations since 925: anointing, followed by coronation, the handing-over of regalia, and an enthronement. Two *un*usual things about the B version, however, are relevant to its dating and the context of its use. First the opening section:

> Here begins the coronation of the king.

> Two bishops lead him by the hand from the assembly of the senior men [the witan] into the church. And the clergy, with the two bishops going ahead and singing, sing the antiphon, 'May thy hand be strengthened', and the Verse, 'Glory to God'.

When the king comes to the church, he prostrates himself in front of the altar, and the hymn is sung, 'We praise thee O God, we acknowledge thee to be the Lord', and when this has been sung through the end, the king is raised up from the ground and let him who is the man elected by the bishops and by the people promise that he will keep these three laws and let him say in a loud voice before God and the whole people:

'These three things I promise to the Christian people under my rule in Christ's name, first that the church of God and the whole Christian people will keep true peace at all times according to our will; second that I shall forbid thefts and all crimes to people of all ranks; third, that I shall command fairness and mercy in all judgements, so that God, the clement and merciful, will grant his mercy to me and to you.'

When this has been performed, all are to respond, Amen.

The meeting of the assembly is not described, as it is in Widukind's account of 936, but the implication is clearly of a non-liturgical election procedure with its own ritual form. Inside the church, the king's prostration symbolizes the 'death' of the 'old' man preparatory to the making of the 'new': the religious meaning of the anointing. Part of this crucial transition is the promise to keep peace and law. This commitment was already present in an earlier Anglo-Saxon coronation ritual (the First *Ordo*), but there it came at the end of the rite and took the form of a program-matic statement of intent. Shifting it to the beginning, and making it into a promise of future action, gave it new significance as a precondition of the inauguration that was to follow. This brought the sequence into line with that prescribed in West and East Frankish rituals, and also with the practice for monks and abbots, priests and bishops, in which a (normally three-fold) promise preceded ordination. The West Saxon equivalent of Hincmar in Francia was Æthelwold, abbot of New Minster Winchester, then bishop of Winchester. It was very probably Æthelwold who produced the B version of the Second *Ordo* in time for Edgar's coronation in *c.* 960 at the beginning of his reign. In 973, he was being re-consecrated, to a wider kingdom, re-imagined as a kind of empire: hence the choice of Bath as the ritual setting, for just as Aachen, in the minds of the organizers of Otto's consecration in 936, evoked memories of Charlemagne, restorer of the Roman Empire in the West, so those who managed Edgar's 'imperial' coronation were inspired by the visibly Roman city of Bath.

Secondly, this *Ordo* is followed by a consecration-rite for a queen which has a short preface:

To do her honour she is anointed on the crown of her head by the bishop with the oil of sacred unction. And let her be blessed and consecrated in church, in the presence of the great men, to consortship of the royal bed, as shown on the following page. We further decree that she be adorned with a ring for the integrity of the faith and a crown for the glory of eternity.

This is not liturgical writing, but a record of a decision in a particular case, and its justification. The likeliest candidate is Edgar's wife Ælfthryth, whom he had married in 964 but apparently without her being consecrated at that time. Ælfthryth had emerged in the intervening years as a powerful figure, with a strong interest in pushing the claims of her son against those of Edgar's son by a different woman who had not been consecrated queen. As in 936, a particular conjuncture in the politics of dynasty, family and legitimacy spurred some hard thinking about the form of the coronation ritual.

A further cluster of points relating to 973's 'imperial' significance include Edgar's minting of a new Roman-style coinage-issue at Bath in 973; new legislation for 'all the nations, whether Englishmen, Danes or Britons' at ritualized submissions – which could also be portrayed as peace-meetings – involving Edgar with Scots, Welsh and Scandinavian chiefs at the border-city of Chester; a greater prominence of high-sounding styles in royal charters; and the building of palace-churches in England designed for imposing liturgical performances on Continental models. An exceptionally large number of the political élite were on the move in 973, involved in a presence culture that the king and his advisers had activated on a new scale. One final symptom of this communicative explosion could be the sermon which Archbishop Dunstan gave in the vernacular Old English, probably in 973, spelling out the nature of the Christian king's 'engagements' and the dangers that would befall if these were not kept, and then spelling out 'the duty of a hallowed king'.[28] Perhaps the sermon was delivered between the coronation and the ensuing mass; but just possibly, the sermon came immediately after, or even immediately before, the promises, and before the ritual process continued with the consecration: if so, it represented an extraordinary prefiguring of early modern coronation sermons in England, in which 'the church spoke prophetically'.[29] This was legitimation – but on terms: terms which, since the sermons were printed and widely distributed, were registered by 'the community of the realm'.

The fourth and last case-study is that of William the Conqueror's coronation in Westminster Abbey in 1066. The contentious issue here is whether the Second *Ordo* was used again on this occasion, thus highlighting continuity with the Anglo-Saxon past for a king who had a very particular need to demonstrate his legitimacy, or a revised and elaborated ritual, the Third *Ordo*. The manuscript evidence leaves open both possibilities; but the argument in favour of the Third *Ordo* can be proposed on three grounds. First, it consists of a splicing together of the Second *Ordo* with items from the German *Ordo* of the Mainz Pontifical used in the eleventh century but derived (in part) from the *ordo* probably used in 936; and this explains how its opening section speaks of a 'king elect', and after the three-fold promise and the responding 'Amen', includes a question-and-answer ritual of the kind used in 869 and 936:

> One of the bishops asks the people if they are willing to submit themselves to such a prince and rector and to obey his commands. Then the response comes from the clergy and people who stand surrounding him: *Volumus et concedimus* (We will [it] and we grant [it]).

UNIVERSITY OF WINCHESTER
LIBRARY

This is a case of belt and braces. It puts added emphasis on the conditional and consensual aspects of kingship, by giving the people a voice that isn't only liturgical – 'Amen' – but legal – 'We will and we grant'. It puts us in mind of the shouting together of 869, and the loud shout of 936. William the Conqueror's contemporary biographer, writing before 1070 the story of the Conquest, recorded this part of the ritual because it gave rise to an accident that almost derailed the Conqueror's whole project:

> The armed and mounted men who had been stationed around the abbey to guard it, hearing the tremendous shouting in a language they could not understand, thought that something had gone wrong, and under this misapprehension they set fire to the environs of the city.

The biographer says no more, heightening the impression of something that actually and inescapably happened, but which simply could not be turned into a 'good' story. If this points to the use of the Third *Ordo* on Christmas Day 1066, a further question then arises of whether this was the first occasion this *ordo* was used. That question needs to be answered with a 'no', if what William needed above all was legitimacy acquired through following Anglo-Saxon precedent, and plugging his regime into that of Anglo-Saxon kings, who could be represented as his legal predecessors. As it happens, the evidence for the dating and context of the Third *Ordo* allows that 'no': in other words, this ritual could have been used for an Anglo-Saxon king, namely, Harold, consecrated on 6 January 1066. The liturgical sources of the *ordo* were certainly available in England by the early 1060s. Ealdred, the Anglo-Saxon archbishop who consecrated first Harold, then William, in the same fateful year, had spent a year at Cologne in 1054–5, during which he may well have witnessed (or if not, surely heard all about) a king's consecration (Henry IV's on 17 July 1054) performed by his host the Archbishop of Cologne. William's initial choice, then, was to underscore continuity with the Anglo-Saxon past, and that was precisely what Ealdred personified. Only later did the Conqueror decide to excise Harold's reign from the historical record.

\*   \*   \*

Chronicles and other historical narratives, despite all their problems of interpretation, broadly confirm that accounts of actual coronations reveal what actually happened on particular occasions and in particular settings. Even though it can seldom be proved conclusively that an extant *ordo* was used on a particular occasion, the fact that it sometimes can be inspires confidence.[30] Beyond that, coronations reflect a profound process of ideological change and re-formation in the earlier Middle Ages, which resulted in Christendom's becoming thereafter more homogeneous, more comprehensively Christianized, more directly and pervasively inspired by biblical examples, and at the same time more committed to a view of rulership as constrained by aristocratic as well as ecclesiastical consensus. The world of assembly politics and presence culture that prevailed in this period accommodated all these characteristics.[31]

It is true that direct evidence for what was generally believed in the Middle Ages is often, and in the earlier centuries, commonly, in very short supply. I have tried not to gloss over the methodological problems, though I have rather played down the difficulties caused by legalistic interpretations, especially in the great tradition of historiography in German to which Anglophone medieval scholarship has owed and still owes so much.[32]

Janos Bak observed that he and Ralph Giesey (I would call them exemplary, in both senses, historians of their generation) had 'gradually given much more attention to the other side of the dualist equation in medieval monarchy – diets, parliaments, estates, electors – than our teachers ever did'.[33] I have followed a similar trajectory in this chapter, but it was not what I set out to do. I began with John Selden's contention about the liturgies as an excellent entrance-way into 'what was generally believed'. Then as I revisited a series of coronation rituals in a few fairly well-documented case-studies where other types of evidence are available, I found that 'other side of the equation' staring me in the face. When the locations of these rituals began to shift to fully-fledged urban sites, and repeats of ritual conjunctures generated rising expectations and notions of consent involved in legitimacy, the possibilities for wider participation seemed to grow. I have on the whole come to agree with Selden. And that means that I end by reversing a question I began with: what I would now want to ask is, how can medieval historians do *without* coronation rituals?

## Further reading

The following list is designed to give readers a sense of the historiography of coronation studies in English over the past half-century. Contributions to the edited works of Cannadine and Price, and Bak, and the special issue of *The Court Historian* for 2004, are packed with further references and cover periods and cultures far beyond medieval western Europe. Of special value are the collected papers of K. Leyser (1994) and T. Reuter (2006). I have put in two recent works in German, which I hope will soon be translated. One is Gerd Althoff's *Die Macht der Rituale: Symbolik und Herrschaft im Mittelalter* ('The Power of Ritual: Symbolism and Rulership in the Middle Ages') which brings together much work of German scholars in this field, his own not least, and provides a broader socio-logical context for coronation rituals. Though his focus is on Germany in the tenth and eleventh centuries, his insights have been more widely applied by scholars writing on France, England and Italy and across the span of the Middle Ages. The other is the modern German historian Barbara Stollberg-Rilinger's *Des Kaisers alte Kleider: Verfassungsgeschichte und Symbolsprache des Alten Reiches* ('The Emperor's Old Clothes: the Constitutional History and Symbolic Language of the Old Empire'), which applies some medievalists' insights and adds original and important ones of her own from which medievalists in their turn can learn a great deal.

Althoff, G. *Der Macht der Rituale: Symbolik und Herrschaft im Mittelalter* (Darmstadt: Wissenschaftliche Buchgesellschaft, 2003).

Bak, J.M. 'Medieval Symbology of the State: Percy E. Schramm's Contribution', *Viator* 4 (1973), 33–63.

Bak, J.M. 'Coronation Studies – Past, Present and Future', in Bak (ed.), *Coronations: Medieval and Early Modern Monarchic Ritual* (Berkeley CA: University of California Press, 1990), pp. 1–15.

Barrow, J. 'Chester's earliest regatta? Edgar's Dee-rowing revisited', *Early Medieval Europe* 10 (2001), 81–93.

Barrow, J. 'Demonstrative Behaviour and Political Communication in Later Anglo-Saxon England', *Anglo-Saxon England* 36 (2007), 127–50.

Buc, P. *The Dangers of Ritual* (Princeton and Oxford: Princeton U.P./OUP, 2001).

Buc, P. 'The monster and the critics: a ritual reply', *Early Medieval Europe* 15 (2007), 441–52.

Cannadine, D. 'The Context, Performance and Meaning of Ritual: The British Monarchy and the "Invention of Tradition", *c.*1820–1877', in E. Hobsbawm and T. Ranger (eds), *The Invention of Tradition* (Cambridge: CUP, 1983), pp. 101–64.

Cannadine, D. and Price, S. (eds), *Rituals of Royalty: Power and Ceremonial in Traditional Societies* (Cambridge: CUP, 1987).

Elze, R. 'The Ordo for the Coronation of Roger II of Sicily: An Example of Dating by Internal Evidence', in Bak (ed.), *Coronations*, pp. 165–78

Giesey, R.E. 'Inaugural Aspects of French Royal Ceremonials', in Bak (ed.), *Coronations*, pp. 35–45.

Jackson, R., 'General Introduction', *Ordines Coronationis Franciae, Texts and Ordines for the Coronation of Frankish and French Kings and Queens in the Middle Ages*, vol. 1 (Philadelphia PA: University of Pennsylvania Press, 1995), pp. 1–41.

Koziol, G. *Begging Pardon and Favor. Ritual and Political Order in Early Medieval France* (Ithaca NY: Cornell U.P., 1992).

Koziol, G. 'The Dangers of Polemic: is Ritual Still an Interesting Topic of Historical Study?', *Early Medieval Europe* 11 (2002), 1–28.

Leyser, K.J. *Rule and Conflict in an Early Medieval Society. Ottonian Saxony* (London: Edward Arnold, 1979), esp. Part III, 'Sacral Kingship', pp. 75–107.

Leyser, K.J. *Communications and Power in Medieval Europe*, 2 vols (London: Hambledon, 1994).

Nelson, J.L. *Politics and Ritual in Early Medieval Europe* (London: Hambledon, 1986) comprising seventeen collected papers, eight of them on coronation rituals.

Nelson, J.L. 'Hincmar of Rheims on King-Making: the Evidence of the Annals of St-Bertin, 861–882', in Bak (ed.), *Coronations*, pp. 16–34.

Nelson, J.L. 'The Lord's Anointed and the People's Choice: Carolingian Royal Ritual', in Cannadine and Price (eds), *Rituals of Royalty*, pp. 137–80, reprinted in Nelson, *The Frankish World 750–900* (London: Hambledon, 1996), ch. 6.

Nelson, J.L. 'Early medieval rites of queen-making and the shaping of medieval queenship', in A. Duggan (ed.), *Queens and Queenship in Medieval Europe* (Woodbridge: Boydell, 1997), pp. 301–15.

Nelson, J.L. 'Carolingian Coronation Rituals', *The Court Historian* 9 (2004), 1–13.

Reuter, T. *Medieval Polities and Modern Mentalities*, J.L. Nelson (ed.) (Cambridge: CUP, 2006).

Reuter, T. 'Assembly politics in western Europe from the eighth century to the twelfth', in Reuter, *Medieval Polities and Modern Mentalities*, J.L. Nelson (ed.) (Cambridge: CUP, 2006), pp. 193–216.

Stollberg-Rilinger, B. *Des Kaisers alte Kleider: Verfassungsgeschichte und Symbolsprache des Alten Reiches* (Munich: Beck, 2008).

Sturdy, D. '"Continuity" versus "Change": Historians and English Coronations of the Medieval and Early Modern Periods', in J.M. Bak (ed.), *Coronations*, pp. 228–45.

Warner, D. 'Comparative approaches to Anglo-Saxon and Ottonian Coronations', in C. Leyser and D. Rollason (eds), *England and the Continent in the Tenth Century* (Turnhout: Brepols, 2011), pp. 275–92.

# Notes

1  See D. Cannadine and S. Price (eds), *Rituals of Royalty: Power and Ceremonial in Traditional Societies* (Cambridge: CUP, 1987); J. Bak (ed.), *Coronations. Medieval and Early Modern Monarchic Ritual* (Berkeley and Los Angeles CA: University of California Press, 1989); *The Court Historian* 9 (2004): a special issue of this periodical devoted to coronations. Full references to papers cited from these volumes are given in Further reading.

2  J. Selden, *Table Talk* (London: 1689), p. 76. Some of Selden's conversational remarks were written down at the time by his secretary, Richard Milward, and published some decades later, to illustrate Selden's ability to 'convey the highest points of religion and the most important affairs of state to an ordinary apprehension'.

3  These examples of rubrical instructions come from the Second Anglo-Saxon king's *ordo* and the queen's *ordo*; the prayer-text comes from the First (i.e. earliest known) Anglo-Saxon king's *ordo*: for references see below.

4  See G. Althoff, J. Fried and P.J. Geary (eds), *Medieval Concepts of the Past: Ritual, Memory, Historiography* (Cambridge: CUP, 2002); also Althoff, in Further reading.

5  See Further reading, B. Stollberg-Rilinger.

6  R. Giesey, in Bak (ed.), *Coronations*.

7  See M. Warner, *Joan of Arc. The Image of Female Heroism* (London: Weidenfeld & Nicolson, 1981); K. Sullivan, *The Interrogation of Joan of Arc* (Minneapolis: University of Minnesota Press, 1999); C. Taylor, *Joan of Arc: La Pucelle* (Manchester: Manchester U.P., 2007).

8  M. Bloch, *The Royal Touch. Sacred Monarchy and Scrofula in England and France* (original French, *Les rois thaumaturges*, Paris: Publications de la Faculté de l'Université de Strasbourg, 1924, English translation by J.E. Anderson, London: Routledge & Kegan Paul, 1973).

9  C. Beaune, *The Birth of an Ideology: Myths and Symbols of Nation in Late-Medieval France*, transl. S.R. Huston, F.L. Cheyette (ed.), (Berkeley CA and Oxford: University of California Press, 1991).

10  When emperors were crowned in Byzantium, the patriarch's prayers included the same quotations from biblical passages about royal anointing as featured in western liturgies, yet these were treated as metaphors of divine blessing, and never translated into literal actions before the thirteenth century, under the influence of western clergy and (short-lived) western conquest. See D.M. Nicol, 'Kaisersalbung: the unction of emperors in late Byzantine coronation ritual', *Byzantine and Modern Greek Studies* 2 (1976), 37–52.

11  See Nelson, in Cannadine and Price (eds), *Rituals of Royalty*.

12  The political context is sketched by Nelson, *Charles the Bald* (London: Longman, 1992), esp. pp. 218–30.

13  *Ordo* of Judith, in R. Jackson, *Ordines Coronationis Franciae*, (Philadelphia PA: University of Pennsylvania Press, 1995), pp. 73–9; *ordo* of Ermentrude, Jackson, *Ordines*, pp. 80–6. Cf. Nelson, in *The Court Historian* (as n. 1 above).

14  I summarize from the text in Jackson, *Ordines,* pp. 87–109, with General Introduction, pp. 24–6.

15  This was the church in which Charles's father had been ritually recrowned in 835 after being deposed.

16  Jackson, *Ordines*, p. 87.

17  Nelson, 'Introduction', to Nelson, transl., *The Annals of St-Bertin* (Manchester: Manchester U.P., 1991).

18  Nelson in Bak (ed.), *Coronations*.

19  P. Buc, *The Dangers of Ritual* (Princeton and Oxford: Princeton University Press, 2001), p. 75.

20  *The Annals of Fulda*, T. Reuter, transl. (Manchester: Manchester U.P., 1992), p. 61; *History and Politics in Late Carolingian and Ottonian Europe. The Chronicle of Regino of Prüm*, transl. S. MacLean (Manchester: Manchester U.P., 2009), pp. 160–1.

21  Charters of Charles the Bald, *Receuil des Chartes de Charles II le Chauve*, G. Tessier (ed.), 3 vols (Paris: Imprimerie Nationale, 1943–1955), vol. II, nos. 328, 329, 330.

22  *Annals of St-Bertin*, pp. 164, 165; *History and Politics* (MacLean), p. 160.

23  Widukind, *The Deeds of the Saxons*, Book II, cc. 1–2, transl. B.H. Hill Jr, *Medieval Monarchy in Action* (London: George Allen and Unwin, 1972), pp. 113–14.

24  This early tenth-century *ordo* seems more likely to have been used in 936 than the *Ordo* of the Mainz Pontifical, of *c*. 950. But see D. Warner, 'Comparative Approaches to Anglo-Saxon and Ottonian Coronations', in C. Leyser and D. Rollason (eds), *England and the Continent in the Tenth Century* (Turnhout: Brepols, 2011), pp. 275–92.

25  T. Reuter, *Germany in the Early Middle Ages* (London: Longman, 1991), p. 149.

26  Warner, 'Comparative approaches', pp. 278–9, 282–6.

27  *The Annals of Flodoard of Reims*, ed. and transl. S. Fanning and B.S. Bachrach (Peterborough, ONT: Broadview Press, 2004), [s.a. 936], p. 28.

28  On 973, and on Dunstan's sermon, see Nelson, *Politics and Ritual in Early Medieval Europe* (London: Hambledon, 1986), pp. 300–3, 337–8. On ritual submissions, see J. Barrow, 'Chester's earliest regatta? Edgar's Dee-rowing revisited', *Early Medieval Europe* 10 (2001), 81–93, and Barrow, 'Demonstrative Behaviour and Political Communication in Later Anglo-Saxon England', *Anglo-Saxon England* 36 (2007), 127–50.

29  D. Sturdy, in Bak (ed.), *Coronations*, pp. 241–2.

30  R. Elze, in Bak (ed.), *Coronations*, pp. 165–78, does this for the *ordo* of Roger II of Sicily, used in 1130. A small number of indicative changes were made in what is basically the *ordo* of the Mainz Pontifical.

31  Reuter, 'Assembly politics in western Europe from the eighth century to the twelfth', in Reuter, *Medieval Polities and Modern Mentalities* J.L. Nelson (ed.), (London: Hambledon, 2006), pp. 193–216.

32  Bak, 'Medieval Symbology of the State: Percy E. Schramm's Contribution', *Viator* 4 (1973), 33–63.

33  Bak, in Bak (ed.), *Coronations*, p. 15, n. 34.

# 9    The sources for manorial and rural history

*Philip Slavin*

The records of rural and peasant life – the records of manorial history – do not become plentiful until the thirteenth century. In England, which is our area of concentration, there are very few records about rural life from the pre-Conquest era (that is, before 1066). This reflects the comparatively low degree of literacy and the undeveloped level of bureaucracy and administration. The Norman Conquest brought about numerous administrative reforms, stimulating the steady growth of official documents. The period of *c.* 1270–1380 was the heyday of manorial records and record-keeping. In these years the royal administration reached the peak of its medieval sophistication, producing innumerable documents of all sorts. It was also a period when the written word in a legal document became more important and authoritative than ever before (as reflected in the famous 1279 *Quo Warranto* statute and proceedings of Edward I). In these years we have a very considerable rise in literacy across much of society, covering both 'scholarly' and 'pragmatic' literacy. And finally – and perhaps most importantly for us – this was the era of direct demesne management. Lords directly controlled their manors, and this required them to keep careful managerial records of their holdings.

Broadly speaking, the primary sources dealing with medieval rural life can be divided into two main categories: those concerning the demesne, or the seigniorial sector (or the lord's sector), and those dealing with peasantry. That is not to say that the two sectors did not overlap or intersect. Indeed, in some instances the same source may reveal information about both the administration and finances of the lord's demesne and also tell us about its peasants. For instance, one manorial court roll can tell us about marriage patterns of peasants and, at the same time shed light on the lord's revenue as received from miscellaneous fines that could be levied on peasant marriage. Similarly, tithe accounts indicate how much the peasants produced and how much the lords received. Manorial accounts may list both revenue received from tenants' rents and also the revenues spent on seigniorial expenditures. Thus, though the distinction between the two types of sources is not clear-cut, we should keep in mind that most of the sources dealing with rural life have a clear 'bias' towards the lords' sector. As a result, it is hardly surprising that there is a wide gap in our knowledge and understanding of the two sectors. This essay will aim to avoid such bias and to provide as balanced a coverage for both sectors as possible.

## Demesne accounts

It is not an overstatement to assert that demesne accounts (often referred to as 'manorial accounts', or 'compotus rolls') represent the single most important source for study of agrarian history of late medieval England. In essence, these were annual agricultural and financial reports, rendered by an official of the lord who oversaw the demesne (he usually being a bailiff, sergeant or reeve). The accounts were on an audit basis and recorded (and preserved for us) by a demesne clerk. The format of the account was that of 'charge–discharge' accounting; the revenue received (the incoming moneys) spelled out in a section that preceded the listing of the expenditures (the outgoing revenues – the expenses). In most cases, the account was rendered on an annual basis, with the year usually running between the Michaelmas (29 September) of previous year to that of the present year. Sometimes, the accounts cover shorter periods (four months or half a year, for instance). Normally, the accounts consist of two main sections: the financial tallies of incoming and outgoing revenues, written on the front side of the roll, and then the agricultural account, written on the reverse or the dorse side.

The financial section of the account deals with cash revenue received and then with the expenditures. The main source of the lord's revenue was derived from rents, court fines, and pannage and pasturage profits, as well as from sales, usually of arable crops, livestock produce and live animals. The expenditure section records various matters, including purchases of grain and livestock, horse shoeing, cart repairs and purchases, soil marling, grain threshing and winnowing, pasture mowing and harvest work.

The agricultural section, compiled on the dorse side of the account, is divided into three parts: crops (*compotus grangii*) , livestock (*compotus stauri*) and labour (*opera*). The first part of the section reveals, in amazing detail, how much was sown and reaped and how the year's harvest was disposed of (mostly through sales and consumption). In some instances the crop yields were recorded in the margins of the account, although often we need two consecutive accounts to calculate yields. The livestock part provides much information about animal husbandry. The demesne animals are divided into five groups: horses, bovids (oxen and cattle), sheep, swine and poultry. For each group the account records detailed patterns of annual gain and loss, including births, deaths, transfers, sales and purchases of the various animals. In addition, the accounts carefully specify the sex and age of the animals. The third part of the agricultural sections records labour; productivity rates, that is, the amount of food and fodder produced by each labourer in terms of number of works per season. It should be noted, however, that not every account includes the information about labour services. Furthermore, in some instances we also have information about fruit productivity from orchards, honey production by local beehives, hay yields from pasture, firewood and catches of fish.

As far as their physical layout or arrangement is concerned, we can speak about three types of demesne accounts: individual accounts, covering a single manor; grouped accounts, covering a group of manors; and enrolled accounts, covering a group of manors that can constitute an entire estate. Perhaps the single best known series of enrolled accounts are the pipe rolls of the bishopric of Winchester. The Winchester pipe rolls are a truly unique source in terms of their chronological coverage. Around 1300 the bishop of Winchester possessed over fifty manors, mostly in Hampshire but also in Berkshire, Buckinghamshire, Oxfordshire, Somerset and Surrey, thereby making him one of the richest land-lords in the realm. With very few gaps, the pipe rolls of these manors or estates run between 1208 and 1472, giving us about 10,000 individual rolls. No other estate can match that record. For instance, of twenty manors owned by Norwich Cathedral Priory only two (Sedgeford and Martham) have a relatively good run. Canterbury Cathedral Priory can boast only about sixteen demesnes for which we have a good chronological string of records, and this is out of a total of some sixty different demesne holdings. And the figure for extant records is even lower for the Abbey of Glastonbury estates; with just under forty demesne manors at hand only two can offer us good chronological coverage (Longbridge Deverill and Monkton Deverill). Roughly speaking, about three-quarters of all surviving manorial accounts relate to ecclesiastical estates, and those dealing with lay lord-ship come mostly from the estates of greater magnates, such as Sir Adam de Stratton (d. 1291/2) or Henry de Lacy (1249–1311). Accounts from petty lords' demesnes are generally rare; we do have a few.

The Winchester rolls also happen to be the earliest extant accounts, and it is likely that it was Peter des Roches, bishop of Winchester (1205–38) who intro-duced the practice of manorial accounting to the estates. His model would have been the royal pipe roll, a kind of financial record that went back at least to the early 1120s.[1] Although there are some surviving manorial accounts from the 1230s, it was not until the 1260s that they gain ground and not until the 1270s that they become plentiful. The decline of direct seigniorial management after the Black Death – when lords were more inclined to rent out their estates for a set sum – meant the decline of (direct) demesne accounting. By *c.* 1420, the majority of demesnes were leased out and hence it becomes more difficult to track their annual accounts. Some lords, however, were more conservative and continued to supervise their estates directly. Several demesnes of the bishop of Winchester (with their accounts) survived into the 1460s and 1470s and some manors of Glastonbury Abbey and Battle Abbey were kept at hand until the 1490s. Even more exceptional were the Durham demesne of Elvethall, in posses-sion of Durham Cathedral Priory, and the Devon manor of Hurdwick, belonging to Tavistock Abbey, whose accounts run all the way to the eve of the Dissolution of the monasteries in the 1530s. But these were clear exceptions and, as a rule, it is difficult to track demesne accounts in large numbers after *c.* 1420.

The survival of accounts across the land also varies considerably from county to county. This is indicated in a database of demesne accounts I am in the process of putting together (Figure 9.1). Though all these figures are preliminary they provide a good sense of the main trends or clusters of surviving records. The thickest coverage is for Norfolk, with about 200 demesnes. Norfolk is followed by Yorkshire with about 140 represented demesnes. Essex, Kent, Somerset, Sussex and Wiltshire each come in with slightly over 100. At the other extreme some of the northern counties standout: Cheshire (five demesnes), Cumberland (six demesnes), Lancashire (nine demesnes), Northumberland (seven demesnes) and

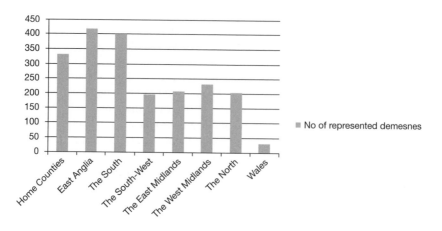

Source: Slavin's database of manorial accounts

Notes
Home Counties = Bedfordshire, Berkshire, Buckinghamshire, Hertfordshire, Middlesex, Oxfordshire and Surrey; East Anglia = Cambridgeshire, Essex, Norfolk and Suffolk; the South = Hampshire, Isle of Wight, Kent, Sussex and Wiltshire; the South-West = Cornwall, Devon, Dorset and Somerset; the East Midlands = Huntingdonshire, Leicestershire, Lincolnshire, Northamptonshire, Nottinghamshire and Rutland; the West Midlands = Cheshire, Derbyshire, Gloucestershire, Herefordshire, Shropshire, Staffordshire, Warwickshire and Worcestershire; the North = Berwickshire (in Scotland), Cumberland, Durham, Lancashire, Northumberland, Westmorland and Yorkshire; Wales = Glamorganshire, Monmouthshire and Pembrokeshire.

*Figure 9.1* Regional distribution of surviving manorial accounts (*c.* 1208–1530)

Westmorland (one demesne), though we note that the nearby county of Durham can offer over thirty demesnes. The only represented demesne in Scotland is Coldingham.[2] For Wales, there are twenty-seven demesnes in Monmouthshire, a further two in Pembrokeshire and one in Glamorganshire.[3] Several factors stand behind this uneven distribution. First, the thickest coverage seems to be in counties where manorialism was at its strongest. Second, there seems to have been a positive correlation between population density and the number of demesne estates in each county. Third, there seems to be a comparable correlation between the net worth of each county and the number of represented demesnes.

Because of their extensive nature (an average fourteenth-century account contains around 8,000 words), very few accounts have appeared in print. However, there are several useful critical editions, including some seventy accounts from Cuxham (Oxfordshire) between 1275 and 1359, several Winchester pipe rolls, and the 1296–7 enrolled account for the earldom of Cornwall.[4] Furthermore, there are some occasional editions of individual accounts, though these can be hard to access and are sometimes below current editorial and scholarly standards.[5] The lion's share of manorial records still remains, unpublished, in various repositories and archives. These fall into three main categories: public record offices and libraries; institutional muniments; and private collections. The single largest corpus of manorial accounts is at the National Archives, Kew Gardens (about 15,000 rolls from all over England). The Norfolk Record Office, Norwich, holds over 2,000 accounts, mostly from Norfolk. Other record offices contain no more than several hundreds of accounts each, at best. Institutional muniments of value include the Westminster Abbey muniments, with some 2,000 accounts; Canterbury Cathedral Archives, with a further 1,800 accounts; Durham Cathedral Priory with about 400 accounts, and Merton College Archives, Oxford, with some 300 accounts. Private collections are usually in the possession of aristocratic families and the degree of access depends largely on the goodwill of the owners and their archivists. The archivists of Longleat House, Berkeley Castle and Arundel Castle proved to be very helpful. Access to some other muniments, on the other hand, remains, at present, closed.

There is still no single central reference guide to demesne accounts. The most comprehensive tool remains the Manorial Documents Register (MDR) at the National Archives. At present, there is an ongoing digitization of the MDR; as of May 2011, fifteen counties with surviving accounts have been computerized. Despite its attempt to be comprehensive, however, the MDR does not cover all the manors with the surviving accounts. Another important handlist is Appendix C to Langdon's PhD dissertation on oxen and horses from 1983, which includes shelf-marks of the 1,565 accounts utilized in his study.[6] In addition, there are several useful guides, including catalogues of manorial documents of Glastonbury Abbey, Bury St Edmunds Abbey and Norwich Cathedral Priory.[7] There is also a comprehensive catalogue of Kentish accounts up to 1350.[8] The majority of record offices have now fully searchable online catalogues where the accounts and their shelf-marks can be spotted. Also, several institutional archives, including those of Canterbury Cathedral, Durham Cathedral and the London Guildhall have recently introduced online catalogues.

The unique nature of manorial accounts has attracted much scholarly attention. Most recently, Bruce Campbell has put together a most valuable database of late medieval crop yields, based on over 30,000 observations between *c.* 1208 and 1492.[9] Similarly, John Langdon produced a national-scale study of horses and oxen, based on 864 sampled demesnes.[10] Macro-history is only one approach, however. In his 2005 monograph *Decision-Making in Medieval Agriculture*, David Stone employed a meticulous micro-analysis of one demesne (Wisbech Barton, Cambridgeshire), to show that late medieval peasants knew to respond rationally to different economic and ecological challenges.[11]

It is perhaps speculative to calculate how many demesne accounts were ever created in the heyday of late medieval manorialism. It is equally difficult to estimate how many have survived into our own days. Assuming that of about 14,350 settlements recorded in the subsidy roll of 1334, about 12,700 were manors and about one-fifth of them kept accounts (judging from the surviving coverage), between 1270 and 1400, we may estimate that over 400,000 separate manorial accounts were produced. At present, each demesne has, on average, seven surviving accounts (a 5 per cent survival rate). This presents us with roughly 20,000 surviving accounts. These estimates, as crude as they are, concur with the overall format and structure of my ongoing database of demesne accounts under the tentative name MAME (Manorial Accounts of Medieval England). As of May 2011, data on agricultural produce, livestock husbandry and prices have been extracted and tabulated from over 20,000 accounts representing 2,023 separate demesnes or manors, though there are more to enter in before the task is complete. The goal is to convert these tabulations into a searchable online database, available for the community of scholars.

## Manorial court rolls

To a considerable extent manorial court rolls represent a complementary source to demesne accounts and it is likely that the two were usually written by the same manorial clerk. Broadly speaking, manorial court rolls are minutes of local courts (*curie*) regulating and dealing with various legal matters that arose within the manor. While earlier court rolls tended to focus mainly on land transactions between free peasants, they soon expanded into other aspects of manorial life, concerning both free and unfree peasants. These included criminal offences, such as violent behaviour, thefts, the reception of criminals and bad work performance; land transactions, such as property sales, purchases and exchanges; quarrels over land; credit and indebtedness; payments of customary fines and dues; and elections of manorial officials.

The frequency of court holdings varied from place to place and from period to period. To a large degree the frequency of courts was dictated by two factors: the physical size of each manor, and the degree of social stability and/or tranquillity in any given year. On average, the courts met between three and five times a year. At Gressenhall (Norfolk), one of the largest and busiest manors in the region, the courts were held, at the close of the thirteenth century, every three weeks. On small manors the courts usually met two or three times a year. The number of court sessions was generally above these averages in the troublesome years of the agrarian crisis of 1315–17 and during (and because of) the economic crisis of the late 1330s–1340s. The frequency of courts also determined the number of manorial court rolls that were produced per year.

Just as was the case for the demesne accounts, these manorial court rolls are without peer among the sources we have for late medieval European society. Their degree of detail and depth make them a unique source for the study of rural life. The range of aspects and topics they cover enables us to study the peasantry in surprising detail. The most obvious issues within their purview include the waning and disappearance of serfdom; agricultural management; land inheritance, tenure and subdivision; the land market; credit and indebtedness; demographic trends (village and family size, age of marriage and death); whether the manor was organized by open fields or whether they had been enclosed; the incidence and patterns of crime; relationships between lords and peasantry; gender roles; peasant culture; and rural crafts.

Apart from their obvious value as a source, we can talk of a number of problems with the records. First, they tend to focus on male tenants and under-represent other groups, including women, minors, serfs and freeholders. Second, they reflect the state of things on the manor and the manor was not necessarily the same as the rural parish in terms of geography, custom and population. As were the demesne accounts, manorial court rolls tend to be formulaic in format. The textual layout is as follows. The roll opens with the general heading stating its location and the date on which the court was held. This is followed by a summary of cases. As a rule, the length of each summary is between one and three lines of text. The summary provides the names of those involved in each case, be they plaintiffs, defendants or transactors. Whenever the outcome was a fine, the exact sum is specified in the left margin. We can divide the court rolls, as documents or artefacts, into several main types. Some are singletons, covering just one court. In other instances one court roll covers several courts from the same manor. Less frequently, one roll will contain minutes from several manors belonging to the same lord. Thus, for instance, there are several early fourteenth-century court rolls covering three or four manors of Norwich Cathedral Priory.[12] The vast majority of late medieval court rolls from Bishop of Durham's manors, known as Halmote court rolls, were also compiled in a grouped format.

It seems that holding manorial courts did not become common practice until at least the late twelfth century. The earliest manorial court rolls appear a bit after the first demesne accounts; the earliest surviving court roll dates from 1237 and is, in fact, a later copy of court proceedings from the manors of St Alban's Abbey. The earliest court roll surviving in its original form is from 1246 and it deals with an estate of the Abbey of Bec. From the 1260s, however, manorial court rolls become plentiful. Unlike demesne accounts, these rolls survived the collapse of manorialism in the fifteenth century and their record goes well beyond 1500. From the late sixteenth century, however, their number, scope and detail diminish and their focus becomes confined to land transactions. It was not until the early nineteenth century that court rolls began to disappear, with some notable exceptions. Thus, at Cockfield (Suffolk), manor court continued to function until the late 1940s.[13] The manorial court rolls that have survived exhibit a much wider geographical coverage than demesne accounts, particularly in regions where manorialism was strong. For instance, surviving demesne accounts cover only some twenty places in Bedfordshire, while many more places (or manors) in that county are represented by court rolls. Similarly, the overall surviving number of manor court rolls from the North is considerably larger than that of demesne accounts. Also, while the majority of demesne accounts come from the estates of greater ecclesiastical lords, court rolls are not, as a rule, biased towards such larger estates. There are a fair number of rolls dealing with estates of minor lords, both religious and lay.

The chronological coverage of the court rolls varies from estate to estate and from period to period. Thus, the court rolls of Hinderclay and Redgrave, two Suffolk manors of Bury St Edmunds, run, with virtually no gaps, from the 1250s to 1710. This was most unusual, of course, and few other manors match such a record. For instance, the surviving Halmote rolls of Bishop of Durham's manors run with almost no interruption between 1365 and 1429 and then again between 1460 and 1507, though we must note the significant gaps between these runs.[14] Paradoxically, on some of the greater ecclesiastical estates the surviving number of court rolls is considerably lower than that of demesne rolls. Only some ninety court rolls, as against 1,800 demesne accounts, are extant for the manors of

Canterbury Cathedral Priory. In other instances, the situation was the reverse, and at Bridport, Dorset, there is a fairly full coverage of court rolls between 1309 and 1496 while not a single demesne account has come down. Similarly, there is a good run of court rolls at Sutton-in-the-Isle (Cambridgeshire), between 1291 and 1480, but only one demesne account from this manor.

As is the case with the demesne rolls, the vast majority of court rolls remain unpublished, to be consulted at various repositories of the UK. However, the number of court rolls that has been published is considerably greater than the number of demesne accounts, by a good margin. Although some of the earliest publications go back to the seventeenth century, the first critical editions began to appear in the first decade of the twentieth century.

So far, about 365 rolls have been published (165 medieval, 200 early modern). The regional distribution is quite uneven. We have forty-seven published rolls for Yorkshire (seventeen medieval, thirty early modern), forty for Lancashire (six medieval, thirty-four early modern). These figures are, however, exceptional. For most part, there are about four manors with medieval and five with early modern court rolls for most counties, though Cornwall, Cumberland, Devon, Herefordshire, Northumberland, Rutland, Warwickshire and Westmorland have no printed manor rolls at all. Nor does the number of printed editions reflect the regional distribution of the surviving rolls.

There are several good guides for manorial court rolls, both those still in archives and those in print. For unpublished materials, Razi and Smith's *Medieval Society and the Manor Court* provides a valuable although somewhat selective (and now rather outdated) handlist of court rolls at various repositories. As with demesne accounts, current repositories and shelfmarks of many court rolls can be located with the aid of the online catalogues of county record offices and institutional monuments. For printed editions, the most comprehensive and useful catalogue is C.J. Harrison's *The Manor Court: A Bibliography of Printed Resources and Related Materials*.[15]

## Manorial surveys: rentals, extents, custumals and terriers

Despite their different names and slightly distinctive functions, these four types of record are either related or interchangeable and therefore are all treated under the heading of 'manorial surveys'. As the name suggests, a manorial survey is, roughly speaking, a description, whether detailed or summarized of a manor, covering both its demesne and its tenancy sectors. These documents are particularly important for the study of peasant holdings and customs. Unlike other manorial documents, which did not really come into use until the thirteenth century, surveys go back to the late eleventh century. The earliest and clearly the single most comprehensive and important survey of all is Domesday Book, commissioned by William I in 1085 and carried out in 1086. With certain caveats, the Domesday Book can be regarded as the first census, recording all landed properties under the king's jurisdiction after the Conquest. Unfortunately, regions outside the king's direct jurisdiction and control – Durham, parts of Cheshire and Lancashire, as well as the northernmost counties of Cumberland, Westmorland and Northumberland (still under partial control of the Scots) – were left unrecorded. The Domesday Book consists of two parts: the Little Domesday Book, covering East Anglia (Essex, Suffolk and Norfolk) and the Great Domesday Book pertaining to the rest of the country, and the former is generally more detailed in its coverage. Collectively, the two parts record landed property in some 13,500 settlement units, including towns, manors and hamlets. Wandering from hundred to hundred, royal officers inquired about the lordship of individual holdings, their size (in acres); their components (arable, pasturage, woodland, mills, saltpans, etc.); and their financial values *c*. 1065 and 1086. In some cases, the inquest records customary dues, the number of plough-teams, the number of slaves and livestock. Although the Domesday Book records only rural lay households, it is possible to estimate that at the time of its compilation the population of England was about 1.6 million. The Domesday Book itself is preserved at the Museum of the National Archives, at Kew Gardens, and is not available for individual consultation. However, its contents are now available online and in translation.[16] Following the Domesday model, in 1183 Hugh de Puiset, Bishop-Prince of Durham, commissioned a similar survey covering landed possessions under his jurisdiction. This resulted in a compilation known as the Boldon Book. To a large degree, the Boldon Book fills in some of the geographic gaps of the original Domesday.

The next great census was conducted between 1274 and 1280, with the survey now known as the Hundred Rolls. These give us a systematic recording of liberties and land ownership as well as villeins' dues and obligations. Though the vast majority of the rolls have been lost, the remainder are preserved at the National Archives and were published between 1812 and 1818.[17] Over the years, many fragments of the lost parts have been re-discovered and a University of Sheffield-based project is now preparing them for publication.[18] Some forty years after the Hundreds inquest, Edward II commissioned another general survey, known as the *Nomina Villarum* (1316). This survey, surviving in its entirety, records the names and lordship in every township under the royal jurisdiction. Despite its laconic format, the survey is still very useful, primarily because it reveals the complexity of land ownership that resulted from the fragmentation of lordship or ownership that came as a result of a growing population and the land pressure it caused in the early fourteenth century. The *Nomina* survey has been published as a six-volume edition.[19]

The Domesday Book, the Hundred Rolls and the *Nomina Villarum* were inquests on a national scale. They were clearly unusual, as the vast majority of surveys were conducted on a local, or at most on an estate level. The twelfth century was a period of economic expansion and growth, in the course of which many lords leased out their demesnes to their better-off tenants in an effort to maximize their economic benefits. This tendency is echoed in an increasing number of surveys compiled in the course of that century. These surveys relate to properties, leased and otherwise, of religious houses, including Ramsey Abbey, Glastonbury Abbey, Saint Paul's Cathedral, Burton Abbey, Peterborough Cathedral, Saint Benet's Abbey at Holme. The year of 1185 saw the birth of two important inquests: the so-called *Rotuli de Dominabus et pueris* and *puellis de XII comitatibus* (Rolls concerning demesnes, boys and girls from twelve counties) and the great Templars' inquest.

The *Rotuli de Dominabus* record the extent and value of landed holdings of widows and heirs of recently deceased tenants-in-chief; in addition, they specify the age of the holders and the number of their children. They cover the counties of Bedfordshire, Buckinghamshire, Cambridgeshire, Essex, Hertfordshire, Huntingdonshire, Lincolnshire, Middlesex, Norfolk, Northamptonshire, Rutland and Suffolk. The Templars' inquest records various services and dues owed by villeins, as well as the size and value of their holdings in various counties.

Twelfth-century surveys tended to be short and at times too generalized. In the course of the thirteenth century, however, they became more plentiful, accurate and detailed. This development can be ascribed to the return by many lords (both secular and ecclesiastical) to direct demesne management and, consequently, to their renewed interest in the potential value and resources of their manors. Though more manors were covered by surveys that we have, their frequency did not increase as much as we might have expected. Thus, the Bishop of Ely conducted only two surveys in the course of the century (1222 and 1251) and there is only one known survey of Norwich Cathedral Priory's estates (known as the Stowe Survey, from 1275 to 1292). Usually, the surveys were connected either to the ascension of a new lord or to the installation of a new estate manager, these being reasonable times to take stock.

The vast majority of thirteenth-century surveys are characterized by centralized organization (that is, each survey covering an entire estate, or a group of manors within that estate). From the late thirteenth century – and through the fourteenth and into the fifteenth – the format of these surveys underwent a pronounced change. In most instances, these were now individual terriers and rentals, pertaining to one manor and recording individual holdings, customs and the dues of individual households. At times, the same manor was surveyed once every generation or so. For instance, between 1289 and 1526, no less than fourteen extents were compiled for the manor of Redgrave (Suffolk), belonging to Abbey of Bury St Edmunds.[20]

Before the mid-fifteenth century the language of such surveys was almost invariably Latin. There are, however, some peculiar exceptions, including a 1315 survey from Cressenhall (Norfolk), being the first known survey to have been compiled in Middle English. Late fifteenth-century surveys could be written either in Latin or English.

What can we extract from these surveys, in addition to the size of holding and customary dues owed by tenants? First and foremost, they reveal much local topographical data. By juxtaposing an earlier extent against its later counterpart, we may see the dynamics of land use and land-holding. In addition, they provide much valuable information about the sub-division of tenurial holdings, an issue still to be studied in detail. Likewise, the surveys can be instructive about population density, a very pressing issue in the first decade of the fourteenth century before the onset of the Great Famine (1314–22) and then of the Black Death (1348–51). The vast majority of twelfth-century surveys are available in print. The later ones are mostly to be found in archives and other repositories. Those in print can be easily traced, with the help of Harrison's catalogue (see footnote 15). Samples of manorial surveys, their history and analysis can be found in Bailey's *The English Manor*.[21]

## Inquisitions Post Mortem (IPM)

Although Inquisitions Post Mortem are a form of extent, they deserve separate treatment because of their special nature. An IPM offers material that is complementary to both manorial surveys and accounts. Like the latter, IPMs pertain to the demesne sector only. Their scope and the level of detail clearly fall behind those of manorial accounts. On the other hand, an IPM supplies information not to be found in manorial accounts or anywhere else.

Basically, IPMs are extents of manors held by lay tenants-in-chief (of the king). As the name suggests, they were compiled and issued upon, or shortly after, the death of a tenant-in-chief. First the king would send a writ to his escheators for the counties in which the tenant's manors were located. Then an inquiry (an inquisition) was held at each manor of the late tenant. Once the relevant data were collected, through local sworn juries, the extents were compiled by local clerks and sent to the royal chancery. Just as were manorial accounts and court rolls, IPMs tended to be formulaic and straightforward. They offer information about the structure of manors, recording their parts or segments such as the arable, pasture, meadow and woodland, all in terms of acreage and values. IPMs also record minor land-uses, such as fisheries, warrens, dovecotes, buildings, mills, granaries, turbaries and orchards. In addition, they indicate dues, customs and revenues deriving from each manor. Furthermore, and perhaps their most unique feature, they contain invaluable demographic information indicating age at death and the age and number of the heirs. Unlike manorial accounts, however, IPMs do not give information about specific crops, animals or the productivity rates and obligations of labour on the manor.

IPMs also vary in coverage from county to county and from estate to estate. Thus, the palatine county of Durham, exempt from royal jurisdiction, has virtually no such documents. Similarly, Cheshire (also a palatine county), parts of Lancashire, Cumberland, Westmorland, parts of Yorkshire, Cornwall and Devon have thin coverage. Parts of Middlesex, Huntingdonshire, Hertfordshire and Hampshire, dominated by ecclesiastical lordship, are also under-represented. But for some counties we have excellent coverage, and in aggregate the IPMs cover one in every three *vills* in England. Just within the half century 1300–49 almost 10,000 were created, including 322 for Wales and 324 for the Lordship of Ireland. In this sense, IPMs become all the more invaluable, since they are the single most important quantitative source for agrarian history of late medieval Lordship of Ireland.

Unlike other manorial records, owing to their origins as instruments of the king's government, the IPMs are deposited in the National Archives at Kew. They run from 1236 to 1677, under the assigned shelfmarks C 132–C 142, with each section divided into sub-sections, arranged according to places and years. References for each extent can be searched or browsed at the online catalogue of the National Archives.[22] The vast majority of the thirteenth- and fourteenth-century IPMs have been well calendared and work is now apace to cover the fifteenth century as well. In addition, select extents have been published, with various degrees of accuracy.[23] An ongoing project, based at the University of

Winchester, proposes to make all IPMs for 1236–1485 available online, in a digital and searchable format.[24]

## Deeds

Deeds, which can also be referred to as charters, are legal documents recording transactions between two or more parties, usually in form of land transfer (via exchange, surrender or sale). There are several types of deeds, including private deeds (that is, issued by a single person); chirographs (contracts written in two or three copies, each to be kept by each party involved); final concordances (agreements between a plaintiff and a defendant); and corporate charters (issued by institutions). Although some deeds provide invaluable information about urban development, the vast majority deal with rural England.

Basically, there are two main formats of deeds: individual and enrolled. Individual deeds can be either the original documents, with attached seal, vouching for its authenticity, or a later copy, with no seal attached. Enrolled deeds are later transcriptions of the original documents as they were copied into cartularies (*cartularia*), compilation volumes, or enrolled into rolls. There are at least 1,500 medieval cartularies from England and perhaps as many as 5,000 from France.[25] In many instances, the text of the original deed survives in later cartulary copies only. It should be noted, however, that many such copies are, in fact, later forgeries. Forged deeds can (sometimes) be spotted because they betray anachronistic terminology and formulas as well as incorporating factual inaccuracies.

Some final agreements regarding land disputes or transfers were copied into centralized documents; we label these *feet of fines*. The feet of fines were recorded in the Court of Common Pleas, in three copies, one of which was retained at the court and subsequently entered into the government's records, arranged by counties. The feet of fines run from 1195 to the 1830s and with little or no interruption. Although only select agreements were recorded into the feet of fines they can be used to track trends in land transfer patterns and practices over a very long *durée*. Most medieval and early modern feet of fines have been either published or calendared.[26] In addition, there is an ongoing University of Houston-based digital project, entitled 'Anglo-American Legal Tradition', which has, in 2010, digitized the vast majority of high and late medieval feet of fines, readily available for consultation.[27]

Deeds survive in astonishingly large number, both in England and elsewhere in Europe. For England alone the original surviving deeds can be counted in millions. What accounts for this remarkably high survival is the fact that the majority of the original deeds were copied into later cartularies. For the pre-Conquest period there are 184 ecclesiastical charters and about 80 deeds issued by laity, and these numbers pale before the 1,163 surviving royal charters. But after the Norman Conquest there was a truly remarkable increase in their number, though only about five per cent of the deeds that antedate 1190 are dated (and but seventeen charters with a known date from between 1066 and 1099, with 966 from between 1100 and 1189, as in Figure 9.2). From *c.* 1190 onwards, more and more deeds were dated and from *c.* 1270 the vast majority of charters bore dates of issue.

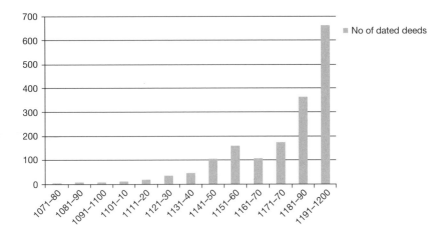

Source: The DEEDS Project (http://www.utoronto.ca/deeds/)

*Figure 9.2* Decennial distribution of surviving private deeds, 1071–1200

There are some 200 printed editions of deeds, whether of individual documents or entire cartularies. Some compilations were edited by amateur historians for local county historical societies and their journals, mostly in the nineteenth and early twentieth centuries. Inevitably, such editions suffer from various degrees of inaccuracy. But against this there are a large number of fine critical editions, published by major academic publishers, and the single most important resource for the late medieval deeds is now the University of Toronto-based project DEEDS. This covers around 8,700 dated charters, issued between 1072 and 1310.[28] This fully searchable database is based on 200 printed editions. Unfortunately, DEEDS only runs up to 1310, which takes us to the onset of a series of socio-economic and environmental shocks in England. Because of the vast number of extant deeds, the majority of the individual deeds remain unpublished. This is especially true for those of the late fourteenth and fifteenth century, documents too often perceived as being only of local concern and therefore of little historical value.

## Taxation assessments

Surveys and charters provide some insight into the size of peasants' holdings but they do not specify how these were used. Our information about peasants' crops and livestock comes, rather, from taxation assessments. In England, these records were created in conjunction with the taxes imposed by the king, usually to finance his ongoing wars. Between 1275 and 1334 the people of England were taxed no fewer than thirty-one times. While the taxation rolls proper survive in full, the surviving assessment rolls are patchy. The earliest extant taxation assessment goes back to 1225 and it covers parts of Wiltshire and Lincolnshire in conjunction with taxation of a Fifteenth. The 1283 valuation, in connection with the taxation of a

Thirtieth, survives for the Blackbourne Hundred in Suffolk. The 1290 assessment covers the Ramsey Banlieu in Huntingdonshire. For the 1297 taxation of a Ninth, we have surviving assessments from Bedfordshire and Yorkshire, as well as from the Spelhoe Hundred in Northamptonshire. Two hundreds in Kent are covered by the surviving roll of 1301. Finally, two assessments survive for Buckinghamshire (1327 and 1332) and one for Sussex (1332).

These few surviving valuations provide a rare glimpse into agro-pastoral arrangements and peasant strategies about land, labour and resources. They reveal, *inter alia*, the structure and geography of tenants' crops and fields and regional variations in the use of both arable land and of animals. A close analysis reveals, for instance, that the tenants' animals tended to be cheaper and hence, perhaps, inferior to those from the demesne sector. The majority of the surviving assessments have been published, usually in accurate and reliable editions.[29] The ones as yet unpublished are in the National Archives.[30]

## Tithe receipt accounts

Tithe accounts, dealing with an ecclesiastical levy imposed on the produce of the laity and equalling approximately one-tenth of the latter, are yet another first-rate material for the study of peasant agriculture. These accounts were composed for the rural rector who owned the tithes (that is, to whom they were owed). These records specify the annual receipt of grains as well as of such smaller-scale crops as flax and hemp. In some instances, they also specify livestock tithes, usually newborn calves, lambs and piglets. Unfortunately, because of their laconic and generalized nature, they specify the quantity of grain or/and animals rendered by an entire parochial community, as opposed to individual parishioners. As a result we can reconstruct general trends but not the level of output of individual households.

A long run of tithe accounts can tell a great deal about general agricultural trends within the peasant sector, as a long run of demesne accounts does for the seigniorial sector. For some estates, tithe accounts survive in large number, as with the more than 1,000 such accounts from Durham Priory, spanning from the 1270s to the 1530s. On the other hand, there is much less surviving material from Norwich Cathedral Priory, Canterbury Cathedral or Westminster Abbey. In some instances tithe receipts were put together with the demesne accounts under the same rubric with the demesne grain and livestock production. We find this, for instance, in certain parts of the Winchester pipe rolls as well as in the account book of Bolton Priory (1286–1325).

In most cases tithe accounts are to be found in the archives of ecclesiastical institutions. Sometimes we can trace them through catalogues but in other cases one has to look for the accounts as they are arranged by locations.[31] One important value of tithe accounts, in contrast to demesne accounts, is in chronology. As we have seen, demesne accounts become quite patchy by the fifteenth century as more and more manors were leased out. Tithe accounts, on the other hand, are found all the way from the thirteenth century through the Dissolution in the 1530s. The importance of tithe accounts has recently been pointed out by Ben Dodds, in his work on Durham tithe receipts.[32]

## Other sources

The list of sources mentioned here is by no means comprehensive. It tends to be selective and biased towards socio-economic and environmental fields and questions that can be dealt with by a quantitative rather than a qualitative approach. There are actually many more sources, and kinds of sources, available for the study of late medieval rural life in England. For instance, wills, starting from the late thirteenth century, can tell a great deal about various aspects, including popular devotion and mentality, personal wealth and living standards. Quite a few late medieval wills, and especially those recorded at prerogative and consistory courts, are available both in print and online. Thus, all wills recorded at the Prerogative Court of Canterbury between 1384 and 1858 are now available online, through the website of the National Archives.[33] These wills cover most of the south of England and many parts of Wales. However, much more detailed and comprehensive overview of wills as a source is found in Chapter 4 in this volume.

Another pathway into peasant and rural life that does not follow manorial records is by way of contemporary sermons. Here a particular genre stands out, sermons *ad status*, that is, sermons addressed to different groups within secular society. Notable names of English preachers addressing or referring to the rural masses include Odo of Cheriton (*c*. 1185–1246/7), John of Wales (*c*. 1220–1285) and John Bromyard (d. 1352), and in addition we have countless anonymous authors of sermon collections. These sermons illustrate the ambiguous and often uneasy relationships between tenants and their lords. They can depict, both satirically and with approval and even admiration, rustic habits and ways of life and they can paint in rich colours aspects of agrarian life and labour. And above all, they reflect the attitude of popular preachers towards the rural class.[34]

Sermons were just one literary genre. We can add contemporary belles-lettres, both poetry and prose. Thus, an anonymous *Poem on the Evil Times of Edward II* (*c*. 1324), William Langland's *Piers Plowman* (between 1360 and 1387), John Gower's *Vox Clamantis* (shortly after 1381) and an anonymous Jack of the North (shortly after 1549) all portray the social reaction of the peasants to economic hardships and to some of the institutional impositions under which they laboured. There are numerous allusions to rustics and rural milieu in the anonymous *Wynnere and Wastoure* (*c*. 1352), in various works of Geoffrey Chaucer (*c*. 1343–1400), and in John Lydgate's *Debate of the Horse, Goose and Sheep* (*c*. 1440).

Textual and statistical sources can always be supplemented by visual ones. There are very few maps before the sixteenth century. However, some isolated late medieval surveys included rough plans of manors or of fields, chiefly in the fifteenth century. It should also be kept in mind that quite a few *vills* remained unenclosed, practising common-field or open-field agriculture up to the Industrial Revolution and beyond. As a result, in many instances early modern sketches and plans of settlements can be instructive. Late medieval and early modern plans can be complemented with twentieth-century aerial photographs that can reveal some surprising facts about the rural terrain that are otherwise invisible to the naked eye, such as remains of Roman villas and traces of deserted villages.[35]

Iconographic evidence can also throw light on medieval rural life practices and experience. In particular, the illustrations (illuminations) in fourteenth- and fifteenth-century liturgical books, especially Psalters and Books of Hours, depict scenes from contemporary life and often from a rural milieu. The Luttrell, Macclesfield, Douai and Gorleston Psalters, all written and illuminated in the 1320s and 1330s by East Anglian artists, include vivid images of harvesting, live-stock rearing, and labour performance, as well as depictions of costumes, tools and buildings.

Material evidence, as reflected through field walking or/and archaeological excavations, adds a great deal to our understanding and appreciation of late medieval rural society. Walking through the sites of medieval villages, whether thriving or deserted, can enable us to visualize the landscapes, buildings, woods and fields that were seen, inhabited by, and worked by medieval peasants. Digging under the surface has revealed much about aspects of their everyday experience, yielding information not otherwise found in textual or visual sources.[36] It seems self-evident, then, that only a broad, inter-disciplinary approach, utilizing many varieties of sources and methodologies, can offer a comprehensive picture of medieval rural experience. Perhaps the lesson is that we should be willing to delve into manorial accounts, court rolls, Chaucer's descriptions, and images like those of the fourteenth-century Luttrell Psalter – either before or after we prepare for a field-walk.

## Further reading

Bailey, Mark, *The English Manor, c.1200–c.1500* (Manchester: Manchester University Press, 2002).

Beresford, Maurice W. and St Joseph, John K.S., *Medieval England: An Aerial Survey* (Cambridge: Cambridge University Press, 1958).

Campbell, Bruce M.S., *English Seigniorial Agriculture 1250–1450* (Cambridge, Cambridge University Press, 2000).

Campbell, Bruce M.S. and Bartley, Ken, *England on the Eve of the Black Death. An Atlas of Lay Lordship and Wealth, 1300–1349* (Manchester: Manchester University Press, 2006).

Dodds, Ben, *Peasants and Production in the Medieval North-East: The Evidence from Tithes, 1270–1536* (Woodbridge: Boydell & Brewer, 2007).

Dyer, Christopher, *Standards of Living in the Later Middle Ages: Social Change in England, c.1200–1520* (Cambridge: Cambridge University Press, 1989).

Harvey, P.D.A., *Manorial Records* (London: British Records Association, 1984).

Miller, Edward and Hatcher, John, *Medieval England: Rural Society and Economic Change, 1086–1348* (London: Longman 1978).

Raban, Sandra, *A Second Domesday? The Hundred Rolls of 1279–80* (Oxford: Oxford University Press, 2004).

Schofield, Phillipp R., *Peasant and Community in Medieval England, 1200–1500* (New York: Palgrave Macmillan, 2003).

## Notes

1 Mark Hager, 'A Pipe Rolls for 25 Henry I', *English Historical Review* 122 (2007): 133–40.
2 The Coldingham accounts were published by J. Raine, *The Correspondence, Inventories, Account Rolls and Law Proceedings of the Priory of Coldingham*, Surtees Society 12 (London, 1841).
3 The National Archives, SC6/1202/7; SC6/920/1–928/28.
4 Harvey, P.D.A., *Manorial Records of Cuxham, Oxfordshire circa 1200–1359* (London: HMSO, 1976); Midgley, L. Margaret, *Ministers' Accounts of the Earldom of Cornwall 1296–7* (London: Offices of the Royal Historical Society, 1942).
5 Thus, an edition of the 1395 account from Newham (Cambs), misreads and translates *pullani* (= colts) as 'fowl' (apparently, confusing with *pulli* = chicks). See, *East Anglian* 4 (1869), p. 91.
6 John Langdon, *Horses, Oxen and Technological Innovation: The Use of Draught Animals in English Farming from 1066 to 1500* (unpublished University of Birmingham PhD thesis, 1983), pp. 416–56.
7 Kate Harris, *Glastonbury Abbey Records at Longleat House* (Taunton: Somerset Record Society, 1991); Rodney M. Thomson, *The Archives of the Abbey of Bury St Edmunds* (Woodbridge: Boydell & Brewer, 1980).
8 James A. Galloway, Margaret Murphy and Olwen Myhill (eds) *Kentish Demesne Accounts up to 1350: A Catalogue* (London: Centre for Metropolitan Studies, 1993).
9 http://www.cropyields.ac.uk/ [last accessed May 2010].
10 John Langdon, *Oxen and Technological Innovation: The Use of Draught Animals in English Farming from 1066 to 1500* (Cambridge: Cambridge University Press, 1986).
11 David Stone, *Decision-Making in Medieval Agriculture* (Oxford: Oxford University Press, 2005).
12 Norfolk Record Office, DCN 60/11/1–4.
13 Mark Bailey, *The English Manor, c.1200–c.1500* (Manchester: Manchester University Press, 2002), p.188.
14 *Halmota Prioratus Dunelmensis containing extracts from the Halmote court or manor rolls of the prior and convent of Durham. A.D. 1296–A.D. 1384* , ed. W.H. Longstaffe and J. Booth, (Surtees Soc. 82, 1889); the online catalogue for the Durham court rolls is available at http://flambard.dur.ac.uk/dynaweb/handlist/ddc/dcdguide [last accessed May 2010].
15 http://www.keele.ac.uk/depts/hi/resources/manor_courts/manbib05.pdf (Fourth web-based edition; Keele University, 2005). [last consulted May 2010].
16 http://www.domesdaybook.co.uk/ [when last accessed, in May 2010, the site was partially under construction]. In addition, there is a most valuable and fully searchable scholarly edition, containing the original images (digitized in 1985), Latin and translated English texts, with maps and commentaries. This edition is published on four CD-ROMs by Addison Publications. Furthermore, there are several good translated editions of the inquest, available in print, the most affordable of which is the paperback Penguin edition (2003).
17 W. Illingworth (ed.), *Rotuli hundredorum temp. Hen. III et Edw. I* (London: Record Commission, 1812–18).
18 http://www.roffe.co.uk/shrp.htm [last accessed May 2010].
19 *Inquisitions and Assessments relating to Feudal Aids* (London: HMSO, 1899–1920).
20 Chicago University Library, Bacon Rolls, 805–818.
21 Mark Bailey, *The English Manor, c.1200–c.1500* (Manchester: Manchester University Press, 2002).
22 http://www.nationalarchives.gov.uk/catalogue/browser.asp?CATLN=3&CATID=2131&GPE=False&MARKER=0 [last accessed May 2010].
23 The editions are noted in Bruce M. S. Campbell and Ken Bartley, *England on the Eve of the Black Death: An Atlas of Lay Lordship, Land and Wealth, 1300–49* (Manchester: Manchester University Press, 2006), p. 352.

24 The current status of the project can be viewed at http://www.winchester. ac.uk/?page=10470 [last accessed May 2010].

25 G.R.C. Davis, *Medieval Cartularies of Great Britain,* (revised by Claire Breay, Julian Harrison and David M. Smith) (Chicago: University of Chicago Press, 2010) [the original edition was published in 1958]; Henri Stein, *Bibliographie générale des cartulaires français ou relatifs à l'histoire de France* (Paris: Picard, 1907).

26 The handlist of published or calendared feet of fines can be consulted at http://www. medievalgenealogy.org.uk/fines/index.shtml [last accessed May 2010].

27 http://aalt.law.uh.edu/IndexPri.html [last accessed May 2010].

28 http://www.utoronto.ca/deeds/ [last accessed May 2010].

29 For instance, Edgar Powell (ed.), *A Suffolk Hundred in the Year 1283* (Cambridge: Cambridge University Press, 1910); J.A. Raftis and M.P. Hogan (eds), *Early Huntingdonshire Rolls*, (Toronto: PIMS, 1976); A.T. Gaydon (ed.), *The Taxation of 1297* (Bedfordshire Historical Records Society, 39, 1959).

30 SC11/531; E179/242/47 and 127; E179/238/119a; E179/123/5; E179/242/12 and 13.

31 For instance, the Durham tithe accounts can be traced through the Cathedral archives website: http://flambard.dur.ac.uk/dynaweb/handlist/ddc/dcdmaccs/ [last accessed May 2010],

32 Dodds, Ben, *Peasants and Production in the Medieval North-East: The Evidence from Tithes, 1270–1536* (Woodbridge: Boydell & Brewer, 2007).

33 http://www.nationalarchives.gov.uk/documentsonline/wills.asp [last accessed May 2010].

34 Gerald R. Owst, *Literature and Pulpit in Medieval England* (Cambridge: Cambridge University Press, 1933), Chapter 6 *passim*.

35 Maurice W. Beresford and John K.S. St Joseph, *Medieval England: An Aerial Survey* (Cambridge: Cambridge University Press, 1958).

36 In particular, Medieval Settlement Research Group (MSRG) is engaged in numerous projects related to medieval settlements in England and Wales and publishes its annual reports. See http://www.britarch.ac.uk/msrg/ [last accessed May 2010].

# 10   Sources for medieval maritime history

*Maryanne Kowaleski*

The study of life and trade at sea and in coastal communities has become more popular in recent years, thanks to growing interest in global history, Atlantic history, and the relationship between environments and people. Scholarly contributions by medievalists to this trend have been limited thus far, due in large part to the scattered nature of the medieval sources, which rarely include the shipboard diaries, naval logbooks and detailed parish register documentation available to later historians. But the potential here is great, especially in terms of interdisciplinary work. This essay outlines the major types of primary sources available to study medieval maritime history, focusing on printed sources that can illuminate our understanding of such central topics as maritime commerce, ships and shipping, mariners and shipowners, navies and naval policy, piracy and privateering, shipbuilding and fishing, navigation and life within coastal communities.

## Maritime law and government regulations

The first medieval maritime sources to be systematically printed and studied were maritime law codes. Although considered a branch of international law, maritime law was generally based on local precedents – how shipmasters, mariners and merchants commonly handled crises at sea or disputes about freightage in their region – which were eventually written down and codified, often long after the oral customs had been in effect, and often with later additions or clarifications. There are striking similarities in all maritime law codes, largely because seafarers faced many of the same problems, such as shipwreck, desertion by a crew member, or when and what to jettison from the cargo in the middle of a fierce storm. These similarities stretch back even to ancient sea law, including the so-called Rhodian Sea Law, large parts of which were incorporated into the maritime law of the Byzantine Empire and Muslim ports. As a result, a great deal of the past scholarship on medieval maritime law has focused on the dating and influence of particular codes and their individual articles.

Many port cities evolved their own maritime laws, but among the most prominent and widespread of the maritime codes were the customs of the cities of Amalfi and Trani in Italy; the *Waterrecht* (Water Law) of the Hanseatic cities around the Baltic Sea, including the compilation known as the Laws of Visby (or Gotland Sea Law); the Laws of Oléron, which governed most of the northern

Atlantic, including France and England; and *The Book of the Consulate*, a Catalan compilation that became particularly influential in the Mediterranean.[1] Most of these were based on judgments in maritime and port town courts, rather than on statute law promulgated by kings or other central authorities. Maritime law is thus more descriptive of real situations than public law, and can provide illuminating details on how sailors were remunerated, the hierarchies and discipline aboard ship, the relationship between shipowners and merchants, and the myriad risks that faced those transporting goods by sea. The Laws of Oléron (article 7), for example, stipulated that a sick mariner should be put ashore with a food allowance and a ship's boy and nurse hired to care for him. If, however, a mariner became injured while drunk or fighting, he could be left ashore with nothing (article 6). The law codes also reveal the different ways that a sailor could be paid: by wage (with set sums for trips on common routes to Gascony for wine or to the Baltic for timber and fish); by sharing in the ship's profits; or by taking part of his wage as free cargo space to ship his own goods or lease the space out to a merchant. Crew members also received food and board, bonuses for loading and handling the cargo, and a whole range of smaller payments for ship-keeping, mending sails and other maintenance duties. There was, moreover, always the promise of prize money from enemy ships and cargoes they captured along the route.

Maritime law is also visible in the proceedings of maritime courts, which survive mainly for later medieval central courts, particularly for English Admiralty juris-diction, which developed early on.[2] The Cinque Ports Confederation of over thirty south-eastern English port towns also had its own courts, which handled arrange-ments for coastal defence, disputes on the ship service the Ports owed the Crown and the defence of the liberties they received in exchange, and huge amounts of debt litigation.[3] Legal rulings on maritime issues are also scattered throughout the minutes of meetings of the Hanseatic League, a trade confederation of mostly German towns, including the major ports of Hamburg, Lübeck, Visby (on the island of Gotland off Sweden), and Danzig (Gdansk in Poland).[4] The Hansa, for example, ruled to suspend all shipping between mid-November and late February, supposedly to avoid the dangers of sailing during the winter in the cold waters of the Baltic Sea.

The Hansa and other state authorities were also heavily involved in adjudicating cases of international piracy, issuing letters of marque (a licence of reprisal for privateers), and recruiting and paying for naval ships and crews to defend their coasts and expand their territorial control.[5] Collections of national and regional records produced by medieval governments contain a wealth of documentation about piracy, navies and political disputes that played out on the high seas.[6] The Calendar of Patent Rolls for England, for instance, records many royal orders to capture pirates, authorize privateering expeditions against enemy ships, recruit men and vessels for the Crown's naval efforts, and protect the coastline against raids during wartime.[7] Proceedings in the court of Chancery, initiated by petitions from injured parties who felt they could not get justice from their local courts, are a particularly rich source for piracy, prize jurisdiction and the problems that plagued foreign trade during wartime.[8] Another fruitful source is the numerous regulations for ships and their crews that were proclaimed by the councils and committees of the Italian maritime republics of Genoa and Venice, whose survival and growth depended on the success of their fleets.[9] The Venetian Senate, for example, promulgated a series of ordinances designed to protect their merchant crews from the dangerous lures of life ashore in London, where a surfeit of taverns, prostitutes and opportunities to lose wages confronted sailors on shore leave. Venetian captains complained of having to visit all the taverns in London to pay off the debts of their galley oarsmen before they could embark for home, or of being forced to hire extra crew to replace those who never reported back for duty.[10]

Medieval governments also produced regulations governing the jurisdiction and structure of their navies, which in the Middle Ages were more often *ad hoc* affairs than permanent fleets with full-time naval officers. Some kings, however, such as Peter III of Aragon and Henry V of England, and port towns such as Venice and Genoa, deliberately pursued political policies that required an efficient navy, paid for from taxes they raised specifically for this purpose. Given how expensive it was to fund a successful naval fleet, it is no surprise that kings, counts and port cities began regulating early on how to assemble, pay and govern the naval forces they employed to impose territorial control, guard their coasts and patrol against pirates. The mid-thirteenth-century law code of Alfonso X of Castile, for instance, regulated everything from the elaborate rituals the admiral had to perform before taking office to the division of spoils and daily ration of biscuit given to naval crews.[11] The growing power of admiralty jurisdiction in late medieval England and France also prompted the dissemination of ordinances and statutes about not only the responsibilities of the admiral, but also the behaviour of men while serving in the navy.[12]

## Fiscal accounts

Account rolls and registers detailing revenues and expenses provide the most precise and quantifiable information about the medieval maritime world. Most of the accounts that survive were generated by state authorities, who needed to keep track of the taxes they raised to fund their naval efforts, as well as the massive expenses they shouldered to build, hire, arm and maintain ships; employ crews and shipyard workers; and purchase and store tackle, armaments, food and drink. Particularly full naval accounts survive for medieval England, many of them in the royal wardrobe accounts because military expenses were often met from the Crown's own funds.[13] As an island nation that fought most of its wars on the continent, England was forced early on to develop an effective system for calling up merchant ships and crews to serve on naval duty. France, which had to defend two very different coastlines that were not part of the same unified government until late in the Middle Ages, has far fewer surviving medieval naval records than England.[14] Indeed, none of the northern European countries could afford to maintain a permanent navy, relying instead on impressing merchant ships and their mariners to serve for two weeks to six months or more at the government's expense, while occasionally constructing purpose-built warships in royal shipyards. Several Mediterranean states, however, were able to fund significant naval fleets for long periods at different times in their history, particularly the maritime republic of Venice and the Crown of Catalonia-Aragon, which also ruled Sicily and parts of southern Italy.[15]

Fiscal accounts also provide the best details about shipbuilding and technological changes in the type, size, rigging, masts and equipment of medieval ships, although the bulk of surviving shipbuilding accounts come from kings or other central authorities, not merchants. The English, French and Spanish royal shipbuilding accounts are particularly thorough in the data they offer about the occupations hired to provide labour, the technology of shipbuilding, the supply of raw materials, and the equipment that every good ship was supposed to have.[16] Although few of its records are in print, the most fully developed medieval shipyard was the government-run Arsenal of Venice, which constructed mainly galleys for both trading and naval voyages.[17] One of the more extraordinary survivals from the Venetian shipbuilding industry is a recently discovered notebook by Michael of Rhodes, a mariner who started as a common oarsman aboard a Venetian galley and rose to be captain and navigator of a convoy of three ships. His writings include the earliest known medieval shipbuilding treatise and a meticulous list of his more than forty voyages.[18]

A particularly valuable category of fiscal accounts are the customs accounts that authorities kept to record the tolls owed by ships and cargoes docking at their ports. Because customs or tolls were usually levied according to the type of cargoes carried, and because merchants from particular ports enjoyed exemptions, customs accounts often carefully record the name of the ship, master and home port, as well as the arrival or departure date, cargo and cargo-owners. This type of information lends itself to quantifying patterns of coastal and overseas trade over time, to a collective biography (through prosopographical analysis) of shipmasters or merchants, and to comparing the shipping and commercial strength and profile of individual ports. Yet these sources also have drawbacks. The most complete set of extant customs accounts, the overseas customs accounts for England, only records overseas trade, not coastal trade, which probably made up half to three-quarters of all ship movements. The local customs accounts usually detail coastal and overseas trade, but also suffer limitations, not least their rare survival. The local port customs accounts of the English port of Exeter, for instance, only document incoming ships and cargoes; those of Southampton exclude local citizens and other merchants who had customs exemptions; and those of Dieppe in France omit the name of the ship and its home port.[19] The *Pfundzollbücher*, customs accounts recording an *ad valorem* tax called poundage (*Pfundzoll*) in such Hansa ports as Lübeck, Hamburg, Gdansk and Reval (Tallinn in Estonia), offer valuable data on Baltic shipping from the late fourteenth century onwards, but the toll was only assessed when extraordinary expenses had to be met, usually during wartime.[20] The Genoese port customs were also assessed only in years when extra income was needed and then only on particular types of goods going to particular destinations.[21] The national port customs of England are the most detailed and comprehensive of the medieval customs accounts, but even they vary in coverage according to the type of custom being assessed. [22] Tonnage accounts, for instance, only record overseas cargoes of wine, while cloth subsidy accounts only document outgoing ships carrying wool cloth.[23]

Despite these drawbacks, port customs accounts have provided maritime historians with not only data to assess overall trends in sea trade, but also incidental detail to illuminate many aspects of the maritime experience. Thus the *Pfundzollbuch* of Hamburg in 1369 reveals that beer represented one-third of the port's exports, valued at 62,000 marks. According to the wine customs accounts of Bordeaux in southern France, the height of the Gascon wine trade was in the first decade of the fourteenth century, reaching exports of over 102,000 tuns (each tun contained 252 gallons), but falling thereafter in the war-torn and plague-filled decades of the later Middle Ages. By the 1430s to 1440s, Bordeaux wine exports averaged less than 10,000 tuns per year.[24] The enrolled national port customs accounts of England, which provide annual sums of customs collected, show the growing dominance of London, which in the early thirteenth century handled roughly seventeen per cent of the value of the country's overseas trade, rising to over sixty per cent by the late fifteenth century.[25] But the customs accounts can also provide insights into other aspects of maritime history. Studies of ship names, for instance, have revealed the devotional and political predilections of shipowners, showing the French fondness for ships named after their sainted king Louis in the thirteenth century, and the Danzigers' preference for ships named St Mary Knight, in honour of the town's overlords, the Teutonic Knights. This name fell into disfavour, however, once the Polish Commonwealth overthrew the Knights in the 1440s.[26]

The industry and trade of fishing can also be illuminated by accounts, such as the tithe accounts of the port of Scarborough (England), which survive for eight years from 1414 to 1442.[27] Tithes were collected by a parish's rector to support his priestly duties, but they were often farmed out to other ecclesiastical institutions which provided a vicar to minister to the parish. Tithes were theoretically worth one-tenth of the value of the fisherman's catch, but customs varied from parish to parish. In Scarborough, for example, the rector was entitled to one-twentieth of the catch, minus expenses, but one-fortieth on the cod fishery and one-tenth (after expenses were deducted) on the Scottish herring fishery. In naming individual fishermen, the types of boats and nets they used in different fisheries, and the value of their catch over several years, tithe accounts offer perhaps the best source we have to evaluate the personnel, locations and profitability of the medieval fishing industry. The fishing trade, including its seasonal peaks during Lent and Advent when the Catholic faith forbade the eating of meat, can also be studied with the help of local customs accounts, such as those at Exeter and Dieppe. Also useful are the accounts of seigniorial lords or towns which were entitled to a share of local fishing profits, such as the town of Rye, where herring accounted for fifty-five per cent of the total paid in 1281–88, plaice twenty-nine per cent, and mackerel ten per cent.[28]

## Notarial and merchant records

Notaries were public scribes authorized to record legal documents between individuals, such as contracts, deeds and wills, as well as official acts by political and ecclesiastical authorities. When disputes arose, the notarial record had the force of law in the Mediterranean region; in northern Europe, however, notaries were mainly scribes employed in the bureaucracy of particular ecclesiastical or lay officials.[29] Notarial registers survive from as early as the twelfth century in Italy; ports such as Pisa and Genoa had over 200 working notaries at any one time in the late thirteenth and early fourteenth century. Thousands of notarial registers survive for Genoa in particular, but they are extant for just about every port in the Mediterranean. Because the notaries recorded all sorts of maritime contracts, including freightage and insurance agreements, the hiring of shipmasters and crews, partnerships, sea loans, recognizance of money owed for specific cargoes, and even shipbuilding, they are an invaluable source for understanding maritime commerce.[30] Their survival can be patchy, however, and the specialization or neighbourhood focus of many notaries means that they can vary tremendously in the amount of maritime material they contain.

Freightage agreements are a particularly valuable record since they shed light on sea transport. Many survive in notarial registers, but fewer are extant in northern Europe since business contracts in general were less systematically recorded there than in southern Europe. When these agreements do come to our attention, it is often because the contract was recorded during the course of a dispute in court. One especially informative type of freightage contract was the 'charter-party', in which a merchant or group of merchants hired a ship for a specific period or specific voyage. In a 1323 English charter-party, for example, a shipmaster from Lyme (Dorset) charged 9s per tun to take a wine cargo all the way from Bordeaux to Newcastle and gave a discount by allowing 21.5 tuns for the cost of 20 tuns.[31] The merchants agreed to pay for towage and petty pilotage and forwarded an advance to the master, presumably for victualling the ship and paying part of the crew's wages. The master was given fifteen days to sail the 750 nautical miles to Newcastle. A late thirteenth-century contract for a Spanish ship to sail by coast from Barcelona to Seville gives even more details, including the stops along the way, the number of anchors (sixteen) and other tackle the ship was to carry, and the number and arming of the crew since the voyage was made during wartime.[32]

The business dealings of overseas merchants are also evident in the merchant account books that survive, particularly for Italy where the Florentines in particular were known for keeping *ricordanze*, a kind of personal and business diary that often contained commercial accounts as well as notes about foreign exchange, particular ports and other items of interest to merchants.[33] Merchant manuals containing advice about the mathematical skills they needed to succeed in trading cargoes sold in one country at a certain weight, but selling it in another where the weights and monetary charges were calculated differently, also offer insights into the business world of overseas merchants.[34] Other manuals offer advice on how to discern the different ships and the quality of particular goods, calculate freightage costs, and compose different types of contracts. Records kept by merchant companies, such as the English Merchant Adventurers (who had extensive trade privileges in the export of cloth) and the Merchant Staplers (who controlled the export of English wool) provide useful details about not only overseas commerce, but also the tensions arising from the political and fiscal policies in which these groups became embroiled.[35]

Commercial correspondence in the form of merchants' letters points to the information that maritime traders and their brokers and customers thought worth sharing, while also reflecting how commercial and maritime information was disseminated. Such correspondence may survive as part of a merchant's *ricordanze*; in his business ledger or diary; noted in a notarial register; or as a separate missive, much like today. Busy merchants could produce massive amounts of commercial correspondence: the archive of Marco Datini contains over 150,000 letters sent between his home offices in Florence and Prato and his branches all over the Mediterranean.[36] Such letters talk about which ships were best to hire on certain routes, which dealers were dishonest, and where the best quality goods (and profits) could be found, and refer in often illuminating ways to the problems that plagued maritime commerce, such as piracy, shipwreck and ships blown off course by violent storms.[37] Towns also sent such letters, to vouch for one of their own merchants travelling abroad, to question the confiscation of one of their citizen's ships or cargoes in a foreign port, or to propose a ransoming arrangement for merchants and mariners captured at sea during wartime.[38]

## Chronicles, travel narratives, literary texts, and navigation

Narrative sources by medieval mariners themselves are extremely rare for the Middle Ages; those that survive tend to be in the form of travel diaries kept by the élite, such as the captain of a Florentine galley fleet.[39] The private diaries of Italian diplomats, like that by the Venetian Marin Sanudo, report in chronicle fashion the arrival, departure, numbers and success of particular naval or merchant fleets, as well as more mundane rumours about the difficulties of finding responsible rowers for the galleys or sufficient hemp and timber for the Arsenal.[40] More common are chronicles and travel narratives, which survive in fairly large numbers to give us an often first-hand account of the conditions of medieval sea voyages. Many of the chronicles documenting the Crusades, for example, spell out the routes, costs and travails of those making the long sea voyage from Europe to the Holy Land or to the Baltic for the Northern Crusades.[41] Chronicles are also our chief source for the strategies employed in sea battles and coastal raids, as well as the thinking behind royal naval policy, and popular reaction to the successes and failures of naval and other maritime ventures. Jean Froissart, the great chronicler of the Hundred Years War, for example, describes the 1340 English naval victory at Sluys over French ships, the sea siege of Calais by the English in 1347, and the garrisons, look-outs and beacons set up on the English coast to ward off a potential French invasion by sea.[42] It needs to be kept in mind, however, that he favoured the English over the French, and his description of sea battles such as Sluys may have been coloured by the writings of the classical strategist, Vegetius.

Chronicles and travel narratives can also offer insights into life aboard ship. A chronicle on the diversion of the Second Crusade to Portugal, for instance, casually refers to the judges that the mariners elected to settle internal disputes, while also giving a blow-by-blow account of the sea siege of Lisbon.[43] The pilgrimage account of an eleventh-century Englishman named Saewulf to the Holy Land speaks eloquently of the fear that gripped the passengers and crew during dangerous storms at sea.[44] The worst destruction, however, came when a huge storm killed over 1,000 pilgrims and destroyed all but seven of a fleet of thirty large pilgrim ships anchored off Jaffa (Israel). Another pilgrim, the fifteenth-century German Dominican friar Felix Fabri, offers amusing comments on seasickness, the difficulties of securing appetizing food aboard ship, and the foibles of travelling companions.[45] Fabri also speaks admiringly of the navigational abilities of the pilots, who relied on the position of the stars, the changing colour of the sea, the flight path of birds, and the appearance of schools of dolphins to steer the right course.

Although few literary texts focus on maritime life, they can often offer valuable incidental detail, as in the miraculous survival of a shipwreck in saints' lives, or the literary motif of Jonah and the whale. A poem describing a pilgrimage voyage to the shrine of St James in Compostela (Spain) contains not only a vivid depiction of how the sailors raised the sails, but also a heartfelt account of the effects of seasickness.[46] Romances often allude to maritime travel, or in the case of the romance biography of Eustace the Monk, portray the exploits at sea of an early thirteenth-century son of a French nobleman who was outlawed and allied himself with King John of England, but then switched his loyalties to the French king.[47] He was hated by the English for his raids on their coastal villages, so they showed him no mercy when he was captured at sea during the Battle of Dover. Storms at sea and disastrous shipwrecks were not uncommon in romances, including the Arthurian romances of Chrétien de Troyes, whose tale of William of England is particularly rich in maritime references.[48] Chaucer's portrayal of the Shipman (by which he meant a shipmaster) rings true in its references to the Shipman's wide travels, his clothing and his navigational expertise.

While chronicles, travel narratives, and literary texts offer some information on medieval navigation, specialized navigational texts and charts provide the best evidence. Portolans probably started as the personal logbooks of pilots jotting down sailing directions to particular ports, which were then copied ashore into larger compendiums to guide other shipmasters and pilots. They were prevalent all over the Mediterranean, but not in northern Europe, where sailing information passed down orally was not recorded much before the fifteenth century. Portolan charts, which were probably in use by the twelfth century in the Mediterranean, were portable sea maps that illustrated coastlines and all the different wind directions to facilitate navigation for pilots.[49] Northern European navigation was aided from the fifteenth century on by rutters, which recorded more detailed instructions about sailing, including lunar information and the tidal currents, the depth of the sea bottom along the coast, and landmarks, among other features.[50] Even more advanced in the nautical data employed was the Portuguese *roterio*, which concentrated on the oceanic sailing that was a fundamental part of the explorations led by the Portuguese. Here too the literature of exploration, from the early voyage of St Brendan to the voyages of Vasco da Gama and Christopher Columbus, provides a wealth of information.[51]

## Artistic and archaeological evidence

Medieval manuscript illuminations are a valuable source of visual data on the appearance of ships, harbours, and quayside facilities, while also supplying insights into the medieval mentality regarding the miraculous intervention of saints to stop storms at sea, sirens attacking a seaborne vessel, or pleasure boating by aristocrats.[52] Images of Noah building the ark have been cleverly employed to track the tools and technology of shipbuilding, while images of ships on town seals have both helped to date developments in ship construction and revealed how particular ports chose to express their maritime identity.[53] Even more valuable has been evidence from archaeology since excavations of shipwrecks are the best source of data on the construction of different types of ships across the medieval world.[54] Shipwrecks are especially important for studying the documentary-poor early Middle Ages because the origin of the surviving cargoes can often be determined.[55] Archaeological excavations have also revealed much about the construction of quays, docks, sea banks and river revetments within individual maritime settlements.[56]

## Maritime communities

Scholars have become increasingly interested in shoreside communities, whether small fishing villages or large seaports. Wills that show bequests of ships or fishing gear (even to women), inventories that record the types of tackle or tools owned by fishers and shipwrights, accounts that show rents from salt pans or the collection of kelp, and deeds and accounts that point to the location and uses of beacons, beaches and quays all provide a window onto what made settlements by the sea so distinctive. Taxes assessed according to age, gender or immigrant status offer insights into the demographic structure of these settlements where male absences may have endowed the women left at home with more autonomy. Also worth exploring are the types of activities found only in maritime communities, such as the scramble for whales or wrecks that came ashore, or the smuggling that was easy to hide in isolated coastal inlets. Kings and other lords generally claimed rights to all wrecks and whales that came ashore, but the business of 'wrecking' was hard to stop since coastal residents were first on the scene and felt it their right to claim the flotsam and jetsam cast up on their shores. Fines for those caught usurping this regalian right, as well as efforts to stop wholesale pillaging by paying one-half the value of wrecked goods as 'salvage' to the finders, offer a snapshot of these maritime activities [57]

A characteristic feature of larger port towns were mariners' guilds, which formed initially to promote religious, charitable and social aims but often acquired occupational monopolies or the right to set standards for the craft in later years. The 1445 ordinances for the fraternity of Masters and Mariners of Ships in Bristol, which named thirty-five members, supported a priest and 'twelve poor mariners' by collecting fees from all Bristol shipmasters entering or exiting the port, with a sliding scale of payments to be made by the lesser yeoman-mariners and servant-mariners. The same sliding scale was applied to fines for those who failed to

UNIVERSITY OF WINCHESTER
LIBRARY

attend the annual election of wardens, the Corpus Christi procession, and the Midsummer watch. The only clause relating to the maritime craft itself required a new member to have some knowledge or 'connyng of his crafte', suggesting that this guild was oriented more towards the care of its elderly and sick than towards training new mariners.[58]

Finally, recent interest in the relationship between people and environment has turned scholarly attention towards ways that the human hand shaped the marine environment. Particularly interesting are the distinctive social and political institutions that developed from efforts to reclaim marshland as farmland and the construction of sea dikes to prevent harmful storm surges. The people of the Rijnland in western Netherlands, for example, formed powerful 'water boards' that supervised the construction of dikes, sluices, dams and canals. The ordinances, contracts and dispute settlements that regulated their activities are recorded in registers from the fourteenth century on.[59] In England, so-called 'dike-reeves' were appointed to collect local taxes ('water-scots') to keep dikes and sluices in good repair and to help adjudicate disputes, while commissions of the sewers were appointed by the central government to administer drainage programmes in places like the Fenland.[60] Landlords certainly played a role in these reclamation efforts, but coastal residents themselves took the lead in initiating and overseeing many stages. The riches of the sea and the marine environment helped to shape life in maritime communities, but cooperative vigilance to hold back the aggressions of the sea was also necessary for their survival.

## Further reading

Dollinger, P. *The German Hansa*, transl. D. S. Ault and S. H. Steinberg (London: Macmillan, 1970).

Haywood, J. *Dark Age Naval Power: A Reassessment of Frankish and Anglo-Saxon Seafaring Activity*, rev. edn (Hockwold-cum-Wilton: Anglo-Saxon Books, 1999).

Kowaleski, M. 'Working at Sea: Maritime Recruitment and Remuneration in Medieval England,' in *Ricchezza del mare, ricchezza dal mare. Secoli XIII-XVIII*, S. Cavciocchi (ed.) (Florence: Le Monnier, 2006), pp. 907–36

Lane, F.C. *Venice and History* (Baltimore: Johns Hopkins University Press, 1966).

Mott, L.V. *Sea Power in the Medieval Mediterranean: The Catalan-Aragonese Fleet in the War of the Sicilian Vespers* (Gainesville: University Press of Florida, 2003).

Pryor, J.H. *Geography, Technology and War: Studies in the Maritime History of the Mediterranean 649–1517* (Cambridge: Cambridge University Press, 1988).

Rodger, N.A.M. *The Safeguard of the Sea: A Naval History of Britain 660–1649* (New York: W.W. Norton, 1998).

Unger, R.W. *The Ship in the Medieval Economy 600–1600* (Montreal: McGill-Queen's University Press, 1980).

Villain-Gandossi, C. and Rieth, É. (eds), *Pour une histoire du 'fait maritime': Sources et champ de recherché* (Paris: Éditions du Comité des travaux historiques et scientifiques, 2001).

Ward, R. *The World of the Medieval Shipmaster: Law, Business, and the Sea, c. 1350–c. 1450* (Woodbridge: Boydell & Brewer, 2009).

# Notes

1  Among the more accessible English translations are: T. Twiss (ed.), *Monumenta Juridica: The Black Book of the Admiralty,* Rolls Series, no. 55, 4 vols (London: Longman, 1871–6); S. Jados (transl.), *Consultate of the Sea and Related Documents* (Tuscaloosa, AL: University of Alabama Press, 1975).

2  For example: R.G. Marsden (ed.), *Select Pleas in the Court of Admiralty, vol. 1,* Selden Society, vol. 6, 1894.

3  Little of this material is in print, but see the minutes of the Brodhull and Guestling courts (which also served as legislative councils) in F. Hull (ed.), *A Calendar of the White and Black Books of the Cinque Ports 1432–1955* (London: HMSO, 1966).

4  There are many sources on Hanseatic maritime issues (albeit written in Low German and Latin), the most important of which are: W. Junghans and K. Koppmann (eds), *Die Recesse und andere Akten der Hansetage von 1256–1430,* 8 vols (Leipzig: Duncker and Humblot, 1870–97); G. von der Ropp (ed.), *Hanserecesse von 1431–1476,* 7 vols (Leipzig: Duncker and Humblot, 1876–92); D. Schäfer and F. Techen (eds), *Hanserecesse von 1477–1530,* 9 vols (Munich: Duncker and Humblot, 1881–1913); K. Höhlbaum, K. Kunze, and W. Stein (eds), *Hansisches Urkundenbuch,* 11 vols (Halle and Leipzig: Hansischer Geschichtsverein, 1876–1916).

5  For example: S. Jenks (ed.), *Robert Sturmy's Commercial Expedition to the Mediterranean (1457/8) with Editions of the Trial of the Genoese before King and Council and Other Sources,* Bristol Record Society, vol. 58, 2006. For translations of English naval records, see R. G. Marsden (ed.), *Documents Relating to the Law and Custom of the Sea,* Navy Records Society, vol. 49, 1915, and J. B. Hattendorf *et al.* (eds), *British Naval Documents 1204–1960,* Navy Records Society, vol. 131, 1993.

6  For example: T. Rymer (ed.), *Foedera, Conventiones, Literrae et Cujuscunque Generis Acta Publica inter Regies Angliae et Alios quosvis Imperatores, Reges, Pontifices, Principes vel Communitates,* 4 vols (London: George Eyre and Andrew Strahan, 1816–69); P. de Bofarull y Mascaró (ed.), *Colección de documentos inéditos del archivo general de la Corona de Aragon,* 41 vols (Barcelona: J.E. Montfort, 1847–1910); J. Paviot (ed.), *Portugal et Bourgogne au XVe siècle (1384–1492): recueil des documents extraits des archives bourguignonnes* (Paris: Touzot, 1995).

7  English translations of the volumes for 1216–1452 are available online at http://sdrc. lib.uiowa.edu/patentrolls/ [accessed Sept. 16, 2010].

8  For example: D.A. Gardiner (ed.), *A Calendar of Early Chancery Proceedings relating to West Country Shipping 1388–1493* (Devon and Cornwall Record Society, 1976), n.s., vol. 21.

9  For example: R. Cessi *et al.* (eds), *Le Deliberazione del Consiglio dei Rogati (Senato) serie 'Mixtorum',* 2 vols (Venice: Deputazione di storia patria per la Venezie), n.s., vols 15–16, 1960–61, and below, n. 10.

10  R. Brown (ed.), *Calendar of State Papers and Manuscripts, Relating to English Affairs, Existing in the State Archives and Collections of Venice, vol. I, 1202–1509* (London: HMSO), 1864, pp. 44–5, 77.

11  R.I. Burns (ed.), *Las Siete partidas,* transl. S.P. Scott, 5 vols (Philadelphia: University of Pennsylvania Press, 2001), vols 2 and 4.

12  Twiss (ed.), *Black Book of the Admiralty,* vol. 1.

13  For example: B. Lyon, M. Lyon and H. S. Lucas (eds), *The Wardrobe Book of William de Norwell, 12 July 1338–27 May 1340* (Brussels: Palais des Académies, 1983). The archival class of E101 naval documents in the National Archives of the United Kingdom contains a particularly large cache of extant naval records.

14  For example: A. Sprot, 'La marine française sous le rêgne de Charles VIII,' *Revue des questions historiques* 55 (1894): 387–454, and n. 16, below.

15  For example: G. La Mantia (ed.), *Codice diplomatico dei re aragonesi de Sicilia,* 2 vols, 1917–19, reprint (Palermo: Ristampa Anastatica, 1970). For Venice, see above, n. 10 and below, n. 17.

16  For example: S. Rose (ed.), *The Navy of the Lancastrian Kings: Accounts and Inventories of William Soper, Keeper of the King's Ships, 1422–1427*, Navy Records Society, vol. 123, 1982; A. M. Chazelas (ed.), *Documents rélatifs au clos des gales de Rouen et aux armées de mer du roi de France de 1293 à 1418*, 2 vols (Paris: Collection de documents inédits sur l'histoire de France, 1977–8), vols. 11–12, section de philologie et d'histoire jusqu'à 1610.

17  F.C. Lane, *Venetian Ships and Shipbuilders of the Renaissance* (Baltimore: Johns Hopkins University Press, 1934).

18  P.O. Long, D. McGee, and A. Stahl (eds), *The Book of Michael of Rhodes: A Fifteenth-Century Maritime Manuscript*, 3 vols (Boston: MIT Press, 2009). See also the Michael of Rhodes website at http://brunelleschi.imss.fi.it/michaelofrhodes.

19  M. Kowaleski (ed.), *Local Customs Accounts of the Port of Exeter 1266–1321* (Devon and Cornwall Record Society, 1993), n.s., vol. 36; H.S. Cobb (ed.), *The Local Port Book of Southampton 1439–40*, Southampton Records Series, vol. 5, 1961; M. Mollat (ed.), *Comptabilité du Port de Dieppe au XVe siècle* (Paris: SEVPEN, 1951).

20  For example: H. Nirrnheim (ed.), *Das Hamburgische Pfundzoll von 1369* (Hamburg: Verlag Von Leopold Voss, 1910); R. Sprandel (ed.), *Das Hamburger Pfundzollbuch von 1418* (Cologne: Böhlau, 1972).

21  J. Day (ed.), *Les douanes de Gênes 1376–1377*, 2 vols (Paris: SEVPEN, 1963).

22  Summaries of totals collected for each port in each year are in the enrolled customs accounts, which survive in a virtually unbroken series from the late thirteenth century. They were compiled from the totals in the 'particular' national customs accounts for each port, but they do not offer the details on individual ships and cargoes that the particular and local port customs accounts record. See S. Jenks (ed.), *The Enrolled Customs Accounts (TNA: E 356, E 372, E 364) 1279/80–1508/09 (1523/1524)* (London: List and Index Society), vols 303, 306, 307, 313, 314, 319, 324, 328, 2004–8.

23  N.S.B. Gras, *The Early English Customs System* (Cambridge, MA: Harvard University Press, 1918). For a recent English translation of the English national customs accounts (E122 class in the National Archives), see S. H. Rigby (ed.), *The Overseas Trade of Boston in the Reign of Richard II* (Lincoln Record Society, 2005), vol. 93.

24  M.K. James, *Studies in the Medieval Wine Trade*, E.M. Veale (ed.) (Oxford: Clarendon, 1971).

25  For these and other comparisons of shipping and maritime trade by port, see M. Kowaleski, 'Port Towns in Medieval England and Wales' in D. Palliser (ed.), *The Urban History of Britain*, vol. 1 (Cambridge: Cambridge University Press, 2000), pp. 467–94.

26  M. Kowaleski, 'Polish Ships in English Waters in the Late Middle Ages,' in R.W. Unger (ed.), *Britain and Poland-Lithuania Contact and Comparison from the Middle Ages to 1795* (Leiden: Brill, 2008), pp. 39–64.

27  P. Heath, 'North Sea Fishing in the Fifteenth Century: The Scarborough Fleet,' *Northern History*, 3(1968): 53–69.

28  For a discussion of primary sources available to study medieval fishing, see M. Kowaleski, 'The Commercialization of the Sea Fisheries of Medieval England and Wales,' *International Journal of Maritime History*, 15:2 (2003): 177–231.

29  Italian merchants brought their notarial culture north to the Low Countries in the fourteenth century; see K.L. Reyerson and D.A. Salata (eds), *Medieval Notaries and Their Acts: The 1327–1328 Register of Jean Holanie* (Kalamazoo: Medieval Institute Publications, 2004), for an excellent introduction to the history of notaries and English translations of representative notarial acts.

30  For examples, see R.S. Lopez and I.W. Raymond (eds), *Medieval Trade in the Mediterranean World: Illustrative Documents Translated with Introductions and Notes* (New York: Columbia University Press, 1955).

31  Robin Ward, 'A Surviving Charter-Party of 1323,' *Mariner's Mirror* 81 (1995), 387–401.

32  L. Mott, 'Aspects of Intercoastal Trade in the Western Mediterranean; The Voyage of the *Santa Mariá de Natzare*,' in *The Byzantine and Crusader Mediterranean (6th–14th centuries): Trade, Cultural Exchange, Warfare and Archaeology* (Aldershot: Ashgate, forthcoming).

33  For a description of the genre and some English translations, see V. Branca (ed.), *Merchant Writers of the Italian Renaissance from Boccaccio to Machiavelli*, transl., M. Baca (New York: Marsilio Publishers, 1999).

34  For example: J.E. Dotson (transl.), *Merchant Culture in Fourteenth-Century Venice: The Zialdone da Canal* (Binghamton: Medieval and Renaissance Texts and Studies, 1994).

35  For example: A.F. Sutton and L. Visser-Fuch (eds), *The Book of Privileges of the Merchant Adventurers of England 1296–1483* (Oxford: Oxford University Press for the British Academy, 2009).

36  For English translations, see Lopez and Raymond (eds), *Medieval Trade in the Mediterranean*, pp. 400–7.

37  For example: S.D. Goitein (transl.), *Letters of Medieval Jewish Traders* (Princeton: Princeton University Press, 1973); A. Hanham (ed.), *The Cely Letters* (Early English Text Society, 1975), o.s., vol. 273.

38  For example: K.M.E. Murray (ed.), *The Register of Daniel Rough* (Kent Archaeological Society Records Branch, 1945), vol. 16.

39  M.E. Mallet, *The Florentine Galleys in the Fifteenth Century with The Diary of Luca di Maso degli Albizzi, Captain of the Galleys 1429–1430* (Oxford: Clarendon, 1967).

40  P.H. Labalme and L.S. White (eds), *Venice, città excelentissima: Selections from the Renaissance Diaries of Marin Sanudo*, L.L. Carroll (transl.) (Baltimore: Johns Hopkins University Press, 2006).

41  For examples of crusade chronicles, see Emilie Amt and S.J. Allen (eds) *The Crusades: A Reader* (Peterborough, Ontario; Broadview Press, 2003).

42  An accessible abridged translation is available in: Froissart, *Chronicles*, G. Brereton (transl.) (Harmondsworth: Penguin Books, 1968); reprint 1979.

43  C.W. David (transl.), *De expugnatione Lyxbonensi: The Conquest of Lisbon* (New York: Columbia University Press, 1916); new edn, 2001.

44  Brownlow, W.R.B. (transl.), *Saewulf, 1102, 1103* (Palestine Pilgrims' Text Society, 1892), vol. 4.

45  A. Stewart (transl.), *The Book of the Wanderings of Felix Fabri (circa 1480–1483 A.D.)* (Palestine Pilgrims' Text Society, 1893–10), vols 7–10,

46  F.J. Furnivall (ed.), *The Stacions of Rome and The Pilgrims Sea-voyage with Clene Maydenhod* (Early English Text Society, 1867), o.s., vol. 25, pp. 37–40.

47  G.S. Burgess (transl.), *Two Medieval Outlaws: Eustace the Monk and Fouke Fitz Waryn* (Woodbridge: D.S. Brewer, 1997).

48  D. Staines (transl.), *The Complete Romances of Chrétien de Troyes* (Bloomington: Indiana University Press, 1993).

49  T. Campbell, 'Portolan Charts from the Late Thirteenth Century to 1500,' in J.B. Harley and D. Woodward (eds), *The History of Cartography, vol. 1* (Chicago: University of Chicago Press, 1987), pp. 371–463.

50  R. Ward, 'The Earliest Known Sailing Directions in English: Transcription and Analysis,' *Deutsches Schiffahrtsarchiv*, 27 (2004), 49–90.

51  W.R.J. Barron and G. Burgess (eds), *Voyage of St Brendan* (Exeter: University of Exeter Press, 2002); J. de Sá, *A Journal of the First Voyage of Vasco da Gama, 1497–1499*, Hakluyt Society, first series, vol. 99, 1898, and the volumes of the *Repertorium Columbianum* series now published by Brepols.

52  J. Flatman, *The Illuminated Ark; Interrogating Evidence from Manuscript Illuminations and Archaeological Remains for Medieval Vessels* (London: British Archaeological Reports International Series, 2007), no. 1616.

53  R.W. Unger, *The Art of Medieval Technology: Images of Noah the Shipbuilder* (New Brunswick: Rutgers University Press, 1991); H. Ewe, *Schiffe auf Siegeln* (Berlin: VEB Hinstorff, 1972).

54   G. Hutchinson, *Medieval Ships and Shipping* (London: Leicester University Press, 1994).

55   See, for example, the sources on shipwrecks listed by the *Digital Atlas of Roman and Medieval Civilization*, M. McCormick *et al.* (eds), at http://darmc.harvard.edu/icb/icb. do [accessed 28 September, 2010].

56   G. Milne, *The Port of London* (Stroud: Tempus, 2003).

57   M. Kowaleski (ed.), *The Havener's Accounts of the Earldom and Duchy of Cornwall, 1287–1356* (Devon and Cornwall Record Society, 2001), n.s., vol. 44.

58   F.B. Bickley (ed.), *The Little Red Book of Bristol*, 2 vols (Bristol: W Crofton Hemmons, 1900), II, pp. 186–92.

59   T. W. TeBrake, 'Hoogheemraadschap Rijnland, Registers OAR 11, 12, 13: 1253–1564' available online (with English summaries) at http://www.janvanhout.nl/tebrake/oar_ frame.htm.

60   A.E.B. Owen (ed.), *The Records of a Commission of Sewers for Wiggenhall 1319– 1324*, (Norfolk Record Society, 1981), vol. 48.

# 11  Sources for medieval urban history

*Caroline M. Barron*

To study a medieval town is to study the medieval state in microcosm. All human life is there. All the materials that historians use to illuminate medieval society in general will be of use to the urban historian: not only written sources such as letters, wills, chronicles and judicial records, but also the results of archaeological excavations and, indeed, aerial photography. Most of the other materials discussed in this volume will, at some point, throw light on medieval towns. The aim of this essay, therefore, is to look at the sources which were generated specifically in, and for, medieval towns.

But first it is necessary to define what we mean when we use the word 'town' in the medieval period. 'A town is a permanent and concentrated human settlement in which a significant proportion of the population is engaged in non-agricultural occupations'. A town therefore normally lives, at least in part, off food produced by people who live outside it. In addition 'the inhabitants of towns normally regard themselves, and are regarded by the inhabitants of predominantly rural settlements, as a different sort of people'.[1] The towns of medieval Europe were not, of course, all the same. Some were ports situated on rivers or by the sea: others were inland hilltop towns. They ranged in size: some significant medieval towns (such as Oxford or Boston in England) may have had no more than three or four thousand inhabitants. Towns such as Osnabruck in Germany, Bristol in England, or the Dutch towns of Leiden or Amsterdam had about 10,000 inhabitants. In 1300, London may have had 80,000 inhabitants, Paris rather more and Constantinople was the largest urban conurbation with some 300,000 inhabitants by the early sixteenth century. Towns varied not only in size but also in their governing structures. Some towns, such as Florence, or Venice or the Flemish towns of Ghent or Ypres, or the German episcopal towns such as Cologne or Mainz were, in effect, city states which governed themselves and acknowledged no superior authority and conducted their own 'foreign affairs'. Other towns, such as those in England, were only allowed to govern themselves because they had been granted the right to do so by a 'higher authority' such as the king who continued to keep a close watch on the towns in his kingdom. Or there might be towns further down the chain of command that had been granted self-government by a great lay or ecclesiastical lord whose authority, in turn, often derived from a ruler still further up the command chain. The larger the town, the more likely it was to have impressive walls and to have a cathedral, the seat of the bishop. Smaller towns might lack these attributes, but could well have a large friary or an impressive market house or council chamber. But however different towns might be in terms of physical appearance, economic functions or systems of government, all townspeople had to find solutions to the problems posed when large numbers of people live together in close proximity. Inevitably, urban communities had to find ways to secure the food supply, prevent riot and discord, control building and perpetuate the conditions which enabled their fragile economies to flourish.

The Roman Empire was essentially an empire held together by its *castra* or garrison camps which often developed into towns. From these bases, connected by the sinews of their remarkable road system, the Romans administered their far-reaching empire and imposed an urban way of life on peoples who had before been largely nomadic and rural. When the Empire began to disintegrate in the fourth and fifth centuries, under the impact of attacks from the men of the east, the towns which the Romans had created fell into decay and disuse as the indigenous peoples and their new conquerors reverted to a less settled way of life. The towns in southern Europe, in Italy, Spain and Southern France maintained some vestiges of cooperative urban life, but in northern France, England and the Germanic lands towns disappeared almost entirely. When the towns of northern and central Europe began to emerge once more in the ninth and tenth centuries, they often made use of the old Roman sites, but they had lost many of the technical skills (such as water supply, hypercausts) which had made Roman town life both sophisticated and comfortable. But the new townsmen reused the surviving Roman buildings and monuments to patch the walls and build their new stone churches.

In this reinvigorated period of town life, as populations began to grow and trade opened up once more across a Europe which had been darkened first by invasions of Germanic tribes, Magyars and Huns, and then by the Viking men of the north, in this spring-time of Christianity, the seeds of town life grew and flourished. Men and women sought once again to live together, trusting that the countryside was sufficiently peaceful to supply them with food, and that there would be a market for goods produced in the competitive and innovative environment of a town. And the growth of more extended (and safer) trade routes opened up a greater range of markets, and economic opportunities, for the skilled and enterprising urban inhabitant and for the merchants who traded their products between towns and across the countryside.

In order to run their own affairs, townsmen usually needed to be granted the right to do so by some 'higher authority' whether a secular or ecclesiastical lord. So some of the earliest materials for studying medieval towns were generated outside those towns, but enable the men who lived inside them, in their turn, to make rules for their common life, impose punishments, and regulate the relationships between those living within the urban community and those outside it. Often the oldest, and most treasured, urban records are charters granted by rulers to towns in these early years. So, in 965 the German Emperor Otto I granted a charter to allow the Archbishop of Hamburg to set up a market, law courts and a mint in his town of Bremen.[2] Within a year of his victory at Hastings in 1066, King William the Conqueror granted a charter to William, the bishop of London, Geoffrey, the port-reeve (or sheriff) and the burgesses 'within London', both French and English, by which he confirmed all their customary rights and specified that they should enjoy hereditary succession to their lands (a privilege later known as burgage tenure, that is, tenure free from feudal obligations). The new king assured the Londoners that he would not allow any man to do them wrong and the brief charter concluded with the words 'God keep you'.[3] In 1155 the French king, Louis VII, granted extensive and detailed rights of self-government to the small town of Lorris, lying some twenty-five kilometres east of Orleans. In this charter the king exempted the burghers from a number of customary royal exactions (although he retained their obligation to carry wine for the royal household twice a year to Orleans), and protected their right to inherit, buy and sell property in the town.[4] This charter to Lorris became as a model for the many royal charters granted to towns in the twelfth century.

Where it is possible to study a series of royal charters to a given town, covering several centuries (as in the case of London, or Dublin) one can see how these urban communities gradually secured (usually at a considerable cost, for charters had to be bought) more and more concessions, such as the right to hold their own judicial courts, to exclude or tax aliens and foreigners, to secure privileges for their own citizens in other towns, to exempt them from military service and to acquire stronger and more authoritarian powers for the governing class of the town who were the people who usually negotiated and paid for such charters.

Medieval townsmen knew that such charters, hard fought-for and dearly-bought, were important and valuable, and they took trouble to preserve them. Although William I's charter to London is a small and inconsequential-looking piece of parchment, most charters were intended to impress those who saw them. When King Alfonso X of Castile in 1256 granted a charter to the citizens of Burgos, it was recorded that the king had drawn up the document 'with the counsel of my court, written into a book and sealed with my lead seal'.[5] Later charters were often not only sealed but lavishly decorated and the initial letter might be enlarged to show the king graciously handing out a document to suitably humble civic recipients.

Charters, of course, only tell us what the king, or grantor, and the town's leading citizens, wanted to happen, or thought should happen. So the charter granted by John, count of Mortain (later King John) to the men of Dublin contained detailed provisions excluding foreigners (i.e. men from outside Dublin) from selling their goods in the city and prohibiting them from remaining longer than forty days; allowing all citizens to arrange marriages freely, for themselves, their children and their widows; and granting them the right to build freely on the banks of the river Liffey.[6] Such clauses were normative, i.e. they were a set of aspirations or ideals, but there is a good deal of evidence to suggest that the detailed provisions of charters were often ignored in practice: sometimes by the grantor who went back on his word; sometimes by other towns which refused to accept the privileges granted to their rivals and, sometimes, by the townsmen themselves. But the charters remain extremely important because by studying them in sequence we can trace the developing aspirations of urban communities as they pressed for greater autonomy, more extensive privileges, and the means to secure more effective civic regulation.

Once they had secured a charter from the higher authority, towns were empowered to draw up their own rules and regulations and they did so with a vengeance.
These voluminous sets of civic ordinances covered every aspect of town life, and
they survive because they were copied into record books, known as registers or
custumals, which towns had compiled and then kept up to date in the burgeoning
civic secretariats. These custumals constituted the 'rule books' of medieval urban
communities and all documents of importance, whatever their source and nature,
were copied into them for preservation and reference. Such record books were
large, impressive and often written up in Latin rather than the vernacular to
ensure permanence, distinction and authority. The governors of the Tuscan town
of Volterra drew up a detailed constitution in 1224 which included the oath to be
taken by all citizens whereby they agreed to obey the consuls chosen to govern
the city.[7] These important custumals acquired special names. In London one of
the earliest custumals, compiled by the City Chamberlain Andrew Horn early
in the fourteenth century, carried his name and was known as *Liber Horn*. The
famous book of city customs put together a century later by the Common Clerk
of London, John Carpenter, was always known as the *Liber Albus*, from the white
leather in which it was bound.[8] The main city custumal in Southampton, compiled
in the early fourteenth century, was known as Paxbred, meaning Pax board. The
main meeting of the Southampton court took place at Easter (Pasche) and the
covers of the book were made of oak, hence Paxbred was the colloquial description of the venerable oak-covered book used at the Easter meeting.[9] When the
Londoners compiled a new (and contentious) book of civic customs, it was known
as the *Jubilee Book* since it was put together in 1377, the fiftieth year of the reign
of Edward III.

In these early custumals the town's rulers and their scribes would record how
officials were to be chosen and when and how often the city's consultative and
judicial courts should meet. Regulations about food prices, building controls,
access to citizenship, guild organization, wage rates, nuisances of all kinds, taxation and civic building projects would all be recorded along with much else. For
example, in the Southampton Paxbred book were entered long lists of the tolls
to be paid on goods coming into the town for sale in the city's markets.[10] In the
Spanish kingdom of Aragon the towns of Borja and Zaragoza drew up detailed laws
about the inheritance of urban property which were included in their custumals or
statute books.[11] On the whole it would be true to say that in these custumals were
recorded matters of importance to all members of the civic community, not issues
of concern only to specific individuals. But these custumals, rich as they are, can
only take us so far: they record how the city rulers thought that life in their urban
communities should be regulated, but not the realities of urban living. For this we
have to look at a lower tier of urban material, also emerging from the civic secretariats, but recording more immediate and short-term events and concerns. These
administrative records, becoming increasingly numerous towards the end of the
medieval period, included minute books of the city's executive councils; financial
records detailing the income and expenditure of urban taxes; judicial records from
a variety of civic courts; rolls and books of property transactions (which might
include wills); and lists of the men (and women) entering into apprenticeships or

taking up citizenship. Not all towns would have compiled, let alone preserved, records in all these categories, but most will have some of these administrative documents, and it is these records which are, perhaps, of most use to the urban historian.

The records, or journals (literally day books) or minute books of the executive councils responsible for town government provide rich material for the urban historian. Royal governments began to keep careful administrative records from the twelfth century and towns followed suit. Many European towns began in the thirteenth century to keep written records of decisions made by their town councils, although many of these early records have not survived. The Spanish town of Cuenca, on the border between the Christian kingdoms and Muslim territories to the south, as early as 1190 drew up regulations about the military obligations of its inhabitants.[12] At about the same time, further south in the Muslim town of Seville, detailed regulations were drawn up to control and regulate market practices which included the prohibition on the sale of truffles around the mosque 'because this is a delicacy of the dissolute'; cats were not to be sold and flour was not to be mixed with the cheese used to make fritters. The man who let blood was always to use a special jar with graduation marks so that he could see how much blood had been taken. Women were not to trade secretly with men and were not to use the same paths as men when they went to cross the river. These remarkably detailed regulations drawn up by the town's rulers tell us a great deal about the economic and social practices of the inhabitants of the town.[13] The concerns of the city's rulers are reflected in the documents which they produced to deal with the day-to-day issues that confronted them in urban life. Many of these decisions relate to the punishments to be meted out to those who transgressed: sometimes this would be imprisonment, but more often a fine or a period in the town's pillory. Public shame was deemed to be the most effective deterrent. These city rulers were omni-competent and their recorded decisions reflect this overarching authority. Their actions ranged from the decision to hold a mass of the Holy Spirit before the annual election of the mayor in London in 1406 to concerns about the activities of single women in Coventry in 1492 to the attempts by the provost, bailiffs and council of Edinburgh to contain the outbreak of plague in the area in 1498.[14] By the end of the medieval period, most towns were probably keeping more than one series of records of the decisions of their governing councils. In London the city was maintaining an impressive series of Letter Books from the 1270s in which all important decisions were recorded in 'fair copy'; from 1416, there also survive the more immediate and informal journals in which the day-to-day minutes of the Court of Aldermen and the Court of Common Council were written down in a highly abbreviated style of note-taking. Finally in 1495 the Court of Aldermen acquired a separate minute book, known as the Repertories, so that by 1500 there were three separate series of books in which the city's executive decisions were recorded.

Not surprisingly, some of the earliest surviving financial accounts for European towns come from the sophisticated cities of Italy. The chancellor of the town of Siena, who was responsible for the city's finances, was elected every six months and assisted by a team of three or four *provisores*. The expenses listed in 1257 included payments for purchasing property, fees to messengers, salaries for civic officials, fees to lawyers and wages to soldiers.[15] Income to fund communal expenditure was raised by tolls or fees (such as licences for non-citizens to sell goods retail in the town) but also by direct taxation. In 1427 Florence instituted a new direct tax on all Florentine citizens and those living in its subject territories, assessed on the value of all their property including real estate, cash, business investments and their holdings in the communal debt fund. This record, known as the *Catasto*, still survives and includes information about the property and wealth of about 60,000 households. The 1427 assessment was followed by similarly detailed assessments later in the century. Historians have been able to use these extraordinarily rich sources to compile many statistics about – among other things – the size of urban households, the number of households headed by women and the age at which men and women were married.[16] The city of Ypres has rich financial accounts surviving from 1267 and these can be exploited in many ways. In 1316, at the height of the 'Great Famine' in Europe, the city fathers used the public finances to pay for the burial of the corpses lying in the streets to prevent the outbreak of disease. The payments made for these burials can be used to chart the impact of the famine: at the beginning of May the city was paying for the burial of fifty corpses a week and this weekly average rose to 190 at the end of July but then began to drop again (perhaps as the harvest was gathered in?) and had been reduced to fifteen a week in early October.[17] In happier times the financial records of civic officials which were presented for audit would reveal payments for feasts and entertainments, liveries of cloth for civic servants, bribes to royal officials and charitable offerings for local good causes.

All towns which had achieved a measure of self-government would establish judicial courts to try cases between citizens and in which to prosecute offenders against civic regulations. In London the oldest court was that known as the Husting where cases between citizens relating to disputes about land or financial transactions were heard and the results recorded on rolls which survive from 1272. This court was also a court of record and so deeds relating to London property and the wills of London citizens were read out in the court and then recorded in rolls which survive from 1252. By 1700 some 30,000 deeds and wills had been enrolled. But other courts were developed to deal with pressing matters of business: the mayor held a court which dealt primarily with matters relating to the specialized business between merchants, although its jurisdiction became much more extensive and the records, which survive from 1298, encompass a wide range of civic business. The two London sheriffs also held courts which dealt with cases of debt and personal actions arising within the city. But because the sheriffs might be called to answer later for the decisions of their courts, the records were considered to be the personal property of the individual sheriffs and so have not survived. Many English towns have records surviving from their judicial courts: the records of the mayor's court in Nottingham survive from 1303,[18] and Exeter from 1390.[19] The importance of the material that survives from these local urban civic courts is that it takes us quite far down the social scale and reveals something of the lives of those who were poor and without property but who sued each other for small debts or were brought before the city officials for trespasses against civic regulation (usually about sharp practices in the sale of goods). Very often we know nothing further about these poorer town-dwellers apart from what it has been possible to glean from these court rolls.

As we have seen, the Londoners kept detailed rolls recording individual property transactions in the city and, contingent to this, the texts of the wills of citizens were also read in the court and then recorded on the court rolls by the executors. Since a fee was payable for such enrolments, executors might choose simply to have the will read out and not pay for it to be entered in the records of the court. In July 1260 the will of Emma the Smerewyf (perhaps she was a tallow chandler) was proved (that is, read out) in the Husting Court of London and this was noted on the original will itself which (very unusually) has survived, but there is no copy of the will to be found entered onto the Husting roll for that year.[20] Emma's executors clearly decided to save money. Some towns kept registers, or cartularies, of the property which was owned by the city communally and which was often an important source of revenue for the town and funded communal enterprises.[21]

It was important for towns to keep a record of those who were its citizens and thereby entitled to enjoy the privileges of the town but also liable for civic obligations. Citizenship, or the freedom, of a town might be achieved in a variety of ways: by patrimony or inheritance, by serving an apprenticeship, or simply by paying for the privilege. The rolls of freemen kept by towns often distinguished between these different forms of entry. The earliest surviving English listing of freemen comes from Leicester, which began to keep these records in 1196, followed by Exeter in 1266, York in 1272 and Lynn in 1292.[22] These early lists of freemen can be used to calculate trends in the size of the population and to assess periods of prosperity. The topographical surnames (such as Ralph de Abingdon) in such listings, taken together with the names recorded in early property deeds (before about the middle of the fourteenth century when surnames tended to become inherited), have also been used to work out the origins of immigrants to the towns and to calculate their zones of economic influence. In the case of Westminster (the main seat of the English government situated in a small but important town adjacent to London), such a study has shown that a high percentage of the men who emigrated to Westminster had travelled a very considerable distance, and that more had come from the north and east of England than from the south and west.[23]

In some towns the ruling élites, in the later part of the period, paid scribes, or local clerics with historical inclinations, to compile official histories of the town. Many German towns paid men to fill the office of *Stadtschreiber*, or town chronicler. These men would be responsible for compiling the official history of the town in Latin or, increasingly, in German. The German-speaking towns of Magdeburg, Bern and Nuremberg all had official historians and official histories by the fifteenth century.[24]

But by no means all the records which we associate with medieval towns emanated from the central or official government of the town, as did those we have been discussing so far. Where people live closely together they are not only more likely to form clubs, guilds and associations of all kinds, but they also have access to the specialized writing skills of scriveners who can be paid to draft legal documents, accounts, lists of ordinances or regulations, rentals and surveys and all the other written records necessary to maintain the organization of such guilds and fraternities. And so towns in the medieval period generated more of these lesser, or subordinate, records than are to be found in small villages, farms and manors. Such records are particularly valuable because they take us to the heart of town life and bring us closer to the realities of urban living and the aspirations of those who were never going to achieve prestigious civic office. Such associations, in origin often informal, did not at first keep formal written records but gradually they found it expedient to do so. And some of the organizations grew to be important and permanent. The smaller units into which towns were divided for administrative purposes might be called precincts, or wards or quarters. In addition there were parishes, and craft and trade guilds which, in the early days, were often linked to the parishes in which members of the craft congregated.

Almost all towns were divided into smaller administrative areas. In London there were twenty-four smaller units known as wards, each presided over by an alderman and with its own administrative officers such as the beadle and constables. All the male householders who lived in the ward were expected to attend the meeting of the ward (ward moot) which met once or twice a year. John Carpenter in his *Liber Albus* describes how these ward meetings were to be conducted. The reality may have been somewhat different, but it is hard to know since so few of these ward records have survived, probably because they were retained by the aldermen as their personal possessions. Some late fifteenth-century ward moot records survive for the London ward of Portsoken and, in this case, they are largely concerned with accusations against prostitutes and other immoral persons.[25] In the town of Nottingham there were similar local groupings in which juries of townsmen reported on the wrong-doing of their neighbours. Here the main concern at the end of the fourteenth century was about those who broke the peace and contravened the price controls imposed by the town.[26] By 1571 Paris was divided into sixteen quarters which formed the basis for tax assessments and the leaders of these quarters were known as *quarteniers*.[27]

Most towns were divided into a number of parishes, although some towns such as Ghent and the Italian towns originally had only a single parish: more were created as the towns expanded. No continental town, however, could rival London's hundred or more parishes which had developed out of small estate churches belonging to individual lords. Very few urban parishes have surviving records from before the fifteenth century. In England the earliest surviving records come from the parish of St Michael without the North Gate in Bath where the churchwardens' accounts survive from 1349.[28] Such financial accounts were kept by the lay churchwardens who were largely responsible for maintaining the fabric and furnishings of the church and who presented their accounts at regular intervals to a gathering of senior parishioners for approval. The churchwardens would receive rents from parish properties, fees for lighting candles and digging graves and offerings from parishioners for particular parish enterprises such as the building of a bell tower or the installation of a parish clock. In turn the wardens spent large sums of money on candles, on repairs to the parish properties, on copying and mending the books necessary for the church services, and paying for extra clergy or singers for the parish festivals.[29] In addition to the accounts, which are the most common parish records to survive from the medieval period, we also find parish books or registers (like the custumals kept by the towns) in which documents of importance to the parish community, such as property deeds, copies of wills in which bequests were made to the parish, or episcopal indulgences were copied down for safe-keeping.[30]

The craftsmen who lived and worked in towns often congregated in the same districts and this meant that their craft or trade associations would focus on a particular parish church or, in Italian towns, a particular friary. These craft associations were of many kinds: some were small groupings of comparatively poor men (sometimes women) and others were composed of the rich and powerful merchants who, in many cases, ran the affairs of the town through their merchant guild. There was a merchant guild in the town of St Omer as early as the twelfth century and the statutes of the confraternity of merchants in Middleburg date from 1271.[31] In England the merchant guild of Leicester has records dating back to the end of the twelfth century: their guild meeting was known as the 'morwenspeche' and the guild took responsibility for the affairs of the town. In 1220 it was the merchant guild which, for six shillings, bought a field for the common use.[32] The statutes of the merchant guild of Berwick which were drawn up in 1249 were later used as a model for other Scottish merchant guilds.[33] These merchant guilds, which often formed the governing structures of towns, were composed of men practising a variety of crafts or trades. But there were also many guilds specific to particular crafts. In Paris in the 1260s Etienne Boileau, the Provost of the city, collected together the rules of over a hundred different crafts guilds that had been formed in the city. Seven of these were guilds of women workers.[34] As early as 1236 the skilled clothworkers of Arras in the Low Countries (known as Shearers) drew up detailed regulations to control the quality of the cloth and the wages and conditions of the workers in the industry.[35] As was usual, these regulations covered not only craft activities but also the social interactions of guild members. In the regulations of the guild of skinners in Copenhagen in the mid-fifteenth century greater emphasis was laid upon the social or fraternal aspects of guild membership, the appropriate behaviour at feasts (including fines for those who were so drunk that they vomited) and the attendance at funerals and services at the city's Franciscan Friary.[36] All such craft guild regulations contained a religious or social dimension: such associations were truly fraternities and their members (and their wives, workers and apprentices) were expected to observe certain norms of social behaviour and religious practice. The emphases might vary from guild to guild but this blend of economic and religious concerns was a characteristic of all these guild regulations. Great numbers of them have survived and they provide a welcome insight into the attitudes and preoccupations of medieval townsmen. As these trade and craft guilds grew in importance, they came to acquire land, halls for their meetings and employees to collect their rents and keep their accounts and the minutes of their meetings. Many of these company accounts and minutes have survived: in London the Mercers, Grocers, Merchant Taylors and Goldsmiths have financial accounts dating back to the fourteenth century and minute books from the fifteenth century.[37] These records demonstrate the wealth, influence, economic self-interest and charitable activities of these groupings of successful urban inhabitants.

But many guilds were not formed by men of the same craft or trade but were simply free associations of men and women who wished to meet together to honour a particular saint, to share an annual feast on their saint's day, to attend each other's funerals and to pray for other members both living and dead. These strictly religious fraternities served also as mutual support groups in which, in return for a small quarterly fee, a member would be helped in case of need by a subvention from the common box and by freewill offerings from other members. Although such fraternities would usually focus on a particular chapel or altar in a church, they often drew their membership from a wide range of visitors to the town or well-wishers who hoped to be remembered in the prayers of the group. Membership was carefully controlled and new members would be expected to take an oath to observe the rules of the fraternity, and it is these rules that, in many cases, have survived.[38] More rarely the accounts kept by the wardens of these religious guilds have also sometimes survived.[39] These religious fraternities are more often (although by no means exclusively) found in towns because there they had sufficient people and some surplus wealth to form and sustain such groups, and also because townsmen were often immigrants to the urban communities and lacked their own kin groups in the towns who would care for them when sick and pray for them after death. A small village was already a fraternity or club, but such groupings had to be artificially created within towns.

Town life generated literate activity: schools, teachers, scriveners, writing materials, manuscripts and, later, printed books, were more readily available within urban communities. For this reason we have a considerable amount of material written by townsmen themselves. Because those who lived in towns had greater freedom to leave their landed property as they wished, there survive large numbers of wills drawn up by town-dwellers from all over Europe. Such collections of wills, many dating from as early as the thirteenth century, provide historians with a rich source of information about the priorities and concerns of those who lived in towns. The wealthy left money for urban public works such as hospitals, bridges, water supplies, street improvements, almshouses, public markets and guildhalls, as well as providing for the poor and needy within urban communities.[40] Those who executed wills were required to draw up an inventory of the goods of the deceased and some of these inventories survive and throw light on the personal possessions, furnishings and household goods of urban households.[41] Many of those who lived in towns were merchants who traded outside the town and, often, outside their own countries. Such businesses required correspondence. The great merchants of the Italian towns such as Venice, Florence and Genoa were the most important international bankers and traders in the medieval period and the largest collections of urban letters survive from Italian cities. One of the most extensive collections of letters is that of the merchant Francesco Datini from Prato near Florence. He built up a business empire which stretched to Spain, Flanders and England and around the Mediterranean; Datini's voluminous correspondence which held his empire together is still preserved in his house in Prato. Many of the letters deal with trade and commerce, but Francesco also writes about his family and his household in Prato.[42] Such surviving collections of letters, although largely written by men, throw light upon the role played by women in urban households and, on occasion, tell us about their priorities and concerns. These Italian merchants often also kept 'day books' in which they recorded their secret business dealings together with more personal information about their families and, sometimes, about their political activities within their own city. One such diary was written by Gregorio Dati, a Florentine merchant born in 1362 who writes with pride of his own rise up the economic and social ladder in Florence and of his business dealings in the silk trade in Spain.[43] Other townsmen chose to write less personal accounts in which their city, rather than their own family, occupied the main narrative. These were not official histories of the town, paid for by the town, but accounts compiled by individuals with their own distinctive viewpoints. In the early fourteenth century Neri degli Strinati, a scion of an old Florentine family, wrote a chronicle account of the politics of Florence in these years and of the changes of fortune experienced by his family who had, for a time, to go into exile.[44] And a century later, an anonymous inhabitant of Paris wrote a vivid account of the vicissitudes of his city during the conflicts between the English, French and Burgundians.[45] In the middle of the fifteenth century Enea Piccolomini (later Pope Pius II 1458–64), and a native of Siena, wrote an account of the factional struggles in his native city.[46] And in the late fifteenth century, the London draper Robert Fabyan compiled his own distinctive account of the tactics of London's aldermanic rulers as they negotiated the cross-currents of the Wars of the Roses.[47] Indeed Robert Fabyan abandoned civic office in order to concentrate on writing history.

The urban communities in which Piccolomini and Fabyan, and countless others, wrote had been created since the twelfth century (and in some cases earlier) by a slow process of trial and error. The growth of these towns and the ways in which they learned how to govern themselves and provide for the needs of their inhabitants can be charted in the written materials which have been discussed in this chapter. Moreover there are, in addition, the material remains of medieval cities: some, such as Bruges, are preserved almost intact whereas others, such as London, have very little of their medieval fabric remaining.[48] It is, however, the written records compiled by townsmen (and -women) for, and about, their communities that enable us to gain some understanding of what it was like to live in a medieval town.

## Further reading

Some of the particular sources available have been indicated in the footnotes to this essay. The best and most accessible collections of documents from medieval towns are to be found in John H. Mundy and Peter Riesenberg (eds), *The Medieval Town* (New York: Van Nostrand, 1958, reprinted, 1979) which contains a useful account of 'medieval urbanism' followed by a selection of documents. More recently, Maryanne Kowaleski has put together an excellent, and very diverse, collection of documents, *Medieval Towns: A Reader* (Toronto: University of Toronto Press, 2008). For a slightly later period, and confined to Britain, there is a useful collection put together by R.C. Richardson and T.B. James, *The Urban Experience: A Sourcebook, English, Scottish and Welsh Towns, 1450–1700*

(Manchester: Manchester U.P., 1983). For general surveys of the medieval town there are the two volumes written by David Nicholas, *The Growth of the Medieval City from Antiquity to the Early Fourteenth Century* and *The Later Medieval City* (Harlow, Essex: Longman, 1997) followed by Christopher R. Friedrichs, *The Early Modern City 1450–1750* (Harlow, Essex: Longman, 1995). All the volumes of the *New Cambridge Medieval History* contain chapters on towns, see for example, 'Urban Life' by Jean-Pierre Leguay in vol. vi: *c.* 1300–*c.* 1415, ed. Michael Jones (Cambridge: CUP, 2000), pp. 102–23; and 'Urban Europe' by Barrie Dobson in *The New Cambridge Medieval History*, vol. vii: *c.* 1415–*c.* 1500 (Cambridge: CUP, 1998), pp. 121–44. The best introduction to the study of English medieval towns remains Susan Reynolds, *An Introduction to the History of English Medieval Towns* (Oxford: Clarendon, 1977) but this can be supplemented by Heather Swanson, *Medieval British Towns* (Basingstoke: Macmillan, 1999). For an excellent, and more theoretical, overview from a human geographer, see Keith D. Lilley, *Urban Life in the Middle Ages 1000–1450* (Basingstoke: Palgrave, 2002).

## Notes

1 David Palliser, 'Introduction' to *The Cambridge Urban History of Britain*, 3 vols (Cambridge: CUP, 2000), i, p. 5 citing Susan Reynolds.
2 Maryanne Kowaleski (ed.), *Medieval Towns: A Reader* (Toronto: University of Toronto Press, 2008), p. 21
3 Walter de Gray Birch (ed.), *The Historical Charters and Constitutional Documents of the City of London* (London: Whiting & Co, 1887), p. 1
4 *Medieval Towns*, p. 41
5 Olivia Remie Constable (ed.), *Medieval Iberia: Readings from Christian, Muslim and Jewish Sources* (Philadelphia: University of Pennsylvania Press, 1997), pp. 225–7.
6 *Medieval Towns*, p. 45
7 Excerpts printed in John H. Mundy and Peter Riesenberg (eds), *The Medieval Town* (Princeton, NJ: Princeton University Press, 1958), pp. 154–7.
8 Henry T. Riley (ed.), *Liber Albus: The White Book of the City of London* (London: Richard Griffin & Co., 1861).
9 P. Studer (ed.), *The Oak Book of Southampton*, 3 vols (Southampton Record Society, 1910–11).
10 Studer, *The Oak Book*, i, pp. 2–17
11 *Medieval Towns*, pp. 191–3.
12 Constable, *Medieval Iberia*, pp. 223–5.
13 Constable, *Medieval Iberia*, pp. 175–9.
14 Caroline Barron, 'Mass at the Election of the Mayor of London, 1406' in *Medieval Christianity in Practice* Miri Rubin (ed.) (Princeton: Princeton University Press, 2009), pp. 333–8; M.D. Harris (ed.), *The Coventry Leet Book*, vol. ii, (Early English Text Society, 1907), pp. 545, 568; J. D. Marwick (ed.), *Extracts from the Burgh of Edinburgh 1403–1528* (Scottish Burgh Records Society, vol. i, 1869), pp. 72–6.
15 *Medieval Towns*, pp. 154–6.
16 D. Herlihy and C. Klapisch-Zuber, *Tuscans and their Families: A Study of the Florentine Catasto of 1427* (New Haven: Yale University Press, 1985).
17 G. Des Marez and E. de Sagher (eds), *Comptes de la Ville d'Ypres de 1267 a 1329*, 2 vols (Brussels: Academie royal des sciences, des lettres et des beaux-arts de Belgique, 1909); Kowalski calculations in *Medieval Towns*, p. 319.
18 James Raine, *Records of the Borough of Nottingham, 1155–1399*, (London: Quaritch, 1882), i, p. x

19  *Medieval Towns*, p. 216
20  Oxford, Bodleian Library, Christ Church Deposited Deeds c. 24: no. 1051. The will is printed in H.E. Salter ed., *Cartulary of Oseney Abbey* (Oxford Historical Society, 1935), no. 838A, pp. 357–9.
21  For example the medieval cartularies kept by English towns such as Coventry and Leicester, see G.R.C. Davis, *Medieval Cartularies of Great Britain and Ireland*, revised by Claire Breay, Julian Harrison and David M. Smith (British Library, 2010), p. 285.
22  H. Hartopp (ed.), *Register of the Freemen of Leicester 1196–1770* (Leicester: Corporation of the City of Leicester, 1927); M.M. Rowe and A.M. Jackson (eds), *Exeter Freemen 1266–1967* (Devon and Cornwall Record Society, 1973); F. Collins (ed.), *Register of the Freemen of the City of York*, vol. i, 1272–1588 (Surtees Society, 1897); *A Calendar of the Freemen of Lynn, 1292–1836* (Norfolk and Norwich Archaeological Society, 1913).
23  Gervase Rosser, *Medieval Westminster 1200–1540* (Oxford: Clarendon, 1989), pp. 182–90, 349–61.
24  See F.R.H. Du Boulay, 'The German Town Chroniclers' in R.H.C. Davis and J. Wallace-Hadrill (eds), *The Writing of History in the Middles Ages* (Oxford: OUP, 1981), pp. 445–69, esp. pp. 465–9.
25  Christine Winter, 'The Portsoken Presentments: an analysis of a London Ward in the 15th century', *Transactions of the London and Middlesex Archaeological Society*, 56 (2005), 97–161.
26  *Records of the Borough of Nottingham,* pp. 293–323.
27  R. Descimon and J Nagle, 'Les quartiers de Paris du Moyen Age au XVIIIe siecle. Evolution d'un espace plurifunctionnel', *Annales E.S.C.*, 34 (1979), 956–83; R. Descimon, 'Paris on the eve of Saint Bartholomew: taxation, privilege and social geography' in P. Benedict (ed.), *Cities and Social Change in Early Modern France* (London: Routledge, 1992), pp. 69–104.
28  C.B. Pearson (ed.), 'Churchwardens' Accounts of the Church and Parish of St Michael without the North Gate, Bath, 1349–1575' in *Somerset Archaeological and Natural History Society's Proceedings*, vol. xxiii (1877), part 3, pp. 1–28 and xxiv (1878), part 3, pp. 29–100.
29  For examples see, C. Burgess (ed.), *The Church Records of St Andrew Hubbard Eastcheap c.1450–c.1570* (London Record Society, 1999); C. Cotton, 'The Churchwardens' Accounts of the Parish of St Andrew, Canterbury, 1485–1509', *Archaeologia Cantiana*, 32 (1917), pp. 201–46.
30  See, for example, A.G. Dyson, 'A calendar of the cartulary of the parish church of St Margaret, Bridge Street', *Guildhall Studies in London History*, i (1974), pp.163–91.
31  C. Gross, *The Gild Merchant. A Contribution to British Municipal History,* 2 vols (Oxford: Clarendon, 1890), i, pp. 290–2; 295–7.
32  M. Bateson (ed.), *Records of the Borough of Leicester, 1103–1327* (London: Clay, 1899), p. 33.
33  Gross, *Gild Merchant*, i, pp. 227–40.
34  R. de Lespinasse and F. Bonnardot (eds), *Les Metiers et Corporations de la ville de Paris: XIIIe siecle, Le Livre des Métiers d'Étienne Boileau* (Paris: Imprimerie Nationale, 1879).
35  *Medieval Towns*, p. 139
36  *Medieval Towns*, pp. 143–5.
37  Caroline M. Barron, *London in the Later Middle Ages: Government and People* (Oxford: OUP, 2004), chapter 9.
38  In England a government enquiry into guilds and fraternities initiated by Parliament in 1388 led to a large number of copies of guild regulations being deposited in the Royal Chancery and so preserved, see J. T. Smith and L. T. Smith (eds), *English Gilds* (Early English Text Society, 1870).

39  For example the accounts of the Fraternity of the Holy Trinity and Sts Fabian and Sebastian established in the London parish church of St Botolph, Aldersgate, see P. Basing (ed.), *Parish Fraternity Register* (London Record Society, 1982).

40  For examples see, *Medieval Towns*, pp. 265–8.

41  See, for example, the inventory of the household goods of Hugh Bever, a London vintner, who was condemned to perpetual imprisonment for the murder of his wife Alice, in 1337, see H.T. Riley, *Memorials of London and London Life* (London, Longmans Green & Co, 1868), pp. 199–200. For a discussion of the use historians can make of such inventories, see John Schofield, *Medieval London Houses* (New Haven and London: Yale University Press, 1994), pp. 128–33.

42  Iris Origo used the Datini correspondence to write her famous biography, *The Merchant of Prato: Francesco di Marco Datini* (London: Jonathan Cape, 1957); and see Helen Bradley, 'The Datini Factors in London, 1380–1410' in D. Clayton, R.G. Davies and P. McNiven (eds), *Trade, Devotion and Governance: Papers in Later Medieval History* (Stroud: Sutton, 1994), pp. 55–79.

43  J. Martines, 'The Diary of Gregorio Datio' in G. Brucker (ed.), *Two Memoirs of Renaissance Florence* (Illinois: Waveland Press, 1991).

44  *Medieval Towns*, pp. 87–8.

45  *A Parisian Journal 1405–1449*, translated by Janet Shirley from the anonymous *Journal d'un Bourgeois de Paris* (Oxford: Clarendon, 1968).

46  F.A. Gragg (ed.), *The Commentaries of Pius II*, Books ii and iii (Northampton, MA: Smith College, 1939–40).

47  *Oxford Dictionary of National Biography* s.v. Fabyan, Robert.

48  See Chapter 16.

# 12  Sources for the study of public health in the medieval city[1]

*Carole Rawcliffe*

The Victorian scholar, Augustus Jessopp, painted a dismal picture of life in the medieval city. For him, as for so many of his contemporaries, history bore witness to the irresistible march of progress, from superstitious ignorance to the scientific and medical advances of his own more enlightened age. These beliefs are strikingly apparent in his most popular work, *The Coming of the Friars*, which was published in 1890 and in which he observed that:

> The sediment of the town population in the Middle Ages was a dense slough of stagnant misery, squalor, famine, loathsome disease and dull despair, such as the worst slums of London, Liverpool or Paris know nothing of. … What greatly added to the dreary wretchedness of the lower order in the towns was the fact that the ever-increasing throngs of beggars, outlaws and ruffian runaways were simply left to fend for themselves. The civil authorities took no account of them as they quietly rotted and died.[2]

He went on to describe how the Franciscans settled 'in a filthy swamp at Norwich, through which the drainage of the city sluggishly trickled into the river, never a foot lower than its banks'.[3] This is a powerful image, frequently invoked by medical historians, although it owes more to fiction than reality. Far from unearthing evidence of urban squalor, archaeological excavations conducted in the 1990s on the site of the friary revealed a highly sophisticated scheme of water management and sanitation. It was clearly planned as an integral part of the precinct, and included an impressive stone-lined underground drain for the removal of waste, several wells, a series of settling tanks and pipes, and, most notably, machinery for the regular cleansing of the system with flushed water. The civic authorities were no less zealous over the creation of a hygienic environment. Contrary to Jessopp's assumptions, they devoted considerable time, energy and resources to schemes for urban improvement, their efforts being documented in the city's remarkably full and well-preserved medieval archives. That they fell short of the standards demanded by central government, from time to time, is nevertheless apparent from the survival of various royal directives criticizing the state of the streets and river. Nor were local people slow to report disagreeable nuisances of an antisocial nature. In short, a study of central and local manuscript sources, along with surviving archaeological remains, clearly demonstrates that, even if they did not always achieve their goals, the rulers of Norwich and most of its residents fully appreciated the importance of health measures and did their best to implement them.

Similar conclusions may be drawn with regard to other major urban centres of Western Europe. Indeed, as we shall see, the comparative study of a cross-section of primary source material reveals remarkable similarities in aspiration concerning such vital issues as the provision of clean water and wholesome food, the elimination of corrupt air, and ready access to properly trained medical personnel. The fact that some European cities appear more 'advanced' than others can generally be explained in terms of their relative size and prosperity, since the amelioration of public services was more often hampered by practical considerations than lack of knowledge or purpose on the part of the ruling élite. We should also bear in mind that standards of record-keeping and preservation varied considerably from place to place. Italian cities such as Venice kept detailed registers of decrees and ordinances, whereas in England longstanding customary practices might only be formalized as circumstances required. The creation of the *Liber Albus* (White Book) of London, which lists many 'ancient' regulations for the elimination of environmental hazards, was undertaken in 1419 because 'all the aged, most experienced and most discreet' magistrates had been 'carried off at the same instant, as it were, by pestilence' leaving their successors 'at a loss from the very want of written information'.[4] On the other hand, the rich but miscellaneous store of memoranda entered chronologically from 1276 onwards in the city's Letter Books furnished Ernest Sabine with the material for three pioneering articles which challenged preconceived ideas about medieval hygiene in the 1930s. In them he set a revisionist agenda which even now remains only partially fulfilled.

In contrast to many of their predecessors, today's medical and social historians share Sabine's desire to avoid what has been called 'the condescension of posterity'. Rather than judging medieval attitudes to sickness and health by the exacting criteria of modern laboratory-based medicine, they seek to understand the particular milieux in which specific ideas flourished and associated sanitary measures were employed. Inevitably, the concerns expressed by fourteenth- and fifteenth-century men and women often differ from our own, not least because they lacked the scientific knowledge and technology that we so readily take for granted. Yet a society without microscopes or any understanding of germ theory can still devise sophisticated strategies for the containment of epidemics. It can also take steps to care for sick and disabled members of the body politic through the medium of subsidized medical treatment and hospitals for the poor.

Before examining in greater detail some of the most common types of evidence currently being used to illuminate the study of public health, it will be helpful to look briefly at the sources from which medieval magistrates derived their information about the prevention of disease. How, for instance, did they come to appreciate the dangers of miasmatic (corrupt) air and the benefits of relegating specific activities to the urban periphery? What convinced them of the need to inspect consignments of meat and fish and punish anyone who sold substandard wares? As literacy increased during the later Middle Ages, educated laymen and women began to demonstrate a keen interest in preventative medicine and related issues. Most of their reading matter was based upon the teachings of ancient Greek authorities, such as Galen (d. 216), which had become familiar in the West from the eleventh century onwards through the work of Muslim physicians and philosophers. In this way, they gained access to a new type of manual known as the *Regimen sanitatis*, or guide to healthy living, which explained how to avoid sickness through the careful management of six external factors known as 'non-naturals'. The two most important, and certainly the most significant in the present context, were food, which Galen had described as 'the first instrument of medicine', and the environment, especially with regard to the quality of the air one breathed and the water one drank.

Initially these guides were commissioned by royalty and other influential figures, being customized to their individual needs (Figure 12.1). The more general advice that they contained was nonetheless clearly applicable to the populace as a whole. A regimen devised by the eminent Catalan physician, Arnald of Villanova (d. 1311), for King James II of Aragon dealt at considerable length with the complex mechanics of respiration. Yet its conclusion – that human health depended first and foremost upon 'the nature of the air', because a polluted or miasma-laden atmosphere would insidiously spread disease – posed few intellectual challenges.[5] Before long, shorter and less theoretical *regimina* began to circulate in the vernacular rather than Latin, aimed at affluent members of the urban élite. The commonplace book of one anonymous fifteenth-century Londoner includes a fairly typical selection of poems on bloodletting and 'the wisdom of physicians', along with a 'noble treatise for man's body' that focused on diet and the dangers of eating contaminated food.[6] Members of the clergy, meanwhile, attempted to instruct their congregations through the medium of sermons and the confessional.

Literature of this kind proliferated from 1348 onwards, often in verse for ease of memorization, as recurrent outbreaks of plague created a growing demand for self-help manuals. Indeed, as soon as the Black Death struck, a more specialist type of *consilium* achieved widespread popularity by concentrating upon the avoidance of epidemics and highlighting the risks posed by such hazards of urban life as dung heaps, stagnant water and butchers' waste. It was on behalf of the entire nation that Philip IV of France asked the medical faculty of the University of Paris for a comprehensive *Compendium de epidemia* in 1348, but many physicians wrote for the benefit of specific communities. Tommaso del Garbo expressed concern for 'the well-being and health of the men who live in the city of Florence',[7] while Jacme d'Agramont produced a concise *Regiment de preservacio a epidemia* in his native Catalan rather than Latin in order to make his recommendations clearer to the rulers of Lerida. Authors soon began to advertise their accessibility. When translating and abridging a popular French plague tract in the 1470s, the Dominican friar, Thomas Moulton, explained that he had decided to 'gather this treatise and write it in English so that every man, both learned and unlearned, may the better understand it and put it into practice, and be his own physician in time of need against the venom and malice of the pestilence'.[8] Hoping to ingratiate himself with the newly crowned Henry VII, Thomas Forestier boasted that his vernacular tract against the sweating sickness of 1485 did 'not prolong of our words, as many before our time have done, the which were

Source: British Library, MS Add. 47680, fo 53v.

*Figure 12.1*  A richly-illuminated regimen produced for the young King Edward III in
1326, shortly before he mounted the throne, stresses the importance of taking
medical advice.

replete with vain glory', but was 'as true and short as it may be done'.[9]

That medical advice all too often falls on deaf ears is a phenomenon as familiar
today as it was in the later Middle Ages, and it would be naïve to assume otherwise. Yet there is, even so, striking evidence to suggest that the ideas enshrined
with varying degrees of sophistication in these *regimina* underscored many of the
measures introduced both nationally and locally throughout Europe for the regulation of urban life. Nor was legislation simply imposed from above upon a resistant
and ill-informed population, at least if the efforts made by local communities to

safeguard their living and working conditions are any guide. There can, however, be little doubt that directives of the type promulgated by French and English monarchs not only placed the issue of public health high on the political agenda, but also increased general awareness of the conditions in which epidemics seemed most likely to occur.

In 1416, for example, Charles VI of France issued letters patent (which were left unsealed, leaving the contents visible) for the demolition of the butchers' market near the royal palace of the Châtelet. Such a radical step was justified on medical grounds, because the stench threatened to contaminate the entire neighbourhood. The letters clearly explained that:

> For the beautifying and embellishment of our good city of Paris, and to provide and take precautions against the infections and corruptions noxious to the human body proceeding from the filth of the slaughtering and skinning of beasts, which for a long time has been done above and quite near to our Châtelet and the great bridge of Paris ... we, by great and mature deliberation in council, have ordained that a certain flesh market lately standing before our said Châtelet, called the great flesh market of Paris, shall be knocked down and razed to the ground, and also that the slaughtering and flaying of beasts shall no longer be done in the accustomed spot, but elsewhere in a place or places less dangerous to the public health of our said city and less likely to corrupt the air of the same.[10]

The move was further necessitated by the pollution of the river Seine with entrails so near the middle of the city; and although, in the event, the market was soon rebuilt, most of the other provisions remained permanently in force.

The majority of these initiatives were more consensual than might at first be supposed. Efforts by Edward I to improve the environment first of London and then York (which temporarily became the administrative capital of England at the turn of the thirteenth century) were less a matter of royal diktat than of collaboration between the king's council and the rulers of the two cities. The York ordinances, which were drawn up in 1301, reveal a predictable anxiety about the provision of fresh, reasonably priced food, the quality of the drugs sold by apothecaries, the competence of physicians and surgeons and the state of the streets. As well as ordering the removal of pigs from public thoroughfares and instituting regular inspections for cleanliness, they also decreed that:

> No one is to put out excrement or other filth or animal manure in the city, nor shall canvas or linen be placed in the drains. Tree trunks and other timbers are to be removed. Ordure is to be carried away and the gutters and drains cleaned. There shall be four public latrines in the four quarters of the city. The people of each trade shall ... remain in a specific place, so that no degrading business or unsuitable trade is carried out among those who sell food for humans.[11]

In England, royal injunctions against insanitary nuisances were frequently initiated from below by aggrieved petitioners. The prior of Coventry secured letters patent in 1380 directed against 'certain evildoers living by the river [Sherbourne], who throw the bones, hides and offal of oxen, swine and sheep, and other things into it, corrupting the water running into a mill in the priory and infecting the air'.[12] When brought to the attention of the king in Parliament, the more serious of these problems might even incur the full force of statute law, thereby assuming national rather than simply local importance. Many of the petitions submitted by individuals or interest groups for consideration by the Lords and Commons related to matters of urban health, and were duly copied onto the Parliament Roll, or official record of the various items of business and private bills that came before each assembly. Again in 1380 (which was, significantly, a plague year), a group of influential courtiers and other 'residents of the streets of Holborn and Smithfield' in London, protested that:

> ... because of the great and horrible stenches and deadly abominations which arise there from day to day from the corrupt blood (*sank corrupt*) and entrails of cattle, sheep and pigs killed in the butchery next to the church of St Nicholas in Newgate and thrown in various ditches in two gardens near to Holborn Bridge, the said courtiers, frequenting and dwelling there, contract various ailments, and are grievously exposed to disease (*tropegrevousement mys a disease*) as a result of the infection of the air, the abominations and stenches above-said, and also by many evils that notoriously ensue.[13]

The royal response simply emphasized the need for stricter enforcement of existing measures against the pollution of the capital's highways and river. But nine years and at least one devastating regional epidemic later, a parliamentary statute comprehensively forbidding the deposit of butchers' waste and similar refuse in or near any English towns or cities seemed necessary because of the continuing threat posed by contaminated air.[14]

Municipal authorities generally assumed a far more aggressive role in the battle against disease. The many ordinances introduced by magistrates across Europe provide a valuable source for the historian of public health, indicating, among other things, that environmental concerns had long predated the Black Death of 1348–50. As early as 1245 the rulers of Bologna insisted that every house should have at least one privy, prohibited the dumping of waste in public thoroughfares and ordered the occupants of every street to keep their gutters and ditches clean. Equally intent on protecting the purity of the air, during the 1320s the government of Florence, rapidly followed by that of Perugia, banned the practice of any noxious trades, such as skinning and butchery, within the walls, while instituting additional measures for the daily cleansing of markets and regular sweeping of streets. Lest it be assumed that Italian city states exercised a monopoly on the introduction of sanitary legislation, we have only to turn to a series of pronouncements from the Crown of Aragon, which reveal that by the late thirteenth century several relatively small Catalan communities were imposing similar controls on butchery and the sale of diseased meat.

The onset of plague gave rise to an unusually well-documented surge of bureaucratic activity in Italian cities, driven by the desire to eradicate any potential sources of miasmatic infection. Records of the Great Council and Senate of Venice confirm that, irrespective of time and place, the initial response to any disaster has always been to set up a committee. On 30 March 1348 three senior officials were deputed 'to consider diligently all possible ways to preserve public health and avoid the corruption of the environment'. Measures for the burial of victims in deep graves outside the city, the removal of infected pork ('which creates a great stench and attendant putrefaction that corrupts the air'), and the exclusion of visitors from suspect areas were duly discussed, approved and recorded by the authorities.[15] Elsewhere, too, the statutes drawn up by civic 'health boards' enable us to trace the development of more innovative strategies, such as the quarantine of shipping, which was first instituted in a directive of 1377 issued by the Great Council of the Adriatic port of Ragusa (now Dubrovnik), and entered in its *Liber Viridis*, or Green Book. It is, similarly, in the Milanese archives that we discover the earliest references to special plague hospitals (*mansiones ad receptum infirmos*) established in 1399 on the orders of Duke Gian Galeazzo Visconti for the segregation and treatment of victims. By the fifteenth century designated offices or departments with responsibility for public health were to be found in most Italian cities of any size. Their primary purpose was to implement the growing number of special ordinances designed to halt the spread of plague, but it made both medical and administrative sense to broaden their remit as agents of sanitary policing. Thus, for instance, the registers of Venice's *Provveditori alla Santià* reveal an ongoing struggle in the face of successive financial and political crises to monitor the city's food and water supplies.

The absence of dedicated administrative structures of this kind at either a central or local level in medieval England has fostered the misleading assumption that no coherent attempt was made to combat plague until the introduction of quarantine in the sixteenth century. But this is to disregard the numerous initiatives taken by local authorities (which often copied each other) and their attempts to crack down on unacceptable activities. In London, the number of orders for cleansing the streets and water courses of noxious waste recorded in the city's Letter Books rose fourfold from just sixteen between 1300 and 1349 to at least sixty-five during the second half of the century. Since the population of London fell by at least half over the same period, and consequently generated far less rubbish, these figures seem particularly striking.

The King's Lynn Hall Books, which record the deliberations and decisions of the ruling élite of this busy East Anglian port throughout the fifteenth century, provide an equally valuable insight into the importance attached to environmental health. The disposal of butchers' waste, the collection of refuse from streets and markets, the distribution of subsidized grain during famines, the control of domestic animals and, crucially, the provision of pure, fresh water, were regularly debated. We can document the protracted and costly process whereby the town acquired a system of aqueducts, pipes and conduits, as well as the effort involved in protecting such a major investment. Between 1431 and 1519 the mayor and council issued at least forty-two separate directives for the repair and cleaning of watercourses either by householders or workmen hired 'at the common cost'. On paper, at least, the penalties for non-compliance were draconian, extending to heavy fines and even imprisonment. Lynn was by no means unusual among English provincial towns: carefully preserved volumes of civic memoranda, such as Little Red Book of Bristol, the Coventry Leet Book and the First Entry Book of Salisbury (each of which is now easily accessible in print), present a similar picture.

Complaints about unpalatable nuisances were often voiced by ordinary men and women, reminding us that members of the urban proletariat were far from indifferent to the state of their surroundings. In 1320, residents of a particularly dirty street in the small Catalan town of Vilafranca objected 'that from the stagnant water and faeces and filth ... there arise infections with attendant illnesses and death', while at about the same time the townsfolk of nearby Berga demanded action against certain dyers who were polluting their water supply.[16] Both communities expected local magistrates to protect them and to safeguard their quality of life. The requirement that all adult male residents of medieval English towns and cities should belong to a tithing (technically a group of ten, but sometimes more) gave rise to a system of local courts, known as leets or ward-moots, at which infringements of regulations were punished, and people had the opportunity to report antisocial behaviour. The lists of potential offences and appropriate penalties that were compiled for the guidance of presiding officials invariably refer to such notorious threats to health as the dumping of rubbish, the sale of substandard food, the contamination of drinking water and the presence of individuals likely to spread infection. One such list, preserved in the Yarmouth Oath Book, describes the questionable practices of Dutch beer-brewers, who were to sell only 'decent stuff ... that is good and wholesome for the human body', or risk three humiliating days in the public pillory which stood in the middle of the marketplace.[17]

Court proceedings reveal a growing sensitivity to questions of public health. In December 1421, jurors from the London ward of Farringdon Without indicted a trader named William atte Wode for causing 'a great nuisance and discomfort to his neighbours by throwing out horrible filth on to the highway, the stench of which is so odious and infectious that none [of them] can remain in their shops'. Their other grievances included dangerous buildings and traffic hazards, whereby pedestrians were 'likely to be dismembered and lose their lives as well by day as by night', at least four blocked gutters and two thoroughfares that were 'flooded and heaped with filth'. Identical problems were reported elsewhere in the City at this time: presentments from Bassishaw Ward began with a complaint about draymen who persistently dumped 'horrible noisome things outside the gate', and went on to report with unconcealed distaste that certain 'rents' lacked privies, thereby obliging the tenants to 'cast their ordure and other horrible filth and liquids before their doors, to the great nuisance of Holy Church and all people passing there'.[18]

On the face of things, evidence of this kind, which was replicated throughout late medieval England, appears to endorse the gloomy views of Augustus Jessopp and his successors. It might, however, be argued that such material actually reflects a widespread intolerance of insanitary conditions and a growing awareness of the risks that they posed. An analysis of the almost complete run of leet court records surviving from Yarmouth between 1366 and 1500 reveals that presentments against suspect lepers (whose 'noisome breath' was mistakenly believed to spread disease) increased dramatically during or just after outbreaks of plague. A mounting sense of anxiety about the dangers of miasmatic air may also be detected in the terminology deployed by court officials. By the later fifteenth century references abound to the airborne infection emanating from not only leprous bodies but also the contaminated meat and fish offered for sale by unscrupulous traders.

The advisability of taking pre-emptive action was not lost on the urban workforce. With the encouragement, if not at the direct behest, of magistrates, many craft guilds sought from an early date to forestall criticism by regulating practices that might endanger communal health. All members would swear to obey specific rules, which would be read aloud at regular intervals and were therefore often written in the vernacular rather than Latin. The *Livre des metiers* compiled in 1268 by the *prévôt* (royal bailiff) of Paris, in an attempt to improve standards of government, brought together in one volume the ordinances of 101 of the city's major guilds ranging from bakers to surgeons. A significant number refer to matters of hygiene, the cooks, in particular, being understandably conscious of the threat to custom as well as health posed by such potentially lethal practices as reheating food and using tainted meat. Even the fripperers, who dealt in second-hand clothes, were influenced by current medical theory, which maintained that the miasmas of disease might cling to fabric and thus be communicated to anyone who wore garments that had belonged to a leper or other infected person. Elsewhere, too, copies of newly promulgated regulations were routinely preserved in municipal archives, as well as in whatever collections might be kept by the guilds themselves. The readiness of the Horners of London to refrain from dismembering the carcasses of animals within the walls, 'in order to avoid the great and corrupt stench, and the grievous annoyance caused to neighbours', was duly noted in both their own and the Corporation's records.[19]

A different approach to communal welfare is documented in the accounts of Florence's many fifteenth-century confraternities, over half of which (like those of Venice) offered subsidized medical help to their members. The latter were mostly artisans, tradesmen or low-ranking professionals, who could not themselves afford the fees of a good physician or surgeon but could club together to fund mutual health insurance. Thus, for example, the Company of San Lorenzo in Piano used some of its revenues to pay the salary of a physician who was expected to treat sick brothers and sisters whenever necessary. His competence was, in theory, guaranteed by his membership of the largest and most powerful of Florence's guilds, which exercised a monopoly over the licensing and practice of all physicians, surgeons, apothecaries and empirics in the city. Its surviving statutes convey a reassuring impression of both the quality and accessibility of care which the medical profession aimed to provide, although it does not necessarily follow that such high standards were actually achieved. A close reading of certain amendments introduced in the late fourteenth century suggests that a combination of plague and the influx of a large number of inadequately trained outsiders had created a crisis in confidence which made it essential to regain public trust. On the other hand, when supplemented by communal taxation records, the matriculation lists kept by the guild confirm that Florence boasted a striking number of fully qualified physicians and surgeons (with seventy-one in 1379 and fifty-eight in

1399, it was better served on a *per capita* basis than nineteenth-century Rome).

Attempts made in London during the early 1420s to replicate this type of system can be traced in one of the city's Letter Books. Despite (or more probably because) of the grandiose plans made for it, this projected 'Faculty of Physic' foundered within a few months, thereby providing another object lesson in the dangers of assuming that statutes and regulations, however well intentioned, must invariably have taken effect. In this instance, a shortage of university-educated physicians and the opposition voiced by lower-status barber-surgeons posed insurmountable obstacles. As artisans jealous of their independence and assured of popular support, English and French barber-surgeons preferred to regulate themselves under the watchful eye of urban magistrates. Concern inevitably focused upon the fundamental issues of training, and licensing, the availability of emergency care and the implementation of effective machinery for dealing with complaints. Inscribed in the second book of memoranda kept by the rulers of York, the late fourteenth-century ordinances of the city's barber-surgeons empowered the wardens of the guild (with backing from the mayor) to examine, inspect and fine any practitioner who failed to meet their exacting requirements. If necessary, they could even close his premises and confiscate his instruments. It is worth noting that, from at least 1480, the oath sworn by all members on admission placed loyalty to the city before any fraternal obligations to 'the science of barbers and surgeons within the same'.[20]

Save for a short-lived attempt to provide free treatment for the poor of London through the above-mentioned 'Faculty of Physic', any subsidized medical or surgical care on offer in English cities came from private benefactors. The situation was very different in continental Europe, where physicians, surgeons and midwives frequently worked as municipal employees. By the early fourteenth century 'communal' practitioners (*medici condotti*) were being retained on a formal basis by most large Italian cities, either to serve in a specific capacity, such as caring for prisoners, or on general contracts for the benefit of less affluent residents. The deliberations of the Great Council of Venice reveal that, because of pressing financial circumstances, it proved necessary in 1324 to reduce the number of surgeons on the official payroll from seventeen to a still impressive twelve, although another physician then joined the existing complement of eleven. In Catalonia, too, abundant evidence survives of efforts by towns to appoint salaried professionals who were competent to practise. A particularly full series of contracts made by the municipality of Castelló d'Empúries with its medical personnel from 1307 onwards furnishes detailed information about the wages and terms of employment of men such as Abraham des Castlar, who agreed in 1316 to 'look at and assess all the urine [samples] brought to me by the inhabitants of the town', to 'give advice on both bloodletting and diet, and more generally on their manner of life', and to 'visit all the sick residents of the said town who wish to see me two or three times'.[21]

Precept and practice were nevertheless often at variance, and we can learn a great deal from civic archives about negligent physicians and surgeons who proved derelict in the performance of their duties. From 1348 onwards, trouble arose over the diagnosis and care of the sick during epidemics, which many practitioners were understandably reluctant to undertake. In December of that year the Venetian Senate authorized a special payment to Master Franciscus de Roma, who alone among his colleagues had not fled to safety. This unfortunate experience may explain why, a few years later, the Great Council prohibited its medical officers from leaving the city in time of pestilence. Such measures were as common in France as they were in Italy. Having been retained by the Syndics of Bourg to treat plague victims, Jean Mye, who was not only a physician and a surgeon but also himself a member of the ruling élite, likewise took to his heels for fear of contracting the disease and was urgently summoned by letter to return on pain of losing all his many privileges and municipal franchises. A few years later, the rulers of Marseilles proved even less tolerant, threatening one such deserter with immediate loss of citizenship and the prospect of incarceration should he ever attempt to practise there again.

Infant mortality, which was always high in medieval towns, could reach dangerous levels during epidemics. As a result, steps were taken in many parts of Europe to provide effective maternity services that would benefit the less advantaged and improve the general health of the population. German midwives, who trained through a process of apprenticeship, were required to swear that they would accept direction from the wives of leading citizens, charge fairly for their services and behave compassionately to everyone, irrespective of wealth or status. From 1417 onwards the *Aemterbüchlein* (register of sworn occupations) of Nuremburg records the name of every midwife who appeared annually before the city council to pledge compliance, the intention being that all expectant mothers, however humble, would receive expert care, if necessary at the taxpayer's expense or as a simple act of charity. Similar expectations were voiced in Frankfurt, where the pious exhortation that each midwife should tend the destitute 'for free and wait for her payment from Almighty God, who does not let works of mercy go unrewarded' echoes the type of advice often given – but not always followed – by the authors of medical textbooks.[22]

These developments made it possible to tackle perceived hazards in a more systematic way. The diagnosis of suspect lepers, which had previously been undertaken by juries of laymen or actual victims of the disease, was increasingly medicalized, as we can see from the formal certificates, either discharging named individuals or recommending segregation, that survive in urban archives. Municipal accounts, such as those of Arras and Béthune in the Pas de Calais, confirm that fees and expenses were regularly assigned to the barber-surgeons and physicians who conducted examinations. In 1491, for instance, two practitioners employed by the commune of Arras reported that, on the command of the authorities, they had thoroughly inspected both the person and blood sample of a local butcher and found him 'clean' (see Figure 12.2). A boy of fourteen, whom they diagnosed at the same time, was less fortunate, being warned that 'he ought not to communicate or converse with healthy people, but should be separated from them'.[23] The appointment of 'health commissioners' in fifteenth-century Frankfurt proved a godsend to the magistrates of neighbouring towns, who referred problematic cases to this central authority. A request by the mayor of Aschaffenburg in 1490 for the expert assessment of one Peter Spengler ends with the encouraging

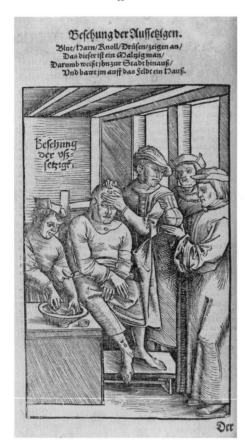

Source: Hans von Gersdorff, *Feldtbuch der Wundtartzney* (Frankfurt, Hermann Gülfferichen, 1551), fo lxxx verso.

*Figure 12.2*
The examination of a suspect leper by a physician (with urine glass), surgeon (touching the patient) and barber-surgeon (filtering the blood sample).

reassurance that, whatever the outcome, 'we also wish to help him with our alms like the other poor folk, since he has lived among us for a long time, has lived piously and honestly, and is really poor'.[24]

A significant proportion of the physicians and surgeons who entered public service were expected to work in municipal hospitals. Most of these institutions owed their origins to the generosity of wealthy patrons concerned for the health of their souls, but by the later Middle Ages the more successful among them had been closely integrated into communal schemes for charitable relief. One of the brightest jewels in the crown of Florence, the Ospedale di Santa Maria Nuova, came to enjoy an international reputation. At the time of its foundation in 1288 by the Portinari family the hospital offered only a modest refuge for 'the poor of Christ', but a combination of public and private investment transformed it into a large-scale medical institution. By the end of the fifteenth century it provided both residents and visitors with a level of care that was celebrated throughout Europe. As the remarkably well-preserved archives reveal, it then dealt with a turnover of about 3,000 male patients a year and an unknown number of women, who together consumed impressive quantities of food, drink and medication. Three resident junior physicians received bed and board in return for attendance on the wards, while six senior salaried practitioners offered daily consultations. That Santa Maria Nuova served as a model for other institutions is evident from a copy of the statutes requested in about 1500 by Henry VII of England from Francesco Portinari. Henry was then planning the Savoy, which was the first English hospital to employ qualified medical personnel and which adopted many of the features of its Italian prototype. Portinari's letter describes in great detail such facilities as the *medicinarium*, or outpatients' department, where 'those with sores and other minor illnesses' were treated by one of Florence's best surgeons, and the hospital pharmacy, which since 1376 had prescribed potions, pills, oils and oint-ments made on the premises freely to anyone who could not afford a physician. We cannot now tell how much of this account was idealized or exaggerated, since Portinari clearly wished to impress the ruler of what he considered to be a poorer and less-developed nation. Even so, the praise heaped by travellers upon 'the first hospital among Christians' would suggest that his pride was amply justified.[25]

The support of influential benefactors remained crucial. In 1327, Charles IV of France assigned a daily allowance of 12d. to the two surgeons who served him at the Châtelet in Paris as recompense for visiting the sick poor in the city's largest hospital, the Hôtel Dieu (Figure 12.3). This type of *pro bono* work was required of all their successors, some of whom took their responsibilities seriously, as their names appear in the hospital records alongside those of the other practitioners

Source: Bibliothèque Nationale, Paris, MS Ea 17rés.

*Figure 12.3*   Royal patronage of the Hôtel Dieu, Paris, remained important throughout the Middle Ages, as is apparent from this woodcut of *c.* 1500. It presents a rather sanitized image of life on the wards.

UNIVERSITY OF WINCHESTER
LIBRARY

and midwives on duty. A bequest made by the London mercer, John Donne (d. 1479), confirms that prosperous English merchants also subsidized the provision of expert care, both in hospitals and the community at large. He was anxious that the surgeon, Thomas Thornton, should:

> continue in his daily business and comfort of the poor, sore and sick people lacking help and money to pay for their leech craft in London and the suburbs of the same: in particular in the hospitals of St Mary, St Bartholomew, St Thomas, Newgate [and] Ludgate, and in other places wherever people shall have need. And [he is] thus to continue by this grace for the space of five years after my decease. For which attendance and costs in medicines, I will that he be paid for each of the five years £5 in cash … and if he happens to be slothful and lacking the diligence to attend the poor people, or if he dies … then my wish is that another able person be appointed.[26]

A striking change in the way that late medieval men and women interpreted their charitable obligations meant that increasing numbers of testators left money for schemes that would protect the urban environment and the health of their fellow citizens. It was common for the more affluent to provide cash-strapped magistrates with the large sums required for important projects. Indeed, wills sometimes enable us to date public works that are otherwise poorly documented. Joan Gregg, a Hull widow, left £20 in 1438 so that the local authorities could begin laying pipes for the transportation of fresh water to the port, while a further bequest of £100 from the wool merchant, Robert Holme, enabled them to complete this costly venture twelve years later. We should, however, note that funds were not always available to implement a person's wishes, which might be disregarded for a variety of reasons. Because Richard de Breccles (d. 1306) had been 'negligent and omitted certain debts' when drawing up his will, it proved necessary to jettison plans for the hospital that he had already started to build in Norwich.[27] Conversely, many individuals, such as the celebrated Londoner, Richard Whittington (d. 1423), gave their executors a free hand, without much in the way of formal instruction. We are therefore dependent on other sources for information about his numerous 'works of piety for the common utility of the city', including improvements to the water supply and the erection over the River Thames of an impressively large public lavatory, known appropriately as 'Whittington's long house'. Urban chroniclers and, at a later date, antiquaries such as John Stow can here prove extremely useful, since their sense of civic pride led them to record acts of generosity that had such a beneficial impact upon the quality of urban life. Stow's *Survey of London*, which appeared in 1598, contains many glowing references to late medieval initiatives, including the construction of the covered market at Leadenhall, where food was sold under supervision in hygienic conditions and grain could be stockpiled in the event of shortages.

Excavations on the site of the Leadenhall market undertaken in 1984–6 revealed that Stow's encomium was richly deserved. This imposing complex of buildings demonstrated wealth, power and concern for the sustenance of the entire civic body. As we have already seen, archaeology can provide a valuable supplement, and sometimes a much-needed corrective, to the written evidence upon which historians customarily rely. It certainly helps us to appreciate the scale of the problems endemic in urban communities. We know, for instance, that vociferous protests about the 'dung and other nuisances' that constantly clogged the Walbrook stream in London, and eventually led the authorities to cover it over, owed little to exaggeration. More often, however, fieldwork can shatter some long-cherished illusions about the filthy state of medieval cities.

Many preconceptions have been undermined by a pioneering collection of essays assembled in 2004 by Manfred Gläser in order to determine the availability of such vital facilities as piped water, latrines, drains, cobbled streets and hospitals in thirty-nine north European towns. These case studies leave us in no doubt of the seriousness with which late medieval men and women addressed questions of public health. From the thirteenth century onwards, houses in the Swedish city of Visby boasted stone-lined cesspits that were regularly flushed clean with running water, while a separate drainage system removed domestic waste and sewage with the minimum of pollution. Predictably, in light of this sophisticated approach to sanitation, the streets were kept free of garbage and regularly repaired. Responses to these challenges could be as ingenious as they were effective. In many towns, ranging from London to Stockholm, waste was used in reclamation schemes or to level uneven land for building, especially during periods of population growth. In Bergen the process was so systematic as to suggest that, between the twelfth and fourteenth century, 'large scale and well-planned operations going far beyond the random dumping of rubbish,' were implemented 'in order to extend the inhabited area and build deeper quays'.[28] The prosperity of this thriving port was, quite literally, founded upon garbage.

Nonetheless, although archaeologists are often better placed to determine the quality of urban life, especially as experienced by the poor, their findings can provoke debate. For instance, the discovery of thick deposits of earth and rubbish between successive layers of paving in Winchester's medieval thoroughfares led Derek Keene to conclude that 'in wet weather most streets and lanes must have been at least ankle deep in refuse'.[29] This assumption has been questioned by Dolly Jørgenson, who cites numerous English and Scandinavian examples of waste being deliberately used to level road surfaces before new paving was laid. Clearly, were this also the case in Winchester, the city must have been cleaner than at first appears, and, indeed, than some of the surviving court records suggest.

It can be difficult for non-specialists to interpret archaeological reports which are couched in technical language and produced for a specialist readership. Perhaps for this reason, historians have sometimes been accused of citing evidence inappropriately, with insufficient regard for the context of production, but when due care is taken in this regard the results can prove illuminating. Excavations in Southampton have established a clear correlation between quantifiable improvements in sanitation and the growing fear of polluted air that prevailed during the later Middle Ages. Whereas before 1200 'cesspits and rubbish pits of all kinds [were] scattered in a disorderly and unsystematic way', the construction of new and improved stone houses meant that 'the whole pattern of waste disposal changed'.[30] Henceforward, as in London, strictly enforced building regulations determined precisely where pits might be situated, while those that were sunk increasingly had solid stone or timber linings, not only to prevent seepage but also to facilitate cleaning (Figure 12.4). Some even possessed vaulted stone roofs to provide better ventilation and eliminate noxious odours. Strikingly, from the 1400s onwards Southampton's wealthier householders seem to have abandoned the use of pits in favour of the immediate removal of waste by the night carts that regularly patrolled their streets. A similar picture emerges in Hull, where the introduction of weekly – and from 1481 thrice-weekly – refuse collections has been linked by archaeologists to the disappearance of back-yard middens during the later fifteenth century. These innovations, together with the growing popularity of purpose-built latrines, made the borough a far healthier place to live.

Histories of the fourteenth and fifteenth centuries are still often characterized by their emphasis upon the passivity of urban populations in the face of death and disease, and the attendant levels of filth that disfigured the landscape. In the words of one Scandinavian archaeologist, 'we like to imagine medieval streets as public rubbish tips and latrines, along which people trudged through drifts of stinking garbage'.[31] The sources considered here paint a rather different picture, suggesting that coherent strategies for environmental improvement, based upon current medical opinion, were adopted at a comparatively early date. So too were schemes to provide at least some of the poorer and less privileged members of society with basic medical care.

Source: Southampton Archaeology Unit.

*Figure 12.4*  Excavations in Cuckoo Lane, Southampton, reveal the construction of a stone-lined cesspit to prevent the contamination of the surrounding area well before the Black Death.

Although many ventures were hampered by the limitations of technological and scientific knowledge, and, as we have seen, might be imperfectly enforced, they reflect a pragmatic and rational attempt to devise constructive solutions to some of the more enduring problems of urban life. By drawing upon a wide range of evidence, from health manuals to archaeological surveys, we can at last begin to move away from the negative image that has so tenaciously endured from Victorian times.

## Bibliography

The following primary sources provide some interesting examples of measures for the improvement of the urban environment and efforts to implement them:

D.R. Carr (ed.), *The First General Entry Book of the City of Salisbury, 1387–1452* (Wiltshire Record Society, liv, 2001).

M. Dormer Harris (ed.), *The Coventry Leet Book*, 4 parts (Early English Text Society, vols cxxxiv, 1907, cxxxv, 1908, cxxxviii, 1909, cxlvi, 1913).

R. Horrox (ed.), *The Black Death* (Manchester: Manchester U.P., 1995).

W. Hudson (ed.), *Leet Jurisdiction in the City of Norwich during the Thirteenth and Fourteenth Centuries* (Selden Society, v, 1892).

H.T. Riley (ed.), *Memorials of London and London Life in the Thirteenth, Fourteenth and Fifteenth Centuries* (London: Longmans Green, 1868).

John Stow, *Survey of London* C.L. Kingsford (ed.) 2 vols (Oxford: Clarendon, 1908).

### *Secondary sources*

C.M. Barron, *London in the Later Middle Ages: Government and People, 1200–1500* (Oxford: OUP, 2004), especially Chapters 10 and 11.

C. Bonfield, 'Medical Advice and Public Health', *Poetica*, 72 (2009), 1–20.

C.M. Cipolla, *Public Health and the Medical Profession in the Renaissance* (Cambridge: CUP, 1976).

L. García-Ballester, R. French, J. Arrizabalaga and Andrew Cunningham, *Practical Medicine from Salerno to the Black Death* (Cambridge: CUP, 1994).

M. Gläser (ed.), *Lübecker Kolloquium zur Stadtarchäologie im Hanseraum IV: Die Infrastruktur* (Lübeck: Schmidt-Römhild, 2004): over half of the thirty-nine contributions are in English.

J. Henderson, 'The Black Death in Florence: Medical and Communal Responses', in S. Bassett (ed.), *Death in Towns: Urban Responses to the Dying and the Dead, 100–1600* (Leicester: Leicester U.P., 1992), pp. 136–50.

J. Henderson, *The Renaissance Hospital: Healing the Body and Healing the Soul* (New Haven and London: Yale U.P., 2006).

D. Jørgensen, 'Cooperative Sanitation: Managing Streets and Gutters in Late Medieval England and Scandinavia', *Technology and Culture*, 49 (2008), 547–67.

D. Keene, 'Rubbish in Medieval Towns', in A.R. Hall and H.K. Kenward (eds), *Environmental Archaeology in the Urban Context* (London: Council for British Archaeology, 1982), pp. 26–30.

D. Keene, *Survey of Medieval Winchester* 2 vols (Oxford: Clarendon, 1985).

R.J. Magnusson, *Water Technology in the Middle Ages* (Baltimore and London: Johns Hopkins U.P., 2001).

K. Park, *Doctors and Medicine in Early Renaissance Florence* (Princeton: Princeton U.P., 1985).

B. Pullan, *Rich and Poor in Renaissance Venice* (Oxford: Blackwell, 1971).

C. Rawcliffe, 'Health and Safety at Work in Medieval East Anglia', in C. Harper-Bill (ed.), *Medieval East Anglia* (Woodbridge: Boydell, 2005), pp. 130–52.

C. Rawcliffe, *Leprosy in Medieval England* (Woodbridge: Boydell, 2006).

E.L. Sabine, 'Butchering in Mediaeval London', *Speculum*, 8 (1933), 335–53.

E.L. Sabine, 'Latrines and Cesspools of Mediaeval London', *Speculum*, 9 (1934), 303–21.

E.L. Sabine, 'City Cleaning in Mediaeval London', *Speculum*, 12 (1937), 19–43.

R.E. Zupko and Robert A. Laures, *Straws in the Wind: Medieval Urban Environmental Law* (Boulder, CO: Westview, 1996).

## Notes

1 I am most grateful to Brian Ayers, Director of the Butrint Foundation, for drawing my attention to much of the archaeological material incorporated into this chapter.

2 A. Jessopp, *The Coming of the Friars and other Historic Essays* (London: T. Fisher Unwin, 1890), p. 6.

3 Jessopp, *Coming of the Friars*, p. 44.

4 H.T. Riley (ed.), *Liber Albus: The White Book of the City of London* (London: Richard Griffin & Co., 1861), p. 3.

5 L. García-Ballester and M.R. McVaugh (eds), *Arnaldi de Villanova opera medica omnia, X.1: Regem Sanitatis ad regem Aragonum* (Barcelona: Universitat de Barcelona, 1996), p. 423.

6 British Library, MS Egerton 1995, fos 74r–81v.

7 J. Henderson, 'The Black Death in Florence: Medical and Communal Responses', in S. Bassett (ed.), *Death in Towns: Urban Responses to the Dying and the Dead, 100–1600* (Leicester: Leicester U.P., 1992), p. 146.

8 British Library, London, MS Sloane 3489, fo 44r.

9 British Library, London, MS Add. 27582, fo 78r.

10 R. Lespinasse (ed.), *Les Métiers et corporations de la ville de Paris I: XIVe–XVIIIe siècle, ordonnances générale, metiers de l'alimentation* (Paris: Imprimerie Nationale, 1886), p. 274.

11 M. Prestwich (ed.), *York Civic Ordinances, 1301* (Borthwick Papers, xlix, 1976), p. 17.

12 *CPR, 1377–1381*, p. 579.

13 G. Martin and C. Given-Wilson (eds), *The Parliament Rolls of Medieval England 1275–1504, VI: Richard II, 1377–1384* (Woodbridge and London: Boydell, 2005), p. 181.

14 R. Horrox (ed.), *The Black Death* (Manchester: Manchester U.P., 1995), pp. 204–6.

15 C.M. Cipolla, *Public Health and the Medical Profession in the Renaissance* (Cambridge: CUP, 1976), p. 11.

16 M. McVaugh, *Medicine before the Plague: Practitioners and their Patients in the Crown of Aragon 1285–1345* (Cambridge: CUP, 2002), p. 226.

17 Norfolk Record Office, Y/C18/1, fo 21v.

18 A.H. Thomas (ed.), *Calendar of Plea and Memoranda Rolls of the City of London, 1413–1437* (Cambridge: CUP, 1943), pp. 126, 117–18, 121–4, 129–30.

19 F.J. Fisher, *A Short History of the Worshipful Company of Horners* (London: G. Becker, 1936), pp. 22–3.

20 British Library, MS Egerton 2572, fo 1r.

21 McVaugh, *Medicine before the Plague*, p. 192.

22 M.E. Wiesner, *Working Women in Renaissance Germany* (New Brunswick: Rutgers U.P., 1986), p. 60.

23  A. Bourgeois, *Lépreux et maladreries du Pas-de-Calais* (Arras: Commission départ-mentale des monuments historiques du Pas-de-Calais, 1972), pp. 216–17.

24  L. Demaitre, *Leprosy in Premodern Medicine: A Malady of the Whole Body* (Baltimore: Johns Hopkins U.P., 2007), p. 44.

25  K. Park and J. Henderson, '"The First Hospital among Christians": The Ospedale di Santa Maria Nuova in Early Sixteenth-Century Florence', *Medical History*, 35 (1991), 164–88.

26  The National Archives, Kew, PCC 2 Logge.

27  W. Hudson and J.C. Tingey (eds), *The Records of the City of Norwich*, 2 vols (Norwich: Jarrold, 1906–10), ii, pp. 17–18.

28  G. Westholm, 'Sanitary Infrastructure in Mediaeval Visby – Waste Disposal and Planning', in M. Gläser (ed.), *Lübecker Kolloquium zur Stadtarchäologie im Hanseraum IV: Die Infrastruktur* (Lübeck: Schmidt-Römhild, 2004).

29  D. Keene, 'Rubbish in Medieval Towns', in A.R. Hall and H.K. Kenward (eds), *Environmental Archaeology in the Urban Context* (London: Council for British Archaeology, 1982), p. 28; and also D. Jørgensen, 'Cooperative Sanitation: Managing Streets and Gutters in Late Medieval England and Scandinavia', *Technology and Culture*, 49 (2008), 547–67, at p. 560.

30  C. Platt and R. Coleman Smith, *Excavations in Medieval Southampton, 1953–1969, I* (Leicester: Leicester U.P., 1975), p. 34.

31  Westholm, 'Sanitary Infrastructure in Mediaeval Visby', p. 491.

# 13 Medieval women's history: sources and issues

*Katherine L. French*

## Introduction: themes and issues

All the sources discussed in the previous section of this volume, and all the types of history discussed in this section can be directed to studying women. Women wrote and received letters, were active in urban life, and accompanied soldiers on military campaigns. Because women were conduits for landed resources and urban citizenship, medieval women are now also understood as important political players. Women are in fact far more visible in medieval sources than historians had generally assumed for much of the twentieth century; once historians started looking for medieval women, they seemed to be everywhere.[1] Having found them, we now need to understand why we have found them where we did, and what finding them means for our understanding of medieval history.

The issues of continuity and change are central to how historians conceptualize women's history. Did women's status change in the pre-modern period? If it did, then when, why, and how did it change? Weighing these issues requires an investigation of primary sources that address the quotidian activities of men and women as well as understanding the legal system and its relationship to Christianity, the reasons why medieval sources were kept, why women appear in them, and what role patriarchy might have played in allowing for changes to medieval women's lives, but without allowing them to achieve equality.[2] In this chapter, I will present some of the classes of sources available for studying medieval women, and discuss ways that historians have used them.

## Sources and methods: descriptive documents

Although we often divide medieval sources between religious and secular texts, these divisions do not reflect medieval experience. Christian values and expectations permeated so-called secular society; kings used the clergy as advisors and bureaucrats, and all believed that the advancement of Christianity was a worthy political goal. Similarly, town leaders supported churches and required church attendance by all officers. Christian values informed civic and royal records. At the same time the Church administered lands, collected taxes and engaged in hard-headed politics. A rigid division between ecclesiastical and government documents creates more confusion than clarity.

An alternative division of medieval sources is between pr3scriptive and descriptive ones. The former are sources that contain some kind of rules of behaviour. They can be law codes, medieval romances, sermons, or even images displayed on walls and in windows and manuscripts. While diverse in their origins and purposes, what they reveal to us is expected behaviour. As such they are important for understanding the assumptions and expectations that shaped medieval people's behaviour. Prescriptive sources do not, however, tell historians how medieval people actually behaved. Scholars assume that when a law was reissued many times, it was because people failed to follow it, but that assumption is not proof of actual behaviour. To understand actual behaviour, historians look to court records, notarial records, financial accounts, letters, tax and other government documents, or leases and other land records. These records are all the result of people's actions, usually created for legal reasons. Historians, whether they are interested in women or not, must question the relationship between prescriptive and descriptive sources and determine how they inform or influence one another.

Descriptive sources have long played a central role in medieval women's history. They are the sources most often used to investigate women's actions but they are not without their challenges and limitations. They do not survive in large quantities until the twelfth century, when governments came to rely more heavily on writing-based administrations. Women seldom wrote such texts themselves and thus whatever information they offer is filtered through the understanding of the male clerks, scribes or other functionaries writing the documents. Before using such sources, moreover, we need to understand why women appear in descriptive records in the first place; this means understanding women's legal status. Regardless of whether women lived in the parts of Europe dominated by Roman law, 'Germanic' law, or English common law, they held a secondary position to men, shackled in large part to their marital status. Typically, unmarried women, whether never or not-yet married, or widows, had greater legal rights than their married counterparts. Whether single women and widows exercised these rights is still a matter of study. For example, female testators constitute only about thirteen per cent of all testators in late medieval England, and of these about ninety-five per cent are widows. In Italy, however, Roman law encouraged women to make wills, even if they did not have direct control over their money and land. Steven Epstein found that in Genoa, women's wills constituted nearly fifty per cent of the surviving wills from between 1150 and 1250.[3] Women's marital status also regulated their appearance in notarial records, manor court rolls, and town and city records. Women's historians also explore ways to see women when they are not directly present in texts. Recognizing that gender also informs men's lives, a concern for gender illuminates women's absences from the documents because men did not act in a vacuum, and concepts of masculinity are informed implicitly by concepts of femininity.

While wives appear less frequently in records, we can still learn a great deal about the circumstances of their marriages, and in some cases their childbearing, family life, and work. In the Mediterranean region, particularly in Italy, Spain, and Southern France, but also in the Low Countries, notarial registers provide important windows into women's lives. Notaries were legal officials with the authority to register contracts. Registering a contract gave it the force of law. As record-keeping grew more important and society more litigious from the twelfth century on, even artisans and others of modest means made use of notaries. As a result, notarial registers contain the legal and economic decisions for a broad range of the population, from rich and well-connected merchants to poor servants. While their survival is uneven and generally urban, they remain an invaluable source for women's history.

Notarial registers contain a great many contracts that have little or nothing to do with women, but the broad nature of the notaries' charge means that their registers contain many contracts that do relate to women, even if only indirectly. Marriage contracts, dowry arrangements, child support, hiring wet nurses and servants, land transactions, the sale and purchase of slaves, and wills frequently or always involved women. The sequential nature of these records makes them ideal for tracking long-term changes and continuities, while the broad range of people who used them, coupled with the wide variety of issues they dealt with allow for comparisons based on social status, wealth and region. For example, comparing dowry contracts from one town or city over the course of a number of decades or centuries shows how dowries changed over time and how artisans or the working poor managed them in comparison to the urban élite. A comparison of the provisions that Genoese artisans made for marriages with those of patricians revealed that artisans gave their widows far greater control of the family's resources. Similarly, comparing contracts for wet nurses not only reveals what sorts of men hired wet nurses, the father's concerns for wet nurses' health and behaviour, but such attention to the names of wet nurses and to the witnesses to the contracts may also reveal networks of wet nurses in a city.[4]

The names and explanations of relationships contained within marriage contracts and wills also allow historians to reconstruct families and connect groups of families through marriage alliances, work relationships, and property. The reconstruction of families means that historians can compare family sizes based on wealth, economic and social strategies, and the role that dowries played in family economic decisions. Even if women are only indirectly involved in notarial contracts, recognition of the important role women played in the family, not only in terms of childbearing and -rearing, but also in terms of their work and their dowries, bring women back into focus in spite of the fact that legally they were on the margins. The presence of contracts dealing with the sale of slaves or the hiring of servants exposes to historical scrutiny an even more marginal population, many of whom were female.[5]

Historians interested in the lives of peasant women have employed research strategies similar to those used on notarial registers. While peasants do not appear as frequently in notarial registers as urban residents, manor records, such as those discussed by Philip Slavin in this volume, are records directly related to the lives and conditions of peasants. Because of England's long history of strong government, such records are abundant for England, providing information on how peasant women lived and how they contributed to their families and to the manorial economy. Ambrose Raftis at the University of Toronto pioneered efforts at reconstructing medieval manors based on their surviving records. Manorial reconstruction became the primary means of understanding the social and economic structure of English manors, including the status gradations among peasants. Judith Bennett took this method and applied it to questions concerning peasant women and their households.[6] Manorial reconstruction uses a method called prosopography whereby historians track individuals through a variety of documents. Originally scholars used a note-card system, writing each name from a document onto a card. Computerized database programs now make this process faster. When sorted by name, all the actions of an individual over the course of his or her lifetime come together. While not biography in a conventional sense, the evidence of a lifetime of interaction with the law and manorial bureaucracy allowed Bennett to assess when women began to enter into the business of the manor, what sorts of work they did, who lived in their households, and how far afield they went to find husbands for themselves or their children. Bennett was thus able to illuminate the life-cycle of peasant women, showing at what stage of their lives they started acquiring land, when they married, and how they survived widowhood. So detailed are some manorial records that Bennett wrote an entire book about a single peasant woman, Cecilia Penifader.[7] Because Cecilia never married, she appeared in the manor records more frequently than her married sisters. While Bennett was not able to address Penifader's emotional or psychological life, the various decisions that Penifader made over the decades reveal a great deal about both the tensions and options facing women as well as the ways in which peasant status and gender worked together to shape women's lives more broadly.

Prosopography also allows historians to recover the networks and kin groups of noble women. Historians interested in the nobility rely a great deal on collections of charters and other records of land transactions. Charters record land sold or given away. They constitute some of the earliest descriptive documents of the Middle Ages. There are charters going back to the sixth and seventh centuries in parts of Europe, and they can shed some light on early medieval women's landholdings. While families would have kept copies of relevant charters, too often these family archives have been scattered or destroyed over time. Monasteries, however, frequently copied charters into a single volume, called a cartulary, thousands of which survive. The occasion standing behind a charter might be a marriage or joining a monastery, or it could be a bequest at death, or a gift to a church or monastery for pious reasons. Whatever the reasons behind their drafting and preservation, taken together, charters reveal a great deal about families' and women's wealth and priorities, such as the parcel of land, how it came to the family, and who would have had rights to it if it were not being sold or given away. Potential heirs were frequently required to witness and approve such transactions so that they could not dispute them years later. Thus, a cartulary or a series of family charters can reveal a great deal about women of the landholding class.

In an effort to reconstruct the household and the networks of supporters, historians working with these kinds of documents not only keep track of the number of times individuals appear as witnesses to charters, but also where on the witness list they appear. This research reveals how often wives participated in land transfers, whether they initiated the transfer and whether the land was part of their marriage portion or not. Amy Livingstone, in her study of eleventh- and twelfth-century noble women in France's Loire Valley, found that they not only participated in the transactions of both their natal and affinal families but also that they often initiated donations. These findings show that women maintained contact with their birth families and also had influence with their husbands' families. Their transactions reveal patronage networks, strategies for family advancement, and the important role women played in this process.[8] Studies of monastic cartularies demonstrate the patronage of women and their interest in particular monastic houses over time, and whether they were shared by their mothers, daughters or sisters. Sometimes donations of land are the only evidence we have for small religious communities of women; tracing these donations shows such convents were more common than we once believed.[9] To be sure, charters and cartularies are not perfect sources. Forgeries are a problem, often the dating is obscure or difficult, many individuals remain impossible to trace, and circumstances surrounding the transactions can be vague. As with the other sources discussed, women are also not the bulk of the individuals listed. Nonetheless, this class of text is a crucial source for understanding noble women's importance in family, political and social strategies.

Witness depositions provide another view into medieval women's experiences. Serving as a witness was not limited by marital status in the way it was with contracts, thus witnesses' testimonies often reveal information about women that is otherwise difficult to find. While witnesses were coached to meet the needs of the court, their evidence still reveals a great deal about attitudes towards love, reputation, work, gender, friends and family. Testimonies explain how people actually inhabited their houses and what spaces were controlled by women. They also show that relationships between employers and servants could be close, but that women were also aware of how difficult it could be for them to maintain their good reputations and legal positions. Even accounting for legal formulae and pressures from attorneys and other interested parties, these records add the element of emotion to the female ties, connections, and networks revealed in other documents. Witness depositions not only appear in court records, but in canonization proceedings. In assessing a candidate's suitability for sainthood the Church called forth witnesses, many of whom were poor or at least ordinary men and women who had travelled to the candidate's shrine for healing. Sharon Farmer's study of the thirteenth-century Parisian poor used witnesses to miracles for the canonization process of King Louis IX of France. Her analysis of their testimony reveals the poor's survival strategies and attitudes towards family, friends, sickness, and neighbours.[10]

Records of misbehaviour, such as coroners' rolls, which report on 'death by misadventure', or visitations by bishops, which report on the behaviour of monks, nuns and parishioners under the bishop's authority, or court records of murder, theft and arson, are also sources which describe the behaviour and actions of women. Looking at incidents of felonies, as recorded in English goal delivery rolls or manorial infractions as recorded in manorial court roles, can reveal the levels at which women were involved with crimes and the kinds of crimes they committed. Studies for example have revealed that women received stolen goods more often than they committed murder.

Many historians working with these kinds of sources make use of basic statistics. For example, Barbara Hanawalt found that among 2,696 cases of homicide from three English counties, in the fourteen century, women were accused in only 7.3 per cent of the cases.[11] Similarly, N. Gonthier found that in Lyon, France between the years 1427 and 1433, twenty per cent of convicted criminals were women.[12] This sort of analysis reveals how widespread illegal behaviour was among the group studied. It also reveals the gender breakdown and it allows for comparisons across time or region. In uncovering patterns of women's behaviour, historians are also able to question how status and wealth interact with gender, the ways in which women's behaviour changes over time, or the ways in which patriarchy continued to assert its power even when women's behaviour or opportunities changed. The combination of statistical analysis and prosopography illuminates the importance of social networks and challenges the stereotypes we have of passive and victimized medieval women. By studying women in large numbers, their behaviour as a group becomes apparent.

Yet studies of women need to go beyond statistical analysis. Historians have to look for the assumptions, biases and expectations behind record-keeping. In what ways did being a woman make it more likely that she would be accused of scolding by her neighbours but less likely to be accused of committing murder? In her study of scolding in post-plague England, Sandy Bardsley not only looked at the rising rates of scolding, but also considered other occasions when women's speech became a legal issue.[13] She found that while women were infrequently accused of treason or libel, they often raised the hue and cry, calling out when a crime or danger was occurring. Bardsley also looked at how the Church especially understood speech, so-called sins of the tongue, such as blasphemy and swearing. She concludes that women's speech carried different weight than men's and that is why scolding came to be a woman's crime by the fourteenth century. It was not that women were necessarily more abrasive than men, but when women spoke out, society perceived their speech differently than men's, because it was considered more threatening to the social order.

Episcopal visitation records, which preserve descriptions of monastic and parochial misbehaviour, are another source that historians can use to understand women's behaviour. Ideally a bishop or his administrator undertook to visit all monasteries, convents and parishes under his jurisdiction every three years. He was checking on their compliance with episcopal statutes, canon law and monastic rules. Visitations are a potentially rich source for attitudes towards religious life, whether in a convent or a parish.[14] Eileen Power used visitations to investigate the quality of convent life in Lincolnshire, England. She finished the project with a dim view of the commitment and sincerity of convent life. More recent uses of visitation reports have considered the ways in which visitation reports were created. The visitor had a list of prearranged questions and frequently only looked for answers to them. Reluctant to air grievances in front of strangers, some participants provided minimal information, while other participants, however, might use the occasion to exact revenge for long-festering disputes. Moreover, in parishes, male leaders had the responsibility of presenting all bad behaviour, whether committed by men or women, and so their own understanding of women's behaviour informed their account. These local details can sometimes be uncovered by attending to rhetoric, or comparing descriptions of misbehaviour. Penelope Johnson, in her study of French nuns, found that the wealth of a house and sexual stereotypes of men and women shaped how visitors interpreted their findings. Once she controlled for these issues, Johnson did not find nuns to be any more badly behaved than monks.[15]

Financial records also constitute a kind of descriptive source. All manner of medieval institutions kept financial records: monasteries and convents, parish churches, élite households, guilds and cities. Financial records can be a good source for studying how work was gendered. Parish churchwardens' accounts, which survive for much of Europe, including France, England, Italy and parts of Germany, reveal that parishes spent a great deal on the physical maintenance of parish church buildings. In the course of doing so they hired a variety of specialized and general labour, some of which might have been local. In tracing the workers hired by parishes we find that women's work for the parish was an extension of their housework; they did laundry, fed workers, cleaned buildings and mended vestments. Yet they also worked with their husbands, sometimes travelling with them to work on location. Tracing workers over the years shows that sometimes the parish dealt with the husband and sometimes the wife, indicating the flexibility of artisan households that might not be otherwise evident.[16]

Household accounts allow historians to study medieval household management. The expenditures and income of a household not only reveal the sources of income, but the varying interests of the members. Expenditures for travel can reveal when the lady of the house was left in charge, giving a more vivid impression of her day-to-day tasks and her managerial skills. Household expenditures are also a gauge of household interest in religion, or involvement in the outside word. Money spent on a pilgrimage, the purchase of a religious book, or on a religious image, indicate some pious interests. Expenditure on gifts helps illuminate the social network and the schedule of socializing.

Using descriptive literature to uncover the group behaviours of women and their families or communities raises the question of the relationship between lived practice and expectation. While uncovering group behaviour reveals one sort of expectation, it does not speak to the assumptions, stereotypes and rules of medieval society. Prescriptive literature, whether created by kings, city councils, or the Church, refers to rules, law codes, and other sources that dictated behaviour. Prescriptive literature in all its many forms helps fill in the pieces missing between ideal and practice. Historians need to be attentive to this because such materials are the sources of the world view of the lawyers, clerks, kings, and others who judged women's behaviour and created descriptive sources.

## Sources and methods: prescriptive sources

The most important prescriptive source for the Middle Ages was the Bible. Theologians taught the laity that the story of creation, and the role of Eve in the Fall, explained women's failings and their need for continual male supervision, whether by fathers or husbands. The story of the Fall also explained why women bore children in pain. Other books of the Bible, such as the letters attributed to Paul, also address women's behaviour. The first letter to Timothy, for example, explains that women were to be modest, were not to speak in church, were not to teach, but were instead to be silent and humble, always seeking their husbands' advice. Such injunctions had wide-reaching ramifications. Yet biblical interpretations did not remain static over the course of the Middle Ages, and changes in emphasis also impacted women's lives. During the Gregorian Reforms of the late-eleventh century, new emphasis on women's pollution eliminated and proscribed the office of deaconess and the ability of priests to marry. Discussion and debate about the Bible's meaning was not only in the hands of male theologians. Christine de Pizan, a fourteenth-century Italian writer who lived at the court of the French king, emphasized the Bible's demands that husbands treat their wives well, and questioned Eve's inferiority to Adam, arguing that Eve had been created in the Garden of Eden out of Adam's rib, whereas God created Adam outside the Garden, and out of the earth; thus Eve was a more perfect creation.[17]

Guided by the Bible, most medieval communities – cities, towns, manors, guilds, or monasteries – issued codes or rules of conduct. They offer a vision for how the group was to regulate itself and the role women were to play in the community. Law codes are perhaps the most obvious form of prescriptive literature. As the Germanic peoples coalesced into kingdoms in the fifth and sixth centuries, kings and nobles had to deal with the Romanized populations living within their borders. One strategy of negotiation was the creation of law codes to address conflicts between barbarians and Romans. Of particular interest to women's historians are the issues of marriage and inheritance, especially as Germanic and Roman traditions blended. Comparisons of the many surviving codes show how women's legal rights came to vary across Europe. Even as the Visigoths were superseded by the Muslims, the Merovingians by the Carolingians and then Capetians, the issues of women's property ownership, dowry and consent in marriage remained fundamental to understanding the evolving position of women in medieval society.

Compared to descriptive sources, prescriptive sources are more common for the early Middle Ages. Church councils, didactic treatises and saints lives all survive in relative abundance. Suzanne Wemple used all these sources to study the changes to women's status from the Merovingian to the Carolingian period.[18] Drawing on saints' lives and church councils, she traced the changing nature of piety advocated for women by the church. Church councils and law codes also changed the rules governing marriage. By the time Charlemagne died (814), monogamy was the norm for nobles, even if men still had concubines. More recently Valerie Garver has looked at late-Carolingian prescriptive literature to access the expectations for noble women.[19] She uncovered a web of contemporary assumptions that connected notions of female beauty, morality, industry and maternal care. All would have shaped the behaviour of women, even though reconstructing their lived experiences remains difficult.

Artisan and merchant guilds also issued statutes which regulated the craft and the behaviour of their members. Some guilds allowed women to be members, others did not. Some guilds allowed widows to practise their dead husbands' craft, but not if they married a non-member. Guild statutes assume that male members were married and that running the shop was a part of a wife's household duties. A few guilds, such as Cologne's yarn makers, gold spinners, and silk makers only had female members. Comparisons between men's and women's guilds show that guild leaders expected women would move in and out of their trade as they married, were widowed, and remarried. Men's guilds had no such expectations for their male members.[20]

Monastic rules are another prescriptive source. While the Benedictine code is perhaps the most famous rule, there are many monastic rules, some of which were written specifically for nuns. Caesarius of Arles' fifth-century rule for his sister is nearly contemporary to the Benedictine code.[21] Rule-writers routinely borrowed from one another and comparisons reveal shared influences and common sources, and differences reveal expectations for nuns, and assumptions about their needs. Caesarius did not want his sister's convent to become a dumping ground for orphans and he wanted the nuns to be literate. When the Benedictine Rule, which enjoyed unrivalled popularity throughout the central Middle Ages, is compared to the rule Clare wrote for her community of nuns in 1253, Clare's rule appears much less hierarchical. The nuns made decisions by consensus and the abbess was the first among equals, rather than the absolute ruler outlined in the Benedictine Rule.[22] Thus the different rules reveal how organizers expected communities to function and their varying assumptions about women's behaviour.

While monastic rules, civic codes, and guild regulations might make behavioural expectations obvious under certain circumstances, medieval society was very interested in regulating the behaviour of women outside the precepts of law. Writers in the Middle Ages created a mountain of prescriptive literature designed to teach manners, piety and social interaction by and with women. Some literature, such as sermons and household guidebooks, was clearly intended to be instructional. Other forms of literature, such as romances or even saints' lives, are less obviously prescriptive but still played that role for medieval audiences: establishing good and bad behaviour and demonstrating the repercussions of both. Some scholars argue that all medieval literature was ultimately prescriptive in one form or another.

Because audiences for sermons were often mixed, sermons provide a chance to explore the ways in which preachers directed their lessons to men and to women. As Anne Thayer's essay in this volume has shown, numerous sermon collections survive for all periods of the Middle Ages. One of the most famous is *The Golden Legend*, a sermon cycle written by the Dominican Friar Jacobus de Voragine in the late thirteenth century. By the time of the invention of movable type in the mid-fifteenth century, there were countless translations and versions of *The Golden Legend*, frequently adapted and modified to suit local audiences and needs. In England, John Mirk, an Augustinian canon, who lived in Shropshire in the fourteenth century, wrote his own sermon cycle, *The Festial*. It was indebted to *The Golden Legend* and it also enjoyed tremendous popularity, surviving in numerous manuscript and printed editions.[23] Both collections were originally intended for parish priests who might not otherwise be educated enough to preach or might not have had the resources to keep up with the laity's demand for sermons. By the late Middle Ages, many lay individuals owned personal copies of these works, showing their growing popularity.

Canon law's prohibition against parish priests teaching theology dictated the contents of sermon collections like *The Golden Legend* and *The Festial*. As a result, their sermons contained explanations of the liturgy, bible stories or saints' lives, and exempla, or short stories containing a vivid moral lesson. Analysis of these stories, the way they were told, the role of women in them, and the metaphors used to describe concepts illustrate how the clergy understood women's behaviour: what it should be and what they thought it was.[24]

Preachers did not preach to men and women in the same way. Influenced by Aristotle and other works of natural history as well as the Bible, medieval theologians understood women as more emotional, physical and irrational than men. Preachers, therefore, embedded gender-specific didactic strategies into their sermons. As the fourteenth-century Dominican, John Bromyard, explained, he manipulated his sermons to reach both men and women.

> It pleases men when they [preachers] preach against women, and the converse. It pleases husbands, when they preach against the pomp of wives, who perhaps spend half of their goods on their ornaments. It pleases wives, when they preach against husbands, who spend their goods in the tavern.[25]

Because preachers assumed that women were wives and mothers and that their interests, activities and obligations centred on their homes and their families, sermons directed women to connect their Christian behaviour to their household and familial roles. Understanding these didactic strategies shows us that sermons did more than pronounce misogynistic messages about women's propensity for sin; sermons taught women how to identify sin and virtue and how to transform this knowledge into meaningful and suitable Christian action.

Another strategy sermon writers employed to reach women was to hold up female saints as models of appropriate female behaviour. The Virgin Martyrs were especially central to this goal. The Virgin Martyrs refer to a group of young female saints who were thought to have lived in the second century, when Christianity was illegal. These women, typically Sts Katherine of Alexandria, Margaret of Antioch, Dorothy, Cecilia, Barbara, Appollonia and Lucy, all suffered horrific tortures in an effort to stave off forced marriages to pagan men. In the end they were martyred for their Christian beliefs and desire to preserve their virginity. They were very popular in the Middle Ages, as demonstrated by the number of chapels and guild dedications to them. In addition to the inclusion of saints' lives in sermon cycles, saints' lives also exist as independent collections, purchased by the laity and the clergy alike. Saints' lives were also popular subjects for civic and parish plays. The outlines of their stories would have been well known to medieval people and played an important role in shaping Christian behaviour.

The relationship between prescriptive literature and its audience was not unidirectional. Over the course of the Middle Ages, hagiographers changed their portrayals of the Virgin Martyrs, making them ever more demure and passive to conform to the expectations of late medieval audiences. In considering how sermon writers used the Virgin Martyrs' stories in their sermon cycles, and how versions differed, we can see that the fashion and tastes of medieval audiences shaped sermon content. Those lay men and women wealthy enough to purchase their own manuscript copies of sermons or saints' lives could choose those they found most meaningful or appropriate. Awareness of the two-way nature of prescriptive literature challenges our understanding of what passivity meant to medieval women. While promoted by men, women too came to value this behaviour in the women they supervised, forcing historians to recognize women's own part in constructing their demure behaviour.

Gender-specific strategies for teaching were not limited to sermons or saints' lives. Advice literature was a common medieval genre of literature, written by both men and women. One of the earliest examples of such literature written by a woman is Dhuoda's manual for her son William.[26] Dhuoda was an aristocratic woman living in the ninth century. Her husband Bernard rebelled against Charles the Bald and consequently Dhuoda's young son William was handed over as a hostage. Unable to advise him personally, Dhudoa wrote him an advice manual, which provides vivid insight into maternal expectations, female education and courtly behaviour.

Advice literature written by men for women, such as the French texts *Le Ménagier de Paris* (*The Goodwife's Guide*), and the *Livre du chevalier de la tour Landry*, translated into English in the fifteenth century as *The Book of the Knight of the Tower*, can all be studied for what assumptions the authors made about women and how understandings of women's physical natures shaped content.[27] *The Goodwife's Guide* is a fourteenth-century book of household instructions for a fourteen-year-old bride, written by her much older (and wealthy) Parisian husband. The book includes not only recipes, cleaning instructions, and lessons on how to manage servants, but also detailed instructions of how the young wife was to treat her husband and behave in the company of others. *The Book of the Knight of the Tower* is a manual of behaviour that the knight wrote for his daughters. Both works used exempla and saints' lives to illustrate their points. Like the sermons, these works emphasize silence and passivity as Christian virtues for women, but they also illustrate the important managerial role wives played in their households, as well as the intimate relationships they had with their husbands.

We can also apply the lessons learned about the mutability of images of the Virgin Martyrs to advice manuals. While heavily influenced by clerical messages, the laity commissioned advice manuals, and did not want inappropriate or alien values in them. The choices of stories, images and metaphors that the authors chose, the way they altered or changed common stories, and the works' overall organization illustrate how lay audiences could modify prescriptive literature to suit their own needs. In teaching women how to find Christian meaning in their daily lives, advice manuals provided models for personal and private introspection in a world that granted women little personal space. Thus, their value lies not only in showing the expectations placed on women, but also on women's own expectations and values. While women did internalize many of the patriarchal values placed on them, how they used the books they owned provides historians with an avenue towards understanding women's lives as they lived them.

# Conclusion

As should now be apparent, much of women's historians' methodology is, broadly speaking, comparative. Women's historians compare activities across time, space and status. They also compare the activities of men to women, looking for changes and continuities across these sites of comparison. Uncovering social expectations not only requires analysing the assumptions behind prescriptive literature, but also comparing assumptions across a variety of kinds of prescriptive literature. Yet we need to go beyond simple recovery and comparisons of women's activities to how gender norms shaped women's activities and behaviour, and how gender norms shaped the very records used by historians. Getting this information comes from considering whether the assumptions laid out in prescriptive literature are present in descriptive literature; does the behaviour recorded in financial records match up with the expectations laid out in sermons or advice literature? What does it mean when it does and when it does not? These sorts of questions lead historians to consider how prescriptive and descriptive sources interact with each other.

Disparities between expectation and practice show us that medieval women were not passive and unthinking adherents to all of medieval society's rules and regulations. These gaps help historians understand women's agency and attitudes. Medieval women may not have viewed themselves as disobedient even if they transgressed social norms. Recognition of women's roles in producing their own behaviour, and their ability to construct their identity, not only sheds light on the ways people reacted to authority, but it also exposes the ways in which gender roles were lived. Gender roles that expected women to stay home and remain silent were impractical for many families. Most families, even aristocratic ones, depended on women's labour, management skills and advice. Locking women away, a scenario played out in many medieval romances, might mean a family lost control of its land, or that household workers exploited their lack of supervision by robbing their employers. For urban artisans, the family was the major unit of production and wives may have done some manufacturing, record-keeping, or dealing with customers. Peasant families also depended on the numerous tasks women carried out on a daily basis. Without women's labour, babies would have died in even greater numbers and families might have starved. Consequently medieval women lived in a world of tension. They were caught between family and personal needs and unrealistic ideals that were related to anxieties about preserving their purity, protecting their chastity, and affirming their husbands' masculinity, which was rooted in control of women. This tension and women's ability to negotiate their world would be less visible if historians did not look for the interaction between descriptive and prescriptive documents.

Medieval women are by no means as invisible as historians had once assumed. By looking for them and asking about their roles in family, religion and the economy, medieval women have become that much more obvious. We also now understand that medieval women were not simply victims, they constructed their own identities, and were essential to the survival of their families.

## Suggested reading

In addition to the secondary works cited in the endnotes see these collections of articles and the following sourcebooks:

Emilie Amt (ed.), *Women's Lives in Medieval Europe: a Sourcebook* (NY: Routledge, 1993).

Derek Baker, *Medieval Women* (Oxford: Basil Blackwell, 1978).

Mary Erler and Maryanne Kowaleski (eds), *Women and Power in the Middle Ages* (Athens: University of Georgia Press, 1988).

Mary Erler and Maryanne Kowaleski (eds), *Gendering the Master Narrative: Women and Power in the Middle Ages* (Ithaca: Cornell University Press, 2003).

Susan Mosher Stuard (ed.) *Women in Medieval Society* (Philadelphia: University of Pennsylvania Press, 1976).

Jacqueline Murray (ed.), *Love, Marriage, and the Family in the Middle Ages: a Reader* (Toronto: Toronto University Press, 2001).

Mary-Ann Stouck (ed.) *Medieval Saints: a Reader* (Toronto: Toronto University Press, 1998).

## Notes

1   For more on the historiography of medieval women's history see *Women in Medieval History and Historiography*, Susan Mosher Stuard (ed.), (Philadelphia: University of Pennsylvania Press, 1987); for more recent discussions see the issue of *Gender and History* dedicated to women's history and periodization, *Gender and History* 20:3 (November 2008): 453–677.

2   For a discussion of the concept of patriarchal equilibrium see Judith M. Bennett, *History Matters: Patriarchy and the Challenge of Feminism* (Philadelphia: University of Pennsylvania Press, 2006), pp. 54–81.

3   Steven A. Epstein, *Wills and Wealth in Medieval Genoa* (Cambridge: Harvard University Press, 1984), p. 38.

4   Diane Owen Hughes, 'Urban Growth and Family Structure in Medieval Genoa', *Past and Present* 66 (February, 1975): 3–28; Christine Klapish Zuber, 'Blood Parents and Milk Parents: Wet Nursing in Florence, 1300–1530', in Christine Klapish Zuber, *Women, Family, and Ritual in Renaissance Italy*, transl. Lydia G. Cochrane (Chicago: Chicago University Press, 1985), pp. 132–64.

5   Rebecca Lynn Wyner, *Women, Wealth, and Community in Perpignan, c. 1250–1300* (Burlington: Ashgate, 2006).

6   Judith M. Bennett, *Women in the Medieval English Countryside: Gender and Household in Brigstock Before the Plague* (Oxford: Oxford University Press, 1987).

7   Judith Bennett, *A Medieval Life: Cecilia Penefader of Brigstock, c. 1297–1344* (NY: McGraw-Hill, 1998).

8   Amy Livingstone, *Out of Love for my Kin: Aristocratic Family Life in the Lands of the Loire, 1000–1200* (Ithaca: Cornell University Press, 2010).

9   Bruce Vernarde, *Women's Monasticism and Medieval Society: Nunneries in France and England, 890–1215* (Ithaca: Cornell University Press, 1997).

10  P.J.P. Goldberg, *Women, Work, and Life Cycle in a Medieval Economy: Women in York and Yorkshire, c. 1300–1520* (Oxford: University of Oxford Press, 992). See also Sharon Farmer, *Surviving Poverty in Medieval Paris: Gender Ideology, and the Daily Lives of the Poor* (Ithaca: Cornell University Press, 2002).

11  Barbara Hanawalt, 'The Female Felon in Fourteenth-Century England', in *Women in Medieval Society*, Susan Mosher Stuard (ed.), (Philadelphia: University of Pennsylvania Press, 1976), p. 129.

12 N. Gonthier, 'Délinquantes ou victims? Les femmes dans la société lyonnaise du XVe siècle', *Revue historique* 271 (1984): 25–6.

13 Bardsley, *Venomous Tongues.*

14 See for example, Eudes Rigaud, *The Register of Eudes of Rouen*, Jeremiah F. O'Sullivan (ed.), transl. Sydney M. Brown (NY: Columbia University Press, 1964).

15 Eileen E. Power, *Medieval English Nunneries, c.1275–1535* (Cambridge: Cambridge University Press, 1922); Penelope D. Johnson, *Equal in Monastic Profession: Religious Women in Medieval France* (Chicago: University of Chicago Press, 1991).

16 Katherine L. French, *The Good Women of the Parish: Gender and Religion after the Black Death* (Philadelphia: University of Pennsylvania Press, 2008).

17 Christine de Pizan, 'The Letter of the God of Love' in *Woman Defamed and Woman Defended: an Anthology of Medieval Texts*, Alcuin Blamires (ed.), (Oxford: Oxford University Press, 1992), 284.

18 Suzanne Fonay Wemple, *Women in Frankish Society: Marriage and the Cloister* (Philadelphia: University of Pennsylvania Press, 1981).

19 Valerie L. Garver, *Women in Aristocratic Culture in the Carolingian World* (Ithaca: Cornell University Press, 2009).

20 Martha Howell, *Women, Production, and Patriarchy in Late Medieval Cities* (Chicago: Chicago University Press, 1986), pp. 124–33.

21 'Caesarius of Arles: Rule for Nuns' in *Women's Lives in Medieval Europe: a Sourcebook*, Emilie Amt (ed.), (NY: Routledge, 1993), pp. 221–31.

22 Elizabeth Alvilda Petroff, *Body and Soul: Essays on Medieval Women and Mysticism* (New York: Oxford University Press, 1994), p. 69.

23 *The Golden Legend: Readings of the Saints*, vols 1 and 2, William Granger Ryan (ed. and transl.), (Princeton: Princeton University Press, 1993); John Mirk, *Festial*, Theodore Erbe (ed.), Early English Text Society, vol. 96 (1905).

24 Karen Winstead, *Virgin Martyrs: Legends of Sainthood in Late Medieval England* (Ithaca: Cornell University Press, 1997).

25 Quoted in Ruth Mazo Karras, *Common Women: Prostitutes and Sexuality in Medieval England* (Oxford: Oxford University Press, 1996), p. 105.

26 *Handbook for William: A Carolingian Woman's Council for her Son*, Carol Neel (ed.), (Washington, DC: Catholic University, 1999).

27 The following are modern English translations: *The Good Wife's Guide: a Medieval Household Book*, transl. Gina L. Greco and Christine M. Rose (Ithaca: Cornell University Press, 2009); Geoffroy de la Tour Landry, *The Book of the Knight of the Tower*, Alexander Vance (ed.), (London: Mofatt and Co., 1868).

# 14 Sources for representative institutions

*Hannes Kleineke*

Simon de Montfort's Idea was to make the Parliament more representative by inviting one or two vergers, or vergesses, to come from every parish, thus causing the only Good Parliament in history.

W.C. Sellars and R.J. Yeatman, *1066 and All That*

By the later Middle Ages, representative institutions had evolved in many of the states and principalities of western Christendom.[1] Among the emerging nation states, the kingdoms of the Iberian peninsula had their *cortes*; England, Scotland and Ireland possessed parliaments; and there were assemblies of the estates in France, its provinces and the territories of the Low Countries.[2] Other bodies with a representative character served as governing organs of the looser federations of central Europe. Thus, for instance, representatives of the towns and cities of the Hanseatic League, delegates of the constituent parts of the Swiss confederacy, and the estates of the Holy Roman Empire periodically gathered for their respective diets. These larger-scale assemblies mirrored the microcosm of the representative, if often oligarchic, bodies that ruled urban communities throughout the Christian West, as well as the greater and lesser collective organs of the Church, the synods, councils and convocations, the chapters of the religious orders and of the cathedrals, colleges and religious houses.[3]

The composition of these representative institutions and their procedures varied widely. In the later Middle Ages the feudal assemblies of tenants-in-chief from which many had evolved still found reflection in separate meetings of the nobility within an institution, as for instance in the English House of Lords, but delegates of the commons, not only of the armigerous lesser nobility but also of the burgeoning mercantile classes, had become an indispensable part of representative assemblies throughout the West. Thus the Castilian *cortes* included delegates chosen by seventeen cities, mostly located in the north of the country. The English parliament contained representatives of a large number of cities and boroughs, many of them concentrated in the ancient heartland of the royal demesne of the kings of Wessex. The diets of the Empire, Switzerland, and even of the Hanse brought together townsmen and nobles, or at least their chosen proctors. In some assemblies, like the Castilian *cortes*, nobles and commoners normally sat as a single body, while in others the different estates deliberated separately. Specific responsibilities, such as the hearing of petitions, or issues such as matters affecting trade, could be and were delegated to sub-committees.

In keeping with their differing procedures, composition and competences the records generated by different representative institutions also varied, as did the practices that governed their preservation. In the Middle Ages representative assemblies tended to be summoned *ad hoc* and at irregular intervals, and many of the working documents created were of little practical use once an assembly had been disbanded. What tended to be preserved for posterity was a record of the decisions taken, rather than an account of the route by which they had been arrived at. Any supplementary materials relating to the discussion that had taken place, and to matters which had been dismissed or delegated to another forum, would frequently be discarded. In other instances, records might be deliberately destroyed. Throughout the Middle Ages, the Commons in the English parliament were concerned that any innovative forms of taxation to which they might agree on a one-off basis should not serve as a precedent for future royal demands, and thus asked that the record of such grants be destroyed. At times of political crisis, the acts of a deposed ruler and his representative assemblies could be invalidated by the destruction of their record by the regime that had superseded them. This, for example, was probably the fate of the official record of the parliament held in 1470–71 during the short-lived restoration of Henry VI to the English throne. The student seeking to investigate the details of the workings of representative institutions must thus seek to supplement the official record with a variety of private and government records. This was recognized at an early date by the editors of the records of the Hanseatic diets, who assembled a range of *Vorakten* (preliminary proceedings) from urban and civic archives, and it has more recently also found reflection in the new edition of the rolls of the medieval parliaments of England, which provides references to relevant material in chronicle accounts, as well as to a range of government records not directly connected with parliament.

\*   \*   \*

Among the representative institutions of the medieval world the English parliament is perhaps the one most readily recognizable to the modern observer. To this day, the parliament of the United Kingdom preserves (in spite of centuries of piecemeal and often badly conceived attempts at reform) many of the structures and procedures of its early precursors. The records of the medieval English parliament are remarkable for their richness and diversity, but they nevertheless serve to illustrate a number of points and problems that are equally relevant to the records of representative institutions elsewhere in Europe.

The origins of the parliament of England have been traced back to the gatherings of the witan, the leading retainers and advisers of the kings of Anglo-Saxon England, and it certainly evolved from the councils summoned by England's post-conquest rulers. In the second half of Henry III's reign, the king's tenants-in-chief were joined by lesser men: first men of knightly rank chosen county by county, and later also by delegates of the merchant communities of the towns and cities. The evolution of parliament was intimately connected with the territorial ambitions of England's rulers, who summoned their subjects to secure grants of taxation in support of their military campaigns, particularly against Scotland and France. In return, the community of the realm gained a forum in which to seek from the king redress of grievances, both individual and collective.

Initially, the core membership of parliament consisted of the greatest of the king's feudal retainers who attended his council, the prelates and secular magnates, summoned individually. From the mid-thirteenth century they were first occasionally, then with increasing regularity, joined by knights representing the English shires (only in the sixteenth century were some Welsh constituencies enfranchised), and townsmen from the cities and boroughs. These representatives were chosen using a variety of electoral systems which became subject to some central regulation only in the fifteenth century. From 1295 to 1340 representatives of the lower clergy, organized by cathedral chapters and archdeaconries, sat alongside the secular commons.[4] After 1340 the representation of the lower clergy ceased, although the bishops in the House of Lords survived even after the Reformation and into the modern period. With the arrival of the Commons, the English parliament became bi-cameral, that is to say, its members deliberated in two separate groups. The Lords, composed of the English and Welsh bishops and archbishops, a number of heads of religious houses, and the secular peers, the barons and earls (and, as the English peerage grew more stratified in the fourteenth century, the viscounts, marquesses and dukes) was in addition attended by a number of law officers: principally, the justices of the courts of king's bench and common pleas, as well as a group of king's sergeants-at-law.

Even after many of the institutions of the English royal administration had become settled at Westminster, parliament met in a variety of locations throughout the realm, usually in towns or cities where a major religious house could provide a suitable venue. Thus in 1328 and 1384 parliament assembled in the cathedral city of Salisbury, in 1301 and 1316 at Lincoln, in 1404 and 1459 at Coventry and in 1330, 1393 and 1449 at Winchester, while on other occasions the sites of great abbeys were chosen: in 1283 and 1398 the Lords and Commons met at Shrewsbury, in 1378 and 1407 at Gloucester; in 1414, 1426 and 1450 at Leicester; and in 1440 and 1453 at Reading. In 1328 and 1380 Northampton was the chosen venue, and in 1388 Cambridge (from where the planned meeting of 1447 was also moved at the last minute to Bury St Edmunds). Several parliaments of the early fourteenth century met at York, while other sessions planned to be held there in 1400, 1464 and 1469 were rapidly aborted, or never took place. The king's principal residence at Westminster was from an early date a favoured venue, but only after 1470 did it become the normal gathering place of the Lords and Commons, and even under Henry VIII sessions were still held in London's Dominican convent, while Mary I's administration initially summoned the queen's second parliament to Oxford, before relenting and changing the venue to Westminster.

If to the modern mind the gathering of delegates of different sections of the community of the realm to bring grievances before the king in itself seems indicative of the representative nature of the English parliament, it is clear that a concept (or concepts) of representation were rather slower to emerge among contemporaries. Into the third century of its existence, parliament was still primarily framed as a body of subjects summoned to advise and supply the king, rather than one intended to represent the community of the realm to him. Thus, the protection from arrest or imprisonment while serving in, or travelling to and from, parliament that was accorded to peers, members of the Commons and their servants was a privilege pertaining to the king, rather than to parliament. It was intended to ensure that the king could receive the advice he sought from his subjects unimpeded, in the same way as a similar custom offered comparable protection to those coming to sue in the royal law courts.[5] Equally, the presentation of petitions formed part of the community's advice to the king, enabling him to rule well, and while the parliamentary Commons might plead poverty when asked to grant taxes to the king, they had no right of direct refusal.[6] Only in the fifteenth century is there a sense that parliament and the local communities developed tangible theories of representation. One indication of this development is found in the stricter delimitations of the electorates of individual constituencies. Thus, in 1427 one of the complaints over the conduct of the Warwickshire elections was that the undersheriff, Edmund Colshull, had permitted a number of burgesses of the town of Warwick, which returned its own MPs, to vote for the county representatives.[7] Before long, a connection also began to be drawn between an individual's stake in the choice of his community's parliamentary representatives and his obligation to contribute to the wages payable to them. So, for instance, in 1419 some of the townsmen of Bishop's Lynn in Norfolk claimed (unsuccessfully) that the entire community, rather than a narrow electoral college, should elect the borough's MPs, since all inhabitants were liable to contribute to their wages, and a similar claim was put forward in 1424 by the inhabitants of Bedford.[8]

One indication of a local community's attitude towards its parliamentary representation may be found in its desire to be kept up-to-date with its representatives' activity in the Commons. From the later fourteenth century towns such as Bishop's Lynn and Colchester in Essex received more or less detailed reports on what had passed in parliament from their MPs.[9] In many communities parliamentary representation was nevertheless regarded as an expensive burden, rather than a privilege to be cherished and defended. Thus, for much of the reigns of Richard II and the first two Lancastrians, Colchester had procured royal exemptions from sending representatives to parliament, and even in 1453 the burgesses of New Woodstock in Oxfordshire had a similar exemption included in their new royal charter.[10]

\* \* \*

A natural starting point for the study of any representative assembly is its official record. In the case of the English parliament, this record was kept in the royal chancery in the form of the parliament rolls.[11] Compiled by the clerk of the parliaments, the parliament rolls preserved the principal acts passed on behalf of the Crown, a selection of the private petitions heard, and a range of procedural matters, such as a summary of the chancellor's opening sermon, occasional royal addresses, prorogations, dissolutions, and the election and approbation of the Speaker of the Commons. Crucially, however, the parliament rolls do not constitute a full record. What was recorded were the decisions that were taken, with little or no indication of how these decisions were reached. No debates, or individual opinions or statements were noted. This is not altogether surprising, since for the conduct of government it was the decision reached, rather than the process, that was of relevance. Moreover, not even every decision reached by parliament found its way onto the roll. No record was kept of private petitions that had been rejected, and even some petitions that had received a favourable response were not enrolled. Finally, the parliament rolls' perspective was somewhat one-sided. As the clerk of the parliaments who compiled them was based in the Lords, it was from there that he viewed proceedings, and he thus gave perhaps excessive prominence to certain items of 'Commons business', such as the approbation and protestation of the Speaker, which took place before the Lords.

The 'official' record of the decisions taken by parliament may in many instances be supplemented by the trail that their implementation left in the records of other government departments. Thus, acts of parliament were in many instances communicated to the law courts for application in subsequent proceedings, while those with financial implications might find their way to the exchequer. As parliament met for only limited periods, there was usually insufficient time available for the consideration of all the matters and redress of all the grievances that were presented. Many of these matters in turn were passed on to other institutions such as the king's council, or officers of state, like the chancellor of England, for resolution, and remain in their archives.[12] The proceedings of parliament itself led to the creation of some subsidiary records which survive. Thus, there were drafts of acts of parliament, and Michael Hicks has recently drawn attention to the bills of proviso that exempted individuals from successive fifteenth-century acts of resumption, and provide information on the interaction of king, lords, clerk of the parliaments and individual suitors.[13]

The bills of proviso form part of the single most important body of subsidiary material, the original petitions submitted to the Crown in parliament, which survive in their hundreds from across the medieval period. Recent studies have sought to demonstrate that from the early part of his reign Edward III actively encouraged his subjects to bring their grievances to parliament, and the result of this development was a considerable increase in the volume of petitions. In order to prevent the business of parliament from being swamped by the redress of the complaints of individuals, the Crown set up special committees, the receivers and triers of petitions, to sift, and in some instances consider, the supplications that were submitted. Clearly, however, many individuals and communities wanted their concerns to be addressed by parliament in time of parliament, and so began to take recourse to collective petitions. Initially, these were no more than petitions brought by groups of individuals or even of communities sharing a particular interest or grievance, but from the second half of the fourteenth century a further development saw the Commons in parliament petition the king and Lords as a body.

If the medieval parliamentary petitions seem at face value a relatively unproblematic source, there are underlying difficulties inherent in their use. In the first instance, it is impossible to know what proportion of the petitions which were presented have survived. As we have already noted, even successful petitions were not invariably copied onto the parliament roll, and failed ones apparently never were. The original medieval files of parliamentary petitions were broken up in the nineteenth century by archivists seeking a more systematic, but ultimately arbitrary arrangement, and mostly cannot now be reconstructed. The nineteenth century reorganization also created other problems. Frequently, petitions were undated, and, having been separated from their (dated) file covers, can only be assigned to a particular parliament on the strength of supplementary, external evidence. Moreover, it is impossible to distinguish in every instance true 'parliamentary petitions', that is, petitions that were submitted and addressed in parliament, from petitions submitted to and considered by the king and his council, or, indeed, from hybrid types, such as petitions submitted in time of parliament, but referred for determination by the council at a later date. Finally, we do well to remember that the events and circumstances described by any given petition, however colourful and attractive their detail, cannot under all circumstances be accepted as fact: they represented the petitioner's subjective version, were coloured by his bias and self-interest, and could be distorted further by being cast in the required format of a petition, or sometimes by being translated into an official language (before the third decade of the fifteenth century usually French or Latin).

Since the parliament rolls largely fail to shed much light on proceedings within the chambers of the English parliament, the modern student needs to look elsewhere for information about what occurred. It is clear that contemporaries themselves took an interest in the proceedings of the Lords and Commons and recorded details in writing. In many instances, this record took the form of an external observer's account incorporated into a wider chronicle. So, to cite just two examples, the St Albans chronicler Thomas of Walsingham had much to say about the parliaments of Richard II and Henry IV, and the chronicle found in the commonplace book of John Benet, vicar of Harlington in Bedfordshire, records a number of events in the parliaments held under Henry V and Henry VI.[14] There were, however, also those inside parliament who kept a detailed record of proceedings. The first known parliamentary diary, kept by the MPs for Colchester, survives from the first session of the assembly of 1485–86, and was evidently designed as a report for their constituents back home.[15] Similar, if rather shorter, reports were sent home by the representatives for Bishop's Lynn even in the first half of the fifteenth century and survive among the borough records.[16] In parallel, some of the clerical staff of parliament began to keep journals containing a day-by-day record of attendance and proceedings. It appears that these journals were initially retained by the clerks who compiled them, and only from 1509 is there a coherent run. For the medieval period, no originals are known, and only fragments survive in early modern antiquarian copies. Of these, the most substantial is the so-called Fane fragment, which covers the proceedings of the Lords during several weeks in November and December 1461, while shorter extracts are known for the parliament of 1449–50. Unlike the later journals, these medieval fragments do not record individual speeches either verbatim or in summary, but instead are restricted to short memoranda of decisions taken and bills read.[17] By the later fourteenth century parliament had become sufficiently established as a normal organ of the governance of the realm to become a literary topos in its own right. The resultant narratives, of which Geoffrey Chaucer's 'Parlement of Foules', William Langland's allegorical description of parliament in the prologue to his *Vision of Piers the Plowman*, and the anonymous *Richard the Redeless* are the best known, provide valuable insights into popular perceptions of and attitudes to parliament, but nevertheless need to be used with considerable care, and without losing sight of their essentially fictional character.[18]

Among the features of these literary sources that have attracted comment from scholars are the apparent characterizations of individual Members of the Commons. While it is clearly impossible to identify conclusively any individual among Chaucer's and Langland's characters, what is and remains true is that parliament was (and is) no amorphous body: it was (and is) a gathering of different individuals whose characters and concerns collectively shaped proceedings. The membership of any given assembly is thus of relevance for our understanding of its proceedings. From the late thirteenth century it is normally possible to determine who should have been in attendance. Copies of the writs of summons sent to the magnates and prelates were enrolled on the close rolls of the royal chancery, while large numbers of the writs addressed to the sheriffs of the English counties and mayors and bailiffs of the cities and boroughs ordering the election of representatives survive in the original, endorsed with the names of the men chosen. In the later part of the fourteenth and the early fifteenth century this information can be supplemented by the enrolments on the close roll of writs *de expensis*, ordering the payment of wages to the (named) county Members and selected burgesses. By the mid-fifteenth century the royal chancery compiled the election returns it had received from around the country into a coherent list of the parliamentary Commons, from which the roll of knights and burgesses could be called at the beginning of a session. No such list is known to survive in the original before the reign of Mary I, but there are early modern copies of at least two from the fifteenth century.[19] Finally, disputes over the partial or non-payment of parliamentary wages and over the conduct and correct outcome of parliamentary elections provide some evidence of the identity of a few additional members of the Commons, as well as giving an indication of some of the underlying political tensions in individual constituencies. These sources are naturally more difficult to interpret than the straightforward lists of members and their wages. Like all legal records they recorded allegations and counter-allegations, rather than proven facts, the account of the circumstances described had to conform to the formulaic conventions of the common law, and, especially where opposing parties told contradictory stories, there is often no way of distinguishing fact from fiction.

Yet, if it is possible to establish with a degree of certainty who should have been in parliament, it is rather more difficult to know who actually attended. The failure of peers and members of the Commons alike to attend parliament was an ongoing complaint. In 1344, Edward III ordered the compilation of a list of absentees from parliament so that they might be punished, in May 1451, so the compiler of Benet's chronicle noted, only 'few lords and commons appeared in Parliament', while in 1454 the council of the incapacitated Henry VI agreed that fines should be imposed on the lords who failed to attend parliament, but details of attenders and defaulters beyond such general statements are hard to come by.[20] In the case of the magnates and prelates, the evidence of the appointment of proctors (frequently recorded in episcopal registers) goes some way to indicate an intention to be absent, but it is difficult to know at what times a peer, bishop or abbot attended in person, and when he chose to be represented by his proctor. The episcopal *acta* recorded in individual bishops' registers allow the construction of a vague itinerary, but we cannot tell, for example, whether the bishop of Winchester, when resident at his manor of Southwark, made the daily journey across the river to the palace of Westminster or not. In the case of secular peers, it is impossible to do much more than to establish their likely presence or absence on particular days.[21]

Even more complex are the sources for the members of the lower house. Here, the evidence of payments of parliamentary wages is often the only indication of a knight's or burgess's presence at or absence from parliament. By custom, the elected representatives of the English shires and boroughs were owed wages from their constituents for their service in parliament. In the early fourteenth century the rates normally payable became fixed at 4s. per day for a knight of the shire, and 2s. for a citizen or burgess. The evidence for the county representatives is frequently inconclusive. It consists largely of records of disputes over the partial or non-payment of a knight's wages, based on a royal writ *de expensis*, which ordered the sheriff to levy contributions towards the wages from the men of his county. Yet, since the writs for the knights of the shires were issued routinely on the last day of a parliament, they made reference only to the officially sanctioned duration of the assembly, rather than to the length of time for which an MP had actually been in attendance. By contrast, the sources for the payment of the parliamentary burgesses are often more helpful in establishing a Member's presence or absence. The writs authorizing the levy of their wages were issued individually, and the urban authorities to whom they were addressed took care to ensure that they paid no more than was owed. Urban financial records thus often specify not only the sums paid to an MP but also the number of days he had served and the rate of pay, which from the later fourteenth century onwards frequently varied from the customary 2s. per day. It is clear, for instance, that some constituencies shared their representatives for some of the time: in the fourteenth and fifteenth centuries the Cinque Ports of Kent and Sussex routinely withdrew some of their representatives from the Commons early, leaving those who remained to look after the interests of all the ports.[22]

Of course, parliament did not exist in a vacuum. It formed a link between the king of England and the shires and boroughs of his realm. Individuals and communities took an interest in its deliberations, and sought to influence its decisions. The streets of the towns and cities where parliament met (not least those of Westminster and the city of London) were often the scene of high drama. Yet, the official records of parliament took no interest in what happened outside the chambers of the Lords and Commons. For events around the meeting-places of parliament local chronicles frequently provide interesting accounts, while in the fifteenth century occasional eyewitness accounts may be found in surviving private correspondence. Thus, for instance, the scenes in the streets of London during the political crisis in the run-up to the parliament of 1450–51 are vividly described in a series of letters sent to the Grand Master of the Teutonic Order by one of his servants.[23]

For the activities of the many individuals who came to parliament to pursue their private interests without being members of either House, the most communicative records are financial accounts which often provide a wealth of circumstantial detail. So we learn from their respective household accounts that Sir John Dynham of Kingscarswell in Devon, as well as the abbess of Syon in Middlesex, rode to Westminster in time of parliament to pursue their own concerns, even though neither of them was summoned or elected to attend. Frequently, we hear of the sums of money expended in the pursuit of particular matters, the promotion of a petition, or the defeat of a rival interest. Copies of relevant documents were purchased, potential supporters in either house of parliament lobbied and rewarded, and legal counsel hired as go-betweens. Urban archives often contain material of this nature, and among the most promising collections are the financial accounts of the London livery companies, which regularly pursued their interests in parliament. Similar material may, however, also be found in the accounts of private individuals or religious institutions, where they survive.[24]

Away from the meeting-places of the Lords and Commons, the summons and meeting of a parliament reverberated in the constituencies, above all at the time of the elections of the knights and burgesses. The parliamentary elections held in the shires and boroughs of medieval England followed a variety of divergent local customs. Perhaps most coherent was the practice in the counties, which was normally conducted by the sheriff or undersheriff in the county court, and which was formally regulated by statute in the first half of the fifteenth century. Yet, even here the presiding officer had some room for manoeuvre, something that successive statutes sought to restrict. Thus, statutes sought to regulate the franchise (the property qualification of voters and candidates) and the method of determining an outcome: it was only in 1429 that a statute explicitly set out that the candidate with the greater number of votes should be deemed elected. Rather more diverse were the practices adopted in the urban constituencies, where frequently the franchise was vested in a narrow oligarchy, to the exclusion of the wider body of inhabitants.

The sources for the study of medieval parliamentary elections are equally heterogeneous, and it is difficult, if not impossible, to draw a coherent picture across medieval England. The official record of parliamentary elections consisted in its entirety of the royal writs issued to the sheriffs of the counties announcing the meeting-place and time of a parliament and ordering the election of representatives. It fell to the sheriff to inform the authorities of any parliamentary boroughs within his bailiwick (no list of which communities these were was supplied) and to return the names of the men elected into chancery. Up to the early fifteenth century, there was no stipulation of the method to be employed either in triggering the elections in the boroughs, or in choosing the knights of the shire. Only in 1445 was a requirement introduced that the sheriff should send a written precept to each parliamentary borough in his county; while somewhat earlier, in 1406, it was determined that henceforth the sheriff should prove the orderly conduct of

his elections by recording the names of the men elected in an indenture countersealed by all those who had participated in the election. Such election indentures survive for most of the parliaments between 1407 and 1455; thereafter their
survival becomes patchy, and no returns at all are known for the parliaments from
1483 to 1504.[25] Yet, even where returns survive, they present considerable problems. In many instances sheriffs made out indentures with the county electorates
in the shire courts, but left their boroughs largely to their own devices. Particularly
in the counties of the south and south-west, each of which contained numerous
urban constituencies, sheriffs simply compiled lists of the names of the borough
MPs and their sureties, the men who guaranteed that those elected would actually
attend the Commons. Frequently, the returns show signs of having been tampered
with, an MP's name being written over an erasure, and sometimes – where the
simultaneous existence of an indenture and a schedule recording the names of
members allows for a comparison – an actual divergence between the two sets
of names. As the fifteenth century progressed, some aspects of the returns lost
their meaning, and became fossilized: thus, the names of the 'sureties' given for
each MP increasingly occur in evidently fictitious rhyming pairs, and in 1432
the county clerk of Wiltshire even amused himself by using the surnames of the
purported 'sureties' to make reference to a number of popular outlaw ballads:

Adam Belle, Clyme Oclow, Wyllyam Cloudesle, Robyn Hode Inne
Grenewode Stode, Godeman Was Hee, Lytel Joon, Muchette Millerson,
Scathelok, Reynoldyn

while a year later he composed by the same method the invocation:

God Save Alle This Faire Compayne Ande Gyffe Theym Grace Weel Forto
Spede, For Fayn Wold They Been Ryght Mery, They Been Ryght Mery This
Too Pray Hyt Hys Nede: Godde Thatte Alle This Worlde Ganne Make Ande
For Usse Dyed Apon Thee Roode Tree Save Usse Alle.[26]

An important source for elections in the English counties is the complaints over
electoral misconduct sometimes found among the parliamentary returns, and the
records of disputed contests that were brought before the royal law courts under
the terms of the electoral statutes of the early to mid-fifteenth century. They tell
often dramatic tales of the 'invasion' of a county court by the armed supporters
of one candidate or another, of the corruption of local officials, and of a variety
of local circumstances. Attractive as these narratives may seem, they present the
historian with the problems common to all legal records. Frequently, they tell
only one side of a story, normally from the perspective of the candidate defeated
in an election. It is rather more rare to have the response of a returning officer.
Furthermore, the need to present the alleged facts of a case in the rigid format
required by the common law often obscures and distorts the true circumstances.
For urban elections, local records often go some way towards illustrating their
conduct, but the poll lists which exist at Grimsby for seven parliamentary contests
between 1455 and 1487 are unique survivals that offer a breakdown of voters and

the candidates they supported. Much detailed prosopographical work is needed to perform a similar analysis of the electorate of a shire county, as reflected by those who countersealed the sheriff's indenture, but this has been achieved for at least one locality.[27]

Two case studies may serve to round off this discussion. The first relates to the parliament of 1431, held at Westminster during Henry VI's minority. During this parliament, so the chronicler John of Agmundesham tells us, there came a number of the tenants of the abbot of St Albans, and staged a noisy demonstration outside the doors of the parliament house, bearing in their hands a range of agricultural implements, including their plough-shares. Their grievances were, we are told, concerned with the oppressive behaviour of a local Hertfordshire gentleman, William Flete, but beyond that, the chronicler has nothing to say. Nor is the roll of parliament any more helpful: it makes no mention of either the protest or the matter it concerned. Yet the story may be fleshed out from the records of the royal chancery. Here we learn that the grievances of the men of St Albans were indeed heard in parliament, but were subsequently referred to the chancellor, Archbishop Kemp, for settlement. We also garner some details of Flete's supposed offences. Flete, himself a former member of parliament, but not elected in 1431, was accused of having abused his office of justice of the peace and generally acting in a high-handed manner in enclosing common land, seizing livestock and making his lesser neighbours' lives hell in other ways.[28]

A second case study illustrates the interplay of the parliament roll with other types of records. During the parliament of 1485–86 a long-running dispute between the canons of the royal college of St George in Windsor castle and a body of royal almsmen known as the 'poor knights' who were nominated by the king, but allocated a pension from the funds of the college, came to a head. The canons had for some time resisted royal demands that they provide pensions for the full complement of twenty-four poor knights provided for in the college's statutes. The poor knights for their part had successfully lobbied Edward IV for formal recognition as a corporate body, with the consequent status before the law. This recognition had been granted in the form of an act of Edward's last parliament of January 1483. This act had been vigorously opposed by the dean and canons of Windsor, who lobbied for its repeal throughout the short reigns of Edward V and Richard III. Finally, in early 1486 the canons secured the repeal of the act from Henry VII's first parliament. Once again, the parliament roll is extremely uninformative, recording little more than the original act of 1483. The diary of the Colchester MPs is equally unhelpful, since it only covers the first session of the parliament held in November and December 1485: the canons' matter is not mentioned, and was thus probably not debated until the spring of 1486. Fortunately, the financial accounts of the college of St George contain a number of detailed references to the canons' pursuit of the matter, and the college archives hold a number of related documents. Here we find the details of the arguments put forward by the canons, we discover the identity of the MPs and law officers who championed their cause in parliament, and we hear of the lobbying activities of individual canons, of rewards paid and drinks bought.[29]

Our two case studies demonstrate how a combination of different sources serves to illustrate proceedings in the chambers of the Lords and Commons, as well as the interplay of parliament and the localities. The case of the peasant protest of 1431 demonstrates the limitations of the 'official record' of the parliament rolls: but for the survival of other sources, we would know nothing of what must have been among the most dramatic scenes of the parliament. It is a combination of narrative (chronicle) and administrative (legal) sources that supplies the details of and background to this particular episode. The matter of the poor knights and canons of Windsor is at least referred to on the parliament roll, but only in a misleading form. While the act of 1483 in favour of the poor knights is enrolled, there is no mention of the debate over its repeal in 1485–86. Only the private archive of the college of St George, and above all its financial records, shed any light on the energetic lobbying activity that went on both in and outside parliament. Between them, the two case studies also illustrate another important point: parliament was not just a place for a social and political élite to debate the high matters of state. It was a place where all ranks of society could bring their grievances and see them addressed.

The sources for the medieval English parliament exemplify the problems inherent in the study of pre-modern representative institutions throughout the Christian West. In common with the sources for other representative assemblies, those for English parliamentary history do not form a single homogeneous body. Rather, the student needs to draw together a wide variety of materials. Across the western world, the survival of such materials is uneven, but there are significant gaps everywhere, even in the official record.[30] Thus, for instance, the Castilian royal Chancery's enrolments of the ordinances promulgated by the kingdom's *cortes* mostly fail to survive, although copies may be found in local archives,[31] while the decisions and acts of the imperial and Hanseatic diets of the Middle Ages need to be collected from a range of local archives, an ongoing task doggedly pursued by German scholars since the nineteenth century.[32] Equally, in France civic archives form an important source of materials relating to the various regional assemblies or estates.[33] Other problems common to the study of representative institutions concern membership and attendance. Lists of members are rare, and even those that survive hardly ever indicate who physically attended a given meeting. Local records of elections and external evidence, such as private accounts, are needed to supplement the few official lists available.[34]

Naturally, the character and survival of the sources for any given representative institution is to some extent affected by the character of the political entity it served. In medieval England, heavily centralized at an early date, many of the records of parliament thus found their way into the government's archives, while a high degree of regional autonomy, as found in France, and even more so in the federal structures of the Hanse and the Empire, resulted in a scattered distribution of archival materials. Rather more haphazard, but nevertheless subject to considerable regional and chronological variation, is the availability of narrative sources. While some English chroniclers, such as Thomas of Walsingham and the author of John Benet's chronicle, took considerable interest in parliamentary proceedings, at times, such as the second half of the fifteenth century, the narrative sources dry

UNIVERSITY OF WINCHESTER
LIBRARY

up almost completely, and equally scholars have with some justification deplored the paucity of similar accounts from medieval France.[35] Where an assembly regularly met in or near a capital city like London or Paris, its proceedings might find their way into a metropolitan tradition of early historiography. Conversely, more peripatetic bodies, such as the imperial or Hanseatic diets, frequently gathered in a variety of different and sometimes insignificant towns and cities which might or might not possess chroniclers interested in their proceedings. What is true for representative institutions throughout the Latin West is that their study involves a degree of detective work. This, however, also means that there are real discoveries to be made, and that (as Sellars and Yeatman might well have agreed) is surely a Good Thing.

## Further reading

C. Given-Wilson *et al.* (eds), *The Parliament Rolls of Medieval England, 1275–1504*, 16 vols (Woodbridge: Boydell & Brewer, 2005).

Clyve Jones (ed.), *A Short History of Parliament* (Woodbridge, Boydell & Brewer, 2009), chs. 2–4, 8.

Hannes Kleineke (ed.), *Parliamentarians at Law: Select Legal Proceedings of the Long Fifteenth Century Relating to Parliament*, Parliamentary History: Texts and Studies 2 (Oxford: Wiley-Blackwell, 2008).

Nicholas Pronay and John Taylor (eds), *Parliamentary Texts of the Later Middle Ages* (Oxford: Clarendon, 1980).

J.S. Roskell, Linda Clark and Carole Rawcliffe (eds), *The History of Parliament: The Commons 1386–1421*, 4 vols (Stroud: Alan Sutton, 1993), esp. the introductory survey in vol. 1.

## Notes

1   I am grateful to Dr Linda Clark and Mr Charles Farris for their comments on a draft of this paper. A discussion of the conceptual and methodological problems inherent in the definition and discussion of medieval 'representative institutions' lies beyond the remit of this essay. A useful introduction to the topic is provided by T.N. Bisson, 'The problem of medieval parliamentarism: a review of work published by the International Commission for the History of Representative and Parliamentary Institutions, 1936–2000', *Parliaments, Estates and Representation*, 21 (2001), 1–14.

2   See e.g. Jan Dhondt, *Estates or Powers: Essays in the Parliamentary History of the Southern Netherlands from the XIIth to the XVIIIth Century* (rev. edn Heule, 1977); J.F. O'Callaghan, *The Cortes of Castile-Léon 1188–1350* (University of Pennsylvania Press, 1989); P. Bierbrauer, 'Die Ausbildung bäuerlicher Landschaften im Raum der Eidgenossenschaft', *Parliaments, Estates and Representation*, 11 (1991), 91–102; T.N. Bisson, 'The Origins of the Corts of Catalonia', *Parliaments, Estates and Representation*, xvi (1996), 31–45; R.J. Tanner, *The Late Medieval Scottish Parliament: Politics and the Three Estates, 1424–1488* (East Linton: Tuckwell, 2001); *The History of the Scottish Parliament* K.M. Brown *et al.* (eds), 3 vols (Edinburgh: Edinburgh University Press, 2004–5), vol. 1: 1235–1560.

3   A full treament of the highly diverse records of the different representative institutions of the medieval world, or even of those of urban communities or of the Church in England, is not possible within the limited framework of this essay, although some of the points to be made in the following are equally relevant to such source materials.

4 J.H. Denton and J.P. Dooley, *Representatives of the Lower Clergy in Parliament 1295–1340* (Woodbridge: Boydell & Brewer, 1987).

5 *Parliamentarians at Law: Select Legal Proceedings of the Long Fifteenth Century Relating to Parliament*, H. Kleineke (ed.), Parliamentary History: Texts and Studies 2 (Oxford: Wiley-Blackwell, 2008), pp. 4–5.

6 G.L. Harriss, 'Aids, Loans and Benevolences', *Historical Journal*, 6 (1963), 1–19.

7 *Parliamentarians at Law*, ed. Kleineke, pp. 112–13.

8 *The History of Parliament: The Commons 1386–1421*, J.S. Roskell, L. Clark and C. Rawcliffe (eds), [hereinafter *The Commons 1386–1421*], 4 vols (Stroud: Alan Sutton, 1993), i. pp. 259, 516.

9 *The Commons 1386–1421*, i. 517; *Parliamentary Texts of the Later Middle Ages*, N. Pronay and J. Taylor (eds), (Oxford: Clarendon, 1980), pp. 185–89.

10 *The Commons 1386–1421*, i. 395; *Calendar of the Charter Rolls vi (1427–1516)* London, 1927; May McKisack, *The Parliamentary Representation of the English Boroughs during the Middle Ages* (Oxford: OUP, 1932), p. 46.

11 In the wake of the re-editing of the English Parliament Rolls in the last years of the twentieth century, there has been much fresh analysis of these documents. Among the most important recent papers on the subject are W.M. Ormrod, 'On- and Off- the Record: The Rolls of Parliament 1337–1377', *Parchment and People: Parliament in the Middle Ages*, Linda Clark (ed.), (Edinburgh: Edinburgh University Press, 2004), pp. 39–56; C. Given-Wilson, 'The Rolls of Parliament, 1399–1421', *ibid.*, pp. 57–72; A. Curry, '"A Game of Two Halves": Parliament 1422–1454', *ibid.*, pp. 73–102, and also see the general introduction to *The Parliament Rolls of Medieval England, 1275–1504*, C. Given-Wilson et al. (eds),16 vols (Woodbridge: Boydell & Brewer, 2005).

12 On the petitioning of Parliament see most recently G. Dodd, *Justice and Grace: Private Petitioning and the English Parliament in the Late Middle Ages* (Oxford: OUP, 2007), and also the same author's 'The Hidden Presence: Parliament and the Private Petition in the Fourteenth Century', *Expectations of the Law in the Middle Ages*, A. Musson (ed.), (Woodbridge: Boydell & Brewer, 2001), pp. 135–49, and for the thirteenth century Paul Brand, 'Petitions and Parliament in the Reign of Edward I', in *Parchment and People*, ed. Clark, pp. 14–38.

13 M.A. Hicks, 'King in Lords and Commons: Three Insights into Late Fifteenth Century Parliaments, 1461–85', in *People, Places and Perspectives: Essays on Later Medieval and Early Tudor England in Honour of Ralph A. Griffiths*, K. Dockray and P. Fleming (eds), (Stroud: Nonsuch Publishing, 2005), pp. 131–53.

14 *The St. Albans chronicle: the Chronica maiora of Thomas Walsingham*, J. Taylor, W.R. Childs and L. Watkiss (eds), 2 vols (Oxford: Clarendon, 2003–10); 'John Benet's Chronicle for the years 1400 to 1462', G.L. Harriss and M.A. Harriss (eds), *Camden Miscellany XXIV* (Camden 4th ser. 9, 1972), pp. 151–234.

15 *Parliamentary Texts*, ed. Pronay and Taylor, pp. 185–89.

16 *The Commons 1386–1421*, i. 517.

17 W.H. Dunham, *The Fane Fragment of the 1461 Lords' Journal* (New Haven: Yale University Press, 1935); *idem*, 'Notes from the Parliament at Winchester, 1449', *Speculum*, 17 (1942), 402–15; R. Virgoe, 'A new fragment of the Lords' Journal of 1461', *Bulletin of the Institute of Historical Research*, 32 (1959), 83–7; A.R. Myers, 'A Parliamentary Debate of the Mid-Fifteenth Century', *Bulletin of the John Rylands Library*, 22 (1938), 388–404, reprinted in *idem*, *Crown, Household and Parliament in Fifteenth Century England*, C.H. Clough (ed.), (London: Hambledon, 1985), 69–85; *idem*, 'A Parliamentary Debate of 1449', *Bulletin of the Institute of Historical Research*, 51 (1978), 78–83, reprinted in *idem*, *Crown, Household and Parliament*, ed. Clough, 87–92. For the later journals, see G.R. Elton, 'The early Journals of the House of Lords', *English Historical Review*, 89 (1974), 481–512.

18 See, for example, F.R. Scott, 'Chaucer and the Parliament of 1386', *Speculum*, 18 (1943), 80–6; C.O. McDonald, 'An Interpretation of Chaucer's *Parlement of Foules*', *Speculum*, 30 (1955), 444–57; E.M. Orsten, 'The Ambiguities in Langland's Rat

Parliament', *Mediaeval Studies*, 23 (1961), 216–39; A. Gross, 'Langland's Rats: A Moralist's View of Parliament', *Parliamentary History*, 9 (1990), 286–301; G. Dodd, 'A Parliament full of Rats? Piers Plowman and the Good Parliament of 1376', *Historical Research*, 79 (2006), 21–49.

19  W. Jay, 'A List of Members of the Fourth Parliament of Henry VII', *Bulletin of the Institute of Historical Research*, 3 (1925/26), 168–75; R. Virgoe, 'A list of Members of the Parliament of February 1449', *Bulletin of the Institute of Historical Research*, 34 (1961), 200–10; A.F. Pollard, 'Thomas Cromwell's parliamentary lists', *Bulletin of the Institute of Historical Research*, 9 (931), 31–43. There is also a partial list of the members of the Commons for the Parliament of 1495, arising from the requirement for MPs to carry standard weights and measures back to their counties: *History of Parliament: Register of the Ministers and of the Members of both Houses 1439–1509*, J.C. Wedgwood (ed.), (London: HMSO, 1938), p. 80.

20  *The Commons 1386–1421*, i. 27; 'John Benet's Chronicle', p. 204.

21  J.S. Roskell, 'The Problem of Attendance of the Lords in Medieval Parliaments', *Bulletin of the Institute of Historical Research*, 29 (1956), 153–204; R.G. Davies, 'The "Earliest Attendance Lists" of the Lords in Parliament, 1402: A Doubt', *Bulletin of the Institute of Historical Research*, 56 (1983), 220–22; *idem*, 'The Attendance of the Episcopate in English Parliaments, 1376–1461', *Proceedings of the American Philosophical Society*, 129 (1985), 30–81. For the attendance of the Lords in the reigns of Richard II and of the first two Lancastrians, see *The Commons 1386–1421*, i. 33–6. For the attendance of some secular lords in the Parliaments of Edward IV, see H. Kleineke, *Edward IV* (London: Routledge, 2009), p. 169.

22  *The Commons 1386–1421*, i. 752.

23  *Parliament Rolls of Medieval England, 1275–1504*, xii. 208–9.

24  M.P. Davies, 'Lobbying Parliament: The London Companies in the Fifteenth Century', in *Parchment and People* ed. Clark, pp. 136–48; H. Kleineke, 'Lobbying and Access: The Canons of Windsor and the Matter of the Poor Knights in the Parliament of 1485', *Parliamentary History*, 25 (2007), 145–59.

25  There is an isolated copy of a Cornish election indenture to the abortive Parliament of June 1483 among the papers of the Trevelyan family.

26  J.C. Holt, *Robin Hood* (London: Thames and Hudson, 1982), pp. 69–70; TNA,C219/14/14,No. 101.

27  A. Rogers, 'Parliamentary Elections in Grimsby in the Fifteenth Century', *Bulletin of the Institute of Historical Research*, 42 (1969), 212–20; S.J. Payling, 'County Parliamentary Elections in Fifteenth-Century England', *Parliamentary History*, 18 (1999), 237–60.

28  *Parliament Rolls of Medieval England*, x. 480–81; *Parliamentarians at Law*, 336–37.

29  H. Kleineke, 'Lobbying and Access'.

30  For a detailed discussion of another geographical area see, for instance, the useful treatment of the records of the regional assemblies of medieval France by Michel Hébert: M. Hébert, 'Les assemblées représentatives de la France médiévale: quelques remarques sur les sources', *Parliaments, Estates and Representation*, 16 (1996), 17–29.

31  *Cortes de los antiguos reinos de León y de Castilla*, 7 vols (Madrid: Rivadenevra, 1861–1903); *Cortes de los antiguos reinos de Aragon y de Valencia y principado de Cataluña*, 26 vols (Madrid: Manuel Tello, 1896–1922).

32  *Hanserecesse* ed. Karl Koppman *et al.*, 24 vols (Leipzig: Duncker & Humblot, 1870–1913); *Deutsche Reichstagsakten*, J. Weizsäcker *et al.* (eds), 28 vols (Munich: Oldenbourg; Göttingen: Vandenhoek & Ruprecht, 1867–2008).

33  Hébert, pp. 23–24.

34  See, for example, Juliusz Bardach, 'L'élection des députés à l'ancienne Diète polonaise, fin XVe–XVIIIe siècles', *Parliaments, Estates and Representation*, 5 (1985), 45–58.

35  Hébert, p. 27.

# 15 Images and objects as sources for medieval history

*Sara Lipton[1]*

Historians tend to think of themselves as 'word people', and the discipline of history is generally conceived of as the study of the past through documents and texts. Since the 1990s, however, as part of a broader 'visual turn' in cultural analysis, many historians have come to recognize that images and objects, too, provide invaluable evidence concerning the human past. Although this 'visual turn' has in large part been prompted by recent technological developments that have rendered images – especially in the form of video and digital media – nearly ubiquitous and increasingly influential, it is nonetheless deeply relevant to the study of the European Middle Ages. Because the majority of its inhabitants were unable to read, medieval Europe was a highly visual (as well as oral/aural) culture. Identity was displayed through clothing and insignia, religion was taught through preaching and pictures, and authority was established through costume, gesture and posture. Agricultural decisions were made not by consulting manuals or calendars but by scanning the fields and the skies. Documents were authenticated not by signatures but by seals: images imprinted on wax. The later Middle Ages, moreover, saw a veritable 'image explosion', as a growing bourgeoisie stimulated the market for art and luxury goods, intensified lay piety broadened the audience for religious imagery, and new techniques of image-making were developed. Medieval images and artefacts thus participated fully in, and constitute rich resources for the study of, medieval politics, society, economy, culture and religion. In some cases they shed light on subjects about which written sources are largely silent.

The tools used to mine visual and material resources are many and varied, ranging from the time-honoured art historical methodologies of stylistic and iconographical analysis to newer approaches influenced by psychoanalysis, anthropology, semiotics, feminism and literary and cultural studies (such as reception theory, queer theory, and performance studies), and to cutting-edge scientific testing of materials and construction. The current scholarly trend is to focus less on what medieval images looked like than on how they were used – to understand the purposes they served and the 'cultural work' they performed for their makers, owners and viewers. Images and objects that profitably have been studied for such information include sculpture on cathedral exteriors, illuminations in religious manuscripts, frescoes decorating castle chambers, weapons and jewellery found in burial mounds, doodles scrawled in the margins of legal documents, liturgical implements and textiles stored in church treasuries, household items such as mirrors, chessmen, and aquamanilia (water jugs), leaden badges sold to pilgrims and tourists, and graffiti scratched on prison walls, among many others. Rather than attempting a comprehensive survey of the vast array of visual and material artefacts created in medieval Europe, this chapter will survey some fundamental ways in which one can learn about history from medieval artworks and also discuss some of the more interesting insights that have been provided by their study.[2]

## Subject and symbol (or iconography and its limitations)[3]

Probably the most obvious question that can be asked of an image is: 'who or what does it depict?' Through the first half of the twentieth century this was taken to be a fairly straightforward question, answerable by reference to the science of iconography, which sought to construct a comprehensive key to deciphering representational art. But for a variety of reasons answering these questions and drawing historical conclusions from the answers are no longer regarded as such simple tasks. On the most basic level, in spite of myriad visual cues developed by medieval artists to facilitate the 'reading' of their artworks (conveniently, if somewhat misleadingly, collected in numerous modern handbooks of medieval iconography), many images remain difficult to identify precisely. For every saint neatly 'labelled' by his or her symbolic attributes – such as St Roch with his bubo and little dog or Magdalene with long hair and an ointment jar – there are numerous other figures less easily given names. The crowned men on the façade of the Cathedral of Notre Dame de Paris are surely kings – but are they ancient Kings of Judah, embodying the human ancestry of the Lady to whom the structure is dedicated, or royal Franks, testifying to the venerability and legitimacy of the ruling Capetian dynasty? Are the faces topped by pointed hats decorating many twelfth-century stone capitals Jewish usurers bearing signs of ignominy or Christian bishops displaying emblems of high office?[4] What are we to call the strange, long-necked, large-eared birds carved on a church capital in Maastricht?[5] What exotic tale or moralistic fable is being narrated along the lower border of the early thirteenth-century fresco once in a Spanish monastery, in which a donkey strums a harp while two companion animals dance on their hind legs?[6]

More fundamentally, scholars have learned to see images not as 'illustration' but as 'representation', and to be wary of assuming that they depict 'reality' or that the meaning of even readily identifiable figures and scenes is transparent, straightforward or stable. Medieval images served many purposes: they glorified God, embodied sanctity, recalled teachings, radiated authority, displayed status, unified neighbourhoods, offered moral example, aided devotion, aroused emotion, and/ or inspired miracles, but they rarely sought to document their surroundings or even simply to tell a tale. We can no more conclude that medieval rulers looked like their portraits, than that a drawing of a lone woman spearing a boar faithfully reproduces contemporary hunting practices; that a thirteenth-century map reliably records a contemporary cityscape; or that peasants toiled in real fields as contentedly as they do in luxurious illuminated prayer books.[7] Nor can one assume that the ideas embodied in an image passively reflected general or uncontested attitudes. Many visual programmes can be considered forms of argumentation or polemic, designed to critique or challenge prevailing mores rather than embody them. So, for example, a fourteenth-century Italian fresco depicting sinners hanged by the strings of their own moneybags testifies as much to the widespread allure and profitability of credit lending, as to official disapproval of the practice.[8] And it has been argued that the strange, grotesque, often obscene creatures inhabiting the margins of manuscripts and the gargoyles leering from the corbels of Gothic structures, once thought to articulate clerical condemnation of vice (or alternately to mean nothing at all), actually satirize mainstream images and concepts, embodying otherwise effaced ideas and amounting to a counter-official discourse.[9]

A further complication arises from the recognition that meaning is by no means limited to the artist's intention: images may embody values, assumptions and thought structures of which patrons and artists are quite unconscious and may move viewers in ways that they themselves barely understand. Moreover, meaning can vary considerably over time: many medieval images repeat themes and forms developed decades or centuries earlier without necessarily replicating or even recognizing their 'original' message. Hebrew prophets first were included on luxurious enamel artworks in the midst of a twelfth-century debate over church ornament so that they might lend their antique authority to a novel art form, but they continued to appear on liturgical vessels long after the debate had subsided.[10] St Paul may originally have been portrayed as a bald, bearded man because he was described that way in a second-century text imbued with eastern Mediterranean ascetic ideals, but within a few centuries the long beard, conspicuous high forehead, and bald crown had simply become standard aspects of Paul's portrait, executed by artists who had never read *The Acts of Paul and Thecla* and had no knowledge of late Roman hair fashions.[11] Successive generations of viewers often ascribed new meaning to old signs. When eleventh-century Anglo-Saxon illuminators depicted horns on the head of Moses, for example, they were signalling his honour and power by invoking headgear associated in Germanic culture with high-status males.[12] But later medieval artists used the same horns to ridicule Hebrew spiritual weakness, and Michelangelo probably endowed his dignified, classicizing Moses with horns in deference to longstanding artistic convention.[13] Though scholars generally strive to identify the visual models on which images rely, this is not because visual sources fix or dictate the meaning of their offspring but because each new use of an image, whether by artist or by viewer, draws upon and is informed by existing connotations, even when they are rejected or changed. Indeed, meaning often lies in the very decision to retain or to modify, even minutely, received patterns.

Multiple meanings can co-exist in different contexts or for different viewers. A man and woman embracing might signify mortal sin on a cathedral exterior but productive generation in the pages of a scientific treatise, and courtly sophistication on a carved ivory plaque. A small-scale scene painted in a private book for a noble lady would be read in the light of the other images in that book, as well as of the lady's own life, social circle, and religious devotions, and would thus take on very different 'meaning' from a similar image in a more public place, viewed by a vastly broader audience living very different lives and surrounded by utterly different scenes and sounds.

In spite of these many challenges, iconographical analysis remains a valuable tool: there is much that can be learned about medieval society by examining which scenes or characters were selected for depiction and how they were depicted. The subjects chosen for representation can indicate current interests and concerns; and the actions, gestures and clothing they are endowed with can illuminate mental structures and cultural assumptions.

One instructive approach is to track iconographical change over time: the shifting forms assigned venerable concepts or figures constitute an eloquent index of socio-cultural change. Christ, probably the most ubiquitous figure in medieval Christian art, varies in aspect from place to place and era to era, and the nature of his portrayal tells us a great deal not only about contemporary Christian theological concerns – a subject discussed in many texts – but also about Christian self-imagining, about which texts are rather less explicit. In early Christian art, Christ was most typically depicted as a humble shepherd, reflecting his worshippers' sense of themselves as a small, tight-knit and vulnerable flock in need of protection from a hostile world.[14] From the fifth century, however, this image was abandoned in favour of his portrayal as a venerable teacher or august emperor, demonstrating the evolution of a new Christian ethos with the political triumph of Christianity and the attainment of dignity and power by the Catholic clergy.[15] Complex images of the crucified Christ from the court of Charlemagne (late eighth–early ninth centuries) combined such vulnerable, mortal features as a humble loincloth, bare torso, and bleeding wound with heavenly attributes such as a halo, staring eyes, and escorting angels to graphically proclaim that the Saviour was simultaneously human and divine, demonstrating how church ritual and furnishings were enlisted in the fight against heterodoxy.[16] An illumination in a fourteenth-century luxurious prayer book possibly made for Philip IV the Fair of France, which sets a poignant, even tragic crucifixion scene within an ornate and elaborately gilded framework, shows how Christ's death and suffering were made meaningful to the late medieval courtly élite, who were accustomed in everyday life to equate status with grace and luxury and to regard the failed, the naked, and the dead with revulsion. In the fifteenth century the proliferation of images of a profusely bleeding Christ, of miraculously bleeding hosts, and of the tools used to draw that blood helped late medieval Christians experiencing unprecedented plague and violence deal with, perhaps even transcend, their fear of death and change.[17] Important devotional, intellectual and cultural shifts have likewise been traced via changing representations of biblical, mythical and historical figures such as the Virgin Mary, St John, Pontius Pilate, Ruth, Alexander, Roland or Cain; of scriptural episodes such as the Sacrifice of Isaac or the parables of Christ; of religious concepts such as hell, vice, or the sacraments; of natural phenomena such as disease; and of social customs such as defacement and rituals of love and marriage, death and burial.[18]

A second important method is to investigate the imagery produced by a distinct group or in a defined context. Particularly rich in this regard has been the study of royal iconography, both portraiture (the clothing, hairstyles, poses, gestures, settings and styles in which rulers chose to have themselves portrayed), and patronage (the scenes and figures selected by rulers for representation in their favoured buildings and artworks). The development of a new periodization for the post-classical Mediterranean world, in which a creative 'Late Antiquity' has replaced the former 'Dark Age of Decline and Fall', rests in part upon changes in visual representation, especially of holy men and inspired leaders. Rather than merely representing artistic and intellectual decay, as was once held, the large eyes, static stance, and otherworldly upward gaze of such men are now thought to signal a major cultural shift, a new sense of intimacy between the divine and the earthly.[19] The characterization of the tenth-century German Ottonian dynasty as promoting a conscious 'renovation of the ancient Roman Empire' is largely based on their evocation of classical robes, headgear, and emblems in a range of artworks, with at least one scholar arguing that more can be learned about Ottonian ideology from imagery than from texts.[20] A study of the construction, embellishment, and use of Westminster Abbey by the English King Henry III (r. 1216–72) argues that the building was designed to serve as a focal point for Plantagenet power and offered a response to French, ecclesiastical and noble challenges, revealing how Henry used architecture to assert and consolidate royal authority.[21] The crusading ideology of King Louis IX of France (r. 1226–70) may be read in the imagery decorating the chapel he built in 1248 to house the Crown of Thorns and other sacred relics: the juxtaposition of scenes from the Old Testament, the New Testament, and the Capetian dynasty constructs a visual link between Paris and Jerusalem – a connection that Louis's Crusade was designed to make real.[22]

Analysis of the artworks created by religious institutions and orders has enhanced and in some cases modified the image of their institutional and intellectual cultures provided by texts. The pride of Benedictine monks in their Order's pre-eminence in biblical study is vividly displayed in their inclusion of notably obscure Old Testament scenes in the typological visual programmes (that is, compositions matching scenes from Hebrew Scripture with New Testament episodes they are said to foreshadow) decorating their manuscripts and buildings.[23] Scenes of Christ washing the apostles' feet were incorporated into Benedictine artworks to trumpet – or perhaps to encourage – the order's commitment to the monastic virtues of humility, hospitality and charity.[24] The Cistercian Order emerges as far less opposed to art in general and colour in particular than is suggested by its statutes when its vibrant walls, windows, books and tiles are examined, despite the well-known fulminations of Bernard of Clairvaux against monastic ornament. Analysis of the visual programmes in two neighbouring monasteries in Zurich reveals a considerably sharper competition for power and spiritual influence between the institutions than is acknowledged in contemporary texts.[25]

The appearance of entirely new motifs and subjects for illustration can signal important social, political, religious or cultural developments. The proliferation of high medieval depictions of Avarice echoes a pattern detectible in contemporary texts (the gradual substitution of Pride by Greed as the most censured vice), but the specifics of the images – showing a man at a counting table or a female clutching money bags – confirm the role of the Commercial Revolution of the twelfth and thirteenth centuries in heightening concern about the sin.[26] The near-obsession with idols and idol-worship that infiltrates high medieval art reveals the growing eagerness of the Church to suppress any and all perceived challenges to Catholic hegemony – including paganism, Islam, Judaism, homosexuality and even sexual desire – and also the logic by which theologians linked very different groups and practices.[27] The prevalence of death and decay in much fifteenth-century imagery (as well as the apparent obliviousness to contemporary suffering displayed by other images of the period) contributed to Jan Huizinga's positing of a general late medieval cultural crisis; although this interpretation has been challenged, the need to account for the imagery has not.[28] The growing prominence of female saints in later medieval art is widely accepted as evidence of a rise in lay, female piety (although, again, one must beware of simplistic equations: the popularity of St Anne, mother of the Virgin Mary, in later medieval art may owe less to women's interests and preferences than to a growing desire among male authorities to regulate secular family life; it has also been attributed to the development of the doctrine of Immaculate Conception).[29] The pronounced interest in visions and ecstasies evident in the art of Counter-Reformation Europe has been seen as part of a conscious clerical programme to refute Protestant theology, which downplayed such extra-rational ways of experiencing the divine.[30] And the introduction of secular themes such as courtship and warfare and of bourgeois concerns such as family, civic life and commerce into late medieval art is a good indication of significant socio-economic change, as lay nobles and urban merchants and craftsmen became able and eager to adorn their homes and public halls with artwork.

Incidental iconographical details are sometimes more informative than the primary scenes or subjects of an image. The famous Bayeux Tapestry (actually an embroidery) depicting the Norman Conquest of England in 1066 is by no means a comprehensive or fully reliable record of the Battle of Hastings: it has been shown that certain figures and episodes are included or excluded for ideological reasons.[31] Even the buildings have been changed – the embroiderers performing a kind of 'visual colonization' in depicting architectural styles not prevalent in England until well after the Conquest.[32] But the Tapestry seems to render some artefacts at least (presumably those less invested with ideological import) with remarkable accuracy, enriching our knowledge of eleventh-century warfare, transport and construction. We learn little about the domestic life of the Holy Family in the first century of the Common Era from *quattrocento* Italian or fifteenth-century Netherlandish religious painting, but we can learn a great deal about how those who made and viewed the paintings imagined and related to the Holy Family from the familiar domestic settings in which they are depicted. The paintings also furnish a rich trove of information about daily life in the medieval city, from the games played by children, to the goods purchased by housewives, the tools used by carpenters, and the shape and placement of the family privy. Of course, we must remain cautious about assuming that even background scenes faithfully replicate medieval life, as the improbably expensive tunic of a shepherd lolling in a field in the *Très Riches Heures of the Duc de Berry* suggests.[33]

Changing academic interests and methods have led scholars to ask a host of new questions of familiar images. The extent to which Christ's genitalia serve as a focal point of medieval and Renaissance art went entirely unnoticed by scholars until psychoanalytic theory taught us to pay attention to sexual signs.[34] Few medieval-ists, however, hold that psychoanalysis can fully explicate the pre-modern past: in his path-breaking work on the sexuality of Christ, Leo Steinberg offers a theo-logical rather than a Freudian explanation for the imagery, suggesting that artists highlighted Christ's sexuality in order to underscore his humanity. Inspired by the insights of feminist and gender theory, which stress that sexuality is understood and experienced differently in different cultures and by different groups, Caroline Bynum offers a somewhat different reading still of such imagery. She suggests that medieval and early modern viewers did not see Christ's penis as erotic but as vulnerable: a 'wounded' (through circumcision) vehicle for salvation.[35] Analysis of the visual syntax (the relative placement of the figures) in the thirteenth-century mosaics in San Marco, Venice, has underscored the misogyny permeating the visual programme: Eve's culpability in the Fall of Man is heightened by her occu-pation of the position of power, to the right of the Tree of Knowledge (the viewer's left), and by her authoritative gesture. This misogyny, which is not dictated by the biblical text, reflects aspects of contemporary Venetian civic culture and demon-strates how the governing élite read their own values and priorities into biblical history and conveyed them to the Venetian public.[36] Further manifestations of the influence of feminist and gender theory include studies of gender role reversal in printed broadsheets, the visual culture of nuns, the representation of sodomy, the visual construction of masculinity, attitudes toward nudity, and depictions of punishment and pain.

Marxist and post-Marxist thought have influenced the study of medieval art in a range of ways; in the realm of iconography such approaches have stimulated investigation into the representation of class and class conflict, into how imagery is shaped by economic conditions, and into how imagery is put in the service of power. So, for example, a study of the vivid agricultural scenes adorning the margins of a fourteenth-century book of hours argues that far from celebrating rural life, the images served as signs of the 'feudal slavery and social control' to which medieval peasants were subjected.[37] Similarly, the aristocratic hunt depicted in the *Très Riches Heures of the Duc de Berry*, once thought to illus-trate an innocent (if expensive) pleasure, is now seen as an affirmation of élite privilege.[38] The distorted Jewish faces doodled on the margins of English royal financial documents may serve less to condemn Jewish religious difference than to highlight royal control over Jews' bodies, and by extension, over the material realm with which they were identified.

Semiotics – the study of how meaning is created through both verbal and visual signs – has encouraged scholars to investigate the relations between signs, to recognize that the same sign can work on various levels, and to look anew at the relationship between words and images. In a set of illuminated biblical commen-taries made for the king of France (*c.* 1225) men with pointed hats and beards and carrying goats, cats, frogs or moneybags are very frequently labelled 'Jews'. However, these 'Jews' function on a range of levels: literally to signify an adherent of the Old Law, metaphorically to signify greed or materialism, metonymically to signify usurers or heretics, and very broadly to signify sin or unbelief. The fact that in these manuscripts 'Jews' and their accessories are associated with a wide range of qualities and practices also common among Christians, from money-lending to philosophical speculation to professional ambition to overly literal biblical interpretation, suggests that the image-makers were not concerned exclusively (or even primarily) with Jewish trespasses.[39]

Medievalists have likewise been influenced in a range of ways by postmodern literary theory and deconstruction, which insist on the instability of language and highlight its ambiguity, fragmentation, incompleteness and contradiction. So, for example, Jacques Derrida's concept of 'erasure' – according to which a crossed-out word highlights the problematic gap between the word itself and the thing it signifies and even brings into question the very existence of the thing – has been applied to the chancel screens in late antique synagogues, which call attention to the inaccessible sacred space beyond and to the absence of the long-destroyed Temple signified by that space.[40] Postmodern influence can likewise be detected in the burgeoning scholarly fascination with images of books and writing, as well as of seals and signatures, relics and reliquaries, broken and unfinished works of art, and hybrid and composite pieces.[41] There was little scholarly interest in the images in cartularies – bound volumes into which earlier individual documents are transcribed – until the work of such critics as Walter Benjamin, Jacques Derrida, and Paul de Man taught us to see copies and translations not as mere echoes of something 'real' but as creative performances in their own right. Inspired by such observations, Robert A. Maxwell has analysed the visual organization and decorative elements of a twelfth-century French cartulary, arguing that they serve to authenticate the transactions recorded within.[42] Scholars influenced by reception and reader response theory have broadened their focus to encompass not only the creation, form and meaning of objects or images but also the nature, expectations and responses of audiences. So, for example, a study of texts describing images of the crucifixion argues that what people 'saw' in a crucifix was conditioned as much by their situations, needs, institutional affiliation and spiritual preparation as by the appearance of the object.[43] A study of late medieval painted altarpieces by Beth Williamson goes further still in promoting 'an open, multivalent reading of the image', noting myriad ways in which people may have perceived an image of the Virgin nursing the Christ Child, some of which may have had little connection to what the image looked like or to where and how it was used.[44] An analysis of the remarkably sensual and dynamic figures depicted in a devotional prayer book of *c.* 1300 argues that they invited 'a mimetic rather than conceptual response', illuminating the embodied physicality of later medieval religious practice.[45]

Perhaps the most powerful example of the influence of current concerns on the study of medieval imagery is the explosion of interest in representations of ethnic and religious minorities and various other 'sub-groups' and 'out-groups'. Images of Jews, Muslims, Africans, peasants, witches, heretics, monsters, couples engaging in same-sex intercourse (sometimes labelled 'Sodomites'), disabled persons, and even the Irish have been analysed for information concerning both specific inter-group relations and broad cultural issues such as the rise of social intolerance, attitudes towards the body, and the nature of subjectivity (conceptions of the self). So, for example, an analysis of visual anti-Jewish polemic in illustrated English manuscripts of the Apocalypse (the Book of Revelation) connects the representation of Jews to contemporary political developments, arguing that the manuscripts' patrons were reformist bishops who used the images to justify violence against and persecution of Jewish communities.[46] By contrast, the historian Robert Bartlett examined images of Jews, Africans, Saracens, and the Irish not to explicate policy but to explore to what extent medieval concepts of human difference were biological or racialist.[47] Some scholars, most notably Debra Higgs Strickland and Ruth Mellinkoff, have focused on identifying a 'pictorial code of rejection' based on imaginings of demons and monsters and eventually applied to a wide variety of non-Christians. Their work consequently emphasizes the anxieties haunting – and the exclusionary nature of – medieval Christian culture and stresses the apparent arbitrariness of the characteristics assigned the 'Other'. Other studies have isolated significant differences in the representation of various sub-groups, arguing that while the depictions of such groups in medieval artworks cannot be considered 'documentary', they are nevertheless driven by some aspects of social reality and betray considerable nuance in how they approach non-Christians.[48] A common thread linking almost all of these works is the conviction that images play a major role in creating stereotypes and generating social intolerance.

Most of the images discussed so far appear in artworks made for the social and economic élite, but the recent rise of popular culture as a legitimate field of study has stimulated interest in such non-élite (and often un-pretty) images as pilgrims' souvenirs, cheap drawings and woodcuts, graffiti, doodles, and the like. Such sources can shed light on areas of medieval society that are otherwise difficult for historians to access, both in illuminating the lives, concerns and image-use of the 'silent' lay majority and in revealing new aspects of familiar practices. Examining the subjects represented on the leaden badges purchased by pilgrims, for example, allows us to gauge the relative popularity of saints, to trace the geographical reach of a cult, to reconstruct the appearance of lost shrines and buildings, to determine which prayers were said in conjunction with certain images, and to glimpse the nature of medieval humour. Analysing both the content and the placement of words, drawings, and defacing marks scrawled on painted walls provides evidence for the preoccupations of the non-élite public (the weather looms large as a topic worthy of note) as well as for how people viewed and responded to art and architecture. Such graffiti sometimes expresses a pilgrim's devotion, but in other cases constitutes rare documentation of resistance to authority.[49] The rough, amateurish drawings of everyday familial and secular life decorating early modern Yiddish books of custom, some of which were made for women unschooled in Hebrew, convey a sense of joy and pleasure not apparent in more 'official' – and 'masculine' – texts and images (though presumably the pastimes depicted were not unknown to rabbis and élite Jewish men).[50]

## Beyond subject matter: style and form

Formal analysis – close examination and categorization of style, composition, and what is sometimes called 'pictorial grammar' – is the bread and butter of art historians seeking to date, locate, relate and explicate works of art. Although as early as the nineteenth century some Marxist art historians began to claim that formal elements could also reveal much about the historical conditions in which they arose, historians were long reluctant to venture into the territory of style. Yet medieval authors themselves held that style bore meaning. The theologian Jean Gerson criticized the sensuality of the language and verbal imagery of the *Roman de la Rose*, but also complained about the elegance of the pictures (and not just their subject matter), fearing that their lavishness and the sheer skill with which they were executed would promote greed and lust among those who viewed them.[51] With the slow erosion of disciplinary boundaries and the renewed postmodern attention to the signifying power of form, style is once again being related to socio-cultural context by art historians and historians alike. Peter Brown, perhaps the leading historian of the late antique world, suggests that the 'brutal novelties' of the style of the Arch of Constantine embody the power and ambition of the new imperial regime, while the 'exquisite neo-classical' style of late fourth-century ivories demonstrates the extent to which the new upper classes had adopted the tastes of the traditional élites they had replaced.[52] Jean Wirth sees the more abstract and schematic, less narrative nature of western art from the late tenth or eleventh century as indicative of a new conceptualization of art's role as making visible sacred truths, such as spiritual hierarchy.[53] Paul Binski argues that the style of thirteenth-century English church art and architecture, which he labels 'tempered magnificence', embodies and helps us understand the mores and values of the clerical élite.[54]

Historians can learn much about travel, cultural contacts, and political and economic ties by tracing the diffusion, preservation, or revival of artistic styles. The appearance of a new style, for example, can indicate the arrival of a new political regime or economic or cultural influence, or, alternately, the evolution of a new ambition or assumption of a new identity within an existing population. A shift in the prevailing style of floor mosaics in the late third- and early fourth-century Galilee (from an illusionistic and naturalistic style associated with Antioch to a flatter, more abstract and decorative style emanating from North Africa) can help us track the progress of Christianization, which introduced a new approach to representation and also expanded ties with the West.[55] The classically naturalistic fish decorating a bowl found in the sixth-century Anglo-Saxon Sutton Hoo ship-burial may signal the continued presence of an indigenous Romano-British tradition.[56] The espousal of Byzantine painting styles by Armenian and Slavic artists furnishes evidence for the political reach of the Byzantine Empire. Rumours of a massive payment to Harold Hardrada by the Byzantine government receive confirmation by the appearance in the late eleventh century of Scandinavian coins modelled on Byzantine styles.[57] The fact that Hebrew manuscripts made for Jews display the same artistic styles – and were often painted by the same artists – as Latin manuscripts made for Christians may point to greater acculturation among medieval Jews than the texts found in those same manuscripts suggest; at the very minimum it shows that religious identity and interreligious relations were considerably more complex than is often assumed.[58] In the ongoing debate about the nature of the Latin Crusader states, the mix of Byzantine, Western and Muslim stylistic elements featured in Frankish (crusader) art and architecture has been cited as a primary reason why the labels 'colonialism' and 'imperialism' do not aptly describe the crusading movement.[59]

The adoption (or rejection) of a certain style can be a conscious ideological statement. Charlemagne, who in 800 became the first Latin Christian to be crowned 'emperor of Rome' in more than three hundred years, modelled his palace at Aachen on classical and Byzantine buildings to underscore his imperial claims (he also had himself called 'Caesar' in an inscription around the dome of the palace chapel).[60] The surprisingly early appearance of the Gothic architectural style (then known as the 'French style') in the late twelfth-century cathedral and palace in Esztergom, Hungary has been related to the pro-French dynastic foreign policy and the Parisian-influenced reformist ecclesiastical agenda of King Bela III (d. 1196).[61] But not all stylistic echoing should be seen as political homage. When Alfonso X the Wise of Castile (d. 1284) selected the Gothic style for his conversion of a former Almohad fort into his royal palace, he was visually trumpeting his military conquests over Muslims and his political aspirations to lead Christendom – and supersede France.[62]

## The image as object: medium, material, technique, condition, scale and location

Archaeologists have long analysed the materials and techniques of artefacts to learn about the societies that left them behind; historians, propelled by the relatively new fields of 'material culture' and 'commodity history', are beginning to do the same. The materials available to (or affordable by) the makers and owners of artefacts provide evidence regarding trade patterns and economic and political conditions; the tools and skills utilized indicate technological and/or organizational characteristics of the society; the layout and construction of buildings illuminate the lives lived inside them; the exchange, display and preservation of objects reveal social networks and cultural values. The introduction of new media can signal major cultural shifts: the revival of bronze casting under Bishop Bernward of Hildesheim around the year 1000, the reappearance of the craft of mosaic at Salerno *c.* 1085, and the re-emergence of enamel-making in Lotharingia c. 1100 – all techniques that had lain dormant in the West for many centuries – must figure prominently in any discussion of the timing and location of the high medieval economic and intellectual revival. The degree of wear and tear on manuscripts or on objects such as a processional cross conveys important evidence about reading habits and liturgical practices; the purposeful erasure of an image sheds light on changing attitudes toward figural art.

A few examples of recent material- and object-based studies offer an idea of the range of insights such approaches can provide. Scientific analysis of Near Eastern ceramics has established that the techniques of potters in the region remained relatively stable until the eighth century, when there was a burst of technical innovation and creativity, perhaps stimulated by the taste for luxury goods among the new urban Muslim élite.[63] On the basis of the distribution and decoration of brooches found in seventh-century grave sites in Greece, which fulfil an apparently increased need for social differentiation, the historian Florin Curta has proposed the emergence of a new kind of high-status Slavic male during a period of Byzantine administrative collapse.[64] The presence in Merovingian graves of artefacts decorated with Christian symbols helps us trace the transition from paganism to Christianity in early medieval Gaul.[65] Analysis of the technical and decorative aspects of silks imported into the Carolingian empire proves that the vast majority of such textiles originated in Asia, lending key support to a recent reassessment of early medieval trade arguing for greater contact with the Arab world under Charlemagne than was long envisioned.[66] A survey of the size, location and spatial organization of English nunneries reveals the extent to which they were patronized by and provided services to the local gentry, indicating greater integration into local communities than the rhetoric of enclosure would suggest.[67] Examining the treatment of stones in Levantine buildings makes it possible to determine which structures were built by Frankish crusaders and which by local Christians, elucidating the extent and nature of Frankish settlement and economic activity.[68] Trace element analysis, which helps identify the geographical sources of the limestone used in cathedral sculptures, has allowed scholars to reconstruct the original programmes of damaged monuments, map patterns of exchange and transport, and gain knowledge of quarrying and building practices.[69]

Scale, too, in terms of the size, quantity, and cost of objects and images conveys information. The privileging of small portable objects suggests that a society or group was itinerant or migratory, whereas the presence of monumental art testifies to a considerable concentration of wealth, the availability of labour, and some sort of centralizing power. The existence of a great amount of imported objects is firmer testimony for trade ties than the presence of a small number. Thus a debate about the extent to which the Roman Empire truly welded the Mediterranean region into an integrated economic unit has been largely settled thanks to studies of the distribution of ceramics, which demonstrate the wide circulation of tableware of all types across the entire area.[70] The appearance of three large, elaborate and expensive German-made carved altarpieces in a single fifteenth-century Norwegian church testifies to a recent burgeoning of the local economy; the fact that paintings became increasingly small (and so more affordable) in fifteenth-century Bruges indicates that an ever-widening circle of middle-class consumers aspired to own artworks.[71] The mass-production (through woodcuts and other forms of printing, introduced in the fifteenth century), standardization, or frequent copying of images can tell us about market demand, production methods, and workshop practices, which in turn illuminate such topics as audience tastes, class relations, literacy levels, economic conditions, and social and religious practices and attitudes.

Although historians and literary scholars long treated their sources (whether laws, poems, sermons, treatises, romances, or commentaries, and so on) as disembodied 'texts', many have now begun to study the physical aspects of the manuscripts in which such texts appear, to consider their overall size, shape, material, arrangement, page layout, and decoration. This approach can significantly add to our understanding of the texts in question. The apparently ascetic and anti-iconic message of the hagiographical text *La Vie de Saint Alexis* (*Life of Saint Alexis*) is complicated (to say the least) when considered in the context of the luxurious twelfth-century illuminated manuscript in which the *Life* first appeared.[72] The large size of the manuscript and illuminations of the *Hortus Deliciarum*, a theological compendium made by the twelfth-century German Abbess Herrad of Hohenbourg, indicates that the work was intended to be publicly viewed and read, suggesting that many members of the female community had achieved a high level of education.[73] Examination of the mixture of classical and Christian iconography in the frontispiece to the little-known Chaucerian poem *The Complaint of Mars* in a fifteenth-century manuscript helps clarify the complex poetic techniques of the poem and also how pious lay readers received it.[74] Analysis of the images and border decoration in a legal manuscript suggests that the laws were copied as part of the Lancastrian king's polemical campaign to critique the dynasty he overthrew.[75]

Centuries of political, religious and social upheaval have rendered it impossible to determine the original location of many medieval artworks, but obviously the geographical origins and final destinations of images and objects can speak volumes about historical circumstances. Moreover, the very fact of displacement can provide historical information. *Spolia* (literally 'booty', meaning here the reused parts of earlier buildings or major monuments) can signal aesthetic, economic or ideological developments; the same holds true for the reuse of smaller objects as well. Of course, careful attention must be paid to the broader physical, social, political and economic contexts; there are many and varied reasons for such recycling. It may sometimes stake a claim to the authority, legitimacy or prestige of an earlier culture. Charlemagne's famous appropriation of columns from Rome and Ravenna for his palace chapel at Aachen must be seen as part of his programme of imperial *renovatio*; similarly, the Lotharingian Abbot Wibald's incorporation of Byzantine reliquaries into his great enamel triptych endows the work – and the monastery that owned it – with the sacred and imperial aura of that great Empire.[76] Alternately, the 'despoiler' may be simply demonstrating his power and right to lay claim to such booty, irrespective of the value attributed to the society that created it, as when in 1140 Pope Innocent II confiscated ancient pagan column capitals for a church he was constructing.[77] The reuse of older materials sometimes demonstrates the evolution of a new aesthetic: Constantine's incorporation of older Roman architectural fragments into his new Lateran Basilica asserts his reverence for the past, but also contributes to and underscores the visual variety so characteristic of Constantinian art.[78] Finally, the practice may simply arise from economic necessity or technological inadequacy: the reuse of twelfth-century stained glass panels in later medieval parish churches probably testifies more to local thrift than to artistic or ideological considerations.[79]

## A thousand words?

The above discussion can offer only a small indication of the rich historical information to be gained from consideration of medieval images and objects. Nor, given the diversity of both medieval images and the questions their analysis can address, is it possible to provide a complete methodological guide to their exploitation as historical sources. But it may be helpful to close with some general observations about the use of images in historical research. First, it should be kept in mind that the divisions laid out above, distinguishing content and representation on the one hand from form and material on the other, are quite artificial; the most compelling and comprehensive analyses of medieval artworks take all of these aspects and more into account. Second, as in any historical endeavour, image-based study should work both diachronically – exploring the artistic models and patterns that influenced or found echo in (or were rejected by) an artwork, and synchronically – delving deeply into the work's contemporary context. Third, the kind of visual analysis discussed here is very different from the (one hopes, outdated) historical practice of using images to illustrate points derived primarily from texts. The point of the 'visual turn' is not to enliven our lectures and publications (though this can be an added side-benefit) but to deepen our knowledge by expanding our source base. Textual evidence will naturally remain vital even to image-based studies. But we look to images not to confirm what we already know but to discover what we don't know, to formulate and then try to answer new questions. Finally, one should not be misled about the difficulty of our task, either by medieval statements about the transparency of images (that is, assertions that pictures are 'the Book of the Simple', or that in contrast to the 'veiled word' they are 'naked and open') or by the still-current clichés that 'a picture speaks for itself' or 'a picture is worth a thousand words'. Images can be eloquent indeed. But we must recognize that the language they speak is quite distinct from verbal communication; as with any language the grammar, vocabulary and idioms of medieval imagery need to be learned. But for the historian who labours to master them, the images and objects of the Middle Ages offer a tale well worth the reading.

## Notes

1  I would like to thank David Nirenberg, Daniel Monk and Joel Rosenthal for their helpful suggestions and comments regarding this essay.
2  I shall also be discussing 'straight' art historical studies designed primarily to illuminate artworks themselves rather than the society that created them, but which nevertheless offer important insights for historians. Indeed, I note with some regret that the majority of works I cite are by art historians, suggesting that the major fruits of the 'visual turn' in medieval history remain in the future.
3  The OED defines *iconography* as 'The description or illustration of any subject by means of drawings or figures; any book or work in which this is done; also, the branch of knowledge which deals with the representation of persons or objects by any application of the arts of design'.
4  Michele Beaulieu, 'Communication sur le prétendu bonnet juif', *Bulletin de la Société nationale des antiquaires de France* (January, 1972): 29–44.
5  Elizabeth den Hartog, 'All Nature Speaks of God, All Nature Teaches Man: The Iconography of the Twelfth-century Capitals in the Westwork Gallery of the Church of St. Servatius in Maastricht', *Zeitschrift für Kunstgeschichte* 59 (1996): 29–62 [50].
6  Fresco of a dragon from the chapter house of San Pedro de Arlanza (near Burgos, Spain) dated *c*. 1200–1220 (The Cloisters Collection, 1931, 31.38.2a, b).
7  On royal portraiture, see Stephen Perkinson, *The Likeness of the King: A Prehistory of Portraiture in Late Medieval France* (Chicago: University of Chicago Press, 2009). On maps, see Evelyn Edson, *Mapping Time and Space: How Medieval Mapmakers Viewed Their World* (London: British Library, 1999). On the hunting image, see Veronica Sekules, 'Women in Art in England in the Thirteenth and Fourteenth Centuries', in

*The Age of Chivalry: Art in Plantagenet England 1200–1400*, Jonathan J.G. Alexander and Paul Binski (eds), (London: Weidenfeld & Nicolson, 1987), pp. 41–8 [47]. On peasants, see Michael Camille, 'Labouring for the Lord: the Ploughman and the Social Order in the Luttrell Psalter', *Art History* 10 (1987): 423–54.

8  Anne Derbes and Mark Sandina, 'Barren Metal and the Fruitful Womb: The Program of Giotto's Arena Chapel in Padua', *Art Bulletin* 80 (1998): 274–91.

9  Michael Camille, *Image on the Edge: The Margins of Medieval Art* (Cambridge, MA: Harvard U.P., 1992).

10  Sara Lipton, *Dark Mirror: Jews, Vision, and Witness in Medieval Christian Art, 1000–1500* (New York: Palgrave Macmillan, forthcoming), Chapter 2.

11  *Acts of Paul and Thecla* 2.3.

12  Ruth Mellinkoff, *The Horned Moses in Medieval Art and Thought* (Berkeley and Los Angeles: University of California Press, 1970).

13  Mellinkoff, *The Horned Moses*. See also Malcolm MacMillan and Peter J. Swales, 'Observations from the Refuse-Heap: Freud, Michelangelo's Moses, and Psychoanalysis', *American Imago* 60 (2003): 41–104.

14  Boniface Ramsey, 'Note on the Disappearance of the Good Shepherd from Early Christian Art', *Harvard Theological Review* 76 (1983): 375–78.

15  Andre Grabar, *Early Christian Art: From the Rise of Christianity to the Death of Theodosius*, transl. Stuart Gilbert and James Emmons (New York: Odyssey, 1968) and Thomas F. Mathews, *The Clash of Gods: A Reinterpretation of Early Christian Art* (Princeton: Princeton U.P., 1993).

16  Celia Chazelle, *The Crucified God in the Carolingian Era: Theology and Art of Christ's Passion* (Cambridge: CUP, 2001), pp. 91ff.

17  Caroline Walker Bynum. *Wonderful Blood: Theology and Practice in Late Medieval Northern Germany and Beyond* (Philadelphia: University of Pennsylvania Press, 2007), p. 252.

18  Some examples include Miri Rubin, *Mother of God: A History of the Virgin Mary* (New Haven: Yale U.P., 2009); Jeffrey F. Hamburger, *Saint John the Divine: The Deified Evangelist in Medieval Art and Theology* (Berkeley: University of California Press, 2002); Colum Hourihane, *Pontius Pilate, Anti-Semitism, and the Passion in Medieval Art* (Princeton: Princeton U.P., 2009); Victor M. Schmidt, *A Legend and Its Image: The Aerial Flight of Alexander the Great in Medieval Art* (Groningen: E. Forsten, 1995); C.M. Kauffmann, 'The Sainte Chapelle Lectionary and the Illustration of the Parables in the Middle Ages', *Journal of the Warburg and Courtauld Institutes* 67 (2004): 1–22; Ann Eljenholm Nichols, *Seeable Signs: Iconography of the Seven Sacraments, 1350–1544* (Woodbridge: Boydell, 1994); Christine M. Boeckl, *Images of Plague and Pestilence: Iconography and Iconology* (Kirksville, MO: Truman State U.P., 2000); Paul Binski, *Medieval Death: Ritual and Representation* (Ithaca: Cornell U.P., 1996).

19  See Peter Brown, *The Making of Late Antiquity* (Cambridge, MA: Harvard U.P., 1978), pp. 13–19, building on the work of H.P. L'Orange, *Apotheosis in Ancient Portraiture* (Oslo: H. Aschehoug, 1947). I thank David Nirenberg for this reference.

20  Reinhart Staats, *Theologie der Reichskrone: Ottonische 'Renovatio imperii' im Spiegel einer Insignie* (Stuttgart: Kohlhammer, 1976).

21  Paul Binski, *Westminster Abbey and the Plantagenets: Kingship and the Representation of Power, 1200–1400* (New Haven and London: Yale U.P., 1995). See also William Chester Jordan, *A Tale of Two Monasteries: Westminster and Saint-Denis in the Thirteenth Century* (Princeton: Princeton U.P., 2009).

22  Daniel H. Weiss, 'Architectural Symbolism and the Decoration of the Ste.-Chapelle', *Art Bulletin* 77 (1995): 308–20.

23  Meredith Parsons Lillich, 'Monastic Stained Glass: Patronage and Style', in *Monasticism and the Arts,* Timothy G. Verdon (ed.), (Syracuse: Syracuse U.P., 1984), pp. 207–54.

24  Susan E. Von Daum Tholl, 'Life according to the Rule: A Monastic Modification of Mandatum Imagery in the Peterborough Psalter', *Gesta* 33 (1994): 151–8.

25   Joan A. Holladay, 'The Competition for Saints in Medieval Zurich', *Gesta* 43 (2004): 41–59.

26   Lester K. Little, 'Pride Goes before Avarice: Social Change and the Vices in Latin Christendom', *American Historical Review* 76 (1971): 16–49.

27   Michael Camille, *The Gothic Idol: Ideology and Image-Making in Medieval Art* (Cambridge: CUP, 1989).

28   Johan Huizinga, *The Autumn of the Middle Ages* (Chicago: University of Chicago Press, 1996; orig. pub. 1919). It is worth noting that Huizinga, acknowledging the beauty and serenity of many later medieval images, downplayed the historical reliability of images. For a different reading of fifteenth-century imagery, see Bynum, *Wonderful Blood.*

29   On female saints in art, see Paola Tinagli, *Women in Italian Renaissance Art: Gender, Representation, Identity* (New York: Manchester U.P., 1997). On St Anne, see Mirelle Veli d'Ancona, *The Iconography of the Immaculate Conception in the Middle Ages and the Early Renaissance* (New York: College Art Association, 1957).

30   Emile Mâle, *L'Art religieux après le Concile de Trente, étude sur l'iconographie de la fin du XVIe, du XVIIe et du XVIIIe siècles en Italie, en France, en Espagne et en Flandre* (Paris: A. Colin, 1932).

31   For example Bishop Odo of Bayeux, the probable patron of the Tapestry, appears multiple times while the equally prominent bishop of Coutance does not appear at all. Lucien Musset, *The Bayeux Tapestry,* transl. Richard Rex (Woodbridge, Surrey: Boydell, 2005) argues that the bishop of Coutance was omitted so as to heighten the prominence of the bishop of Bayeux. He also suggests that the deaths of two English royal relatives are included to confirm that William was the only surviving claimant to the throne.

32   Suzanne Lewis, *The Rhetoric of Power in the Bayeux Tapestry* (Cambridge: CUP, 1999), p. 44.

33   Jonathan J.G. Alexander, 'Labeur and Paresse: Ideological Representations of Medieval Peasant Labor', *Art Bulletin* 72 (1990): 436–452.

34   Leo Steinberg, *The Sexuality of Christ in Renaissance Art and Modern Oblivion* (New York: Pantheon, 1983).

35   Caroline Walker Bynum, 'The Body of Christ in the Later Middle Ages: A Reply to Leo Steinberg', *Renaissance Quarterly* 39 (1986): 399–439.

36   Penny Howell Jolly, *Made in God's Image? Eve and Adam in the Genesis Mosaics in San Marco, Venice* (Berkeley and Los Angeles: University of California Press, 1997).

37   Camille, 'Labouring for the Lord'. Not many historians would today use quite this terminology to describe the manorial economy.

38   Alexander, 'Labeur and Paresse'.

39   Sara Lipton, *Images of Intolerance: The Representation of Jews and Judaism in the Bibles moralisées* (Berkeley and Los Angeles: University of California Press, 1999).

40   Joan R. Branham, 'Sacred Space under Erasure in Ancient Synagogues and Early Churches', *Art Bulletin* 74 (1992): 375–94.

41   See for example Brigitte Bedos-Rezak, 'Medieval Identity: A Sign and a Concept', *American Historical Review* 105 (2000): 1489–533 and Cynthia Hahn, 'The Voices of the Saints, What Do Speaking Reliquaries Say?', *Gesta* 36 (1997): 20–31.

42   Robert A. Maxwell, 'Sealing Signs and the Art of Transcribing in the Vierzon Cartulary', *Art Bulletin* 81 (1999): 576–97.

43   Sara Lipton, '"The Sweet Lean of His Head": Writing about Looking at the Crucifix in the High Middle Ages', *Speculum* 80 (2005): 1172–208.

44   Beth Williamson, 'Altarpieces and Images: Liturgy and Devotion', *Speculum* 79 (2004): 341–406.

45   Jeffrey F. Hamburger, *The Rothschild Canticles: Art and Mysticism in Flanders and the Rhineland c. 1300* (New Haven and London: Yale U.P., 1990), p. 106.

46   Suzanne Lewis, 'Tractatus adversus Judaeos in the Gulbenkian Apocalypse', *Art Bulletin* 68 (1986): 543–566.

47  Robert Bartlett, 'Illustrating Ethnicity in the Middle Ages', in *The Origins of Racism in the West*, Miriam Eliav-Feldon, Benjamin Isaac, and Joseph Ziegler (eds), (Cambridge: CUP, 2009). Bartlett nonetheless does not ignore policy, noting that Gerald of Wales's description of the Welsh was written as an aid to conquest.

48  See Francisco Prado-Vilar, 'In the Shadow of the Gothic Idol: The *Cantigas de Santa Maria* and the Imagery of Love and Conversion', Ph.D. diss., Harvard University, 2002 and Sarah Salih, 'Idols and Simulacra: Paganity, Hybridity, and Representation in Mandeville's Travels', in *The Monstrous Middle Ages*, Bettina Bildhauer and Robert Mills (eds), (Toronto: University of Toronto Press, 2003), pp. 113–33.

49  Véronique Plesch, 'Memory on the Wall: Graffiti on Religious Wall Paintings', *Journal of Medieval and Early Modern Studies* 32 (2002): 167–97; Marcia Ann Kupfer, *The Art of Healing: Painting for the Sick and the Sinner in a Medieval Town* (University Park, PA: Pennsylvania State U.P., 2003).

50  Diane Wolfthal, *Picturing Yiddish: Gender, Identity, and Memory in the Illustrated Yiddish Books of Renaissance Italy* (Leiden and Boston: Brill, 2004).

51  Sandra Hindman, *Christine de Pizan's 'Epistre Othéa': Painting and Politics at the Court of Charles VI* (Toronto: Pontifical Institute of Mediaeval Studies, 1986), p. xviii.

52  Peter Brown, *The World of Late Antiquity, A.D. 150–750,* (New York: Norton, 1989), p. 29.

53  Jean Wirth, *L'Image à l'Époque Romane* (Paris: Cerf, 1999).

54  Paul Binski, *Becket's Crown: Art and Imagination in Gothic England, 1170–1300* (New Haven: Yale U.P., 2004).

55  M.W. Merrony, 'The Reconciliation of Paganism and Christianity in the Early Byzantine Mosaic Pavements of Arabia and Palestine', *Liber Annus* 48 (1998): 441–82; Zeev Weiss, 'The Mosaics of the Nile Festival Building at Sepphoris and the Legacy of the Antiochene Tradition', in *Between Judaism and Christianity: Art Historical Essays in Honor of Elisheva (Elisabeth) Revel-Neher*, Katrin Kogman-Appel and Mati Meyer (eds), (Leiden and Boston: Brill, 2009), pp. 9–23.

56  Carola Hicks, *Animals in Early Medieval Art* (Edinburgh: Edinburgh U.P., 1993).

57  Philip Grierson, 'Commerce in the Dark Ages: A Critique of the Evidence', *Transactions of the Royal Historical Society*, 5th ser., 9 (1959): 123–40 [136].

58  See the essays collected in *Imagining the Self, Imagining the Other: Visual Representation and Jewish–Christian Dynamics in the Middle Ages and Early Modern Period,* Eva Frojmovic (ed.), (Leiden and Boston: Brill, 2002); Katrin Kogman-Appel, *Illuminated Haggadot from Medieval Spain: Biblical Imagery and the Passover Holiday* (University Park, PA: Pennsylvania State U.P., 2006); Marc Michael Epstein, *Dreams of Subversion in Medieval Jewish Art and Literature* (University Park, PA: Pennsylvania State U.P., 1997).

59  Adrian J. Boas, 'Archaeological Sources for the History of Palestine: The Frankish Period: A Unique Medieval Society Emerges', *Near Eastern Archaeology* 61 (1998): 138–73 [153].

60  Kenneth J. Conant, *Carolingian and Romanesque Architecture*, 4th edn (New Haven: Yale U.P., 1994) and Charles McClendon, *The Origins of Medieval Architecture* (New Haven: Yale U.P., 2005), pp. 108–19.

61  Ernö Marosi, *Die Anfänge der Gotik in Ungarn. Esztergom in der Kunst des 12. –13. Jahrhunderts* (Budapest: Akadémiai Kiadó, 1984).

62  D. Fairchild Ruggles, 'The Alcazar of Seville and Mudejar Architecture', *Gesta* 43 (2004): 87–98 [95].

63  Rob Mason, 'Analytical Techniques in Near Eastern Archaeology: Materials and the Scanning Electron Microscope', *The Biblical Archaeologist* 58 (1995): 237.

64  Florin Curta, 'Female Dress and "Slavic" Bow Fibulae in Greece', *Hesperia* 74 (2005): 101–46.

65  Yithak Hen, *Culture and Religion in Merovingian Gaul, 481–751* (Leiden and New York: Brill, 1995), p. 146.

66  A. Muthesius, *Byzantine Silk Weaving AD 400 to AD 1200* (Vienna: Fassbaender, 1997), cited in Michael McCormick, *The Origins of the European Economy: Communications and Commerce AD 300–900* (New York: CUP, 2001), pp. 714–25.

67  Roberta Gilchrist, *Gender and Material Culture: The Archaeology of Religious Women* (London: Routledge, 1994).

68  Adrian J. Boas, *Crusader Archaeology: The Material Culture of the Latin East* (London: Routledge, 1999).

69  See the articles published in 'The Limestone Project' issue of *Gesta* 33 (1994).

70  Chris Wickham, 'The Mediterranean around 800: On the Brink of the Second Trade Cycle', *Dumbarton Oaks Papers* 58 (2004): 161–74 [164].

71  Jan von Bonsdorff, 'Is Art a Barometer of Wealth? Medieval Art Exports to the Far North of Europe', in Michael North and David Ormrod (eds), *Art Markets in Europe, 1400–1600* (Aldershot and Brookfield, VT: Ashgate, 1998) and Jean C. Wilson, *Painting in Bruges at the Close of the Middle Ages: Studies in Society and Visual Culture* (University Park, PA: Pennsylvania State U.P., 1998).

72  Michael Camille, 'Philological Iconoclasm: Edition and Image in the Vie de Saint Alexis', in R. Howard Bloch and Stephen G. Nichols (eds), *Medievalism and the Modernist Temper* (Baltimore and London: Johns Hopkins U.P., 1996), pp. 371–401.

73  Fiona J. Griffiths, *The Garden of Delights: Reform and Renaissance for Women in the Twelfth Century* (Philadelphia: University of Pennsylvania Press, 2006).

74  Jessica Brantley, 'Venus and Christ in Chaucer's *Complaint of Mars:* The Fairfax 16 Frontispiece', *Studies in the Age of Chaucer* 30 (2008): 171–204.

75  Rosemarie McGerr, 'A Statute Book and Lancastrian Mirror for Princes: The Yale Law School Manuscript of the Nova Statuta Angliae', *Textual Cultures: Texts, Contexts, Interpretation* 1 (2006): 6–59.

76  Holger Klein, 'Eastern Objects and Western Desires: Relics and Reliquaries Between Byzantium and the West', *Dumbarton Oaks Papers* 58 (2004): 283–314 [299–300].

77  Dale Kinney, 'Spolia from the Baths of Caracalla in Sta. Maria in Trastevere', *Art Bulletin* 68 (1986): 379–97.

78  Beat Brenk, 'Spolia from Constantine to Charlemagne: Aesthetics versus Ideology', *Dumbarton Oaks Papers* 41 (1987): 103–9 [105].

79  Meredith Lillich Parsons, 'Remembrance of Things Past: Stained Glass Spolia at Châlons Cathedral', *Zeitschrift für Kunstgeschichte* 59 (1996): 461–97 [461].

# 16  Medieval archaeology

*David A. Hinton*

Archaeology has been defined as 'the study of the human past from its material remains'. For prehistory, no evidence can exist other than the tangible and visible – flint tools, pottery sherds, bones, banks and ditches, pits, house foundations – but prehistorians draw upon social anthropology for their interpretations of what these remains reveal about the societies that found, hunted, grew, made and used them. For medieval archaeologists, documentary records, such as those discussed elsewhere in this book, provide a further dimension because they give a context for artefacts and ecofacts – the former being the objects that people shaped and used, the latter being the record that they leave in organic, biological residues, such as of the foodstuffs that they ate or of the agriculture that they practised.

## Survival: from buildings to bones

Things may survive from the past for various reasons. Although archaeologists are usually regarded as people who study what gets dug up, the standard definition is not so restrictive; 'material remains' are physical things that survive from the past, and that includes things that have never been buried. Reasons for above-ground survival vary. Religious buildings, for instance, may be looked after because they are revered, like the sixth-century mausoleums in Ravenna, Italy. Masonry structures like those have a better chance of outlasting a short period of neglect than timber ones, which need to be regularly maintained, but Norway's stave churches show that wood can stand for a thousand years provided that it is not allowed to rot away. Durability of the materials is not the only factor, however; most buildings come to be regarded as superfluous and are dismantled for their materials. Another factor is status, as stone is often regarded as more prestigious than wood, partly because a masonry building is nearly always more expensive to construct in the first place. It also suggests permanence, and may become sacred as a relic and a perpetuation of the memory of the people responsible for its creation, often saints or founder-members of a powerful family.

Because buildings are material remains, understanding them is a joint enterprise for archaeologists and architectural historians; the latter may regard style as their prerogative, but even that depends on principles of typological study that are shared with archaeologists, and indeed with art historians. Mostly, however, archaeologists are concerned with constructing information about society from what people threw away, abandoned, lost or deliberately placed in the ground and did not dig up again. Survival for anything that passes out of use depends upon its condition at the time, and the conditions that it then encountered. A pig bone from a joint of ham is likely to be much less robust when it is thrown away than one from a roasted piece of loin, because ham is salted and therefore the structure of the bone is already weakened. Furthermore, the ham bone may be (even) more attractive to gnawing animals such as dogs, so may be further damaged before it is discarded. Thereafter, the fate of both bones depends upon what happens to the accumulation of rubbish that they land in; a few may get thrown into a pit deep enough not to be completely destroyed when a site is redeveloped, and remain there. Yet even if the pit is permanently waterlogged and not acidic, neither bone will survive for ever, though the ham bone will usually decompose quicker than the roast loin bone.

Survival bias affects archaeologists' ability to reconstruct fully the meat part of people's diet, as the ratio of pig meat to beef and mutton will seem to be lower than it really was if the ham bones have an extra factor militating against their survival. It is also difficult to get a proper representation of birds and fish, because even if they survive at all, excavators can only recover most of them by sieving soil through water and picking them out by hand, which is very time-consuming.[1] Some species of fish do not have bones, so are even less likely to be found; documentary records of fishing and toll payments give more detail. Another source of information about the amount of sea-fish in people's diets is coming from stable isotope analyses of collagen in their bones; inland medieval peasants in the twelfth to fifteenth centuries had less access to a fish market than townspeople, for instance. Fast-days promoted fish eating, but these analyses show also that secular people were less strict in their observance than clerics.[2] Collagen in bone slowly changes during a person's or animal's lifetime, but can still contain elements consumed while growing up. One recent study of fifth- and sixth-century Bavaria has shown that many women had come from various different places, some far way, while the men had been more stationary – which is consistent with the objects found with them in their graves.[3]

Some animal parts – teeth, ivory, and antler – are denser than bone, and are likely to survive better. But survival can also depend on whether a material is useful: dead animals provided hides for leather, and the parts of the carcase that went to the tanner took a different route to ultimate disposal than the ones that went to the butcher. Another factor is that some animal parts were used to make a variety of small tools, such as combs, which were usually a combination of bone plates into which the teeth were sawn, held in place by more robust antler ribs. A few later medieval ones were made of ivory, a scarce material in western and southern Europe, and therefore sought after. It was also valued for such things as writing tablets, some elaborately carved. Although churches and great houses would be where their use would be most expected, one probably carved in France was found in a pit in an English port; it raised the issue of the way that merchants may have used exotic things that they could obtain on their travels as ways to enhance their status and self-esteem.[4]

Most bones did not go into pits; some were thrown into gutters, streams or rivers – medieval documents frequently complain about filth and the blocking of water channels; most went into a midden outside a house, and were carted away and spread on to fields as useful manure, where turning over by the plough wore them away.

A few things survive because they were never thrown away – many ivory writing-tablets were kept in church treasuries, for instance, as many treasures still are. Almost certainly preserved in this way is the wonderfully carved Franks Casket, made of whale-bone probably in late seventh- or eighth-century Northumbria – though it was discovered in a French farmhouse in the nineteenth century; this shows that even for special things preservation can be a matter of chance. Its importance lies in what it reveals of cultural ideas and influences, while its runic and Latin inscriptions make it both an archaeological artefact and a historical document.[5] Manuscripts can be regarded in the same way, not only for the information that their texts convey, but as objects to be studied for the materials used in their production, even, if made of vellum, the quality of the herds from which the skin came.[6]

Because many manuscripts and books have survived in libraries, there is probably more vellum extant than leather from everyday boots and shoes, knife sheaths and scabbards, though modern conservation is balancing the record.[7] Other organic materials especially susceptible to decay are wood and textiles, both probably even more common than leather. Wood has the extra disadvantage of burning well, so an old cup or a broken post would end up in the fire below an oven, or on an open hearth. Inorganics, such as metals, are likely to be recycled; even iron can be reforged. Lead glass can survive quite well, as can soda glass; so it is frustrating that the commonest in medieval western Europe, potash glass, flakes and decays so readily. Even pottery is not always durable, particularly if fired only to a low temperature.

## Recovery: deposits, losses and throw-aways

Inventories like those described elsewhere in this book show that richer late medieval households had quantities of gold and silver plate, and even the less well-off often had a few silver spoons. The documents usually record the metal from which something was made, because they were interested in its value. Even though many hoards of coins have been found, and many of those from the later Middle Ages contain jewellery, few have any other objects.[8] Large plates and cups were more difficult to conceal, so were probably much less often buried or hidden, making the archaeological record less representative. Most of what little plate survives is ecclesiastical because of church treasuries.

Later medieval hoards were concealed by people who for one reason or another did not return to collect them as they had almost certainly hoped. Particularly in the early Middle Ages, some objects were deliberately buried, usually as grave-goods, so what is found may be more representative of people's best gear, not their everyday things. For the seventh century, Mound 1 at Sutton Hoo shows how gold and garnets were valued by the élites, but the 2009 discovery of the Staffordshire hoard is changing ideas about how much actually existed: the eighty-five or so gold sword pommels, and the many other gold and silver fittings, put a new perspective on quantities.[9] As it was not in a grave, the reason why the hoard was abandoned remains debated; someone may have intended to come back for it, but it might have been deliberately disposed of, because it had come to be thought of as unlucky, or because gods needed to be propitiated. Some of the objects in it were Christian, for it belongs to a melt-down period of beliefs. Even though the practice of burial with valuable grave-goods died away in the face of Christianity's teaching that things should be given to the Church in this world as they would be no use to anyone in the next, the large number of swords found in streams and rivers suggests that the idea that someone's best weapon should 'die' with them may have taken up to the eleventh century to fade away. Another long-living deposition practice is hinted at by hoards of ironwork, such as one found buried at the bottom of a post-hole as though in some way to bless the tenth- or eleventh-century building above it.[10]

The Staffordshire hoard was found by the user of a metal-detector, an instrument that in the last forty years has made the recovery of metal objects a widespread pastime, legal in some countries, illegal but undoubtedly practised in others. Unfortunately, the 'value' of some things is not just in their importance for changing ideas about the past, but in their 'value' in the modern market, which certainly leads to things not being reported, or being given a false provenance or none at all. Nevertheless, most finders have nothing to lose by passing on reliable information, so in most cases it is fair to assume that at least an approximate find-spot is accurate. From such records, distributions of different types of metal objects can be mapped, for instance of early medieval coins found in Britain.[11] Distributions suggest the areas in which coins circulated; the numbers indicate the volume of circulation, and therefore the extent to which the economy was using money for its everyday activities such as buying and selling, or whether most coins were held in reserve for special occasions or regular needs like paying the rent. For the later Middle Ages, hundreds of silver pennies and halfpennies have been found scattered across fields, clearly lost by people working the land, and putting a new complexion on the extent of their disposable wealth, which is confirmed by finds of gold and silver finger-rings and brooches reported annually to the Portable Antiquities Scheme.[12]

Metal-detecting has not only led to the discovery of new objects, but also of new sites. Some early medieval material found on the ground surface has come from graves in previously unknown cemeteries (and, it has to be said, some detector users have disturbed graves in their searches, so that the relationship between an object and the body with which it was buried has been lost). Equally, finds that might have been expected to come from graves have proved on excavation, or other archaeological work such as geophysical prospection, not to have derived from a cemetery but seemingly to have been casual losses. Metal-detecting has also been largely responsible for the recognition of a whole new seventh- to ninth-century site-type, where quantities of coins and other metalwork have been found. Excavations at some of these concentrations have shown that there were buildings, and in at least two cases probably for a while a church; other sites have not revealed any structures, and may have been where fairs were held. This has changed ideas about the amount of trading that took place before the Viking period, particularly in eastern England.[13]

A pot-detector has yet to be devised, so archaeologists trying to find sites that are unlikely to be revealed by the amount of metal coming from them, and which do not show up on air photographs as lighter (usually because drier, as above a buried wall) or darker (because wetter, as an underlying ditch or pit may be) lines and patches in the soil round them have to resort to other techniques. Some archaeologists have the patience to walk up and down and back and forth across ploughed fields, bent over double while they peer at the surface trying to see broken sherds which are often as dark as the soil around them. This can be the only way to find ephemeral places where people lived in small numbers, leaving little rubbish behind. Finding them is essential if a settlement pattern is to be established, however; it is no longer enough for archaeologists to focus on the great buildings and sites when the goal is to understand society as a whole. Individual farmsteads and hamlets that existed even in well-documented periods were not necessarily recorded, as landlords were interested in the profits of an estate overall, not in its individual components.[14]

Air photography has been used by archaeologists for a hundred years, at first spasmodically but from the 1930s more systematically. An exciting new technique is Lidar (Light detecting and ranging), which sends a succession of rays down to earth from a moving aeroplane and measures how long they take to bounce back; the tiniest surface variability can be picked up, showing for instance the ridges and furrows of medieval strip-field systems, even if they now appear quite flat when viewed from the ground. It can even penetrate through tree-cover, so that surface features hidden where woodland has grown over them can be picked out. Ground-penetrating radar is another very new technique; if the pulse hits a wall below the ground, a plan can be obtained. Unfortunately, earth-filled features such as ditches and post-holes are not picked out by GPR; magnetometry is better for those, as they are likely to have components that register differently from the earth around them. Resistivity sends a current in a downwards parabola between probes pushed into the ground; a wall resists the current. Other geophysical devices are beginning to appear.

A second reason to field-walk for sherds is to understand manuring, because broken pots were, like the bones discussed above, usually thrown onto middens and carted out with the rest of what is politely termed 'night-soil'. This is not an infallible method, as some pottery is friable and quickly breaks down, but the effort that went into carting the midden material out to the ploughed fields has proved a way in which archaeologists can chart the increase in tenth- to thirteenth-century arable, and assess how much less labour went into maintaining it thereafter.[15]

## Excavation and recording

Everyone associates archaeology with planned digging, though field-walking, geophysics, and recording standing structures are all archaeological procedures. Excavations can be on sites which are not imminently to be destroyed by farming or development, but most take place where evidence is soon to disappear. In most towns, redevelopment is usually the only time when such an opportunity is presented. The few 'failed' medieval towns are usually protected, and permission to dig in them is rarely given. That is true also of many sites such as medieval monasteries and castles, though work can take place in those sometimes so that they can be better explained to visitors, or when conservation of standing remains requires below-ground work around the foundations. Farms, hamlets and villages present problems when they are still occupied, but 'community archaeology' projects are now exploring them, for instance opening small trenches in back gardens to plot the spread of occupation, and its contraction.[16]

The quantity of material from medieval (and indeed other, notably Roman) sites is often daunting – thousands of bones and pot sherds, hundreds of different features. A feature may be anything from a pit or wall like those already mentioned, to the ephemeral trace of where a horizontal timber beam once rested on the ground as the sill of a building, or of a layer of earth no more than a millimetre thick that may be all that separates features hundreds of years apart in date. In poor light, or when the ground is very dry or very wet, it is easy to miss subtle distinctions. Burrowing animals may have caused sherds from higher up a stratigraphical sequence to get intermixed in earlier layers. Urban excavations can be even more complex than rural ones, if the volume of activity within them has led to the build-up of much deeper deposits than in rural sites.[17] Waterfronts, as in medieval London, present extra hazards from flooding, but extra rewards from the high level of preservation.[18] Cemeteries need great care because of human bones.

Another sort of archaeological recording is of standing structures, again making a record for the future, but also interpreting how the building was constructed, in different periods or even by different work-gangs. Photogrammetry is increasingly used, as well as the old-fashioned stone-by-stone or timber-by-timber measured drawing. Again, these are not techniques exclusive to the medieval archaeologist, but since there are thousands of medieval buildings, even quite modest ones from the thirteenth century onwards, there is a huge database. 'From the thirteenth century' has become possible to say because of tree-ring dating (dendrochronology),[19] which is of greater use to medievalists than is radiocarbon because of its greater precision. A tree normally grows a new ring each year, the width of which depends on the amount of water absorbed; this may reflect rainfall, but complications include a year in which insects eat the leaves through which the tree absorbs some of its moisture, or if the tree has roots that go into standing water. At least fifty rings are usually needed to be sure that the timber can be fitted into a sequence, and often a further problem is to know how many rings have been removed by a carpenter trimming off the soft outer sapwood. Nevertheless, dates to within a three-year period are often obtained from standing buildings and waterlogged timbers.

## Interpretation

Many archaeologists now feel that defining their discipline as a 'study' is no longer enough; a report on an excavation or a descriptive catalogue of a particular type of artefact in a particular museum are studies, but only become a contribution to knowledge if the information in them is used to construct a better understanding of the human past. Some medievalists consider that too much work on the archae-ology of the Middle Ages has not kept abreast of modern thinking about the past in general, and avoids discussion of issues that are central to prehistory, such as 'agency'.[20] Others consider that their period is different because of the framework that documents provide about narrative history and social conditions, and that because so few societies have social and economic structures like those of the later Middle Ages, comparisons are not really valid.

Medieval archaeology has certainly moved on from a time when its focus was on the upper echelons of societies, through excavation to find out a little more about the plans of the castles that they lived in or of the monasteries that they patronized. Castles have become hotly debated territory, as archaeologists and historians argue over the extent to which they were built for defence or for status, to be a last refuge for their cowering owners when attacked or to be a permanent and visible symbol of their lordship. How that affected the landscape and lives of those around them is explored; different lifestyles are shown by the castles' venison, glass, and riding equipment compared to the tools and stews of the country people round about, though mixing of rubbish within a castle blurs the distinctions between its internal social levels, from the lord's family down to the servants. Another aspect is the extent to which castle-building was part of a general 'feudalizing' European movement.[21]

Trying to force archaeological data into a particular narrative can certainly be misleading. The single mention by Gildas of a British victory at Mons Badonicus has led to endless speculation about its site and its significance, colouring and distorting ideas about the spread of Anglo-Saxon culture in the fifth and sixth centuries. On the other hand, Bede's description of eighth-century London as a busy place, when archaeology could find no trace of activity within the old Roman walls, spurred on research that led to the explanation that the trading area was extra-mural, a conclusion triumphantly justified by subsequent excavation. An ongoing University of Southampton project involving research into Tidgrove, a royal house that is documented as having money spent on it only in the 1170s, has produced the conundrum of pottery and other evidence showing that it remained in use well into the thirteenth century. The assumption was that in the 1180s the king built a new house, Freemantle, not far away; it now seems possible that the site remained the same, but its name was changed. So far, however, no one has found a parallel for that, and uniqueness is suspicious. 'Freemantle' derives from a French name;[22] English sites often enough had French names if they were new, like Beaulieu Abbey, but changing the name of an existing place seems unparalleled.

Parallels give confidence to interpretation. Prehistorians take them from social anthropology; medievalists on the whole prefer documents. The two are not anti-thetical, as the case of some curious animal leg-bones with one side planed down to a flat surface shows: their interpretation as ice-skates illustrates three types of analogy. Documents suggested the first: a twelfth-century writer described how Londoners tied shin-bones to their feet and poled themselves on the frozen River Thames. Next, skating in that way was still practised until recently outside modern Britain, so anthropology suggests their use. Thirdly, replicas have proved not only that it is a feasible technique, but subsequent inspection of the undersides of the bones used has shown similar striations to those on the archaeological examples. All this does not disprove that some could have been used in other, unrecorded ways, however, such as for smoothing leather hides, which could have left similar wear-marks.[23] The documents reveal one function, but that should not preclude consideration of other possibilities.

Bone skates are not world-changing, but they throw a little light on leisure activities, and provide one of the very few ways of finding out about how ordinary people used any free hours that they had; documents say much about the aristocracy's hunting and game-playing, but only record the lower orders' pastimes if they were riotous or too time-wasting. Skates were cheap to make and so are like very many things in the archaeological record, not costly enough to be recorded in people's wills, discussed elsewhere in this book. These show how people considered their possessions, for financial value and personal association, and room-by-room inventories reveal where they were kept, but it is not always clear from inventories what things looked like. In the Anglo-Saxon wills, for instance, words like *preon* may refer to what would now be classified as a brooch, as a pin, or as any other sort of clothes-fastener.[24] Later in the Middle Ages, *ouche* was used in ways that make it clear that a fastener was intended, but not what specific sort was being listed. Many Anglo-Saxon and later medieval dress fittings survive, but associating a particular type with an entry in a particular inventory is unfeasible; therefore the exact value of a surviving brooch, either in monetary terms, or in terms of its meaning for its owner, cannot be precisely known. By showing the range and numbers available, and the effort that went into their manufacture, however, archaeology gives a general idea of things' importance and availability across the time-range, not just at the particular moment that an inventory was drawn up.

Because so few inventories recorded everyday low-value items, pottery is rarely mentioned in them, whereas it is what the medieval archaeologist finds most of. It can therefore be used to investigate what the documents convey little information about, the peasants' market and their purchasing power. Surprisingly large amounts of pottery, made at a number of different kilns, is consistent with the emerging evidence of large numbers of coins being found; both suggest that peasants had more to spend than used to be thought. When they went into the nearest market town, or to a fair, they had a range of choice. A cooking-pot may have cost very little, a glazed jug slightly more, though prices are not recorded; what is significant is that overall numbers of both coins and pottery sherds are high, especially in the thirteenth century. Peasants' houses, too, were not the flimsy structures once taken for granted; at least the better-off were using solid timber, and had chambers and an open hall. This plan was like a reduced version of a manor-house. Exactly what sort of timber framing they used depended in part on the region in which they lived, but both the hall and the choice of timber style raise major questions about the extent to which peasant culture was a reflection of the aristocracy's, or whether 'emulation' is only one of the ways in which peasants expressed themselves.[25]

'Peasant culture' is a term that implies uniformity, which obviously medieval Europe did not have; agriculture, resources, transport systems, market demand, and peasants' ability to make any sort of profit from their work varied. There could be surprisingly wide variation even within a limited compass: one recent study has compared three deserted rural sites within ten miles of each other in central England, and has pointed out how much they differed in their planning, the durability and outside appearance of their buildings, and their agricultural practice and field systems, so that their inhabitants' experiences of their world would have been very different.[26]

One experience that would seem to have been common to all peasants, and indeed to the whole of society, was the demographic of population rise and, particularly dramatically during plague episodes in the sixth, seventh and fourteenth centuries, population fall. Rise led to new settlements being established, or expansion of old ones, fall to abandonments and shrinkage. In most medieval societies, increase led to some surplus people being available to create and swell the numbers of towns, where on the whole populations were not self-sustaining.[27] Archaeology's role in understanding towns ranges from the obvious one of revealing their origins and expansion to explanation of the lifestyles and expenditure of their inhabitants. Extremes of wealth may be easier to recover than of poverty; in the larger towns, stone houses and expensive goods show how the richest merchants set themselves apart. Timber-framed urban houses survive from the thirteenth century onwards to show the investment aims of the middling sort; the hovels and overcrowded chambers of the poor are harder to find, as those who owned little leave little behind.

Even the poor leave their bodies behind, however. Until recently, archaeology seemed to be interested only in the early medieval dead who were buried with grave goods. Work on disease, living conditions and diet has changed that focus,[28] and a study of the detail of burial in the later Middle Ages has shown wider variation in practice than supposed, and a degree of 'superstition' carried on into everyday lives.[29] Studies like that show that archaeology can throw light even on areas of medieval life that seem so well-known because so well-documented; 'official' statements and actual practice were not necessarily the same thing.

## Further reading

The best book on the Migration period in Europe remains Philip Dixon, *Barbarian Europe* (London: Phaidon Press, 1976), because of its maps and coloured images, as well as for a short text which has not been made outdated by subsequent, much more detailed studies. For the next part of the period, a book recently edited by James Graham-Campbell with Magdalena Valor, *The Archaeology of Medieval Europe. Volume 1: Eighth to Twelfth Centuries* (Aarhus: Aarhus University Press, 2007), has at last risen to the challenge of producing an authoritative, multi-author overview; Volume 2 is in preparation, but meanwhile Roberta Gilchrist and Andrew Reynolds (eds), *Reflections: 50 Years of Medieval Archaeology, 1957–2007*, Society for Medieval Archaeology Monograph 30, has contributors from many different countries as well as discussion essays on many aspects of archaeology, several of which are referred to in the text above. The Oxford Bibliography On-Line is an up-to-date resource for a wide range of medieval topics, not just archaeology.

## Notes

1 Dale Serjeantson, 'Birds: Food and a Mark of Status,' in *Food in Medieval England. Diet and Nutrition*, Christopher M. Woolgar, Dale Serjeantson and Tony Waldron (eds), (Oxford: Oxford University Press, 2006), pp. 131–47; Dale Serjeantson and Christopher M. Woolgar, 'Fish Consumption in Medieval England,' in *ibid.*, pp. 102–30.

2 Gundula Müldner and M.P. Richards, 'Diet in Medieval England: the Evidence from Stable Isotopes,' in *Food in Medieval England*, Woolgar, Serjeantson and Waldron (eds), pp. 228–53.

3 Susanne Hakenbeck *et al.*, 'Diet and Mobility in Early Medieval Bavaria: a Study of Carbon and Nitrogen Stable Isotopes,' in *American Journal of Physical Anthropology*, 142 (2010), 1–15.

4 Nigel L. Ramsay, 'Writing Tablet', in *Age of Chivalry. Art in Plantagenet England 1200–1400*, Jonathan Alexander and Paul Binski (eds), (London: Royal Academy of Arts /Weidenfeld and Nicolson, 1987), pp. 384–5.

5 Leslie Webster, 'The Franks Casket,' in *The Making of England. Anglo-Saxon Art and Culture AD 600–900*, Leslie Webster and Janet Backhouse (eds), (London: British Museum Press, 1991), pp. 101–3.

6 Richard Gameson, 'The Archaeology of the Book' in *The Oxford Handbook of Anglo-Saxon Archaeology*, Helena Hamerow, David A. Hinton and Sally Crawford (eds), (Oxford: Oxford University Press, 2011), pp. 815–36.

7 Esther A. Cameron, *Sheaths and Scabbards in England AD 400–1100* (Oxford: British Archaeological Reports British Series 301, 2000).

8 Jørgen Steen Jensen *et al.*, *Danmarks Middelalderlige Skattefunde c.1050 – c.1550* (Copenhagen: Det Kongelike Nordisk Oldskriftselkab, 1992), pp. 143 and 146–7 for Danish examples; E. Descatoire (ed.), *Treasures of the Black Death* (London: The Wallace Collection, 2009) for Colmar, France, and Erfurt, Germany, both of the mid-fourteenth century.

9 Kevin Leahy and Roger Bland, *The Staffordshire Hoard* (London: British Museum Press, 2009).

10 Gabor Thomas, 'The Symbolic Lives of Late Anglo-Saxon Settlements: a Cellared Structure and Iron Hoard from Bishopstone, East Sussex,' in *Archaeological Journal*, 65 (2008), 334–98.

11 www.fitzmuseum.cam.ac.uk/dept/coins/emc.

12 www.finds.org.uk; David A. Hinton, 'Deserted Medieval Villages and the Objects from them,' in *Deserted Villages Revisited*, Christopher Dyer and Richard Jones (eds), (Hatfield: University of Hertfordshire Press, 2010), pp. 85–108.

13 Tim Pestell and Katharina Ulmschneider (eds), *Markets in Early Medieval England. Trading and 'Productive' Sites, 650–850* (Macclesfield: Windgather Press, 2003).

14 See the chapters on manorial history and rural history in this book.

15 Richard Jones, 'Signatures in the Soil: the Use of Pottery in Manure Scatters in the Recognition of Medieval Arable Farming Regimes,' in *Archaeological Journal*, 161 (2004), 159–88.

16 Carenza Lewis, 'New Avenues for the Investigation of Currently Occupied Medieval Rural Settlement: Preliminary Observations from the Higher Education Field Academy', in *Medieval Archaeology*, 51 (2007), 133–64.

17 Martin Carver, *Underneath English Towns. Interpreting Urban Archaeology* (London: Batsford, 1987).

18 Gustav Milne, *The Port of Medieval London* (Stroud: Tempus, 2003); and see Kowaleski in this volume.

19 Nat W. Alcock, 'The origins of crucks: a rejoinder,' in *Vernacular Architecture*, 37 (2007), 11–15.

20 Roberta Gilchrist, 'Medieval Archaeology and Theory: a Leap of Faith,' in *Reflections: 50 Years of Medieval Archaeology, 1957–2007*, Roberta Gilchrist and Andrew Reynolds (eds), (Society for Medieval Archaeology Monograph 30, 2009), pp. 385–408.

21 E. Svensson, *The Medieval Household. Daily Life in Castles and Farmsteads: Scandinavian Examples in their European Context* (Turnhout: Brepols, 2008).

22 Keith Briggs, 'Freemantle,' in *Journal of English Place-Name Studies*, 40 (2008), 97–111; the project is directed by Kristian Strutt, in partnership with the Kingsclere Heritage Association.

23 Arthur MacGregor, *Bone, Antler, Ivory and Horn. The Technology of Skeletal Materials since the Roman Period* (London and Sydney: Croom Helm, 1985).

24 Gale R. Owen-Crocker. *Dress in Anglo-Saxon England*. Revised and enlarged edition (Woodbridge: Boydell & Brewer, 2004), pp. 340–1.

25 Alcock, 'Origins of Crucks'.

26 Sally V. Smith, 'Houses and Communities: Archaeological Evidence for Variation in Medieval Peasant Experience', in *Deserted Villages Revisited*, Dyer and Jones (eds), pp. 64–84.

27 See Barron in this volume.

28 Müldner and Richards, 'Diet in Medieval England,' in *Food in Medieval England*, ed. Woolgar, Serjeantson and Waldron, pp. 228–53; Charlotte Roberts, 'Health and Welfare in Medieval England: the Human Skeletal Remains Contextualized,' in *Reflections*, Gilchrist and Reynolds (eds), pp. 307–26.

29 Roberta Gilchrist, 'Magic for the Dead? The Archaeology of Magic in Later Medieval Burials', in *Medieval Archaeology*, 52 (2008), 119–60.

# Index

UNIVERSITY OF WINCHESTER
LIBRARY